The Gun Digest Review of
CUSTOM GUNS

Edited by
Ken Warner

DBI BOOKS, INC., Northfield, Illinois

Staff

EDITOR
Ken Warner

ASSISTANT TO THE EDITOR
Lilo Anderson

ASSOCIATE EDITOR
Robert S. L. Anderson

COVER PHOTOGRAPHY
John Hanusin

PRODUCTION MANAGER
Pamela J. Johnson

PUBLISHER
Sheldon L. Factor

Photo Credits: Cloward, Fischer, Lind, Ottmar, and Yee gun photos by Mustafa Bilal; Dave Miller guns by International Photographic Associates.

ISBN 0-910676-10-0   Library of Congress Catalog Card #80-67745

CONTENTS

INTRODUCTION

YOU HAVE in your hands our GUN DIGEST REVIEW OF CUSTOM GUNS. It is a review, and not an encyclopedia. We are attempting here to take a quick look at almost everything that affects custom guns, stopping here and there to take closer looks at some things. There has not been such a broad-gauged attempt before, so there are bound to be gaps in the coverage. I hope not many.

First you'll see several feature articles, heavily illustrated, on the joys and the few sorrows of owning custom guns. Stuart Williams and John T. Amber contributed here, and there are reports by me on a seminar on custom guns and on an interesting collection of modern rifles. At the back end, you'll find a catalog and directory section. And between are reports on the state of the art we hope will bring you up to date on the custom gun work now going on.

This latter effort was prepared by myself and C.E. Harris, and which of us wrote what is indicated by our names appearing at the end of each segment. Obviously, to do the work at all we needed the help of a great many people, but happily we know a great many people. To even begin to try to acknowledge all that help, some of it direct and some of indirect, some of it brand new and some of it decades old, would be impossible. We are grateful, however.

THE GUN DIGEST REVIEW OF CUSTOM GUNS defines "custom guns" more broadly than have, in their separate articles, John Amber and Stuart Williams. The reason for this is not wholly a matter of semantics. There is a great deal of confusion over the term "custom gun," true enough, but we believe perhaps less so in the minds of the many shooters than in the minds of those of us who write of guns. To a degree, it seems to us that a gun which is no longer as the factory built it, having been restocked, rearranged, rebarreled, or whatever, and at whatever level of circumstance, can be considered a custom gun. That is, although the word is unfortunate, any such gun has been, unarguably, "customized." Therefore, we have attempted throughout this work to treat all the facets that distinguish the special gun from the standard gun, and at the same time try to indicate at what level such work may be done, leading us, therefore, to agree with

Mr. Williams and Mr. Amber that the very best of custom guns are the guns they describe.

Therefore, you find that we discuss, soberly and without disdain, the semi-inletted stock. You will find hints that custom guns can be the work of their owners; you will even discover that cheap guns can be custom guns; and you will find a deep respect throughout, we believe, for the work and effort and accomplishment of the very top craftsmen.

That is our definition then: Custom guns, which may be found at various levels of quality in terms of workmanship and style, are those guns which have been particularly adapted to the use of a particular owner.

As for why such a work as this will find a market and how it comes to be that so much material on the subject is available, I believe custom guns to be an expression of the general affluence in the United States over the past several decades, and a reflection of the changes in hunting and shooting opportunities for American shooters. There are more shooters, and even possibly more opportunities, than ever, but they are not those same opportunities our fathers and grandfathers had.

Certainly, more men are spending more money on their toys than once was the case. (And I must add, of course, that more women are spending more money on their toys, as well.) And it follows that they become increasingly particular about those toys.

That is, in the end, where the potential for the increasing sophistication comes from. There has never been any shortage of artists and craftsmen, no matter what you have read bewailing such shortages. In the history of the world, whenever there have been patrons, there have been artists. And when there are no patrons, in the widespread sense of their presence, there have been only the most dedicated of artists and craftsmen.

In short, there are a great many Americans ready, willing and able to pay for fine guns, and being involved in the creation of fine guns is an immensely satisfying way to put bread on the table, and so we have them and we have this book.

Most of the information herein comes from the people who do the work. We have tried to report it accurately. Where there are mistakes, and omissions, they are mine.

Ken Warner

WHY BUY A CUSTOM GUN?

by STUART WILLIAMS

An older Sako action, still in 222, but with a Titus barrel displays many Al Lind talents. The Tacoma, Washington, maker chose a point pattern with borders fore and aft as appropriate over this handsomely grained piece of New Zealand walnut. Note that the bolt handle has been reshaped and checkered.

NOT MANY years ago, I was one of a rather rare breed which I shall call the Custom Gun Cognoscenti. Hardly one gun owner in 10,000 owned a "bespoke" gun. Today, however, the breed is vastly more numerous, and its numbers are growing apace. What's more, the demand they have generated has created a minor renaissance of sorts. There are far more outstanding gun craftsmen today than at any time in our history, and new talents are coming along all the time.

Yes, the custom gun revolution is in full efflorescence. The word revolution may seem to be a misnomer in this context, but that is precisely what it is—a revolution against the standardization and drabness of most factory-made guns. It is—to borrow a term from the social sciences—"a revolution of rising expectations." In the past decade gun publications have elevated the tastes of many gun buyers to such a level that they simply are not content with *any* ready-made gun.

Please note that I am not speaking of a handful of plutocratic gun connoisseurs. Their numbers are certainly insufficient to constitute a revolution in any meaningful sense. No, the phenomenon is much more democratic. It includes policemen and firemen, salesmen and journeymen, butchers and bakers and candlestick makers. Whereas formerly the privilege of owning a "bespoke" gun was—to quote from Benjamin Disraeli in a very different context—"for the few and the

This 1909 Mauser in 300 Magnum, with Douglas Premium barrel, is a Miller-Crum creation. The California English stock is checkered in a fleur-de-lis pattern, 24 lpi. Note that the pistol grip is just a shade more open than the pair might use on a less powerful rifle.

quality in food, wines, cars, guns and things in general than Americans, but this is changing rapidly with the growth of the consumer movement in this country. Now Americans are the finickiest gun buyers in the world. An ever-growing number of American hunters and shooters have developed tastes and demands that cannot be satisfied by *any* factory rifle.

Their preeminent demand is for a carefully designed, crisply detailed, contemporary classic stock. The metalsmiths and many of the stockmakers themselves never tire of saying that a custom stock, classic or otherwise does not make a custom gun. But in the minds of most men ordering a custom rifle a good classic stock is the *sine qua non* of the whole production. As of this writing only a few factory-made sporters—the Mossberg RM-7, the Ruger 77, the Remington Classic, and the newer Sakos—carry classic-style handles, and there are persistent rumors that Winchester is about to introduce a variation of the Model 70 with a classic stock. (These are, to be sure, not highly refined classic

very few,'' today all kinds of men are ordering guns built up to their specifications. What's more, the very elevated prices—$1,000-$2,000 and up—have not depressed the demand. Neither has the current recession nor the bleak long-term prospect for the economy. If anything, such factors have stimulated demand. Many custom gunsmiths report that clients will place an order for a gun, giving precise specifications as to what they want, without even asking the price. They say: "Just tell me how much money you need."

Consequently the grand gurus and the ascended masters of the stock-whittling craft—Dale Goens, Lenard Brownell, Jerry Fisher, and their confreres—are booked up far into the future. Some makers are so besieged with orders that they have to turn away all but their old, repeat clients. Some clients—rather unfairly, I think—judge the quality and desirability of a man's work by the length of time they have to wait for the gun, and the longer, the better.

Let us consider some of the reasons for this burgeoning demand for custom guns. I would say custom rifles—because this discussion will focus on rifles—except for the fact that I am going to consider custom-ordered shotguns briefly.

The first of these reasons is an ever-increasing quality-consciousness among Americans in general. Europeans have traditionally been more demanding of

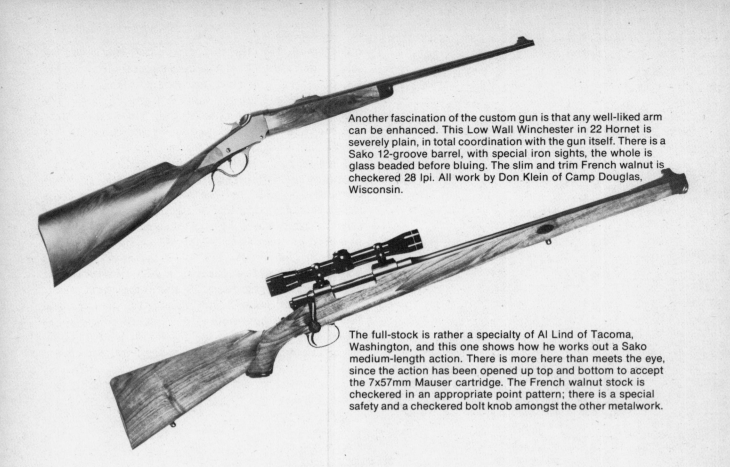

Another fascination of the custom gun is that any well-liked arm can be enhanced. This Low Wall Winchester in 22 Hornet is severely plain, in total coordination with the gun itself. There is a Sako 12-groove barrel, with special iron sights, the whole is glass beaded before bluing. The slim and trim French walnut is checkered 28 lpi. All work by Don Klein of Camp Douglas, Wisconsin.

The full-stock is rather a specialty of Al Lind of Tacoma, Washington, and this one shows how he works out a Sako medium-length action. There is more here than meets the eye, since the action has been opened up top and bottom to accept the 7x57mm Mauser cartridge. The French walnut stock is checkered in an appropriate point pattern; there is a special safety and a checkered bolt knob amongst the other metalwork.

designs.) I would estimate that at least 95 percent of the custom rifles being built today are built with classic-style stocks. In fact, people like Don Allen, Al Lind, and Jim Cloward—all of whom have precise stock-carving pantograph machines and do a large amount of wood-machining for other stockmakers—tell me that virtually *all* of the orders they get are for the contemporary classic design.

The second feature most demanded by buyers of custom rifles, a feature likewise prominently absent from production rifles, is top-quality metalsmithing. In this respect most production rifles are only half-completed. The trigger guards and floorplates may well be of pot metal. The locking lugs may make contact over less than half of their bearing surfaces. The bolt and safety may operate stiffly, the trigger pull may be heavy and creepy, and the bolt handle may have awkward and ugly contours. However, a first-rate metalsmith like Dave Miller or Phil Fischer will refine an action to the ultimate degree of beauty and functional efficiency. He will hone and jewel the bolt; lap in the locking lugs for maximum contact; true up the bolt face; reshape the bolt handle or install a new one; checker the bolt knob; slenderize and recontour the trigger guard, or build an entirely new trigger guard-floorplate assembly; and perform other operations that give the action the slickness and surety of operation of a Rolex watch. Many of these operations will be apparent only to the man who did the work.

Another feature that buyers of custom rifles are seeking, and cannot generally find in production rifles, is the beauty of embellishment. To such buyers a fine custom rifle is as John Keats wrote, " . . . a thing of beauty and a joy forever." Such beauty may well include a very elaborate checkering pattern, covering a large area and cut 24, 26, 28, or even more lines to the inch and may also include engraving, an octagonal barrel, a quarter rib with express leaf sights, cold rust bluing, color case-hardening, an exotic wood fore-end tip, and skeleton grip and butt fittings. There might also be custom-built scope bases and rings. Almost certainly custom gun beauty includes a piece of wood carefully chosen for figure, flow of grain, color, strength and stability.

In all fairness, it must be admitted that some factory rifles do carry rather nice wood—the Colt-Sauer, the Weatherby Mark V, the Steyr-Mannlicher Model ML79 Luxus—but even these are certainly not of the quality seen on most fine custom rifles. The cost of fancy walnut precludes such a luxury on any production-made rifle. A very fancy piece of French or California English walnut will, in rectangular *blank* form, cost more today than two ordinary *completed* factory rifles.

Another quality often stipulated by buyers of custom rifles is lightness. The ordinary production-made bolt-action sporter, when outfitted with scope, mounts, sling, and a magazine full of cartridges, is, comparatively, a clunker. It will weigh *at least* 9 pounds and usually

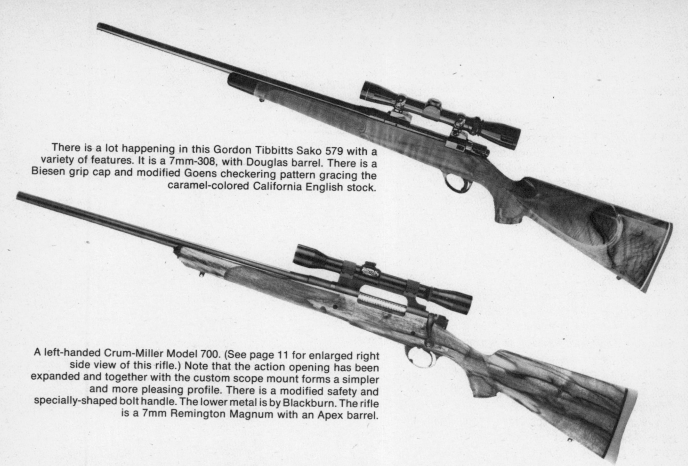

There is a lot happening in this Gordon Tibbitts Sako 579 with a variety of features. It is a 7mm-308, with Douglas barrel. There is a Biesen grip cap and modified Goens checkering pattern gracing the caramel-colored California English stock.

A left-handed Crum-Miller Model 700. (See page 11 for enlarged right side view of this rifle.) Note that the action opening has been expanded and together with the custom scope mount forms a simpler and more pleasing profile. There is a modified safety and specially-shaped bolt handle. The lower metal is by Blackburn. The rifle is a 7mm Remington Magnum with an Apex barrel.

closer to 10 pounds. If the rifle happens to be a magnum and carries one of those big 3x-9x variable scopes so dear to the hearts of dudes, it will probably weigh *over 10* pounds. To a man who has long labored up the steep escarpments of the Cassiars or the Wrangells or the Ruby Range after sheep or goats, or up the Rockies after elk or mule deer, the Gredos after Spanish ibex, or the Alps after chamois, such a weight is hideous and obscene. Such a man wants a rifle that is as light and lithe as a magic wand, as dynamic as a conductor's baton. This means a total weight not to exceed *8* pounds, preferably somewhat less.

The only way to get such a light rifle is to have it custom-built. The weight is arrived at by very careful planning and workmanship: selecting a light barrel, action and stock blank; Swiss-cheesing the magazine walls; hollowing out the bolt knob; building a new slenderized trigger guard and a blind magazine; boring out the buttstock and routing out the forearm, and other such measures that no large-scale manufacturer can or will take. Custom gunmakers who specialize in precisely such operations routinely build rifles weighing— fully equipped—only about *7* pounds! Dietrich Apel, president of Paul Jaeger, Inc., is one of these. Steve Billeb is another, and Al Lind a third. For example, a typical Al Lind mountain rifle is built around a highly refined Czech G33/40 Mauser action and a 22-inch featherweight barrel, stocked with a piece of fairly straight-grained but very light and strong California

English walnut. The rifle is outfitted with custom-built lightweight scope bases and rings, and a Leupold 4x Compact scope. Total weight? Six pounds, 13 ounces! Moreover, Al's dainty little rifles scotch forever that arrant bit of balderdash that light rifles won't shoot. His will, without exception, shoot into an inch, and many will shoot into ¾-inch.

Other qualities increasingly in demand among purchasers of custom rifles are precise fit and balance and dynamic handling. Heretofore these were qualities that only customers for made-to-measure shotgun stocks were concerned with, but the rifle stockmakers of the land tell me that more and more of their clients are insisting on meticulous fit and dynamic balance. Bill Dowtin says that in response to such demand he is building more and more rifles on Ruger Number 1A barreled actions. The Ruger Number 1A with 22-inch barrel offers the between-the-hands balance and the handling qualities of a fine English game gun no bolt-action rifle can match.

To digress for a moment to the matter of made-to-measure shotgun stocks. Briefly rehearsing the obvious, I will start with the premise that no man can shoot his best with an ordinary factory-made stock. All factory-made stocks are made to standard dimensions for a hypothetical "average" man and therefore won't fit any man perfectly. Some very good shooting can be done with a factory-made stock, but I insist no man will ever shoot his best with anything less than a made-to-measure stock. In this sense the British, as a nation of shotgunners, are far more sophisticated than we. A serious British shotgunner, a man who will fire at least 5,000 rounds a year at clay targets and live birds, would no more buy a ready-made gun than he would buy a ready-made suit.

The made-to-measure shotgun has never really caught on in this country, but there is increasing interest in it. Those few men who specialize in stocking shotguns—Don Klein, Mike Yee, Bill McGuire, Al Lind, Maurice Ottmar—are much in demand. All concentrate on stocking fine sidelock double guns, and their work is equal to anything coming out of the London "best" gun shops or the best Italian workshops, and superior to most of it, particularly the fit-to-metal and checkering.

There is a significant demand for highly specialized guns that can only be had by custom order. Let us say a man wants a fast-handling, full-length-stocked saddle carbine for hunting elk in the timber. Steve Billeb or Dave Swenson—both former elk guides and therefore familiar with the requirements of such a rifle—are the men for him. Perhaps he is going off to the Central African Empire in quest of a pair of 100-pound plus elephant tusks, or to the Alaska Peninsula for brown bear. Then he might well turn to Don ("Doctor Sunshine") Bartlett or Jim Cloward or Dave Miller, who specialize in big-bore slammers for dangerous game. If he is a freak about esoteric single shots he would certainly wish to consult Don Klein. I have already discussed lightweight mountain rifles, which are the most frequently requested of all specialty rifles.

Another considerable source of demand for custom rifles comes from clients who wish rifles in calibers that have been dropped by the large-volume gunmakers because they did not find favor with the multitude. The 7x57 certainly leads the list of these oldies but goodies, and is one of the most frequently requested chamberings for custom rifles. Jim Cloward and Al Lind tell me that the 7x57 ranks third in popularity among their clients, and Steve Billeb builds up more rifles in 7x57 than in any other chambering. The 250 Savage is another neglected number for which custom rifles are built. Phil Fischer, who does a beautiful job of shortening Mauser actions to accommodate the 250 Savage, builds more rifles for that cartridge than any other. Many custom rifles are built up in 280/7mm Express Remington, 257 Roberts, and 22 Hornet.

There is still a lot of interest in wildcat cartridges. Cecil Weems, Gordon Tibbitts, and Steve Billeb—among others—inform me that they put together almost as many rifles in wildcat chamberings as in standard factory chamberings. Finally, there is a steady small flow of orders for some of the more useful British and metric cartridges such as the 416 Rigby, 7x64, 9.3x62, and 9.3x64. Jim Cloward gets quite a few requests for the 9.3x64 from Alaskan guides wishing to

This is the Model 98 Mauser 404 shown on page 12 in close-up. This is a classic big rifle in all the details. Dave Miller and Curt Crum provided this 404 Jeffery with British-style sling swivels, Miller iron sights, and over-all a general impression of refined British styling. It is undeniably an American stock, but its ancestry is clear.

This is the other side of the Miller-Crum 1909 Mauser in 300 Magnum which shows much more Miller metalsmithing. The scope mount is his, of course, and the Model 70-shaped bolt handle has been hollowed and plugged. Note the Model 70-type safety also installed, and the five checkering panels on the bolt knob.

California English walnut of high quality, checkered 26 lpi by Curt Crum, distinguishes this left-handed Remington Model 700, with metalwork by Dave Miller. The Tucson, A2, artisans furnished, to order, a Wilson of Connecticut barrel, lined magazine stock, custom trigger bow and altered safety, together with their own scope mounts.

The trademark of Gordon Tibbitts is the intricate one-of-a-kind checkering pattern, in this case 24 lpi on an English walnut stock. Furniture includes Biesen skeleton butt and cap. The FN Supreme action has a Douglas Premium barrel, caliber 25-06.

back up their fishing clients or their hunters out for brown bear. He calls these rifles his "Yakutat varmint rifles."

There is a less common but very real motivation for the increased demand known as one-upmanship. Let us say that a famous television personality or politician or professional athlete has a fine rifle. Peter Plutocrat, every bit as well-heeled as the celebrity but not basking in the refulgence of frequent publicity, sees the gun at the celebrity's house or at the gunmaker's shop. He cannot stand to be outdone, so he orders up a rifle with fancier wood, more elaborate metal work, more extensive and expensive engraving, and any other features that will clearly distinguish his rifle as the finer of the two. If the men are rivals, this motivation is doubly strong.

The opposite side of the coin is what I might term camaraderie. Let us say that two men are longtime hunting buddies and the best of friends. One of them gets a custom rifle. In many cases, he simply will not rest until his friend has also ordered a custom rifle. This gives them a shared experience and strengthens the bond of friendship. It gives them something that they can enjoy together on a hunting trip or just sitting around the fireplace.

Then there is another wholly different phenomenon at work to increase the demand for fine custom firearms. I will call this phenomenon the Europeanization of hunting in the United States. For decades—centuries in fact—quality hunting has been a more elusive commodity in Europe. As quality hunting has become more and more inaccessible in Europe, hunters—or would-be hunters—have directed more and more time, devotion, and money to those appurtenances and experiences surrounding the sport and closely associated with it—hunting dogs, hunting art, music of the hunt, furniture and home decorations with hunting motifs, and most notably, fine guns. In the Germanic countries, one of the more exotic combination guns or double rifles, lavishly engraved and inlaid with gold and silver, and stocked with an opulently figured piece of walnut that has been embellished with carvings of wildlife or hunting scenes, assumes almost the status of a fetish or a sacred object. Such a gun will rarely—if ever—be used for hunting.

Much the same phenomenon is happening in this country. It accounts for, I think, a large part of the demand for custom rifles. Many such guns are ordered not with the intention of using them as means to more successful, enjoyable hunting, but as ends in themselves, as beautiful and precious objects to be admired and caressed and shown off, which will provide years and years of pleasure, whether they are ever taken afield or not.

There is yet another motivation for the swelling demand for fine custom guns, and that is purely economic. As the rate of inflation soars and the dollar is debased,

Refining a Mauser 98 to this level takes some doing, and it was done here by Stephen Billeb who provided a Model 70-style safety lever, a reshaped Model 1909 Mauser trigger guard, and a good pistol grip coverage for this 35 Whelen.

A big rifle can be graceful up close. This is a Model 98 Mauser in 404 Jeffery, and shows Dave Miller's five-panel bolt knob, on a handle shaped to Model 70 style. The straight-grained California English wood befits a heavy-recoiling piece.

One of the delights of the fully customized rifle can be embellishment. This Ruger No. 1 was engraved and gold-inlaid by Angelo Bee and is destined to be stocked and completed by Mike Yee. The caliber, one can tell from the style of the engraving, will be a heavy one.

people lose faith in banks and in paper currency. They turn to tangible investments such as gold coins, works of art, and oriental carpets as repositories of lasting and concentrated value. Fine custom guns make excellent repositories of value.

This statement must of course be qualified. As in many areas of taste and aesthetic judgement, there is some snobbery involved. Guns made up by the demi-gods of the gunmaking art, those who happen to be in vogue at the moment, fetch extortionate prices. Other guns, equal or perhaps even superior in every way, but built up by less fashionable makers, bring much lower prices. The value sometimes lies more in the name than in the gun itself. Buying custom guns as an investment is a very tricky business; one must be an excellent judge of gun values, a skilled negotiator, and an opportunist in order to succeed. Each custom gun is one-of-a-kind, and therefore sale of any one custom gun does not automatically help to establish parameters of value for

other custom guns. My advice is to buy a custom gun for the pleasures of owning and using a custom gun and not with any forethought of resale. If at a later date you do sell and make a good profit, well and good. Just don't count on it when you are having the gun built.

Another very potent motivation for owning custom guns is simply the acquisitive, or collector's, instinct, with a goodly admixture of what the Bible calls "the lust of the eyes." This instinct remains latent until you have taken delivery of your first fine custom gun, "the stuff that dreams are made of." It is something rich and strange, a rare and unique artifact. You fondle it endlessly, you admire the total mastery of form and design and the exquisite detailing of wood and metal work. All the love and care that went into it seem to radiate out from it. You are content—at least for a while. Then perhaps you visit a gun show and stop by some custom gunmakers' displays. You see some absolutely ravishing custom rifles there, and you realize that yours is not

Taken together, these three rifles reveal that Fred Speiser of Missoula, Montana, knows the classic look. The two Model 70s are barreled with Douglas barrels and stocked in French walnut, checkered in similar patterns. The Ruger No. 1 is stocked with an exceptional piece of feather crotch black walnut in the butt, and a matching fiddleback pattern in the forearm.

the only really splendid custom gun in the world. At this time your acquisitive instinct begins to rouse from its slumbers. A fellow whose work you have been admiring pulls out the most seductively figured piece of Californa English walnut you have ever seen, jet black streaks meandering in a maze through honey. You are weakening.

Then the man says: "I happen to have a Czech G33/40 action in very good condition." By this time your resistance, if you had any in the first place, is just about done for.

You rationalize: "Well, what the hell—it's *only* $2500! I guess I can always refinance the house . . . or sell my wife . . ."

By that time, my friend, the hook is sunk deeply. Your lust for acquisition is awakened to its full ferocity and insatiability. Hardly has the rifle been completed and delivered than you start dreaming of the next one. You think: "Well, I'm missing a 222 at the lower end of

my line-up and a 375 H&H at the upper end. I don't understand how I've gotten by all these years without *either* of them."

Then you start planning again. Will it be a piece of wildly figured New Zealand walnut or a stick of very rare multi-colored hard Claro? An FN Mauser or a pre-64 Model 70 action? Or perhaps for variety a single shot this time around? Perhaps you'll have Don Klein build you one of his nifty little full-stocked Martinis in 222 or Bill Dowtin do one of his regal Ruger Number 1s in 375 H&H. After the pleasures of planning, and the even sweeter pleasures of anticipation, your prize is delivered. Once again, you've got your fix, but once again it's only temporary.

You visit a gun store and you see an extraordinary piece of Bastogne walnut as fine-textured as bone, as hard as teak, rich and variegated with black and gold and ochre and amber. Then you think to yourself: "Aha! There's a great gap right in the middle of my

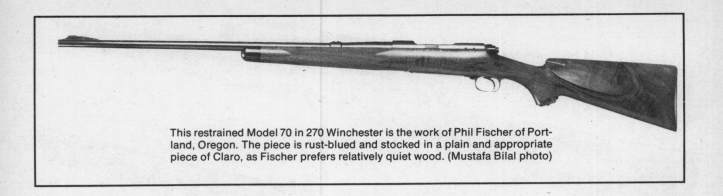

This restrained Model 70 in 270 Winchester is the work of Phil Fischer of Portland, Oregon. The piece is rust-blued and stocked in a plain and appropriate piece of Claro, as Fischer prefers relatively quiet wood. (Mustafa Bilal photo)

This Ruger No. 3 is gotten up as a heavy using gun. That slick receiver has been chrome plated; the Douglas Premium barrel has been octagoned, with London Gun Express sights. The caliber is 375 Holland & Holland Magnum. Note the special action lever and the leather-covered butt pad. All work by Don Klein of Camp Douglas, Wisconsin.

From this angle, one can see the inter-relationship of metalwork and woodwork, here all accomplished by Gordon Tibbitts. This is the 25-06 shown elsewhere, but in this picture one can see the genuinely intricate checkering pattern, and the handsome metal finishing. The stock is English walnut, with Biesen furniture.

line-up—the 7x57! How could any sophisticated rifleman survive without at least *one* good 7x57?''

Once again you drool like Pavlov's salivating dog, and once again you start planning your next fix. Such is the addiction to fine custom rifles. To my knowledge, there is—happily—no known cure. What's more, the addiction is becoming epidemic, a happy state of affairs for the custom gunmakers of the land. For example, Dave Miller has a client who now owns 20 of his rifles and another who owns 15.

The bottom line of the burgeoning demand for custom guns is that more and more gun buyers are rebelling against the sameness and mediocrity of mass-made merchandise. In an age when quality is selling out to quantity, and everything—houses, cars, clothing, cameras, movies etc. ad infinitum and ad nauseam—is

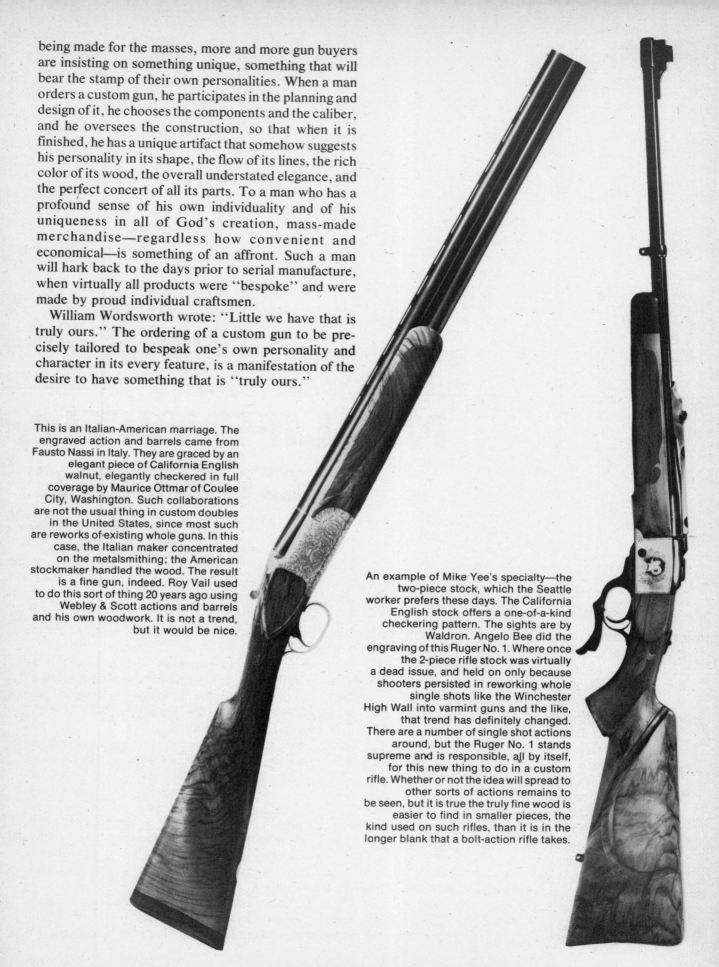

being made for the masses, more and more gun buyers are insisting on something unique, something that will bear the stamp of their own personalities. When a man orders a custom gun, he participates in the planning and design of it, he chooses the components and the caliber, and he oversees the construction, so that when it is finished, he has a unique artifact that somehow suggests his personality in its shape, the flow of its lines, the rich color of its wood, the overall understated elegance, and the perfect concert of all its parts. To a man who has a profound sense of his own individuality and of his uniqueness in all of God's creation, mass-made merchandise—regardless how convenient and economical—is something of an affront. Such a man will hark back to the days prior to serial manufacture, when virtually all products were "bespoke" and were made by proud individual craftsmen.

William Wordsworth wrote: "Little we have that is truly ours." The ordering of a custom gun to be precisely tailored to bespeak one's own personality and character in its every feature, is a manifestation of the desire to have something that is "truly ours."

This is an Italian-American marriage. The engraved action and barrels came from Fausto Nassi in Italy. They are graced by an elegant piece of California English walnut, elegantly checkered in full coverage by Maurice Ottmar of Coulee City, Washington. Such collaborations are not the usual thing in custom doubles in the United States, since most such are reworks of existing whole guns. In this case, the Italian maker concentrated on the metalsmithing; the American stockmaker handled the wood. The result is a fine gun, indeed. Roy Vail used to do this sort of thing 20 years ago using Webley & Scott actions and barrels and his own woodwork. It is not a trend, but it would be nice.

An example of Mike Yee's specialty—the two-piece stock, which the Seattle worker prefers these days. The California English stock offers a one-of-a-kind checkering pattern. The sights are by Waldron. Angelo Bee did the engraving of this Ruger No. 1. Where once the 2-piece rifle stock was virtually a dead issue, and held on only because shooters persisted in reworking whole single shots like the Winchester High Wall into varmint guns and the like, that trend has definitely changed. There are a number of single shot actions around, but the Ruger No. 1 stands supreme and is responsible, all by itself, for this new thing to do in a custom rifle. Whether or not the idea will spread to other sorts of actions remains to be seen, but it is true the truly fine wood is easier to find in smaller pieces, the kind used on such rifles, than it is in the longer blank that a bolt-action rifle takes.

BY JOHN T. AMBER

MY LIFE WITH CUSTOM GUNS

CONSIDERING the times and my precarious financial condition—it was the early 1930s—I bought my first custom-made-to-order rifle in 1934. No, it wasn't made for me. The original owner of the rifle—a Model 54 Winchester—had had it restocked in handsome fashion, its caliber the then-new 22 Hornet. I wasn't that fond of the 54 in factory form but I couldn't resist this one, and the price, which included a 16-power Fecker scope sight, much ammo and loading tools, was right.

Griffin & Howe had made the stock in 1931, which was another reason for my wanting it; I'd seen their ads, I'd received brochures from them, and their name was well and favorably known. To refresh my memory I just looked at my bound copy of the 1931 *American Rifleman*. My friend Don had paid G&H about $100, which included a bit better piece of walnut, a checkered steel buttplate and a steel grip cap. The Sedgeley Springfield 22 Hornet, newly sporter stocked and with Lyman 48 micro sight, was $75, as shown in the same issue.

I'd got into rifle shooting as a youngster of ten or so

when an uncle had given me a 22 Winchester pump repeater. A ceaseless reader—my mother used to drive me from the house to go outside—I began devouring everything then available on guns and shooting, not that there was much compared to today's flood of publications. Nevertheless in a few years I was a fairly well-informed enthusiast. During that time I'd put together a small lot of shootable firearms, handguns as well as rifles, and my chief interest now was in centerfires.

I was forced to sell that lot when the depression hit hard, but by 1933 I'd landed a good job, one that paid well for long hours and tough work, at least for that time. I've never been idle since. I went into Marshall Field's Gun Shop in 1935, which further increased my opportunities to expand my knowledge, and when I wanted to buy anything from our stock, the 20 percent discount helped.

At this point, I think, a couple of things need clarification: what I believe the genuine custom stock should consist of, and the reasons for my very long love affair

This is how Amber shoots, these days. Problems with the right eye were solved only by the creation of special firearms so that he could shoot from his right shoulder using his left eye. It takes only a little getting used to, so it works.

This is the entirely conventional in appearance bent-stock Model 70 created for John Amber by Don Allen and numerous others. One might say this is the most custom of all of John Amber's custom guns.

Seen from above, the bend in the Don Allen-created rifle becomes quite apparent. The recess in the cheek area plus the bend in the stock provide most of the correction needed to allow Amber to shoulder the gun naturally and shoot with his left eye.

So as not to wind up with a completely grotesque gunstock, which would not be Amber's style, Herman Waldron offset the scope with this special set of scope mounts, which got the rest of the correction needed. This photograph was made while the rifle was in the white.

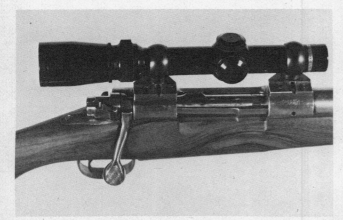

with such work.

Unless the rifle (or shotgun) is made to the order and specifications of the customer—within reasonable limits, to be sure, and with the approval of a qualified gunmaker—I don't consider anything else worthy of the words "custom-made."

With no intent to impugn their undeniable usefulness and cost appeal, I don't consider that semi-inletted stock blanks, for example, which are usually of standard form and dimensions, no matter the variety of style offered, meet the test. They are not, by definition, *custom-made*. Their dimensions are, often, not adjustable to fit the user except they may be made smaller— it's a hard task to add height to a comb except via new wood or whatever. The shape, length and circumference of the pistol grip—on a given profiled blank— can hardly be altered appreciably. I could go on!

At the time of which I write, some 50 years ago, *all* rifles offered were stocked in traditional classic form. Some were less well done than others, of course, but

For John Amber, a custom gun would not really be a custom gun without some embellishment, and here is the principal embellishment of the Don Allen rifle, a gold mouflon and monogram, together with tasteful scroll, all done by Tommy Kaye. Note the special Waldron magazine floorplate release immediately ahead of the trigger guard.

none showed the exaggerated Monte Carlo combs so prevalent later and now; no closely-curling pistol grips dropping well below the line from toe to guard, no broadly-splayed fore-ends, no white-line spacers anywhere. Some years later, my hunting partner and I had a hell of a time getting Roy Weatherby to make us a pair of 375 Weatherby Magnums with classic stocks; we didn't quite succeed either.

My experience with and knowledge of custom rifles, then, was clearly colored by the times in which I lived. A large factor in developing my bent for the classic stock form was one book, E. C. Crossman's *Book of the Springfield,* which I read and re-read. I thought it a great work then, and I still do. I reveled in its descriptions and illustrations of fine rifles, from simple examples to elaborately done, engraved versions. Chapter 2, "The Sporting Springfield," is worth the cost of the book, and as valuable today as it was in 1932.

Crossman's best rifle, by far, was a fully engraved Springfield sporter made for him by the legendary R. L. (Bob) Owen. It is pictured full length and in close-ups in this book. How I yearned for a like rifle; it was the epitome of the classic rifle, done just right—slim, trim, elegantly simple in its flowing lines. Crossman noted, more than once, that it was the best fitting, best feeling rifle of any he'd handled.

There were few excellent custom gunmakers in those days. Crossman mentions only a handful besides Owen—Ross King, Griffin & Howe, James V. Howe, August Pachmayr, Wolff and Worthen. He might have mentioned Clyde Baker in his short list (he does in other contexts) and the famed Alvin Linden.

Nor is Louis Wundhammer included, the man who made the first Springfield sporters in 1910, barring the one made at Springfield Armory for Theodore Roosevelt. Wundhammer made four of these rifles to the co-design of Crossman and Stewart Edward White, a popular writer then and an African game hunter. The other two were made for two friends, Rogers and Colby. Some years ago, by mere chance, I bought the one made for White, as pictured in Crossman's book.

I must say I was dismayed when the first California school stocks appeared after WW II. (The May, 1946, *American Rifleman* shows a Weatherby type in an article by Roy Weatherby on scopes by way of precise dating.) Later, when I put together the Custom Guns section of *Gun Digest,* I selected a fair number of such non-classic styled rifles for display. I did this deliberately, thinking that their juxtaposition with the classics shown might, I hoped, illustrate the superiority of the latter. I don't think I fully succeeded—the gaudy, overblown, graceless styles proliferated like weeds, which is not an inapt simile.

Nevertheless, our best and best-known stockmakers today rarely do stocks that are not classic in line, form and general treatment. Several of these talented and hardworking craftsmen, not very well paid really,

When Heym of Germany began to make special projects of Ruger rifles, the Number 1, of course, it probably was inevitable that John Amber would get one and this is it. Fitted with sideplates to increase the expanse for engraving, the whole effect is ornate in this photograph and in reality.

simply will not produce a non-classic stock.

As the years rolled by, and the state of my purse permitted, I had custom stocks and rifles built to my order. An early one was by Al Biesen, and took a mere 5 years to complete. Dale Goens did a matched pair of full-stocked rifles for me, one for an old hunting partner. Both classics, of course, but a mite gaudy, too! These have silver buttplates, grip caps and fore-end tips, each well engraved. John E. Warren, the once triple-threat worker—superbly skilled in metalsmithing, stocking and engraving, but now doing only engraving—made two rifles for me: an earlier one with a massive but classic stock for bench rest shooting, and later a light full-stocked rifle, both showing his mastery of three skills. Maurice Ottmar, who did much of the stock work for Champlin Firearms, made a sporting rifle for me, a BRNO 270 bolt-action, as well as a fine over/under shotgun.

A while back Frank Pachmayr made for me a semi-bent stock for a Model 12 Winchester in 20 gauge—it worked out very well. Made to a pattern designed by Frank's father, August (Old Gus), the buttstock is not fully bent to the right; rather, one's cheek is placed *over* the comb, to a degree, and excellent alignment of the left eye with the rib is easily achieved.

That success got me to thinking: would a similar treatment work on a bolt-action rifle? I asked Don Allen, the custom gunmaker of Northfield, Minnesota (who markets an excellent stock copying machine he devised) about this. Don was intrigued by the idea, though a bit wary of success; he'd never heard of a bent stock bolt-action, nor had I, and digging into old books and periodicals failed to turn up an example. Now, having said that, I'm pretty sure that one or more of our readers will correct me?

To his surprise and pleasure, he'd found the task rather easy, he told me, but rather than adopting the

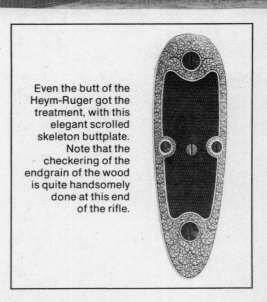

Claw mounts, of course, distinguish the Heym-Ruger, but these claw mounts are decorated in keeping with the rest of the style of the rifle. The large-belled scope is a necessity for Amber's latter-day weak eyesight. Note that the checkering is standard European fashion.

Even the butt of the Heym-Ruger got the treatment, with this elegant scrolled skeleton buttplate. Note that the checkering of the endgrain of the wood is quite handsomely done at this end of the rifle.

Here are both sides of an Al Biesen 7mm Remington Magnum sporting rifle of impeccable design and execution. One thing that Amber always notes about this rifle is that it was 5 years in the making.

Pachmayr plan, Don suggested a different treatment —he'd put minimal bend in the buttstock, make a cheek depression therein on the left side, and ask Herman Waldron, well-known as an arms metalsmith, to make scope bases offset leftward about ½-inch.

I'd sent Don a pre-'64 Model 70 Winchester action, rebarreled by David Huntington to 280 Remington. A little later I received the rifle for trial, metal in the white and stock sanded but not finished. About ⅛-inch more wood needed to be removed in the shallow, curving cheek area, I saw, but otherwise all was fine. Then came the waiting! Don Allen is a full-time pilot with Northwest Airlines, so his gun work is a sometimes thing. I told him I'd wait; better a well-done job, however delayed, than a rushed one.

Besides, I'd *have* to wait. I also wanted this answer-to-my-prayers rifle, a first of its type as far as I could learn, to be something special. I wanted it engraved. As you'll see, I got that and more!

Don sent all the metal to T. J. (Tommy) Kaye of Beaumont, Texas, for the embellishment, after which Tommy and I talked several times about what would be done. I suggested he put a gold moufflon in relief on the floorplate, sending him a photo of the good one—almost a full curl—I'd shot in Czechoslovakia. I wrote about that hunt in *Gun Digest* 32nd/1978 ed. (Hunting in Europe—1976).

A few weeks ago the completed rifle was in my hands, its deeply-rich rust blue gleaming. Don, Herman and Tommy had done a hell of a fine job. Don's metalsmith, Mark Lee, had done some work on it, too—the ramp front sight and the forward swivel on a barrel band.

I suppose I'm prejudiced, naturally, but this is a beautifully-done rifle in all respects bar one, and that aspect was insurmountable if I were to have the rifle without even more delay—the project had taken some

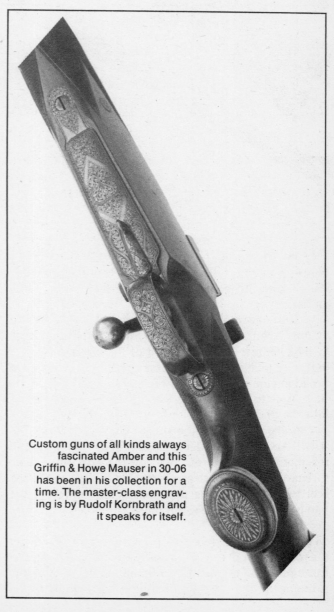

Custom guns of all kinds always fascinated Amber and this Griffin & Howe Mauser in 30-06 has been in his collection for a time. The master-class engraving is by Rudolf Kornbrath and it speaks for itself.

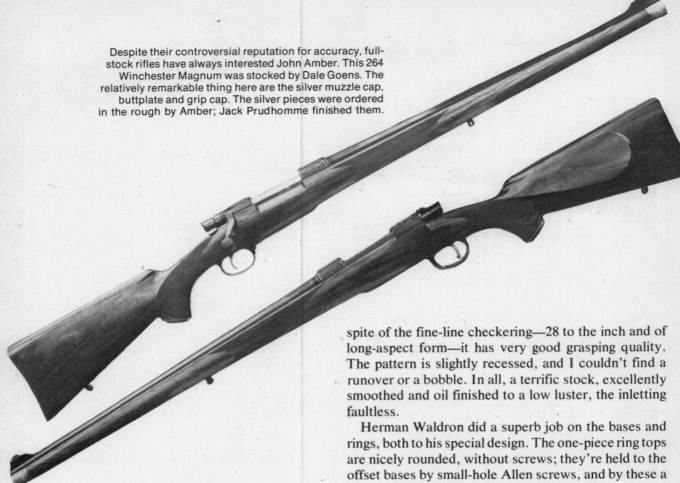

Despite their controversial reputation for accuracy, full-stock rifles have always interested John Amber. This 264 Winchester Magnum was stocked by Dale Goens. The relatively remarkable thing here are the silver muzzle cap, buttplate and grip cap. The silver pieces were ordered in the rough by Amber; Jack Prudhomme finished them.

2 years, about par. Don needed about a 3-inch thick blank to manage the bend—a size not commonly found—and the best such blank he had carried only moderate figure. Nice enough, certainly, but not an exhibition piece of walnut.

Don Allen shaped the stock top in a quite unusual fashion—a few inches forward of the checkered steel buttplate (a Niedner type from Al Biesen), there's a broad-angled ridge atop the cheek-recess area. This ridge runs forward, drops into the hand hole to blend into the checkering of the pistol grip; the checkering covers the grip top, three small points showing at the front. Another low ridge, one on either side, picks up the motif and runs from beneath the grip checkering forward to the bolt-release button on the left and to the bolt handle cut on the right side. Quite different yet highly effective. The comb-nose flutes are perfectly cut.

The checkering, done to a multi-point pattern, covers the fore-end from top to top, and extends about 7 inches fore and aft. The pistol grip is fully covered, the line forming the rear slightly curved, English fashion. In spite of the fine-line checkering—28 to the inch and of long-aspect form—it has very good grasping quality. The pattern is slightly recessed, and I couldn't find a runover or a bobble. In all, a terrific stock, excellently smoothed and oil finished to a low luster, the inletting faultless.

Herman Waldron did a superb job on the bases and rings, both to his special design. The one-piece ring tops are nicely rounded, without screws; they're held to the offset bases by small-hole Allen screws, and by these a degree of lateral adjustment can be made.

The 23-inch round barrel, 0.585″ at the muzzle, is snugly inletted into the fore-end—and perfectly done. A well-angled ramp front sight is fitted; the sling-strap band ahead of the fore-end tip about 1¾ inches. Weight with the Leupold 1-4x variable scope and rings is a scant 8¼ pounds, empty.

The bolt release button is checkered, as is the bolt knob, top and bottom; the top panel is pear shaped. The new steel floorplate is of straddle type, and the guard, also created by Waldron, is nicely rounded and narrowed. The trigger face is grooved for non-slip holding. The bolt body is engine-turned to small whorls, and the extractor is blued.

Waldron did an unusual and effective job on the floorplate release, a near copy of one I'd seen years ago. Rather than fitting the traditional swinging-lever type (as on some old Mauser sporters) or using a push button in the guard, Herman installed a steel, rounded-top sliding release, sharply checkered, that locks or opens the floorplate. Recessed into the floorplate, close to the guard, it's all but invisible in profile; the plate and guard are left clean, uncluttered. Important from a practical view, it is not vulnerable to inadvertent release; a small effort must be made to work it.

Tommy Kaye did a handsome job indeed. The

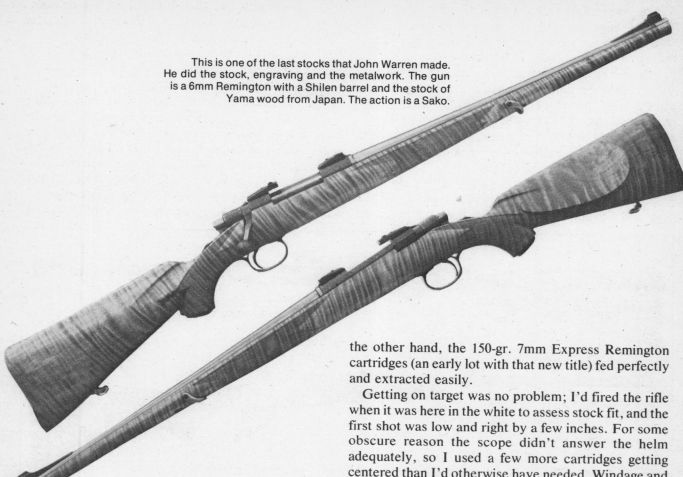

This is one of the last stocks that John Warren made. He did the stock, engraving and the metalwork. The gun is a 6mm Remington with a Shilen barrel and the stock of Yama wood from Japan. The action is a Sako.

floorplate, guard, grip cap, scope rings/bases and the barrel breech are scroll-engraved—large and small. What I hadn't expected was the extra gold inlay work. Tommy did a gold band around the muzzle, two such at the barrel breech, one around the top bolt-knob checkering and another around the steel grip cap and finally, a graceful monogram of my initials in gold on the guard. The moufflon was there, too, of course.

My first shooting test of the new rifle was made on March 20; the temperature was above 50 degrees Fahrenheit for a while, the wind light out of the southwest. The day was dark though, and the two targets at 100 yards rather blurry. I had no trouble getting the Leupold cross hairs sharp, but that floating mass in my left eye—my one and only good glim—prevents my seeing the bull's-eye crisply. Nevertheless, as I've indicated, it was a joy and a satisfaction to sit down at the bench and, once more, shoot from the right shoulder.

I'd found a few rounds of old Peters 280 with 165-gr. bullets, loads I intended to use to settle the barrel and condition it. But none of them would chamber, so it appears that this barrel has a rather tight chamber. On

the other hand, the 150-gr. 7mm Express Remington cartridges (an early lot with that new title) fed perfectly and extracted easily.

Getting on target was no problem; I'd fired the rifle when it was here in the white to assess stock fit, and the first shot was low and right by a few inches. For some obscure reason the scope didn't answer the helm adequately, so I used a few more cartridges getting centered than I'd otherwise have needed. Windage and elevation controls exhibited the same tendency—a couple of division changes in either turret showed little or no change at the target until I'd fired the second or third shot after the change.

It was getting darker now and threatening to rain, so I ran the remaining 11 rounds of the new R-P 150-gr. loads through the rifle rather quickly—or I meant to do that! Another problem arose now—two misfires (neither of which caught me out, I'm pleased to say; the cross hairs remained on the bull).

I had noted from the first shot that the firing-pin depression was quite shallow; the form of the imprint was somewhat flat, too, not hemispherical. Firing-pin protrusion, I'd guess, is minimal, and its point shape incorrect. A "new" pre-'64 firing pin should fix all that.

I thought both groups very good, considering the shooter—the first five, with one of the misfires intruding, went just an inch; the other four shots, again with a misfire, printed at 1¼ inches. I'm sure that a younger eye would better those figures by 25 percent or more, and it must be remembered that this very special rifle has had so far less than 40 cartridges through it.

To sum up, the new rifle is a delectable essay in craftsmanship. All of the elements in its make-up are excellently coordinated, and it feels wonderful.

I'm afraid I got carried away here with the bent wood M70; but it seems to me so completely designed for me and me alone, I don't mind. It is a *custom* rifle.

There have been others, of course. Joe Balickie stocked a Ruger No. 1 single shot to my measurements, the wood a terrific piece of California walnut and the handsome engraving by Ray Viramontez. Clayton Nelson (give the devil his due) made a great stock for my 416 Farquharson; Hal Hartley, using his beloved fiddleback maple, stocked my first Model 70 Winchester, a 30-06 bought in 1937, and recently Phil Pilkington put a Ruger M77 rifle together for me, a beautiful job indeed (See *Gun Digest* 32/1978).

I own several other custom rifles, but not made for me—a 7x57 Springfield, as trim and graceful a rifle as I own, and a Sauer Mauser in 30-06, the latter engraved by R. Kornbrath (see *Gun Digest* 23/1974), and both made by Griffin & Howe in that firm's golden years, the 1930s. I don't, alas, own any rifles by Jerry Fisher, Earl Milliron or Len Brownell, though Len has done some fine custom work for me.

Among my custom-made foreign guns are these: two Famars 12-gauge doubles, one their Castore 270 external hammer gun, the other their best-grade Venere hammerless; a Francotte sidelock 12-bore, the engraving an American game scene by Joseph Fugger; his first full-scale job for Abercrombie & Fitch, and a recently done Ruger S.S. rifle, rebarreling, stock work and metalsmithing by Fr. W. Heym of Germany. Dummy sideplates were fitted to this handsome rifle, and the

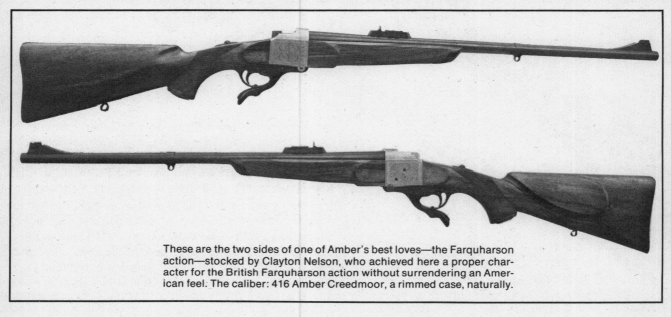

These are the two sides of one of Amber's best loves—the Farquharson action—stocked by Clayton Nelson, who achieved here a proper character for the British Farquharson action without surrendering an American feel. The caliber: 416 Amber Creedmoor, a rimmed case, naturally.

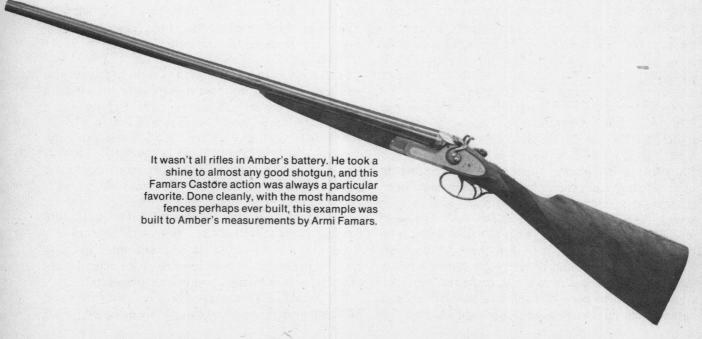

It wasn't all rifles in Amber's battery. He took a shine to almost any good shotgun, and this Famars Castore action was always a particular favorite. Done cleanly, with the most handsome fences perhaps ever built, this example was built to Amber's measurements by Armi Famars.

whole engraved and gold inlaid by Eric Bössler (see *Gun Digest* 34/1980 ed.). Not least in my rack is a beautifully done break-open single shot rifle made for me by Renato Gamba of Brescia; the engraving was done by Angelo Galeazzi in the very demanding *bulino* technique—see *Gun Digest* 32/1978. Perazzi, some years ago, made a most handsome upland game gun for me, an over-under with detachable trigger system and an extraordinarily colorful stock and matching fore-end of Circassian type. Last, for now, a side-by-side sidelock double rifle by John Fanzoi of Ferlach—see *Gun Digest* 30/1976.

I don't know that I can adequately convey to you my lifelong love affair with the custom-crafted rifle or shot-

the precise fit of the mating parts, metal or wood, the small niceties of design elements that took so long to evolve, it is the *completed* gun that arouses me—the feel under the hand of smoothly polished wood, its warm color softly glowing; the tactile qualities of the gun between the hands as it is brought up, the satisfaction experienced as the butt snugs solidly into the shoulder; the perfect pointability of a gun properly fitted, and the crisp breaking of a well-tuned trigger.

A display of emotion, coupled with physical gratification? I suppose so. But for those of you who don't look upon best quality custom guns as I do, my sympathy, sincerely. For those who share my views, who know what I'm talking about, I need say no more.

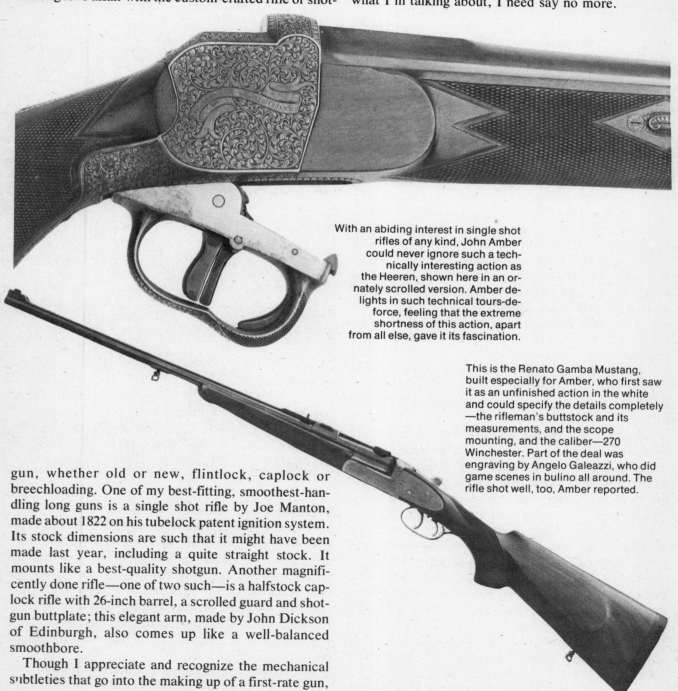

With an abiding interest in single shot rifles of any kind, John Amber could never ignore such a technically interesting action as the Heeren, shown here in an ornately scrolled version. Amber delights in such technical tours-de-force, feeling that the extreme shortness of this action, apart from all else, gave it its fascination.

This is the Renato Gamba Mustang, built especially for Amber, who first saw it as an unfinished action in the white and could specify the details completely—the rifleman's buttstock and its measurements, and the scope mounting, and the caliber—270 Winchester. Part of the deal was engraving by Angelo Galeazzi, who did game scenes in bulino all around. The rifle shot well, too, Amber reported.

gun, whether old or new, flintlock, caplock or breechloading. One of my best-fitting, smoothest-handling long guns is a single shot rifle by Joe Manton, made about 1822 on his tubelock patent ignition system. Its stock dimensions are such that it might have been made last year, including a quite straight stock. It mounts like a best-quality shotgun. Another magnificently done rifle—one of two such—is a halfstock caplock rifle with 26-inch barrel, a scrolled guard and shotgun buttplate; this elegant arm, made by John Dickson of Edinburgh, also comes up like a well-balanced smoothbore.

Though I appreciate and recognize the mechanical subtleties that go into the making up of a first-rate gun,

HOW A COLLECTOR

EXPLAINING the collector's passion is probably beyond the reach of the noncollector, but it ought to be possible here to see what has made Erich Lengyel such a passionate collector of fine handmade guns. Quickly, as he does most of the things he does, Lengyel has, in a few short years, amassed a collection of 100 fine guns, most of them rifles by top American craftsmen.

A hunter since high school, Erich Lengyel is a young man with a very good business and a very good business sense, which explains where the funds come from. In recent years, he has hunted Alaska every year, besides shooting on Chesapeake Bay and in most local deer seasons. He lives in Virginia.

The man is a collector, regardless. He came to collecting custom rifles after collecting other kinds of guns. He began with working guns, buying guns with which to hunt. That is certainly a reasonable beginning.

Soon, Lengyel was into Smith & Wesson handguns. Beginning in 1971, he collected a rather large number of Smith & Wessons, but either found that limiting or felt there were better investments to make, and by this time he had to think of investments. He was doing better, he found, in guns than in other financial interests and opportunities.

He began then to buy Brownings and sell Smith & Wessons. The Browning handguns led to Browning shoulder arms and when other collectors began to bid up Brownings, Lengyel already had dozens. He bought only high-grade guns and felt that Brownings were the best way to go because they were absolutely a known quality to any potential buyer.

"A Browning new in the box," Lengyel puts it, "was very much like a deposit in a bank account. It was, and is, a known quality, and there was a market in Brownings."

All during this period, Lengyel was hunting every year, and not ignoring other guns completely. It was during this time, perhaps around 1975, that he bought, from the estate of a local man, a set of four Jaeger rifles. On his first Alaska trip, he hunted with a pre-'64 Model 70 rifle stocked and engraved by the Jaeger firm.

From that beginning, Lengyel began to dabble, as it were, in better grade guns. Each time he found a gun that was a little out of the ordinary at the right price, he would buy it, and then he would consult with local dealers, like Fred Davis of Falls Church, and other knowledgeable friends, and find out, in detail, just what he had bought.

"The more I found out about any given gun, the more I knew about other guns," Lengyel says, "and the more I found out about fine guns, the handmade guns, the one-of-a-kind guns, the more I was interested in them,

both to shoot them and to own them."

As an investor, Lengyel calculated that 1977 and 1978 were good years to sell off Brownings, and he did so. In many cases, he found that his Brownings were excellent trading material. It goes without saying that Brownings bought during 1971 to 1974 and held for several years and then disposed of were indeed good investments. Certainly, with his gun collection that far, Erich Lengyel was able to outperform the general investment marketplace and did so.

As the Brownings left, over a period of many months, Lengyel explored all the opportunities he could for

COLLECTS by Ken Warner

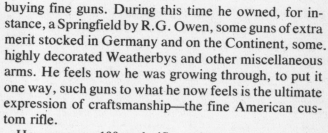

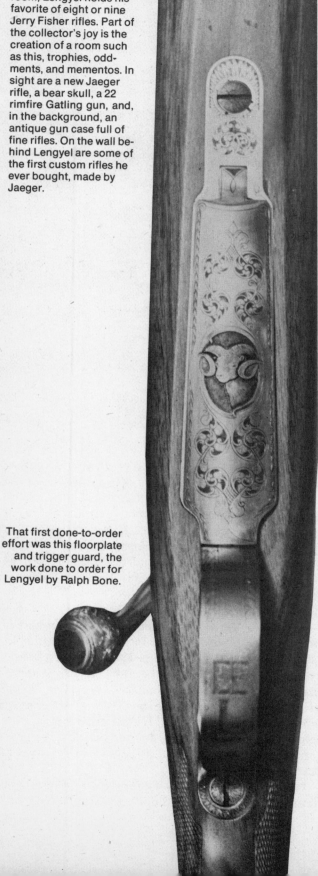

(Opposite) In this gun room, Lengyel holds his favorite of eight or nine Jerry Fisher rifles. Part of the collector's joy is the creation of a room such as this, trophies, oddments, and mementos. In sight are a new Jaeger rifle, a bear skull, a 22 rimfire Gatling gun, and, in the background, an antique gun case full of fine rifles. On the wall behind Lengyel are some of the first custom rifles he ever bought, made by Jaeger.

That first done-to-order effort was this floorplate and trigger guard, the work done to order for Lengyel by Ralph Bone.

buying fine guns. During this time he owned, for instance, a Springfield by R.G. Owen, some guns of extra merit stocked in Germany and on the Continent, some highly decorated Weatherbys and other miscellaneous arms. He feels now he was growing through, to put it one way, such guns to what he now feels is the ultimate expression of craftsmanship—the fine American custom rifle.

He now owns 100 such rifles, with a few shotguns. If the words "custom rifle" mean that the gun must be made to order for the individual who owns it, then much of Lengyel's collection includes fine rifles, not custom rifles. However, he did not buy them on the open market, but almost always, either himself or through an agent, from those people who had originally ordered them. In several instances, rifles made for someone else did not fit him and went back to the makers to be fitted.

Lengyel is a good shot, but he is not of average build. He is short, wide-shouldered, and heavily muscled with short arms. He has and dispenses a great deal of energy, but he also carries plenty of weight for his height. These days, artisans who make guns for him work to a standard—for Lengyel—set of dimensions; early on, he bought fine rifles of whatever dimension.

I mentioned passion, and passion it is. Lengyel repairs cars for a living. He doesn't repair so many himself these days, although he is a master of that particular trade. There are, depending on the time of year, seven to ten top mechanics working in his shop. His father began the business, and Lengyel continues it and it is, deservedly, a most successful business. Lengyel's is a German-speaking family, having emigrated to the United States after WW II out of the morass of eastern Europe. Out of the family background, the hard work, the fair dealing, the profitmaking, has come a drive and an energy which, in that part of his life concerned with firearms and with hunting, amounts to no less than a passion.

There is hardly any other way to explain how someone would come along and in the space of a few short years, perhaps 4, even find, let alone buy and acquire, 100 fine guns.

What sort of guns are we talking about? Well, he still has those Jaegers, although they are distinctly overdecorated for his tastes these days. He owns 11 rifles by Jerry Fisher, and of those six were made for him. He owns rifles by Monte Kennedy and Clayton Nelson and Keith Stegall and several by Lenard Brownell and five by Dale Goens and rifles by Shelhamer, Milliron, Pilkington, Biesen, Fashingbauer and Labatchni and Goudy. He has a rifle on which John Warren did the whole job—stock, metalsmithing and engraving. He has metalwork by Burgess and Blackburn and Wiebe and Talley. He has engraving by Churchill and Warren and Marktl and Willig and Goens and Alvin White and Arnold Griebel and Huff and Tommy Kaye. Ralph Bone is considered a personal friend and Lengyel has several of his rifles and much of his engraving. He still builds rifles from Jaeger, engraved by the Willigs.

Some of these rifles are guns made some time ago, but the majority are guns of the last several years. Knowledgeable people have to agree that over the past 5 years or so, the detailing in American custom rifles has taken several strides, and this is certainly visible in the guns on Lengyel's walls. The guns themselves have, over the past several years, advanced Erich Lengyel's tastes in guns and desires for the future.

Like every other collector of excellence, at least in this field, Lengyel buys every good rifle action he can, invests in wood in advance, meets every new artisan he can, and keeps six to 12 jobs in work all the time.

There in the middle years Lengyel used standard factory arms on his hunting trips, with a great fondness for Ruger 77s. They delivered perfectly well, but now he sets aside suitable fine guns for such trips. The investor in him won't let him take the very best to the field, so those that go along tend to be relatively plainer models, but that is certainly understandable.

A fellow who owns 100 rifles obviously does not shoot them all. In the collection are rifles in virtually all the common, and some of the uncommon cartridges, ranging from 22 Hornet to 458 Magnum. Lengyel does shoot perhaps three or four out of ten of his fine rifles and for good reason.

"These rifles, as pretty as they are, are meant to be shot," he says, "and if they do not shoot well are not really fine guns. Therefore, you have to shoot them to be sure, and I have never been disappointed. When a Fisher or a Kennedy or a Biesen stocks a rifle, and a Blackburn or a Burgess does the metalsmithing, the result will shoot.

"All these are hunting rifles and I expect them to shoot a 3-shot group from a cold barrel into 1-inch at 100 yards and they do." Lengyel adds, "In one case, with a rifle that I had remodeled to suit me, it took an extra trip back to the makers to reach that standard, but that is the only such case connected with this collection. A lot of them are very pretty rifles, I certainly hope, but they will all shoot because that is what they are for and that is how they were built."

Those advanced tastes have already begun to crimp Lengyel's style. He still buys rifles, but they are harder to find at the level he wishes to find them. There are plenty of handmade, good quality guns around, but they have to be as good as the guns he already has for him to buy these days. If it gets really difficult, he feels he may be reduced to upgrading the guns he already has by having them engraved, and there he has a problem since he wants only top engraving and there are only so many top engravers around.

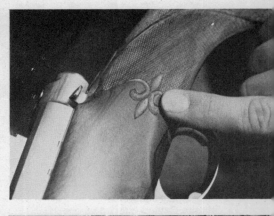

Still in the white, the currently in-work 375 exhibits the highest grade of custom work in every detail, checkering, wood finish, all facets.

At his garage workbench, getting ready to go to Alaska, Lengyel mounts his scope on an Al Biesen hunting rifle. He keeps a considerable supply of scope mounts and scope mount parts as well as scopes to insure he does not wind up with any scopeless rifles.

Erich Lengyel is in a position beyond most of us to know what he likes in a custom rifle. Unlike many, he has not refined his tastes until there is only one kind of thing that appeals to him. He is not, for instance, caliber conscious, nor action conscious. He merely insists that the action and furniture and weight of the rifle be suitable to its caliber. The bulk of his rifles are pre-'64 Model 70s and Model 98 Mausers. However, there is at least one Husqvarna, a Sako or two, even a Weatherby Mark V in the collection.

When it comes to wood, Lengyel likes watermarked or marble cake walnut, but considers, where suitable, straight grained fine French or English walnut just as pretty. In checkering, well, the craftsman in him appreciates the 32-line master patterns. He likes 26-line checkering on a hunting rifle, but 32-line checkering on what he calls a "show gun." His pattern preference is a multi-point pattern, but the fleur-de-lis and ribbon patterns suit certain rifles and if they do he approves of them.

He accepts carving only if it is part of a maker's style already established, and "I don't go in for that baroque

The rifle starts with the action, and, taken all in all, Lengyel likes the Argentine 1909 Mauser. This sample he is working on himself, not to go in competition with metalsmiths, but probably because he can't keep his hands off it.

Traveling with fine guns takes something special, and Lengyel had Cargo Carrier construct this special four-rifle case, wheeled and handled for easy air transport. The unit has a full set of locks.

stuff," he says, meaning inlays and strange stock patterns and exaggerated features of any kind.

"In fine guns, styles change," he notes. "They don't get any better, in my opinion, but they do change and are different. By now, these stockmakers have taken the time element about as far as they can go. Detailing is so advanced, it is very difficult to conceive that they can get a lot more time into stocks in the future.

"Engraving on firearms today is the best ever. Not all of it is the best, of course, but the masters, the very best people, simply are not going to improve greatly. And that is true for metalsmiths, also. No one is ever going to polish better than a Lampert or a Burgess, or any of the hundreds of people who have seen their work and have a talent themselves to carry fine work that far.

"The whole field is going to go up, but that will be mostly evidenced in prices in the future. To the extent that the purchase or, if you prefer, assembly of a fine rifle is an investment, the best investments will be the very best makers. Inevitably, those people are going to command very high prices for their work and be worth it.

"That is where the newcomer—both the newcomer artists and newcomer buyers—will find opportunity," Lengyel observes. "The very high prices of the masters and the very long waits for their work will tend to push those new buyers toward the newer craftsman, who can deliver at lower prices and quicker. Many of those, of course, will be every bit as good as today's masters, perhaps even better, in terms of actual workmanship. They will not have the name, and therefore will not be such good investments, but the rifles themselves will, beyond a doubt, be first-class rifles."

Lengyel is probably not going to get out of fine guns as he has the other sorts of guns he collected. Now the passion continues unabated, and there is enough going on in the field to keep an interest going, even an advanced collector's interests. There is still an adventure in each gun, even after 100 guns.

For instance, Lengyel now finds that certain actions, as acquired, and certain pieces of wood speak to him. A 375 he is now having built is one such. He found the wood first. It was one blank among many, but as he got it, and later as it cured, he kept thinking that it would make a perfectly good 375. When he located and bought a square bridge Mauser action, he thought that it and the piece of wood went together perfectly well, and then he began to search for the right artisans to assemble the gun, and it is under way. Approximately the same thing happened once when he decided that a given piece of wood would greatly suit a 220 Swift varmint rifle, and eventually had the gun built.

Erich Lengyel is an impatient man. He drives hard at about everything he does, and is known to pay premium prices in order to see the work completed as fast as it can be done. He will also go to considerable length to find what someone needs and furnish that instead of money, if that will get the job done quicker. When all else fails, he resorts to patience, but that is not easy.

This general interest in fine guns has led him into other kinds of collecting, of course. He collects handmade knives, and Americana, and, now, the great sporting books, both British and American. The tastes acquired for good workmanship have led him, with his wife Beverly, to buy sound antique furniture to use in their home. Again, none of these things are bad investments, but none are chosen solely because of that.

As for defining that passion, it seems to be rooted in a competitive nature. Erich Lengyel uses guns and uses them well, he hunts seriously and he hunts hard and he trains seriously to hunt each year, and he has the space and the money it takes to collect seriously, and he makes the time to do so. All of those things are so, but they do not explain this particular passion. Lengyel himself probably gives the best clue: "You can, now, find things that are the very best of their kind and they are only one of a kind and so you can own things that no one else can own."

STUDYING

by KEN WARNER

With adjustable lights—very important, Pilkington feels—and the furnished abbreviated checkering cradle, Rich Wahl concentrates on a fleur-de-lis forearm pattern. With what was there at the seminar, any student who wanted to could accomplish a checkering job.

THE STATE OF THE ART

In his session on stock design, Pilkington made the point with this sketch that the principles worked on anything. He never built the stock sketched here, designed for one of John Amber's British single shots, but the drawing shows the system works.

(Opposite page) During the work phases of the seminar "Seminar of the Masters," students got the direct attention of Phil Pilkington, here about to provide some specific instruction. Pilkington furnished cradles, tools and the right kind of wood for this exercise.

SEMINAR OF THE MASTERS is a rather grand name for an accelerated course in the fine points of fine gun making, but it makes sense. If your purpose is to teach the best techniques by best teachers to the people most interested, and that *was* Phil Pilkington's purpose, the name fits.

It was not a big event, but it was an extraordinarily well-prepared event and, in the opinion of most who attended and this writer, a bargain at $500. Apart from all else, the art and the craft and the technique of fine gun making and fine gun acquiring has gotten to the point where someone needed to start a school.

Doing a seminar came naturally to Phil Pilkington, who is widely acknowledged to be among the very best practitioners of the fine art of stockmaking. Pilkington has been a teacher before, and an orator as well. He did not orate in the 5-day meeting he put together at the fairgrounds in Enid, Oklahoma, where he lives and works. Academically, Pilkington regards a seminar as an informal atmosphere, with an agenda and no rules.

The agenda for the week included: learning to finish wood as Pilkington finishes it; learning to blue metal as Pilkington blues it; learning to lay out a stock as Pilkington does it; and then learning to lay out and perform a checkering pattern as Pilkington does it. That is actually not how it happened, nor is that all there was to the seminar, because following those instructional efforts, acknowledged master metalsmith Ron Lampert arrived on the scene to impart his special viewpoints on the proper finishing of rifle actions and barrels and accessories. Among the little stunts Lampert demonstrated was the checkering of bolt knobs and polishing and jeweling of bolts, together with a look at the solid techniques of polishing and finishing for which he is so well-known.

The seminar was intended for anyone with an interest

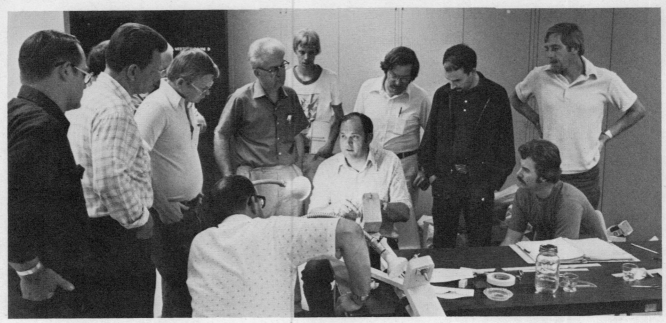

Phil Pilkington instructs in the principles and practice of checkering fine guns—one session of the 5-day course.

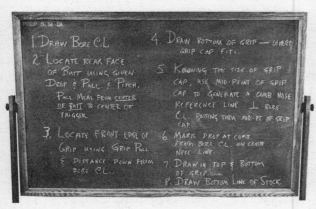

Designing a gun stock is more than an 8-step process, but this blackboard shows the main points in the Pilkington approach to the subject. Each student got to design a stock.

At the drawingboard, Pilkington took questions from his students, each of whom followed every step of the process as this picture shows. Among those in the picture at top center left is Bill Dowtin, himself a well-known stockmaker.

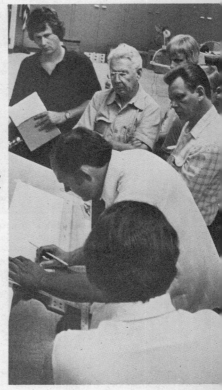

Pilkington started with a blank piece of paper, just as his students had, and then as they gathered around, created this sketch. There is about as much figuring as there is drawing in a proper stock design.

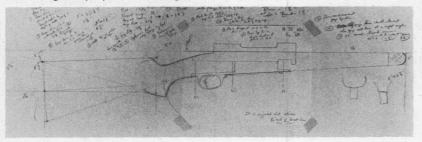

in fine rifles, be he or she a buyer, or fabricator or collector of same. That is exactly who came—a selection of men, this time, whose interest in the subject was amateur, semi-professional and professional. They came from Arizona, North Dakota, Texas, and North Carolina—in short, they came from all over. About a third were users and collectors, serious people interested in the fine instruments for and of themselves; another third are best described as semi-professionals,

meaning men who earn their basic living in other ways, but also earn some money as gunsmiths every year; the remainder were professionals, either professional general gunsmiths, or fine stockmakers of repute, or owners and operators of sporting goods stores specializing in guns. There were only 15 of us, and two were writers, Jim Carmichel and your reporter, neither of whom can be said to be uninterested in fine guns.

There was a great deal to learn, and it was fully

Part of the course, and one much enjoyed by the students, was the collection of fine custom rifles from Champlin Firearms Company and the subsequent examination and critique thereof. Despite his expression, Pilkington found little wrong with the rifle in his hands.

Who Was There?

This was the first Seminar Of The Masters, and it is likely there will be a second, managed by Phil Pilkington. Perhaps there won't be, but I am convinced there will be, whether or not this one is repeated, other seminars, other courses in appreciation and courses in technique offered as time goes on. Therefore, for the historical record, I think a list of the first 15 names ought to be published:

Jim Carmichel, Jonesboro, TN—*enthusiast, writer.*
Willis R. Dortch, Tucson, AZ—*enthusiast.*
Bill Dowtin, Celina, TX—*professional stockmaker.*
Pete Forthofer, Avon, OH—*professional smith.*
Charles R. Joines, Sparta, NC—*part-time smith.*
Charles D. Marine, Marion, IN—*enthusiast.*
Douglas Mongeon, Rolle, ND—*enthusiast.*
M. W. Murphy, DeSoto, MD—*professional smith.*
Dennis Pearson, Charlotte, NC—*enthusiast.*
David Schwarze, Ft Wayne, IN—*professional smith.*
John Sones, Denver, CO—*part-time smith, instructor.*
Ronald Toews, Enid, OK—*enthusiast.*
Rich Wahl, Lyons, KA—*part-time smith.*
Ken Warner, Falls Church, VA—*enthusiast, editor.*
John Westrom, Des Moines, IA—*part-time smith.*

The course was organized, of course, by Phillip Pilkington of Enid, Oklahoma, who taught the stockmaking and bluing portions of the instruction. Ron Lampert of Guthrie, Minnesota, taught the metal finishing.

The seminar took place in the Hoover Building on the fairgrounds at Enid, Oklahoma June 16 to June 20, 1980.

Not a gunsmith, Willis Dortch, did what most of us do when looking over a gun. This one is an excellent older Biesen. Dortch took the course because he likes rifles.

presented. This is not the place for a description of techniques, but it is probably a place to talk of what Phil Pilkington thinks is important about custom rifles and the details of their construction and finishing.

This seminar was to concentrate, Pilkington said, pretty largely on the surface of the gun stock and the metal. "What you see" is the way he put it. Not much time was wasted in telling those in attendance how to reduce a stock to its final shape nor, indeed, what that

final shape ought to be, except that the word "classic" was used a great deal. And Pilkington did get into that, of which more below.

First, however, he described his oil finish, which he says is in the wood and not on it. It was not to be a simple lecture course, for each student had sample pieces of English walnut, some of it already started, and had finish and the proper finishing tools. Pilkington mixes a short-lived finish from marine spar varnish and other ingredients, and there is a 12-step finishing process, which may be terminated about half-way along if the stockmaker wishes.

Certainly, the Pilkington method is simple enough, consisting of sanding in successive coats of the finish. In just two applications or so, the pores in the wood are largely filled, and from thereon it is refinement. That is something that Pilkington aims at in most of the things he does with guns—refinement.

The students had very little trouble following the directions, and it was plain to see that Pilkington's system does exactly what it is intended to do. The end result is an in-the-wood oil finish of considerable merit.

When it comes to bluing, Pilkington, a former chemist, takes much the same tack. He sought the simple way. He regards his stock finishing technique as simple because you never have to sand away a whole layer of finish to start over. You simply apply the finish in a manner that uses it and the sanded-away wood and some of the sanding grit to fill the pores quickly, and, one might say, you never look back.

With the bluing, Pilkington sought a finish that would work equally, and to the right color, on all kinds of all steel, could be interrupted at any time without damaging the job, and did not require either painstaking attention to the details of the process, or an extraordinary amount of work in carding off red rust and the like. The end result is what Pilkington calls fume bluing. As a chemist, he was able to assure his students that what happened on the surface of the metal was the same process as happened in other forms of rust bluing. However, Pilkington's method seemed, to this viewer at least, to be a good deal simpler and more certain than other bluing methods he has seen.

In essence, Pilkington simply exposes properly polished and prepared metal to the fumes—the mixed fumes—of nitric acid and hydrochloric acid. This is done in a clear plastic box. The parts are simply placed in the box and a few drops of the acids are now liberated within, and the cover is set down. After a time, the action of the fumes slows, and the parts may be removed from the box, boiled in water, mildly carded to remove a sort of bluish fur, and returned to a fresh batch of fumes. The number of repetitions required to achieve the desired rich, slightly soft-to-the-eye blue varies with the kind of metal being blued, but five to ten repetitions is all it takes.

Of course, getting the repetitions and the fine results is not as simple as those paragraphs might indicate. Pilkington is a demon on degreasing. He believes that most of the problems with bluing jobs result from inefficient and insufficient degreasing procedures. He greatly prefers, and can cite sound chemical reasons for his choice, to soak the parts to be blued for a long time in solvents rather than to attempt to scrub them physically. For instance, he says it is very often the case that oils will be trapped under the rib of a pair of shotgun

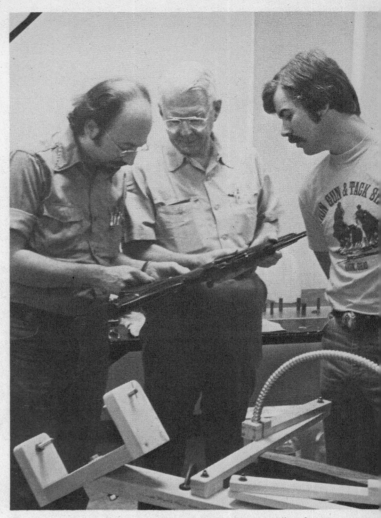

Students at the seminar learned from each other as well as from Pilkington. Here Sones, Dortch, and Pete Forthofer team up on a custom rifle during the course. Sones is a gunsmithing school instructor; Dortch is an amateur enthusiast of the fine rifles; Forthofer, as his T-shirt shows, is a working gunsmith —but all found common ground in the discussion of a custom gunstock. The bluing set-up is behind the trio, and in the foreground can be seen the checkering cradle used by students in the seminar.

barrels and then, during the bluing process, escape through pinholes and the like to mar the eventual finish. Similarly, some rifle actions, particularly those that are cast, can occasionally weep lubricant during bluing and the result is a spot. Pilkington thinks that lacquer thinner would be about the best solvent for this job, but he finds it too expensive to use in the quantities he uses it, and so with a great deal of precaution, he degreases with gasoline, followed by another solution.

Through all this, Pilkington had as attentive an audience as I have seen in any seminar anywhere. He spoke, of course, with authority, but he also spoke to people who wanted to hear what he had to say. There were few people in the room paying closer attention than, as an example, Bill Dowtin, whom many consider a master stockmaker in his own right. Certainly, he is a full-time and very busy stockmaker. And there he was.

Ruger Number 1 or the Winchester High Wall, the actions absolutely demand certain starting points for the stock and there is not a lot of room for deviation. Pilkington regards that as a simpler and easier situation than what is provided by the magazine rifle.

In any event, any given action can have a comb line only so high, and the human body demands that the drop at the heel and pitch fall within certain limits, and the right hand on the grip insists that, for instance, the distance from the center of the trigger to the forward edge of the grip can probably be somewhere between 3⅜ and 3¾ inches.

Talking as he worked, Pilkington drew out a complete plan for the profile of a sporting rifle stock to be built on the Model 70 action, which was the drawing provided.

It was then the student's turn, and this writer took a turn. Deciding the system Pilkington had provided looked good, I set up a different kind of problem than the standard stock just to see how it worked. My intention was to create an open-gripped heavyweight stock for a large man to shoot a 458 Winchester or similar cartridge. I wanted something that might well work and look vaguely Continental/English with a touch of the African safari about it. I opted to have a much longer than normal trigger-to-grip-cap distance, to have a rounded bottom on the pistol grip and to have a thick and relatively short forearm.

I am now convinced the Pilkington system is a sound system since, with no skill whatever as a draftsman, I

Here Rich Wahl returns a Biesen grip cap to the bluing box while Pilkington demonstrates carding technique in the background. Once bluing started, classes were interrupted throughout in order to complete the various steps.

Moving along into what he called the "art" phase of stockmaking, Pilkington showed everyone how to begin with a drawing of the action and then working from absolutely required base lines, such as trigger pull length, and comb height, how to establish the points of references and gradually build up, on paper, a stock design to suit. At the moment, stockmakers across the country are pretty well agreed on what makes a classic form of stock for a bolt-action magazine rifle. The magazine rifle, Pilkington says, is the most difficult for which to design, since lines may go anywhere, so to speak. That is, a little subtle shaving at the tangs of almost any bolt-action and the lines of departure of the top and bottom of the stock can be almost as the stockmaker wills. This means that the stockmaker has complete freedom to make an ugly stock or a handsome one. With other actions, Pilkington says, such as the

Another portion of the course delivered by Pilkington was fume bluing, which is accomplished in a plastic box with a mixture of acids. The many samples in sight from all different sources proved conclusively that the method provides a close match, regardless of steel, when properly done. The high polish of the rectangle will become a soft-looking, tough blue. The jar at left holds one of the acids used in the process.

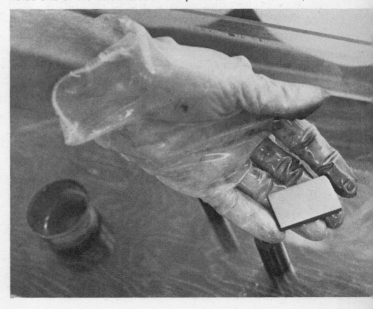

was able to churn out the profile of a sporter stock that looked as if it might be built and not be the ugliest stock on the block when finished. It would not, admittedly, carry the delicate refinement of what has come to be the current classic American sporter rifle stock, but it had its own look, and it did appear to be a good handle for a heavy rifle meant to be manipulated quickly. Beyond that, I make no claim, for there is no accounting for tastes. And that explains, my mother used to tell me, why the lady kissed the cow.

There was also a session on checkering, and many of those present took to it like ducks to water. This reporter does not and did not. The instructions for the procedure to lay out a checkering pattern seemed perfectly clear, and certainly the results attained by the students bore that out. Some had more experience than others, but all did in fact accomplish a fairly regular set of scratchings on their sample pieces.

We now take time out at this point to tell you that this was not a simple classroom situation. Pilkington had

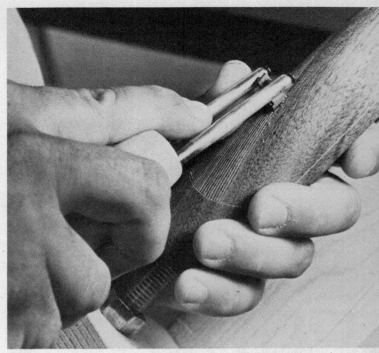

Here is the beginning of one good student effort. Hardly any student dared confess to already knowing how to checker, but some of the patterns grew suspiciously fast.

Here are some of the materials supplied students at the seminar. The wood squares were fine walnut which students finished according to the Pilkington recommendations. The assorted checkering tools are handmade by Pilkington and use glued-in standard commercial cutters.

prepared checkering cradles, checkering tools, sample forearms of the proper kind of English walnut, in short all the tools needed to do any of the things he taught were present there for the students to use.

And it is also worth noting that he has his own kinks about tools, preferring the kind he makes that use standard cutters to the kind that are sold generally. And he put his effort where his opinion was by making a set of such tools for use during the seminar of every student there.

Ron Lampert, the other Teaching Master at the seminar, had a whole different problem in presentation. Metal finishing is either done by hand or with very expensive tools, and not much inbetween. Lampert did bring some of his highly specialized jigs and fixtures, and in particular the machinists among the students got a great deal out of his two days of presentation.

Lampert is a perfectionist and a very highly skilled and patient polisher of rifle actions. In his own shop he is equipped to reach a high degree of sophistication and

does so regularly, if the samples he showed were fair samples, and indeed they are. It is not too difficult to find a Lampert metalworking job among custom rifles, and all I have seen have been superlative.

Thus far, we have seen what this seminar—this very well-prepared seminar—actually offered its students. The larger question it answers is: How interested are American shooters in fine custom guns? The answer, from my point of view, is that they are very interested indeed. What went on at this seminar is not nearly so important as that there was a seminar, that it did draw a paying crowd, and that no one in that crowd was unhappy with what they learned. There simply were no complaints among the assembled group and, in fact, quite the contrary situation existed: Everyone thought it was well worth the trip and the time and the money.

So we have come, on the evidence, to a state of the art in the manufacture and fabrication of fine custom guns where they have become a separate and very sophisticated subject, one worth the study. During one session

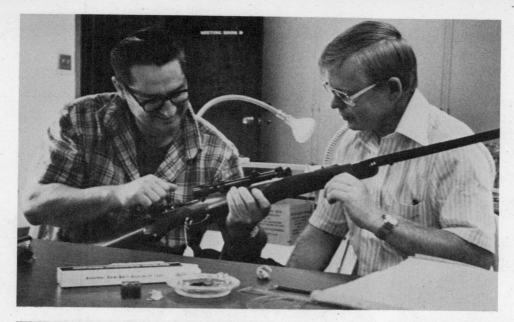

Waiting for his part of the program, Ron Lampert (checked shirt) enjoyed looking at rifles with Ron Toews of Enid, who took the course. The points of view of a master metalsmith about jobs he has never seen before are often interesting.

This indexing fixture, made from a typewriter, is one of Ron Lampert's tools to acquire precision in the refined and delicate jeweling of bolt bodies—part of the secret, Lampert says, is to have the right setups. (Toews photo)

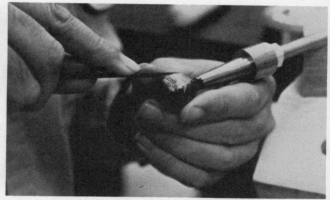

The hands of Ron Lampert demonstrate the checkering of bolt handles, a finished detail highly thought of in the custom rifle ranks. (Toews photo)

in the seminar a number of custom rifles were borrowed from the inventory of the Champlin rifle company, also of Enid, and all were compared in the atmosphere of the seminar. The trends of the past and their pathway to the present were clear in the lines and details of these guns, some of which were 20 years old and some of which were brand new.

It is obvious that all concerned are putting a great deal more time and refinement into details. And it is plain that we may well be reaching a plateau of sorts in the degree of refinement to which wood and metal can be carried. A case in point was an Al Biesen custom rifle, some 20 years old, from the Champlin collection. Compared to the work done these days, the old Biesen stock is rounded and soft and, not to speak too bluntly, quite undetailed compared to what is going on these days, doubtless in Mr. Biesen's own shop.

That is not to say, and this was pointed out by Pilkington to the crowd, that the older gun was any less a custom rifle, or any less a fine achievement in design. It

Lampert, suffering from a broken ankle, discussed action smithing techniques during the seminar. Here, a pair of students find out how to get into the crevices of a Mauser 98 action.

It didn't take a whole rifle to draw a crowd during the seminar. This scene took place one minute after a full complete Lampert polish job was handed over to the student body for examination.

From above, the same two actions reveal even more of the Lampert magic, including the Model 70 style safety, the specially-made scope mounts, the bolt jeweling and, of course, a fine bolt handle.

The before and after of a Lampert job can be seen here in the bottom of a Mauser action, the one cleaned to a better profile and a high polish; the other as-issued.

was a more friendly gun than most, which has to be one of the aims of the custom rifle maker. The rifle had been well-used and cared for and seemed an entirely competent effort. Certainly there was no evidence that it had ever warped or gotten out of line or been anything but a useful tool during its whole life, and there was little reason to think that its next owner will not get full value.

There will likely be a point, down the road, when classic rifle design will get static and the opportunity for further embellishment will be limited by the available surface. One cannot, after all, checker an entire gun stock.

It is at that point that new designers and new eyes will come to the scene, and we will be off on a new round of design refinement, doubtless reaching some day unto a new classic style.

For now, the first Seminar Of The Masters has passed; there will doubtless be a second one; and all of those to come for the foreseeable future will doubtless concern themselves with that most classic of stock designs—the American classic sporting rifle stock.

STATE OF THE ART

by Ken Warner and C. E. Harris

Rifle Stocks   Sights and Mounts   Other Shotguns   Metal Finish
Rifle Actions   Rifle Furniture   Revolvers   Wood Finish
Metalsmithing   Doubles   Autoloaders   Buying Wood
Barrels   Hunting Handguns   To Buy the Work
        Embellishment   Match Rifles
            Match Handguns
            Skeet and Trap Guns

What is The Art?

THE ART of the gun craftsman is to provide a gun that better suits its function, and achieves or retains the highest standards of what must be called beauty and elegance. All specially made, carefully remodeled, or refurbished guns should reach some elevated standard but only the very best reach the highest standards.

We are trying here to help define what that very best is. And, necessarily, we are defining what might not be the very best, but might be entirely suitable for a given purpose or might be as much as a given pocketbook could stand.

Why call it art? Well, that is a debate among the people who do this work. Some of them take a hard line and say that if it shoots it cannot be art; others believe that a working tool can be a piece of art as well. That is,

probably a philosophical discussion. We will leave it that. There are a great many guns today which, if they are not art, are at least artistic.

Certainly, as with any art, what is accomplished with custom guns is accomplished by the application of specific techniques. We intend to go in great detail into that technique, both in metal work and wood work. This is not a how-to-do-it book, but a book to help its readers to be able to judge fine guns and the workmanship in them. To a degree, therefore, it is a work of criticism, almost in the same sense that poetry and drama and fiction and architecture are the subject of books of criticism.

Herein, then, are discussed those techniques followed by those who do the best work being done on guns—this is the state of the art.   *Ken Warner*

STATE OF THE ART

Rifle Stocks

THE BARREL and action of a rifle make it work, and the stock is its personality, that which makes a rifle assume the character of its owner. You can tell a lot about a shooter by the stocks on his rifles. Not everybody is a Jerry Fisher, however, so we have to either accept the weaknesses of our own work, or get it farmed out to somebody who knows how. Some hobbyists do quite acceptable stock work and can be justifiably proud, even though they don't rank up with masters of the trade. Personally, I don't have the patience to do much painstaking handwork, so I'm rarely content with what I do myself. I feel better paying somebody who does good work to do it for me.

Some shooters who have seen really top work by professionals judge lesser names or their own work harshly. This isn't realistic. There is a great deal of difference between stock work as a hobby or as an adjunct to other gunsmithing work, and doing stock work as a professional specializing in wood and nothing else. An example is a 375 Magnum Winchester Model 70 owned by George Martin of the NRA. Jim Carmichel, Shooting Editor of *Outdoor Life*, stocked this rifle some time ago, and while George says Jim wasn't happy with it, neither of us can see why, for we wouldn't be embarrassed to show that rifle in any company. It looks good and shoots even better. Personally, I think it's Jim's way of quietly bragging. It's good work.

Of course, when you start paying top dollars, say over $1,000, for a stock, then you should be picky about little things, since for that kind of change you shouldn't

take any less than the best. In 1980 though, $1,000 won't go the whole course toward a best quality stock by the top names if you do everything "right." It's not even hard to spend $500 or $600 on a rather standard, but nicely done stock for a hunting rifle. Serious shooters spend as much as $300 on hunting, silhouette or target stocks (which are machine made from standard patterns) by the time they are bedded, finished and given a minimum of checkering. You have to decide how much you expect to pay, and what you should get for it.

If you are handy with tools and are content with standard patterns and few alterations, you might be happy with a semi-inletted stock from somebody like Fajen or Bishop. Here the stock is roughed out to shape and has "90 percent of the easy work done." Usually you can have minor changes made to the basic pattern for an extra setup charge, such as longer length of pull up to a certain maximum, longer or wider fore-end, higher or wider comb, etc. Most such stocks have enough wood left on them that you have considerable latitude in the final dimensions of the stock. It's quite normal for two otherwise identical semi-finished stocks finished up by two different people to look entirely different. One fellow may just drop in the barreled action, knock off the tracer marks and finish it as-is, leaving it a bit chunky, while another fellow spends a lot of time in slimming it way down, keeping all the lines straight where they should be and carefully contouring the butt, wrist, underbelly and fore-end. The difference can be as dramatic as comparing a fence post to a

This matching pair of Jerry Fisher stocks are among the very best such ever made, in the opinion of many experts. The impeccable line of the stocks, the good detailing, but, above all, the rightness of the whole ensemble are the marks of the master. The metalwork here is all Burgess; the engraving is John Warren.

At a famous NRA meeting, the sign on the Oakley & Merkley booth said, "Meet America's Finest Gun Craftsmen" and there they were. From the left: Jay Frazier, Joe Oakley, Dick Hodgson, Tom Burgess, Thomas Wilson, Larry Amrine, Bob Winter, Gary Goudy, Duane Wiebe, Steve Billeb, Phil Pilkington, Joe Balickie, Herman Waldron, Bob Swartley, Al Biesen, Byrd Pearson.

baseball bat. A really skillful fellow can take a semi-inletted stock and mould its character so that it takes close examination to determine for sure that it wasn't a from-the-block job. Those guys are the exception, however, and there are others who should stick to whittling tent pegs and leave rifle stocks to those who know how.

The average shooter thinks of a replacement stock made from a semi-inletted blank to a standard pattern as a "custom" stock, since it's different from the one the factory put on his rifle. Perhaps in a broad sense this is correct, though it's worlds apart from a handmade, from-the-block stock, by about $600-$1,000 depending on how far you go with it. For hunting rifles which will see a lot of use, a machine-made and hand inletted/finished stock is completely satisfactory. But there are times when the standard patterns won't accomplish what you want. Then you have several options on how to go about it.

For instance, on target rifles, it's common practice for shooters to make a pattern from a standard stock, gluing on chunks of wood here and there, whittling and rasping them, then shooting these patchwork monsters in matches for a season or two, and continuing the puttying, rasping, gluing and whittling process until they are sure they have what they want. After a few seasons they have the ugliest rifle on the whole line, *but it fits*. Those smart fellows take that cobbled up stock and send it to Fajen, or Bishop, or somebody else with a pantograph (a mechanical tracer made to copy gunstocks) and have the beast duplicated in a decent piece of wood. This is one of the least expensive ways to get a custom-fitted stock if you know what you want and how to go about it. I have done this on several of my rifles, and I like it. Cost varies, but you can generally have your pattern duplicated (not counting wood cost) for about $75 and up, depending on whether you do the inletting, buttplate fitting, etc., yourself, or have the man do it for you.

Some outfits do quite a business of duplicating

This Cecil Weems 6.5-06 on an FN Mauser action with Conetrol mounts has a particularly slim appearance. The Circassian walnut stock in a fiddleback grain pattern, almost a striping pattern, has a skeleton buttplate; its other details are inside. It is a rather nice, long slim rifle.

Here is a striking piece of English walnut done up by Joe Hollingsworth in classic style. He keeps the forearm particularly slim in this example, and furnishes it with a rather short tip. The rifle is a Mauser in 270 Winchester with a Jack Childress barrel and some Jantz features.

This Stanley Kenvin sporter, a Model 70 in a striking piece of tiger tail myrtle, has Griffin & Howe rib, mounts, trigger guard and front sight with Biesen grip cap and trap buttplate. All lines and detailing are quite properly restrained in the classic mode here to let the remarkable grain pattern have full play.

This Stanley Kenvin rifle is a Model 70 with Douglas barrel, installed by Jaeger; mounts by Brownell; trigger guard by Blackburn; grip cap and trap butt by Biesen. The classic stock is made from an exceptionally hard and dense piece of American walnut and the lines and detailing are excellently carried out.

stocks, and done well they can be very good, even copying inletting so closely that very little, if any, handwork is required. Therefore, if you break a stock, save the pieces, since if you can glue them back and fill them with plastic wood, you have a usable pattern. If you have one stock you like, you can make a similar one for another rifle, even if the actions aren't the same. I

with a piece of wood resembling a railroad tie more than a rifle, and he whittles away everything that doesn't look like a stock. He usually starts by making a slightly oversized template of aluminum or plywood in your dimensions and to the shape of the stock, which is laid out on the blank and placed so as to get the grain running straight through the grip, with the figure all in the butt and straight or upward rising grain in the fore-end. After checking the grain by planing and wetting, and once satisfied with the way the pattern will lay out, he traces

Don Klein of Wisconsin did this Model 70 in 280 Remington with a darkly handsome piece of English walnut. He checkered it with a recessed pattern, and solved the problem of the short forearm with a barrel band sling swivel.

Here is a Paul Jaeger rifle with very restrained furnishings and relatively plain design over-all, which is a tribute to the remarkably patterned wood of the stock blank. There is not much need to embellish such a piece of wood.

This is a Fred Speiser stock job in Claro and ebony. The rifle is a Model 70 in 270. The stock is checkered 22 lpi and offers a fleur-de-lis pattern. The comb nose appears to be ahead of the center of the grip cap because of the photo angle. The stock is strictly classic.

once copied a Ruger 77 stock for my Remington 788. The tracing machinery used has a stylus which follows the contour of the stock, guiding the cutter on the opposite station. In some setups it's not wise to use a finished stock, since the stylus will scratch it, though sometimes they can put a plastic cap on it to avoid marking the finish. You don't get as much detail in the copy this way, so it will require more handwork.

The class way to go (and the most expensive) is the "from the block" stock. Here the stockmaker starts

around the template with a pencil, and saws off the excess material outside the lines, using a table saw for the straight cuts and a band saw for curved cuts. The blank is planed smooth on the right side, then the top where the action will be inletted is planed square to the right face. The underbelly of the stock should also be square to act as a guide to inlet the trigger guard to avoid canting it. Next the centerline is laid out, for the barrel and action, and continued over the butt, taking into consideration the amount of wood needed for the cheekpiece, offset or cast-off. This generally requires blanks be at least 2¼ inches thick, though a plain stock with no cheekpiece can be made from a blank 2 inches thick. The cast-off or offset may be constant, though most good stockers cant the butt slightly, which gives a more comfortable stock. Once the offset centerline is measured and drawn, the action reference marks are erased from the butt to avoid confusion. The canted butt is governed by position of the buttplate, which appears slightly to the right and twisted from the rear.

Most stockers then flip the blank over and inlet the trigger guard first, using another template having the outline of the trigger guard. The outline is made with a scriber, first outlining the dimensions of the magazine box and removing this wood. If attempting this yourself, it's a good idea to have the action screw holes drilled and the magazine cutout roughed by machine, leaving the major portion of the inletting and shaping to be done by hand, since it will save a lot of handwork and minimize the risk of a botched start.

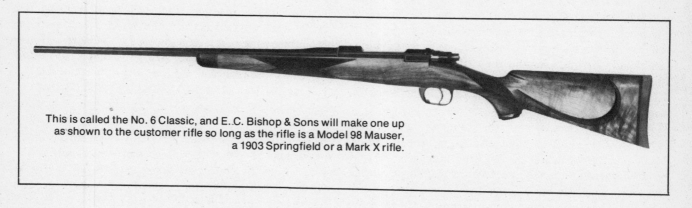

This is called the No. 6 Classic, and E.C. Bishop & Sons will make one up as shown to the customer rifle so long as the rifle is a Model 98 Mauser, a 1903 Springfield or a Mark X rifle.

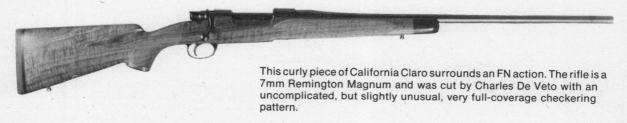

This curly piece of California Claro surrounds an FN action. The rifle is a 7mm Remington Magnum and was cut by Charles De Veto with an uncomplicated, but slightly unusual, very full-coverage checkering pattern.

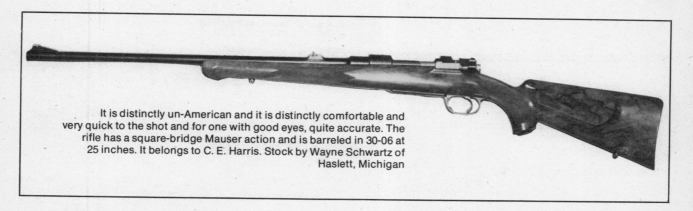

It is distinctly un-American and it is distinctly comfortable and very quick to the shot and for one with good eyes, quite accurate. The rifle has a square-bridge Mauser action and is barreled in 30-06 at 25 inches. It belongs to C. E. Harris. Stock by Wayne Schwartz of Haslett, Michigan

Once the layout lines are done, the real work begins. Most important is establishing the correct location for the front guard screw hole. This is checked against the template and action and the dimension obtained by the measurement from the butt. Once the hole is located, the front guard screw hole is drilled using an angle vise and drill press to keep the hole square and straight. This is drilled from the top and in actions such as Mausers, which have parallel guard screws, the rear screw hole is drilled at the same time.

It isn't necessary for the magazine box to be tightly inletted and isn't a good idea anyway. On hard kicking rifles you should have some clearance of the wood around the magazine box at the corners. The magazine box shouldn't fit too loosely, though, especially on Mausers or others which have a small floorplate, since an enlarged magazine opening would leave an obvious gap. Master stockers get a very close fit of wood to metal with no obvious gaps at all. This is what you pay for, though you don't always get it. An old trick to hide minor gaps is to smear wood-colored grease in the inletting. It always irks me to see this done, though it's a common practice in many European factory-made and even some presumably "higher grade" guns.

The way good stockers obtain a close fit of the trigger guard in the stock is by tapering the trigger guard so it is slightly wider at the bottom than on the top, so it wedges in just-so. This beveling is called "draft." The trigger guard is inletted until it is slightly below the surface of the stock all around, less the floorplate. It is then spotted into the wood later by coating it with Prussian blue, lampblack, or lipstick, and then trying the guard and inletting the bearing points until full contact is obtained. It's essential not to cant the guard. Check it with a square, lest the action screws not fit.

After the guard is inletted, the front guard screw hole is used as a guide to align and locate the receiver. Mauser and Winchester Model 70 actions have the rear guard screw entering the receiver at a right angle like the front one, so both screws are used for guides. Headless inletting screws with handles are inserted

through the stock and into the receiver so the bottom of the recoil lug contacts the stock. Then the shoulder is marked around with a pencil and just hogged out to let the action contact at the front and rear tang to locate those. This initial rough hole will eventually be removed in the action inletting, so it doesn't have to be neat.

Once the action fits down close against the wood, the stockmaker will scribe all around it to get the outline of the receiver bottom. The action opening is roughed out inside the scribed line to nearly half the diameter of the receiver ring, and the barrel channel scribed and roughed as the action sinks deeper into the blank. Once the receiver is lowered to the sidewalls the stocker will switch from straight chisels to round gouges for the receiver and barrel channel. Guidelines are rescribed as the receiver and barrel sinks deeper, then the hard work begins as the stocker starts spotting in everything.

The difference between a really fine stock and a simple gun handle is the close inletting, which is one place where the master stocker earns his pay. Here he switches to scrapers, sharp edged metal plates ground to various contours. These are used on the bottoms and

This magnificent Ruger No. 1 rifle depends wholly on the quality of the wood, impeccable line—note how the shaping of the fore-end and the front end of the buttstock makes an oval of the section around the action—and the clarity of execution. The wood is perfectly balanced by the plain color case-hardened receiver.

Stephen Billeb stocked this left-handed 270 Weatherby with feathercrotch black walnut. Perhaps to demonstrate his abilities, he added some non-classic features, such as the diagonal of the forearm tip, and the shape of the pistol grip.

This left side of a Jaeger rifle shows what the grain pattern ought to be for strength; it also shows that something a little different can still be classic. The line of the buttplate looks purposeful, although it is a little unusual.

Again, the typical Gordon Tibbitts checkering pattern gives this one away. This is a 243 Sako stocked in a very dark piece of Claro for a lady. The deep drop of the pistol grip is no doubt intentional.

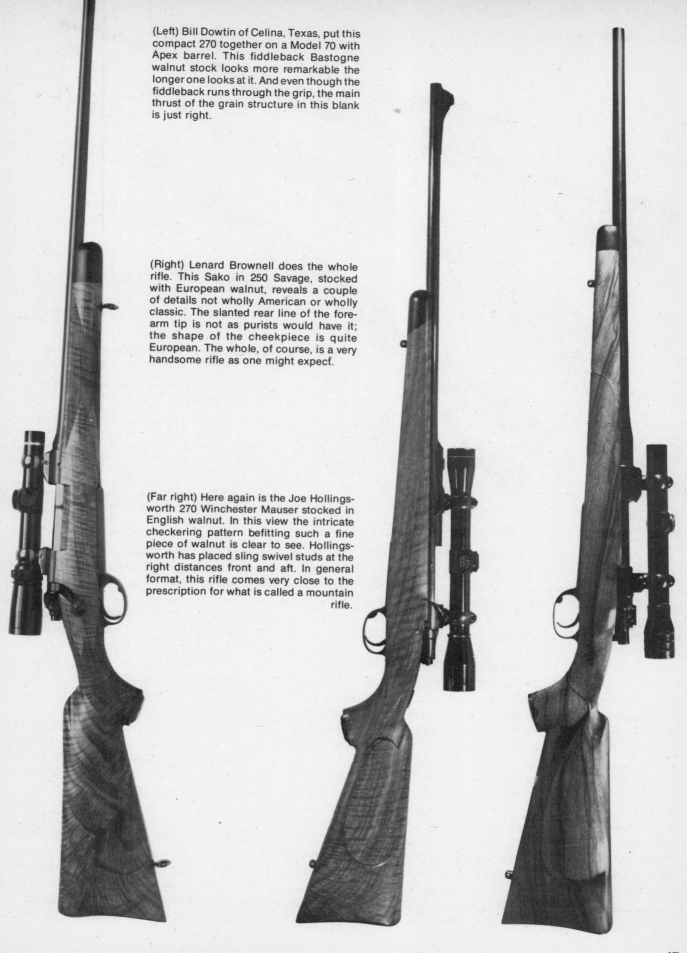

(Left) Bill Dowtin of Celina, Texas, put this compact 270 together on a Model 70 with Apex barrel. This fiddleback Bastogne walnut stock looks more remarkable the longer one looks at it. And even though the fiddleback runs through the grip, the main thrust of the grain structure in this blank is just right.

(Right) Lenard Brownell does the whole rifle. This Sako in 250 Savage, stocked with European walnut, reveals a couple of details not wholly American or wholly classic. The slanted rear line of the forearm tip is not as purists would have it; the shape of the cheekpiece is quite European. The whole, of course, is a very handsome rifle as one might expecf.

(Far right) Here again is the Joe Hollingsworth 270 Winchester Mauser stocked in English walnut. In this view the intricate checkering pattern befitting such a fine piece of walnut is clear to see. Hollingsworth has placed sling swivel studs at the right distances front and aft. In general format, this rifle comes very close to the prescription for what is called a mountain rifle.

(Top) This side of the Jaeger rifle evidences even more handsome grain on the right side than on the left side, which is not unusual even in very fine wood, as this is. The rifle over-all is a severely classic design.

(Middle) This vaguely African style custom rifle began in its most recent guise as a square-bridge Mauser action not suited to magnums. The decision was made to have it as a true classic, without scope, and that decision has not been regretted. Stock by Wayne Schwartz of Haslett, MI.

(Bottom) Another C. E. Harris gun, designed and built by consensus some years ago, is this rather heavy 35 Whelen built on a pre-war Model 70 target rifle action. The long forearm was demanded by its owner since it suits his shooting stance. It has a Westley Richards trap grip cap and ramp front sight with night sight. Somewhat huskier than the average custom rifle these days, its owner finds that an advantage—he can shoot rapidfire with heavy loads and maintain full control.

sides of chisel cuts to remove the last few thousandths of an inch of wood and to make the surface smooth. They are used with light finger pressure only. The entire underside of the receiver and barrel will be coated with spotting compound (lipstick is good) to the bore centerline, and the inletting edges inspected, and lines scribed where a few light chisel cuts are still needed. The recoil shoulder of mild recoiling rifles up to 308 Winchester will be spotted in, but the shoulder is cut back a bit in heavier caliber rifles so it can be reinforced with a steel or fiberglass bearing. Once the receiver has bottomed in the stock there should be no gaps between wood and metal. The guard screws are then inserted into the receiver through the trigger guard and tried in the rifle to be sure they are in line. The magazine box should come as close to the receiver bottom as it can without touching, within $1/64$-inch on well seasoned wood, more if you have wood which might shrink a little. When the inletting is finished, the receiver should bottom solidly from the tang to ring, the recoil shoulder having slight clearance at the sides and bottom. Unless you wish a free-floating barrel, the barrel should bear in full contact the last 3 inches or so, and require 8-12 pounds to pull the fore-end away from it.

The labor entailed in hand inletting is what makes a custom stock cost, since the job, if done right, takes a hell of a lot more time than simply hogging out everything and pouring glass in to fill the gaps.

The role of fiberglass should be explained here, since many people use it as a substitute for good inletting. For target rifle stocks, however, stability is more important than looks. Wood in the bedding areas of target rifles is removed entirely except for locating areas under the ring and tang, and along the magazine well. The wood here is machined away and replaced with a stable bedding material. In the popular "pillar" system, end mills are run clear through the stock so there can be no wood compression when the guard screws are tightened. The action and trigger guard are supported by solid columns of epoxy or fiberglass, with the screw holes relieved so they slip freely as they should. If accuracy is the only aim and you don't care if the glass shows, this is fine, and is a stable, accurate system.

In a classy sporting rifle, though, any glass used shouldn't show. Purists shun use of synthetic bedding materials at all. A good, tight inletting job is the hallmark of a master stockmaker. To them, asking for glass bedding is like going into a deli and asking for

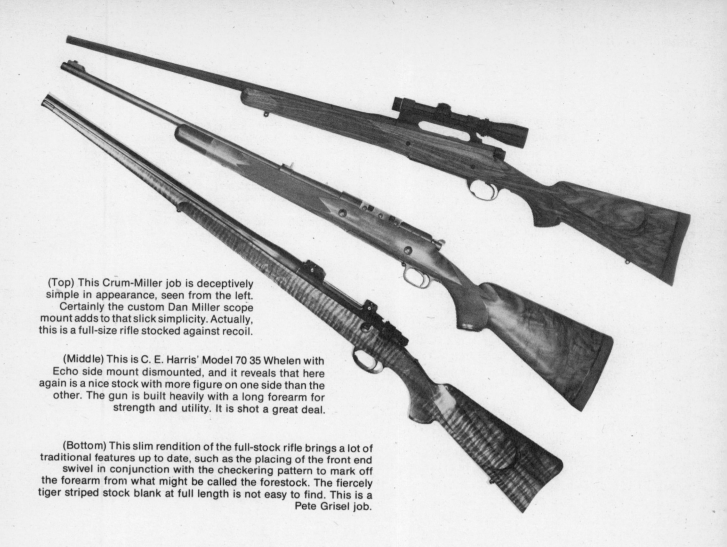

(Top) This Crum-Miller job is deceptively simple in appearance, seen from the left. Certainly the custom Dan Miller scope mount adds to that slick simplicity. Actually, this is a full-size rifle stocked against recoil.

(Middle) This is C. E. Harris' Model 70 35 Whelen with Echo side mount dismounted, and it reveals that here again is a nice stock with more figure on one side than the other. The gun is built heavily with a long forearm for strength and utility. It is shot a great deal.

(Bottom) This slim rendition of the full-stock rifle brings a lot of traditional features up to date, such as the placing of the front end swivel in conjunction with the checkering pattern to mark off the forearm from what might be called the forestock. The fiercely tiger striped stock blank at full length is not easy to find. This is a Pete Grisel job.

mayonnaise on your hot pastrami . . . it just ain't done (or so people will tell you). Actually, on a rifle which will actually be *used* afield, and not just kept for fair weather shooting or for show, glass bedding makes a lot of sense. My classy hunting rifles are glassed. However, you should start with good inletting to begin with. Fiberglass should be used to augment the field utility of a good inletting job for extreme field conditions. It should not be used to cover up a shoddy job. Fiberglass is great for the amateur to salvage a home-botched inletting job, but professionals don't use it that way. They shouldn't need to. The good stocker using well seasoned wood may use thinned fiberglass or epoxy to cement fore-end tips and recoil pads, and to "paint" the surfaces of already good inletting on hunting rifles, so the exposed wood grain will be entirely sealed once the action is set into it. High stress areas like the recoil lug will be relieved to permit a reinforcing layer of glass ¼-inch thick at minimum, though you'll only have a thin layer elsewhere. If done right no glass will be visible at all until you take the rifle out of the stock.

When having a custom stock made, you could consider several styles depending on your personal taste. The most popular form in the U.S. is probably what has become known as the "classic" stock. This is an adaptation of the style practiced by the masters of the period from the 1920s until after WW II, such as Alvin Linden, Bob Owen, Leonard Mews, and Tom Shelhamer. Today's "classic" stock has been refined and the combs straightened to accommodate scope sights. The basics of styling remain much the same. These are a straight comb or only a slight Monte Carlo, long, gently curving grip, and the underline of the stock forming a straight line from the toe to where the grip meets the trigger guard. The grip doesn't "hang" below the underline, but is blended smoothly with it, with the grip cap being perpendicular to the arc of the grip at the point of tangency. A vertical line drawn through the center of the comb nose should go through the center of the grip cap. The fore-end is round in cross section, or nearly so, and is a straight taper from the receiver ring to fore-end tip. The length of the fore-end is rarely more than slightly longer than half the distance from the receiver ring to muzzle. The fore-end tip, if there is one, meets the wood in a joint that's perpendicular to the barrel. The buttplate and grip cap are usually steel, and the fore-end tip horn or ebony, though plastic is sometimes used today. The finish is usually oil or a dull-rubbed synthetic. White-line spacers are anathema to the classic rifle buff.

The next most popular style is the so-called "California" stock popularized by Roy Weatherby. The lines here are more "modern," with high Monte Carlo combs, roll-over cheekpieces, flattened fore-end bottoms, with the fore-end tip usually meeting the stock at a pronounced angle. The grips are deeper and closer than in a classic stock, and the stocks may be inlaid with contrasting wood. White-line spacers usually separate the wood and recoil pad or fore-end tip. Where classic stocks are quiet and subdued, these are loud and flashy.

Not very popular in the U.S. is the European stock, which is typified by the pre-war Mauser or Mann-licher-Schonauer rifles and carbines. These are typically skinny, minimum stocks which are very light. The fore-end isn't a straight taper but usually thins abruptly forward of the ring and then often flares toward the muzzle in a schnabel tip. Combs on European stocks are usually low and straight without a Monte Carlo. Some stocks have a gently curved comb called Schweinsrücken or "pig's back." Many German or Swiss rifles have what is commonly called a Bavarian-style cheekpiece which is somewhat square or angular in shape, rather than being oval or rounded, as are British or U.S. sporters.

European stocks are entirely functional with iron sights, but they require the shooter to raise his head to obtain a full field of view even with relatively low-mounted scopes. In heavy recoiling calibers the thin combs and fore-ends are unpleasant to shoot much, though their handling qualities in general are excellent. In Europe the low comb isn't considered a detriment to shooting with scope sights, as the shooting is planned and deliberate. The scope is usually carried separately, the hunter mounting it only after he is placed on a stand. Snap-shooting as practiced in the U.S. is rare. Quick detachable scope mounts, generally used, often place the optics high enough that the iron sights may be seen beneath them. Although some U.S. shooters have tried this arrangement, low mounted scopes and properly dimensioned stocks which let the shooter mount them naturally and find a full field are far more practical.

British style stocks have some popularity in the U.S. and probably served as models for what later became the American "classic" stock. What is known today as the British-style stock is exemplified by Mauser sporters made by English makers for the African trade between the World Wars, or similar guns by European makers, such as the Mauser Type A. These stocks generally have short, rounded fore-ends, which are thicker than on most European guns, but straight tapered as on American rifles, and not as full. The fore-end tips are small, meet the wood at a right angle to the

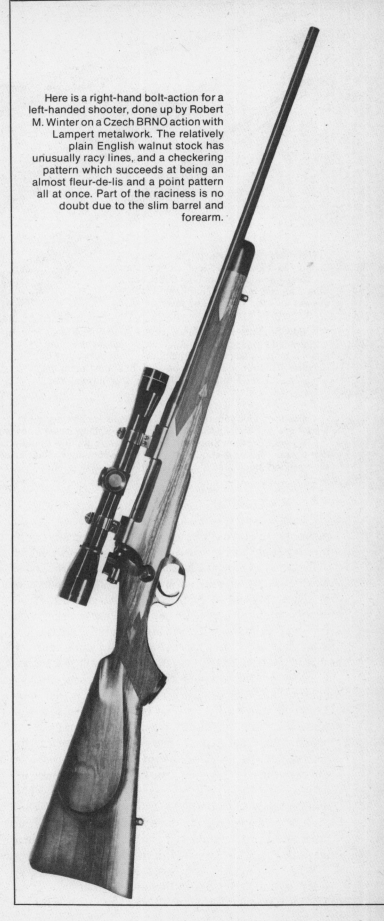

Here is a right-hand bolt-action for a left-handed shooter, done up by Robert M. Winter on a Czech BRNO action with Lampert metalwork. The relatively plain English walnut stock has unusually racy lines, and a checkering pattern which succeeds at being an almost fleur-de-lis and a point pattern all at once. Part of the raciness is no doubt due to the slim barrel and forearm.

This piece of French walnut is fitted with a 1909 Mauser action refined by Waldron with an Atkinson barrel. Keith Stegall did the stock in severe classic style with no forearm tip. The checkering pattern is called a panel point.

barrel and are usually horn or ebony. Straight grained walnut with an oil finish was the standard, since these were intended as "low-priced" (compared to a double) rifles. While most early sporters of this type were "utility grade" guns, they are still high-grade guns by the standards you would judge factory rifles today. The wood was usually good quality, and while plain, it was usually dense and darkly striped, quarter-sawed Circassian or European walnut, which is expensive today. This style seems to be gaining in popularity. Factory rifles such as the Interarms Whitworth and Sako Safari Grade have stocks of this type. It is good functional design and is pleasing to the eye.

When planning a custom stock, you should decide carefully whether you wish to have it made-to-measure, or whether you will simply get one made to a standard pattern. A standard pattern doesn't necessarily mean standard dimensions, since a stocker on knowing your build, facial contour, shooting style, etc., will make allowances. But making allowances is a lot different from having a stock made from scratch especially for you. The difference is analogous to getting a custom tailored suit, or having an off-the-rack one altered. Few people can get a perfect fit with an unaltered off-the-rack suit, and similarly, factory stocks are a compromise for the theoretical "average" person. The altered, standard pattern may fit you fine and be satisfactory, but the custom fitted stock can incorporate subtle changes and accommodations not possible in a standard stock. There's no substitute for being able to handle and maybe actually shoot the rifle, having the man right there to take rasp in hand, and cut the comb down, adjust the size and contour of the comb flutes, to clear the thumb and heel of your hand the way you grasp the wrist, and to see where you hold your hands so as to be sure to get checkering in the right places. At this same time he can watch how tightly you cheek the stock if you tend to shoot with your head back and erect or if you mash it down hard and forward up close to the scope. If you work the bolt vigorously from the shoulder, he'll insure the pitch is right to keep the butt into your shoulder through recoil and against the upward and backward motion of your hand working against the bolt. That way, you can get off that second shot without losing the butt or your head position on the stock.

An experienced stocker can find out more by watching you handle a rifle than you can think to tell him. If you contemplate owning more than one custom stocked rifle, it's worth it to go through the ritual once, since once you have a stock that's right, you have a base to work from in the future. In rifles made for snapshooting game in close cover, particularly dangerous game, it's not a bad idea to take a page from the shotgunner's book and play with the rifle *sans* sights, and adjust the stock dimensions so you can stare at a target, throw the rifle up without regard to looking at the barrel or sights at all, and hit relatively close to what you are

State of the Art: Rifle Stocks

(Top and middle rifles) If one Model 70 isn't enough, one might have two. This pair by Bill Dowtin use wood matched and cut from the same tree. They are checkered on the grip in his hunt pattern. The wood is seedling English walnut; the lower metalwork is by Blackburn.

The single word, perhaps it doesn't do it justice, that fits this rifle is *cute*. It just is. Built on a Martini rimfire target rifle action by Don Klein using New Zealand walnut, the stock and metalwork together solved many problems inherent in the action and the little piece handles very well.

aiming at. This seemed far-fetched to me until a fellow had me try it. Lo and behold, he had me throwing up the rifle like I was mounting a shotgun and within a few minor adjustments I was hitting a quart plastic bleach bottle at 25 yards *with no sights* rather consistently.

When we finally put sights on the gun, low over the barrel (this was to be an iron-sight-only gun) things really began to click. The sights were "there and lined up" instantly when I mounted the gun. You should try this yourself, closing your eyes, throwing the rifle up and opening them, and adjusting as needed until you get a natural sight picture. With a shotgun this type of thing is usually done with an adjustable "try stock" in which the pitch, cant of the butt, length of pull, etc., can be adjusted and the measurements recorded. This can be done with a rifle also, but is less common, though that would be the best way to do it.

In my case, I started out handling as many good custom rifles as I could get my hands on, and shot those which I could. When I found one that felt right, which I also shot well, I made careful measurements and recorded them. After I had three such sets of measurements from different rifles, a continuity of dimensions came through. I took these to my stockmaker friend and from there he came up with a very close approximation on the first try, after making allowances for my shooting style. It's interesting, though, that of all the stocks I tried, the ones which looked and felt best were really "class acts." They were a Roy Vail Mauser, a Jerry Fisher Winchester Model 70 and a Tom Shelhamer Winchester Model 70. All owned by different folks, they had the qualities I was looking for.

There's no substitute for *knowing* what you want. This makes the work a lot easier. Most stockers end up making the stock to suit themselves, since the customer seldom knows what he wants. Others think they know, but they aren't knowledgeable enough to distinguish between fad and need. When the silhouette rifle game first got going strong, everybody came up with ideas for what made the right stock. The most memorable comment I ever heard on pull length was when Roy Dunlap, veteran gunsmith and designer of (probably) the best target rifle stocks ever made, broke into a conversation and said, "Gentlemen, the correct offhand pull length for anyone is exactly ½-inch shorter than he thinks he needs."

There's a lot of truth in this, since most shooters, hunters in particular, tend to get stocks too long. I'm guilty of this myself to an extent. We all are. You need a shorter stock to compensate for cold weather clothing, not to mention the fact you should be able to shoulder the rifle naturally without consciously pushing the butt forward to keep it from hanging up on your coat or in your armpit. You will find you need a long pull length on a prone varmint or target stock, about an inch shorter than that for a standard stock used for over-the-course, position or most hunting, and probably an inch shorter

(Top rifle) Stephen Billeb did this military Mauser 98 up with a Model 70 type safety and a much refined Model 1909 trigger guard. The rifle still has the military barrel, bored out to 35 Whelen.

(Middle rifle) Al Lind used his New Zealand walnut to do up this Mauser in lightweight rifle style, stocked for the quick shot. Walter Koluch of McMinville, Oregon, was the engraver.

(Bottom rifle) This Stephen Billeb full-stock is left rather full through the forearm and up to the tip because the Sako action on which it is built carried a heavy barrel to control the 7mm Remington Magnum cartridge. The stock blank is very contrasty California English. The total effect is very competent.

still for one used purely for offhand shooting. Similarly, a stock used purely for bench shooting can be quite short, and is usually more convenient if it is.

Stock finishes deserve a lot more consideration than you think, since they determine most of a stock's utility and character. A good stock finish is a beauty to behold and durable in service. Although for pure elegance it's hard to beat a good rubbed oil finish, others are more durable for field use, though an oil finish will hold up very well if taken care of. It is easily touched up after each outing and keeps its good looks. The minor dings and scratches are less noticeable when blended into an oil finish, than with varnish or other materials, such as shellac and oil.

When building a pretty rifle, you don't want a dark, dull finish which hides the grain, you'd like it to show through. While the European oil finish is fine on hunting guns, it will hide the beauty of fancy wood. However, a bright, slick, shiny finish isn't desired on a hunting rifle, since it shows every scratch and minor ding, and can reflect enough sunlight to spook game. There are some finishes which are strictly for show, and others for field use, while a majority of them can look good and be functional too.

Nearly all stocks will require filling, which should be done after the stock has been well sanded, the grain raised repeatedly and cut down so the surface is smooth and the pores open, ready to fill. Most commercial wood fillers work fine. Those containing silicon work particularly well, though they are hard on checkering tools. A good filler is to use casein glue or shellac mixed with wood dust sanded from the stock. A good filling job will hide minor gaps in the inletting also.

Stock finishes used on custom rifles can be oils, such as linseed or tung oil, or mixtures of shellac and oil, such as the "French polish," or rubbed varnish, besides the popular synthetics used today. The rubbed oil finishes and the French polish look best in the rack, though they are time-consuming to apply and not as durable afield. The new synthetics are easy to use, can look good, and are durable.

Linseed oil is traditional and is still a good finish though there is a lot of synthetic linseed oil which isn't suitable for gunstocks sold in paint stores. Let your nose be your guide. Pure linseed oil is chemically treated to separate the impurities, then a drying agent is added. Tung oil is also good, but in pure form is expensive and hard to get. Some commercial tung oil finishes, such as Formby's Tung Oil Varnish, are satisfactory for use on gunstocks. The disadvantage of most tung oil finishes, though, is that they dry quickly, must be applied lightly and rubbed in immediately as they otherwise dry, leaving a film which looks like a quickie varnish job. Another disadvantage is the fact that some people are allergic to tung oil and break out in a rash after handling a stock finished with it.

Tru-Oil, Lin-Speed or tung oil finishes should be

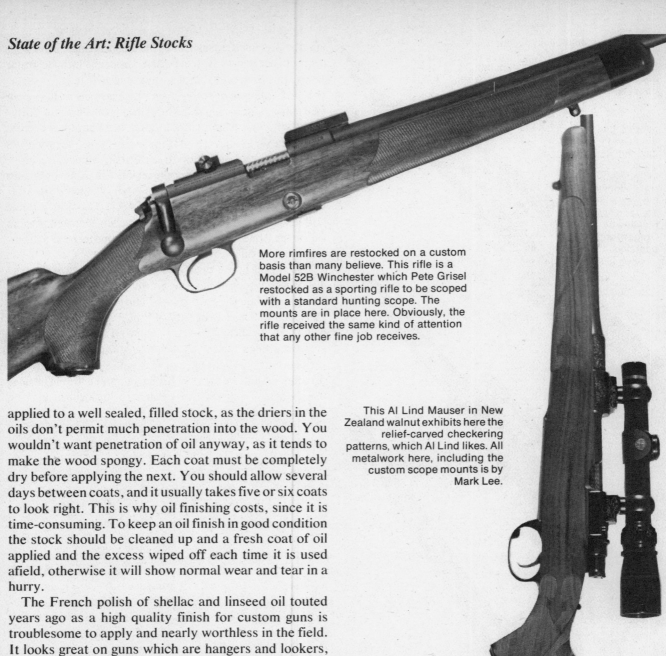

More rimfires are restocked on a custom basis than many believe. This rifle is a Model 52B Winchester which Pete Grisel restocked as a sporting rifle to be scoped with a standard hunting scope. The mounts are in place here. Obviously, the rifle received the same kind of attention that any other fine job receives.

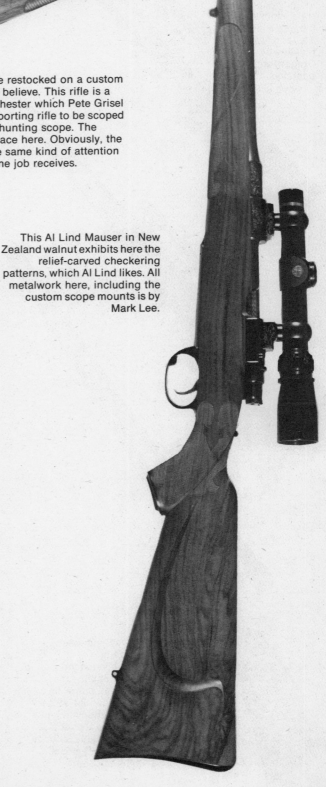

This Al Lind Mauser in New Zealand walnut exhibits here the relief-carved checkering patterns, which Al Lind likes. All metalwork here, including the custom scope mounts is by Mark Lee.

applied to a well sealed, filled stock, as the driers in the oils don't permit much penetration into the wood. You wouldn't want penetration of oil anyway, as it tends to make the wood spongy. Each coat must be completely dry before applying the next. You should allow several days between coats, and it usually takes five or six coats to look right. This is why oil finishing costs, since it is time-consuming. To keep an oil finish in good condition the stock should be cleaned up and a fresh coat of oil applied and the excess wiped off each time it is used afield, otherwise it will show normal wear and tear in a hurry.

The French polish of shellac and linseed oil touted years ago as a high quality finish for custom guns is troublesome to apply and nearly worthless in the field. It looks great on guns which are hangers and lookers, but not for utility guns. A modified varnish and oil finish is far more durable and achieves a similar effect. Here the stock is well oiled first and then finished with a mixture of spar varnish and linseed mixed half and half, cut down with denim or burlap between coats. The final coat is usually oil only, and it's hard to tell the resulting finish from straight oil. However, I've also seen a final coat of mostly varnish used and worked down to a good shine if desired.

Synthetics have almost replaced varnish or shellac finishes used 25-30 years ago, the most popular ones today being derivatives of polyurethane or epoxy. Applied straight, these finishes give a high shine which many find objectionable. In appearance this finish is similar to the slippery factory finish simply sprayed on many rifles today. However, if the synthetic finish is built up, and then cut down nearly to the wood surface with 400 grit paper and lubricated with mineral oil or

This is the right side of the Keith Stegall 1909 Mauser. It can be seen that the fiddleback figure continues all the way up the right side of this blank, although it does not on the left side. The panel point checkering pattern is clearly revealed here.

The left-handed shooter gets a break and this remarkable 6mm Remington is built around a Remington 700 left-hand action with Wilson barrel. The stock is California English, checkered 26 lpi in a point pattern and furnished with a blind box magazine. Though the barrel is 22 inches long, the graceful rifle is a lightweight tool.

This gleaming sporter reveals a Gordon Tibbitts trademark—the intricate one-of-a-kind checkering pattern, here fully realized. The rifle is a 25-06 on an FN Supreme action. The wood is dense English walnut. Note the detail around the bolt release and how it is complemented by the rear lines of the forearm checkering pattern and flows thence into the lines of the cheekpiece. Very handsome.

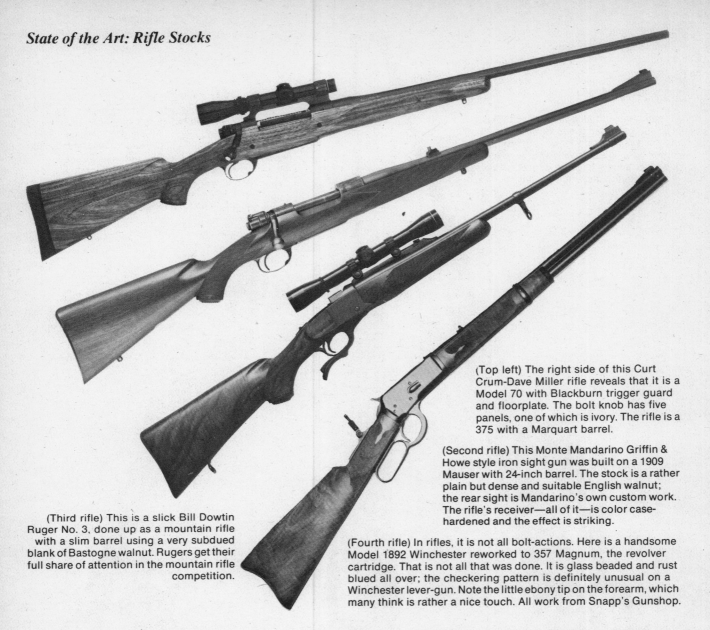

(Top left) The right side of this Curt Crum-Dave Miller rifle reveals that it is a Model 70 with Blackburn trigger guard and floorplate. The bolt knob has five panels, one of which is ivory. The rifle is a 375 with a Marquart barrel.

(Second rifle) This Monte Mandarino Griffin & Howe style iron sight gun was built on a 1909 Mauser with 24-inch barrel. The stock is a rather plain but dense and suitable English walnut; the rear sight is Mandarino's own custom work. The rifle's receiver—all of it—is color case-hardened and the effect is striking.

(Third rifle) This is a slick Bill Dowtin Ruger No. 3, done up as a mountain rifle with a slim barrel using a very subdued blank of Bastogne walnut. Rugers get their full share of attention in the mountain rifle competition.

(Fourth rifle) In rifles, it is not all bolt-actions. Here is a handsome Model 1892 Winchester reworked to 357 Magnum, the revolver cartridge. That is not all that was done. It is glass beaded and rust blued all over; the checkering pattern is definitely unusual on a Winchester lever-gun. Note the little ebony tip on the forearm, which many think is rather a nice touch. All work from Snapp's Gunshop.

water, a very smooth, non-glossy finish is obtained. This is an easy way to dress up factory stocks too. I use 400 grit and water, letting the stock dry between sessions until all the irregular "orange peel" texture is gone. Done this way the stock is uniformly smooth and no unsanded areas remain. Then a final light finish is applied, usually with an oil finish containing a drier, such as GB Lin-Speed, Tru-Oil or Formby's Tung Oil Varnish. Rubbed in well, this will make the cut-down epoxy or polyurethane finish look very much like a rubbed oil finish, though the trained eye can tell. However, it is attractive and very serviceable. The rubbed oil finish is still traditional for fine custom guns which are kept mostly on the rack, but more practitioners are going to rubbed synthetic finishes on rifles they know will actually be used afield.

Checkering deserves careful attention on a custom stock, since the quality of its execution affects the overall impression of quality in the stock. A less than perfect checkering job can spoil the effect of an otherwise perfect stock. Good checkering is expensive, but it's worth it to pay the price for good work, rather than to try it yourself if you can't do it right. Some hobbyists do good checkering, provided they stick to simple patterns. A few others can do real professional work. Those who don't have the skill or patience to do good work should hire the job done.

Quality of checkering depends to a great extent on the quality of wood. Soft open-grained wood can't take as fine or as deep checkering as dense, close-grained hard wood. With the high cost of custom stock work, it is poor economy *not* to get good wood. It hardly makes any sense to lavish from $350-600 labor on a $100 piece of wood, let alone a $50 or $75 piece.

A lot of checkering is for show, but it should be functional too. The purpose of checkering is to provide a good grasp of the rifle, and therefore, you should seek to have it where your hands will be. This seems

(Below) Those who feel they have to go to the factory for something special can get a custom-built Remington Model 700 like this one, done up with fancy American walnut and skipline checkering.

(Second rifle) This is what some cherry wood can look like. The rifle started as a Savage Mark Ten target 22 at modest price. It is a tackdriver, so Ed Harris thought it was probably worth having it done up to suit him, which this good looking stock does. Stock by Wayne Schwartz of Haslett, Michigan.

(Third rifle) A big gun, an FN Mauser action with a Douglas Premium barrel in 458 Magnum, almost requires express sights and that certain style. Talmage Enterprises gives this one that look with French walnut, an ebony fore-end tip, steel grip cap and classic 20 lpi working checkering.

(Fourth rifle) When you turn loose a group of workmen, they come up with an extraordinary composition sometimes, and Dave Miller and Curt Crum did so with this handsome rifle. The ejector port is opened, there is a special quarter rib and iron sights and a barrel band front swivel. It is all-over immensely practical, but executed very cleanly in the severely classic style.

elementary, but you'd be surprised how many people get stocks made to standard patterns, and they don't suit their shooting style at all. For instance, when snap-shooting I often extend my left hand forward to guide the rifle, much as I do when shooting a shotgun. With a traditionally proportioned classic stock, though, my hand may be out over the fore-end tip, and I'd get no benefit whatever from the checkering my hand never touches. My woods rifle, therefore, has a bit longer than standard fore-end, and a generous amount of checkering on it. This looks only a little unusual, and works fine for me. Actually the fore-end would be in perfect proportion for a longer 25- or 26-inch barrel, and it looks long with this 22-inch barreled bolt-action. I live with it easily though, since it handles as I want it to.

Fine checkering, more than about 22 lines-per-inch is generally more for show than for grip. Fine checkering is where a skillful craftsman can boast his skill, and where the rifle owner can boast the quality of wood and

workmanship, since you must have both or it doesn't work.

For hunting rifles, though, checkering of 16 lines-per-inch is entirely adequate, and when well done it looks good. With less than perfect wood the diamonds will be stronger with coarser checkering, and this is often a factor on many do-it-yourself jobs. Most ordinary American walnut won't take checkering finer than about 18 lines-per-inch, though good hard American walnut will take up to about 24-line checkering satisfactorily. The best European walnut or hard maple will take 28-line checkering. A good trick on questionable wood is flat-top English style checkering or "scoring," which doesn't quite bring the diamonds out full, but leaves a small flat on top of each one. This is hard to do uniformly, but works on almost any wood and looks good when well done. Old English dueling pistols, muzzle-loading fowling pieces, and some early breech-loading guns are checkered this way. This tech-

Curt Crum, as many other stockmakers, uses machines for precise wood cutting when he can and whenever the wood is hard enough to machine well.

nique is often used on rifles having substantial recoil, where you don't wish the sharp diamonds of a checkering pattern to dig into your hand. Of course, finer checkering can be used for the same purpose with good wood.

Checkering patterns vary, but some basics hold true for most of them. Typical checking patterns consist of two side panels on the fore-end and grip, though on fancier jobs the panels are connected over the top of the grip and under the bottom of the fore-end. "Point" patterns are often used on classic rifles and have the borders coming to a pointed outline on the front and rear of the panels on the fore-end and grip. Most good checkering is of the borderless type, where the pattern is brought out to the edges of the panel. Bordered checkering has a double-line cut around the edges, the main purpose of which is to hide runovers. Sometimes the borders of a checkering pattern will be embellished with S curves to create larger panels on the fore-end for more checkering, or with carved uncheckered areas inside the pattern outline in the shapes of acorns, fleur-de-lis, etc. Another technique to dress up a pattern and provide a better grip is the use of "French" or skip-line checkering, which is done by using two widths of spacing tools, the main pattern being laid out with a fine tool, such as 24-line, and every fifth or sixth space laid out with a coarser 18-line or 16-line tool.

With all checkering be alert for the hallmarks of good work: straight, clean lines; symmetrical full, sharp diamonds; and smooth contours. The diamonds should be full and even right to the edge of the pattern, and the borders should be "clean," without runovers. The grain should show through the pattern if well done.

Walnut is the "standard" wood for rifle stocks, and its many varieties are used more often than all the other

This is a truss for bedding the barrel action used by Dave Miller. He feels he can bed with pre-determined upward pressure without stressing the action.

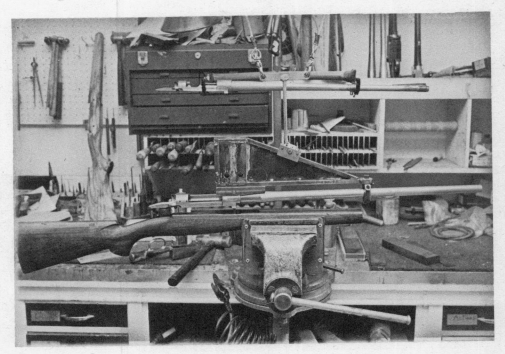

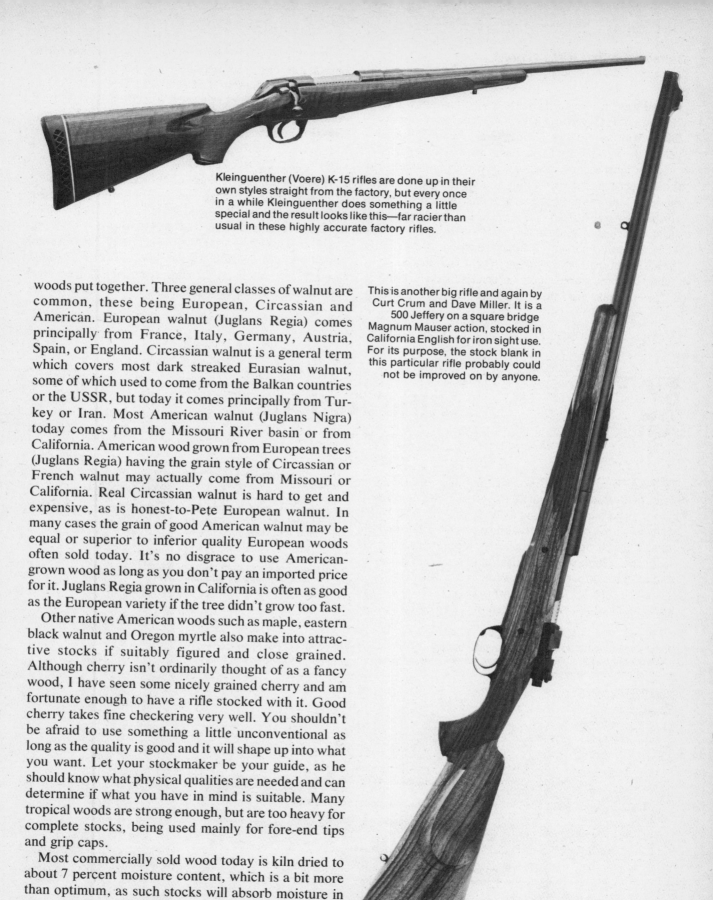

Kleinguenther (Voere) K-15 rifles are done up in their own styles straight from the factory, but every once in a while Kleinguenther does something a little special and the result looks like this—far racier than usual in these highly accurate factory rifles.

This is another big rifle and again by Curt Crum and Dave Miller. It is a 500 Jeffery on a square bridge Magnum Mauser action, stocked in California English for iron sight use. For its purpose, the stock blank in this particular rifle probably could not be improved on by anyone.

woods put together. Three general classes of walnut are common, these being European, Circassian and American. European walnut (Juglans Regia) comes principally from France, Italy, Germany, Austria, Spain, or England. Circassian walnut is a general term which covers most dark streaked Eurasian walnut, some of which used to come from the Balkan countries or the USSR, but today it comes principally from Turkey or Iran. Most American walnut (Juglans Nigra) today comes from the Missouri River basin or from California. American wood grown from European trees (Juglans Regia) having the grain style of Circassian or French walnut may actually come from Missouri or California. Real Circassian walnut is hard to get and expensive, as is honest-to-Pete European walnut. In many cases the grain of good American walnut may be equal or superior to inferior quality European woods often sold today. It's no disgrace to use American-grown wood as long as you don't pay an imported price for it. Juglans Regia grown in California is often as good as the European variety if the tree didn't grow too fast.

Other native American woods such as maple, eastern black walnut and Oregon myrtle also make into attractive stocks if suitably figured and close grained. Although cherry isn't ordinarily thought of as a fancy wood, I have seen some nicely grained cherry and am fortunate enough to have a rifle stocked with it. Good cherry takes fine checkering very well. You shouldn't be afraid to use something a little unconventional as long as the quality is good and it will shape up into what you want. Let your stockmaker be your guide, as he should know what physical qualities are needed and can determine if what you have in mind is suitable. Many tropical woods are strong enough, but are too heavy for complete stocks, being used mainly for fore-end tips and grip caps.

Most commercially sold wood today is kiln dried to about 7 percent moisture content, which is a bit more than optimum, as such stocks will absorb moisture in most parts of the country, unless well sealed. Good air-dried wood is probably better, though it's hard to get. The most stable target and varmint rifle stocks I've owned were made from air-dried wood which was over 20 years old. I have one rifle made from a walnut board taken from an old barn, which hasn't changed zero in years, despite the fact the barrel isn't free floated.

Other approaches to stable, non-warping stocks are those impregnated with polyethylene glycol (PEG) or made by laminating sheets of wood of the same type, or contrasting ones, with epoxy or fiberglass. Laminated stocks are often chosen for varmint or target rifles. They are seldom used for fancy sporting rifles, though they are about tops for strength and stability.

The ultimate stable stock material is fiberglass. While it doesn't make up into a fancy rifle, it is very strong, light and stable. The most practical application for fiberglass stocks if for bench rest or target rifles where you wish the weight in the barrel, rather than the stock, or for hunting rifles to be used in extremes of weather conditions. The U.S. Marine Corps has switched from wood or laminated wood to fiberglass stocks on their bolt-action sniper rifles and nearly all top bench rest rifles today are stocked with fiberglass.

Wood is still the material of choice for most builders of custom rifles, though, and will continue to be for some time. To many people there is something "fake" about fiberglass. While I admit the superiority of the synthetics for sheer stability and accuracy in target and bench rest guns, I still like my hunting rifles to "look like a rifle," having a pleasing contrast of blued steel and nicely grained brown wood.

C. E. Harris

Rifle Actions

IT'S SAFE to say that Americans build more custom rifles on bolt-actions than all the other types combined. For many years following WW I, the '03 Springfield was *the* action on which to build a custom rifle, and the number of Springfields used far outnumbered the '98 Mausers, which were the Springfield's main competition until introduction of the Winchester Model 54, and later the Model 70. An important feature of the Springfield which endeared it to the likes of Townsend

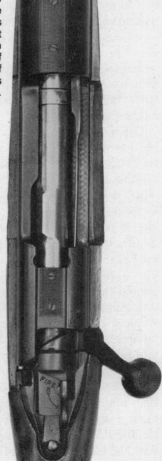

The pre-1964 Model 70 Winchester is held in very high regard by those who will make custom rifles. This example has a sideplate for an ECHO sight mount in view. It has been reworked with mild touches of checkering and a little oakleaf engraving here and there and is now a 35 Whelen.

Polished and ready this FN commercial action is thought by many to be one of the nicer looking available Mauser 98s. The scope mount screw holes in the top are original. The bolt handle seems to be altered in this example.

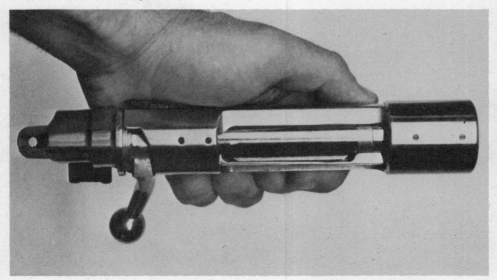

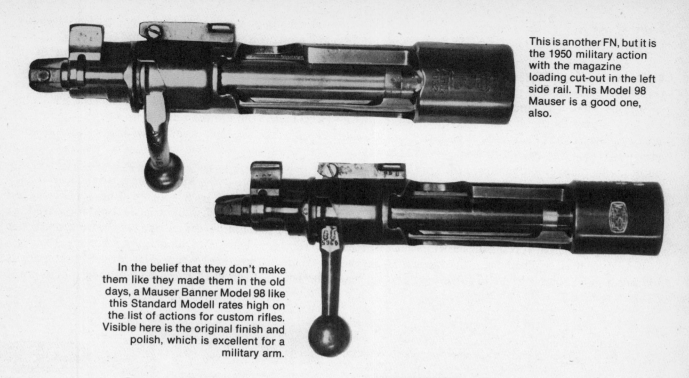

This is another FN, but it is the 1950 military action with the magazine loading cut-out in the left side rail. This Model 98 Mauser is a good one, also.

In the belief that they don't make them like they made them in the old days, a Mauser Banner Model 98 like this Standard Modell rates high on the list of actions for custom rifles. Visible here is the original finish and polish, which is excellent for a military arm.

Whelen, Jack O'Connor, and other notables, was its smooth operation from the shoulder. Its reduced opening effort, and swept back bolt handle favorably positioned with respect to the grip and trigger, simply beat the Mauser '98. That the Winchester Model 54 and later Model 70 were successful competitors to the Springfield was due mainly to their retaining the Springfield's smooth operating characteristics.

Although the Springfield was much preferred then over the Mauser, and still is by some, both actions share a common characteristic which is noteworthy. Their nonrotary hook extractors provide a "controlled round" during the feeding and ejection cycles. On both rifles the lower lip of the bolt rim is machined away so the cartridge is forced up under the extractor hook as it is stripped from the magazine. This causes it to be held against the bolt face, while being supported by a projection opposite the extractor, until the action is opened, and the bolt retracted far enough for the ejector to drive the case off the bolt face and out the right side of the receiver. Fundamental differences are that the '03 extractor will snap over a round placed directly into the chamber, whereas the one on the Mauser '98 generally will not, unless it has been modified to do so. With either rifle a positive grasp of the cartridge from the magazine is achieved before it is completely chambered, which effectively prevents double loading. Double loading is otherwise common when a nervous shooter short-strokes the bolt and chambers one round on top of another. This factor has been forgotten by many designers and users of bolt-action rifles today, but shouldn't be, since it is of prime importance for anyone who needs a firearm which will work reliably when

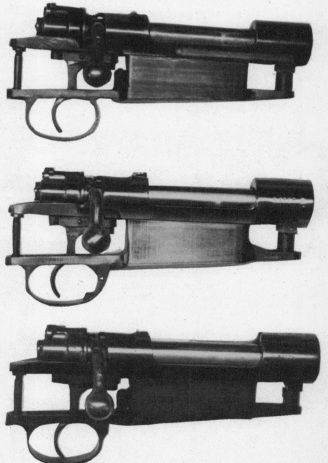

Top to bottom, these are the G33/40, Argentine 1909 large ring and FN military large ring Mauser actions. The FN 1950 was available in 30-06, a relatively long cartridge for the Mauser action. Minor differences—only minor—are clearly visible.

State of the Art: Rifle Actions

called upon. Its worth is obvious in a military rifle, or one used on dangerous game.

Serious hunters and many target shooters, therefore, are not happy with bolt-actions other than those featuring the "controlled round." Today this means the pre-1964 Winchester Model 70, Mauser '98, and its true copies, which haven't abandoned the controlled round in favor of a plunger type ejector, such as the FN Mauser, or Interarms Mark X. Most recent Sako rifles and the Ruger 77 don't qualify here, since, while they may have the nonrotary extractor, their plunger ejector defeats its function by forcing the cartridge ahead of the bolt face as it is stripped from the magazine, so the extractor must snap over it. If I live long enough and

find a willing machinist, I'm going to take my Ruger 77 and convert it to a controlled round type similar to the Winchester pre-1964 Model 70, '98 Mauser or '03 Springfield.

Of the bolt-actions desired for building custom rifles, the pre-1964 Winchester Model 70 tops the list. It has been called the utmost refinement of the Mauser '98. It's hard to beat for fineness of line, smoothness of operation, and reliability of function. Because it is in such demand, prices are high and you can expect to pay dearly. The pre-1964 Winchester action has all the refinements needed in a sporter, fine finish, hinged floorplate, good adjustable trigger, bolt contoured for low scope mounting, drilled and tapped for scope bases or receiver sights, and all steel, machined parts.

While the pre-1964 Winchester Model 70 probably is the action of choice for most who build a high-grade

These are typical markings on a genuine Mauser Standard Modell. Actions so-marked that have not been abused may be relied on to deliver the full benefits of the marvelous compromise that the Mauser 98 action is.

Many believe that the Mauser 98 action offers the best compromise of the important factors that make a bolt-action rifle a sound and reliable instrument. Others are smoother, have cleaner lines, permit larger cartridges, and claim tighter breeching, but the Mauser does it all.

Perhaps the favorite, because it is widely available and because it is a very good action, is the Argentine Model 1909 Mauser 98, shown below from the left. The elegant Mauser solution to the floorplate catch is the principal attraction of the 1909 over others. This trigger guard may be simply reshaped and does not need replacement.

This is how Fabrique Nationale (FN) marked its post-World War II military Mausers. Note the Liege Tower on the front ring.

The Czech 33/40 small-ring Mauser action was greatly favored by the Germans who, as soon as they could, utilized it for rifles for mountain troops and the like. Here the standard and original factory lightening cut is shown. This normally appears on no other Mauser action.

(Below) Here is the difference between old production technique and new production technique in Mauser 98s. The older model on the right had the inner shroud of the action cleared on one side only for the extractor. The newer model, on the left, is broached clean through on both sides because it is more sensible from a production point of view. Many prefer the older method.

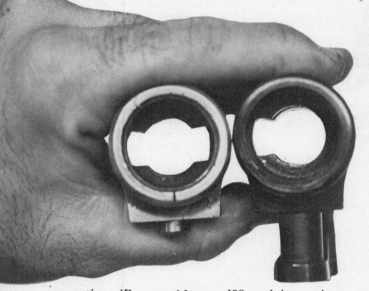

sporting rifle, the Mauser '98 and its variants outnumber it, and are also good choices. The Winchester is a slicker action to operate from the shoulder in rapid-fire, but this isn't always important in a hunting rifle. GOOD Mausers can be very smooth from the shoulder, giving up very little in ease of bolt manipulation to the prized Winchester Model 70s or '03 Springfields, so this argument is one mainly of personal preference.

The '98 Mausers fall into two general categories, "old" Mausers, and "new" ones of current manufacture. "Old" Mausers are the pre-war Oberndorf sporter actions, and the finely made pre-war military actions such as the Argentine M1909, or pre-1942 German military actions. They also include the Mexican Model 1910, Czech VZ24, VZ33, G33/40 and FN military actions, such as the Venezuelan Model 24/30, or postwar FN military actions like those made for the Dutch

It is not all Mauser 98s and Model 70s, of course. Some very fine rifles, like this stocked by Al Lind get attention also. This is a Sako action, a Mauser derivative, of course, with a great deal of metalwork by Herman Waldron, not the least of which was to open up the action to accept the 7x57mm cartridge.

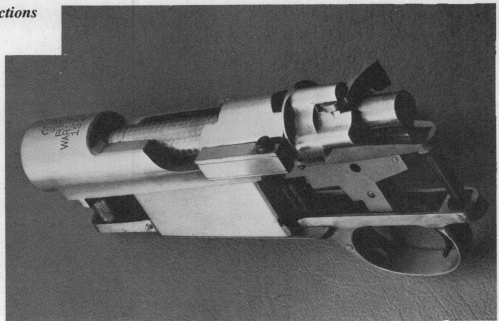

The jokes don't count when it comes to Polish Model 98 Mauser actions. They are very good actions, or Phil Fischer would not have gone to all the trouble and expense to shorten this one down to accept the 250 Savage cartridge. The magazine and floorplate-trigger guard assembly is custom built. The trigger guard and special safety are not original, either.

This is obviously a Model 98, but it never saw the Mauser factory or the factory of any licensee. This is a double square bridge magnum Mauser with integral side scope mount manufactured in its entirety by Fred Wells of Wells Sport Store, Prescott, Arizona. Such a production, machined from the bar stock, is undeniably expensive, but one can get exactly what he wants in a Mauser action this way.

Here is how the 1909 Mauser magazine floorplate release works and this is why people like this particular action. Often, the assembly is lightened considerably, but in its essentials left alone.

and Belgians.

Original Oberndorf sporter actions are greatly prized for building custom rifles, because of their fine workmanship and the variety of action lengths and magazine sizes which accommodated cartridges from the 250-3000 up through the 416 Rigby. The small ring short action used to accommodate the 6.5x54 or 250-3000 Savage was 8⅛ inches long, whereas the standard-length, large ring action used for military 8x57 rifles or 30-06 commercial sporters was 8¾ inches long. The large Mauser or later Belgian Brevex Magnum actions used for cartridges such as the 10.75x73, or 416 Rigby were 9¼ inches long. Mauser actually made 20 different configurations of sporting actions for various cartridges, using one of these three receivers, and different sizes of magazines.

Original Mauser sporting actions are recognized by their longer, heavier cocking piece than military '98s, their lack of guard locking screws, and by their pear-shaped bolt knob with bent down handle. They also had hinged floorplates with either a tab release inside the trigger bow, or a lever beneath the floorplate. Prior to

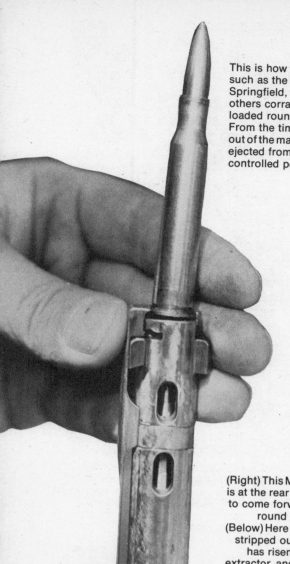

This is how the older actions, such as the Mauser 98, the Springfield, the Model 70 and others corral and control the loaded round during feeding. From the time the round rises out of the magazine box until it is ejected from the gun, it is controlled positively.

(Right) This Mauser action's bolt is at the rear of its stroke, ready to come forward and move the round into the magazine. (Below) Here the round has been stripped out of the magazine, has risen up and under the extractor, and has entered—in a straight line—its chamber.

WW II some Mauser sporter actions were made without the thumbcut in the left receiver wall, and many of these have the receiver bridge raised for better adaptation to European scope mounts. Double-square actions with the receiver ring raised as well are highly valued these days.

You may encounter Original Mauser sporter actions which don't seem to fit a standard pattern. A case in point is a square bridge action I own, which was originally made for the 318 W.R. cartridge. It has a standard-size large ring action, but the rear of the receiver ring has a clearance cut to let the long noses of 318 cartridges pass when clip loading, and unlike most square bridge actions I've seen, it has the thumbcut in the left receiver wall to facilitate clip loading. The action has no markings other than serial number, British proofs on the left of the receiver ring and a Mauser Banner trademark under the recoil lug. This is the action pictured on page 284 of *Mauser Bolt Rifles* by Olson. The 318 magazine is long enough to accommodate a 375 H&H cartridge with ease, which I had hoped to do with it. When the old barrel was jerked out, however, we found the receiver didn't have the standard 1.1-inch-12, 55-degree V thread, but instead had a smaller diameter thread, the same as small ring actions like the G33/40 or VZ33. All things turned out for the best, however, since I decided to build an iron-sighted 30-06 sporter, which I now use and enjoy a lot more than if I had built a 375 Magnum.

Small ring Mauser actions such as the Mexican M1910, Czech VZ33 or German G33/40 are often chosen for sporters, since they are lighter than standard '98s. They make up into nice light mountain rifles. The German G33/40 rifle was a variant of the Czech VZ33, used for mountain troops. Both rifles had the small ring action, thinner receiver sidewalls and lightening cuts along the receiver sides covered by the stock. The bolt handles were hollowed out and the trigger guards and magazine boxes were made of lightweight alloy, rather than steel. Rifles of this general type were also purchased in large quantities for use by police in Brazil, Ecuador, El Salvador, Guatemala, Nicaragua, and Peru, so they are fairly common. A small ring Mauser is probably a top choice for a lightweight hunting rifle in calibers such as 6mm Remington, 257 Roberts, 7x57mm or 308 Winchester. Use of a "blind" magazine permits even further weight reduction.

"New" Mauser actions are those made after WW II for the commercial trade. The factor which distinguishes "new" Mausers from "old" Mausers is the mode of manufacture. Until the 1950s the receiver diaphragm was cut through only on the right side to clear the extractor. Then it was found easier to manufacture the receiver if the locking lug guideways were cut

Among lever-actions, Winchesters are the most often changed around to suit their owners. This Model 92 by Snapp in 357 Magnum presents all the problems of such conversions, and Snapp has solved them. The rifle loads, feeds, extracts and ejects without a bobble.

Single shot actions have their admirers, and attempts to provide an outside-hammer single-action of vaguely Winchester High Wall proportion come along relatively often. This is the Falling Block Works action, which may be purchased as shown, ready to make a traditional single shot without chopping up a genuine old rifle.

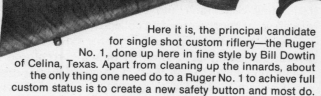

Here it is, the principal candidate for single shot custom riflery—the Ruger No. 1, done up here in fine style by Bill Dowtin of Celina, Texas. Apart from cleaning up the innards, about the only thing one need do to a Ruger No. 1 to achieve full custom status is to create a new safety button and most do.

The factory doesn't offer it, but one can make quite a nice 22 rimfire out of the Ruger No. 1 rifle and more than a few people have done so. There are several techniques, including off-center boring of the barrel, to get the chamber in the right place to be struck by the standard firing pin; others change the leverages and camming to change the position of the block in the frame to achieve the same result. That they will go to that much trouble is tribute to the No. 1 Ruger.

through the receiver diaphragm on both sides. Most FN commercial Mausers, such as those sold in this country by Browning are of this type. The Interarms Mark X, made in Yugoslavia by Zastava is also made this way. Although these actions are quite strong and serviceable, they are theoretically less rigid than the original '98s. Husqvarna and Sako sporting rifles sold in this country into the 1960s used FN Mauser actions and were manufactured in this manner.

No discussion of "new" Mausers would be complete without mention of the custom-made actions produced by Fred Wells in Prescott, AZ. Wells manufactures complete actions and rifles in his own shop, machining the receivers, trigger guards and floorplates, and even the bolts, from scratch. His actions are patterned after original Oberndorf sporter actions, in sizes from the small ring, short actions to the large magnum ones, for his 510 Wells Express. Everything is made to order, so there are a lot of variations from original Mauser patterns, such as integral scope mounts, larger receiver rings, and left-handed actions. These are understandably expensive, complete rifles starting around $5000, and actions from about $1650, but that's not bad for a half dozen steel parts requiring over 50 separate machining operations. Owners of Wells' rifles think they are worth the wait and expense.

Of course, there are custom rifles built on other than bolt-actions, and to neglect the single shots, and the other repeaters, such as lever-actions, would be a grave omission. Single shot rifles have a particular appeal, and they are enjoying a renewed popularity. Interest in them waned as shooters hungered for more powerful rifles and higher pressure cartridges in the decades after WW I. As the supply of Winchester High Walls and their contemporaries dried up, there were few good single shot actions available, starting in the 1960s, except for surplus Martinis and Remington rolling blocks, which weren't always well finished or suited for the cartridges people wanted.

Introduction of the excellent Ruger No. 1 helped

rekindle the interest in single shots, which is still growing, prompting a variety of competitors. These include the Browning 78, which resembles the Winchester High Wall in appearance (though it is entirely different), Falling Block Works, and the Wickliffe, (which both resemble the Stevens 44½, but aren't true copies), and the Reidl, an interesting modern design.

The current generation of single shots offers suitable strength for modern cartridges, such as the 243 Winchester, 30-06 or 22-250, and have better extraction leverage than older actions such as the Martini or Winchester High Wall. Also, their firing pin diameters are smaller and the openings in the breechblock are reduced accordingly, so problems with punctured prim-

State of the Art: Rifle Actions

There is a vogue to make, these days, a using rifle by doing a full custom job on a 1922 M2 Springfield 22 rifle. Bob Emmons did this one in strict accord with 1931 Griffin & Howe styling.

(Middle rifle) Any good action is grist for the custom rifle mill. This one is the Shilen DGA, fitted with a Model 70 guard and floorplate by Bob Emmons. Such high-accuracy-potential actions as the Shilen make a great deal of sense in a very special rifle.

(Bottom rifle) This is the deHaas-Miller specialty single shot as gotten up in American walnut by Miller. Single shots have their own distinction and this one demonstrates it.

ers so prevalent with older actions (unless they are bushed) are entirely eliminated. Though many custom rifle enthusiasts cobbled up choice old Stevens, Winchesters, Remington-Hepburns and Martinis in the 1940s and 1950s for varmint or target rifles, the increasing value of unmodified single shots today is enough to discourage the practice. The availability of new single shot actions should insure the continued survival of remaining collectable old ones. Old rifles, already modified, of course, are of no collector interest, but this means they can continue to delight the single shot buff who wants an old action, rather than a current one.

The Winchester High Wall or Stevens 44½ actions are favored among single shot target shooters who compete with plain-based, breech-seated cast bullets in the traditional style practiced by the American Single Shot Rifle Association. A few are used by varmint shooters also, though for cartridges operating at over 48,000 c.u.p., actions like the Ruger, Browning, or Reidl are better choices.

Of the available single shot actions made today, the Ruger No. 1 probably offers the most potential in building a custom rifle. It can be successfully adapted to any rimmed, or rimless, centerfire, or even rimfire cartridge. I have seen Ruger single shots converted to just about everything from 22 Long Rifle, to 577 Nitro Express. They are incredibly strong, and when properly set up, will shoot right along with the best bolt-actions of that same caliber and weight. One of the nice advantages of the Ruger, and most of the single shots in general, is the short action length, which permits a longer barrel length for the same size rifle. A Ruger No. 1 with 26-inch barrel is no longer than most bolt-actions with 22-24-inch barrels. Another feature I like about the Ruger is that you can change the ejector to a plain extractor by simply taking out the ejector spring. This permits easy recovery of brass for bench shooting, or quick reloading in a hunting situation.

I have to admit a certain prejudice in favor of the Ruger single shot. I have never owned one, but have coveted several Rugers belonging to friends and have shot them a great deal. The No. 1 has a certain fineness of line which is more attractive to me than any of its competitors. The large receiver flats have lots of potential for engraving, and the basic gun looks and shoots pretty well without doing a thing to it. Sometimes it's hard to improve on a good thing, but enough people are customizing Ruger 1's that it must be fun trying.

Lever-actions offer considerable possibilities for customizing, though you don't see quite as many custom lever-guns as you used to. Probably the most popular lever-action conversions are those on the Winchester Model 92, converting it from the original 25-20, 32-20, 38-40 or 44-40 calibers to 357 or 44 Magnum. Although there may not be as many of these done in the future, thanks to availability of factory-produced lever-actions in these calibers, those desiring a slick operating, accurate rifle will still seek original Winchester Model 92, converting it from the original 25-20, the current Marlin lever-actions in 44 Magnum or 357 Magnum, have Micro-groove barrels which don't handle cast bullets well, and compared to the old guns, they are nowhere near as smooth. A replacement barrel and an action job on one of these would more than double the cost of the rifle, and the fellow contemplating that much work may as well start with a classier action to begin with. Even with factory jacketed loads, the new guns may not always feed all types of ammo, or shoot better than about 3 inches at 50 yards, but a good custom job should digest almost anything. Good 357 conversions on the Winchester 92, like Snapp's, will group about as well at 100 yards as out-of-the-box Marlins will at 50. There's a big difference in cost, but you get a really smooth working, trim, classy and accurate gun for the money.

Custom lever-actions also provide you with options you'd never get at the factory. I've seen Winchester 92s converted to 45 Colt, which is an interesting idea if you have a revolver or two in that caliber. I've also heard of them or the Marlins done to 45 ACP, which has obvious appeal to the auto pistol enthusiast. The appeal of common rifle/pistol ammunition, popular 100 years ago, is being revived, and has a certain utility for small game, varmints, plinking, and even for deer-sized game at very close ranges.

While the pistol-caliber rifle conversions are mostly small game and plinking guns, lever-actions offer even more possibilities in real big game and meat getting calibers. The Savage 99 has a great deal of potential since its rotary magazine permits use of spitzer bullets and handles rimless cartridges from the 22-250, 243 Winchester, or 250 Savage quite easily. My experience has been that the Savage 99 is potentially far more accurate than the Winchester 94 or Marlin 336. This accuracy potential has prompted a good many varmint rifles on the Savage 99 which are used with good effect by coyote and fox hunters in calibers like the 22-250. Such a rig carries very well in a saddle scabbard and handles fast like all lever-guns, but groups as well out to about 200 yards as most bolt-actions. Some gunsmiths really gussy up the 99, making full-length Mannlicher stocks, half ribs, with express sights or integral scope bases and the like. I heard once of a German fellow who liked his 99 so much he put claw mounts on it.

The Winchester 94 somehow doesn't fit the usual profile of actions to be customized, since the fellows who use them a lot generally prefer them the way they are, but I've seen a few of those customized too. The most common things to do here are long barrel, half-magazine, cosmetic stuff, and action jobs. Occasionally people adapt them to interesting wildcats, like the 35-30, which is a 30-30 necked up to 35, giving ballistics like the 35 Remington. It is adapted easily to the Winchester 94, which the 35 Remington is not.

Winchester lever-actions have all sorts of things done to them to create special rifles. The big ones are sometimes made into big-bore rifles; the little ones, like this Model 92, are often set up to handle revolver cartridges. This one by Snapp is a 357 Magnum.

The Winchester Model 71 is highly prized by some lever-action buffs and is essentially a modernized Model 1886 with a heat-treated receiver. It was made only for the fat, rimmed 348 Winchester cartridge, from 1936-1957, but 71s draw big-bore, lever-action enthusiasts like honey draws flies. It can be converted to many of the large-bore, blackpowder cartridges, such as the 45-70 or 45-90, which were used in 1886, and will give the user a strong-actioned rifle suitable for heavier handloads than original guns. There is also a whole family of wildcats on the 348 Winchester case, Ackley Improved versions, and such. The 35-348 Ackley Improved really isn't much different from a 35 Whelen or 350 Remington Magnum. I know of one fellow who lived in British Columbia and had a Winchester 71 converted to 50/348 Winchester, which blew the case out straight. This round looks like the old 50-70, but with a big difference, since he could drive a gas-check 450-gr. bullet at real shoulder stomping, bear busting velocities with a substantial charge of RL-7.

Although there isn't a lot of custom work done these days on pumps or autoloaders, if you fancy these types of actions there's no reason not to go ahead if that's what you want. I've seen some interesting work done on Remington 760 slide-actions, to 35 Whelen and such, and I've seen Ruger Mini-14s or Colt AR-15s reworked to heavy barrel target rifles and varmint guns in 25 caliber or 6mm wildcats on the 223 case. Just think it all out and make sure it will work before you start.

There's almost no limit to what can be done to a good action, but the trick is to find the BEST one, suited to your purpose, and then get a quality action and seek quality work.

C.E. Harris

Metalsmithing

THE METAL parts of a gun are what makes it work, and everything else is just a handle. Consequently, what you do to them has a profound effect on the function, accuracy, safety and overall satisfaction derived from a custom firearm.

Some metalsmithing is purely functional, some mostly cosmetic. Some are actually for both reasons. In a broad sense, metalsmithing can mean a mere adjustment, cosmetic improvement, or a complete rebuild of a rifle. What you do and how you go about it depends on what you start out with, and how far you decide to go with it. The latter is determined by your requirements and capabilities. There are many metalsmithing jobs within the ability of most gun owners such as installing new triggers, streamlining trigger guards, or installing scope safeties on military rifles. Other jobs can be done by the advanced hobbyist who has skills in machine tool operation or welding, though the average guy would probably be wise to have this farmed out, unless he's well versed in what he's doing.

There is a big difference between adjustments, the installation of new replacement parts, and the complete design and manufacture of new parts. This is where simple gunsmithing and custom metalsmithing depart. It's quite one thing for a fellow to do the basic alterations on a military Mauser or Springfield action for sporterizing, and yet another to build a new hinged floorplate, magazine and trigger guard assembly from scratch for that rifle. Though the advanced hobbyist may do his own drilling and tapping, safety and trigger

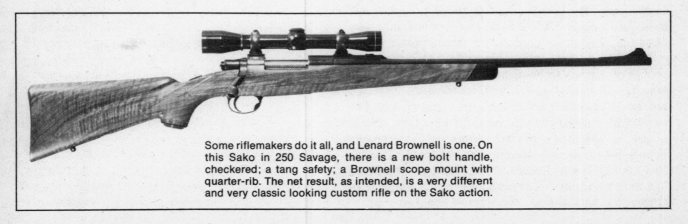

Some riflemakers do it all, and Lenard Brownell is one. On this Sako in 250 Savage, there is a new bolt handle, checkered; a tang safety; a Brownell scope mount with quarter-rib. The net result, as intended, is a very different and very classic looking custom rifle on the Sako action.

Bob Emmons says that just about everything that could be done to a Mauser was done to this VC-24 action with Apex barrel. The front ring has been ground; there is a Jantz Model 70-type safety, guard, floorplate and bolt. In addition the bolt knob has been checkered; the rear receiver tang lowered. Inside, the magazine box has been skeletonized and a Biesen skeleton buttplate and Talley skeleton grip cap and swivel bases have been installed. The rifle is a 7x57mm.

This Shilen DGA in 6mm Improved, has been fitted with a Model 70 guard and floorplate by Bob Emmons. Stock is in Bastogne with 24 lpi checkering with Biesen furniture. The mount is a Len Brownell.

installation, and perhaps even alter the bolt handle and do his own barrel-fitting work, it takes a skilled, experienced craftsman to perform major alterations which work well and look right. That's why even top gunsmiths farm out some of their custom metalwork, since a fellow who specializes in certain jobs can usually do them better, and in less time than a fellow who doesn't.

That's why you have few "general practitioners" in the gun trade. Gunsmiths who do a really respectable job in more than two areas, such as stock work, barrel and action work, engraving, custom metalsmithing, accuracy modifications or general repair, are few and far between. Some masters, however, have a market among those who want only one name on the work. The gunsmiths who usually make out best are the ones who specialize in bench rest and target rifles, since they specialize mostly in precision machine work, barrel fitting and stock bedding. They don't have to cater to the select crowd who shun fiberglass or wood stocks devoid of checkering. This isn't to say that the target gunsmiths are less skillful, they just specialize in a different game. If you want a rifle to shoot a ⅛-inch group every time, see a bench rest specialist. If you want to draw crowds in snobby company, see one of the glamour guys. But, if you want to do both with the same rifle, you'd better get both fellows together, for neither can do it by himself.

Most home gunsmiths get into general metalsmithing as a do-it-yourselfer, often sporterizing a military action for their first custom gun. This is great fun and can provide a real sense of accomplishment when the completed job turns out right. Just be sure you don't pick up somebody else's mistakes for a "bargain" at your local hockshop, for you may end up buying more than you figured on.

Bolt handle alterations are a pet peeve of mine, since I once had the misfortune of having a bolt handle come off, leaving the body still in the rifle. I didn't mess up that job myself, but somebody else did, and it made me a lot more careful of home gunsmithed jobs in the future. Bolt handle alterations are done either by forging or welding. Most jobs are generally the same, differing mainly in the shank size and shape. The shank thickness determines the strength of the handle. If it is made too thin and streamlined where it joins the body, it might yield if considerable force were required to extract a stuck case. However, if the handle is made really heavy and strong, it looks like the devil and requires a larger cut in the receiver and stock to accommodate it. This can get tricky, for if the notch isn't deep enough it can hold the bolt partially open, or if it is too deep, the bolt handle will jump when the firing pin falls, and firing pin protrusion may be excessive. The notch should be cut just deep enough so when the bolt is turned down, the military safety on Mausers or Springfields can be turned to the full locked position. When installing a new bolt handle or altering an old one

This Model 70 in 280 Remington shows the slick and careful work a metalsmith has to go to when he is looking for light weight. The barrel band swivel and very slim barrel go together well. There is a custom mount and a new trigger guard and floorplate. It is a Don Klein job, with finish by Mark Lee.

by welding, the strength of the weld is important. If the handle isn't to come off, the weld must start in the middle and work out all the way through and not just run around the edges. Properly done, a welded-on bolt handle is as strong as if it were integral.

Another method of altering bolt handles, usually on military rifles, and the preferred method for doing those, is by forging. The bolt is held in a fixture and clamped at the root of the bolt handle. The fixture acts as a heat sink while the handle is heated red hot and beaten until it conforms to the contour of the fixture.

Aside from altering or replacing a bolt handle to accommodate a low scope, you might choose to replace one in an effort to relocate the knob closer to the trigger for easier manipulation, or to improve its appearance. Years ago, M1917 Enfields were instant candidates for bolt handle alterations, since the ones which came on them were so darned ugly. Today, people customize Remington 600s or 660s for the same reason. Of course you sometimes get yourself into a whole series of alterations to accommodate the others. With the Remington 600 series you usually end up restocking, replacing the bolt handle and trigger guard, and repositioning the trigger before it begins to "look right." Folks go to this trouble because they like how their rifles shoot, but can't stand to look at them. Most have felt the trouble worthwhile.

The outcome of a bolt handle alteration and how it is done is a good reflection on the gunsmith's skill and sense of line. Not all bolt handle jobs look the same. There is an immense difference between the ordinary job and the great one. Top men in the field have a certain dignity or refinement in their work so that even this so-called "standard" job takes on a different character. It not only works well and is done smoothly, it looks great, having just that right shape and curvature. It is strong and functional, yet elegant. It stands out in a crowd because it's far above the ordinary, being perfectly executed. Of course, fellows in this league don't weld on a mass-produced bolt handle, they make them from scratch and will often make a special one with a particular sweep or length of handle or shape of knob to create just the desired effect.

When building a high-grade custom rifle you should consider the functional aspects first before the cosmetic ones, though. Even when customizing "ordinary" hunting guns, attention to detail pays great dividends in reliability and accuracy. I judge a gunsmith by the way he spots little things wrong, and how he explains the what, how and why of it all. A real craftsman will generally insist on making what he considers essential corrections needed for safety or reliability. He may also suggest optional, useful, but nonessential improvements.

If all rifle actions were perfect, there wouldn't be much need for this exercise, but tool wear and normal tolerances in manufacture, combined with normal human frailty, mean that all firearms are not created equal. Tolerances can stack up the wrong way, which cause both good guns and not-so-good ones to be made in the same factory on the same day. Many times, however, a little care in fitting and adjustment can take

This Model 70 with a Titus barrel in 30-06 has considerable metal work. The tang has been recontoured; the bolt stop has been built up and checkered; not visible here is a new bolt handle, checkered in two panels. Altogether, the rifle weighs 7¼ pounds, Lind says.

Dave Miller of Tucson sometimes goes to some length in creating fine metalsmithing. Here there is a custom trigger guard on the Model 98 with unusual external contours. The 5-panel bolt knob is another metalsmith specialty. The grip cap is an Al Biesen model.

an ordinary rifle and make it into a smoother working and more accurate one.

It's hard for me to understand why some shooters skimp on the functional handwork and just dress up a rifle, when it is the nitty-gritty stuff that matters when a six-point bull elk appears 300 yards away, or a big buck breaks for the tall timber. You shouldn't be tempted to think of all these little "nits," which aren't as obvious to the untrained eye, as things gunsmiths think up to get more of your money. They are usually important details which are indicative of the kind of care you should learn to expect from one who takes pride in his work. No real craftsman would put his hallmark on a half-baked job. He'd feel justified in refusing work rather than cutting corners against his better judgment.

Most of the better gunsmiths and metalsmiths consider these refinements to be standard jobs, part of the process, ordinarily done in the course of the work. They wouldn't think of fitting a barrel to a customer's receiver without squaring it up, smoothing any little rough areas, spotting or lapping the bolt lugs in, and so on. Maybe I'd better explain these in a bit more detail so you'll understand what your money buys.

It isn't unusual, when rebarreling a bolt-action rifle, to find the bolt face out of square with the chamber, or that the locking lugs bear unevenly. You might also find that sometimes the front of the receiver ring is out of square, so the barrel shoulder bears unevenly when it is tightened. Any of these minor defects, either singly or in combination, will hurt accuracy. While many people might not ever notice it in an ordinary hunting rifle, the improvement in accuracy is often noticeable when such defects are corrected, though you usually don't have a chance to ascertain the effect directly, since most often the gun has usually been rebarreled or rechambered.

When squaring the bolt face, a fixture made from an old barrel is screwed into the receiver and a dial indicator placed against the bolt face in the locked position. If the bolt face is out of square, a lap is inserted through the polished hole of the fixture and the bolt face polished with oil and 400 grit. The lap must be squared often in the lathe. The lap is touched to the bolt face only lightly, polishing just enough to make it clean up all around, removing as little metal as possible.

In spotting locking lugs in, the rear faces of the locking lugs are polished with crocus cloth, and coated with a visible compound and the bolt closed in the receiver while pulling back against the handle so the lugs will bear against their seats in the receiver. After removing the bolt you can readily see where they contact, and then polish the lug seats of the receiver with more crocus epoxied onto the end of a squared rod, and again spot and examine. This is repeated carefully until full lug contact is obtained in the locked position. It is important to remove as little metal as possible, particularly on Mauser actions which have the locking areas only surface hardened—if this is overdone, the lugs will

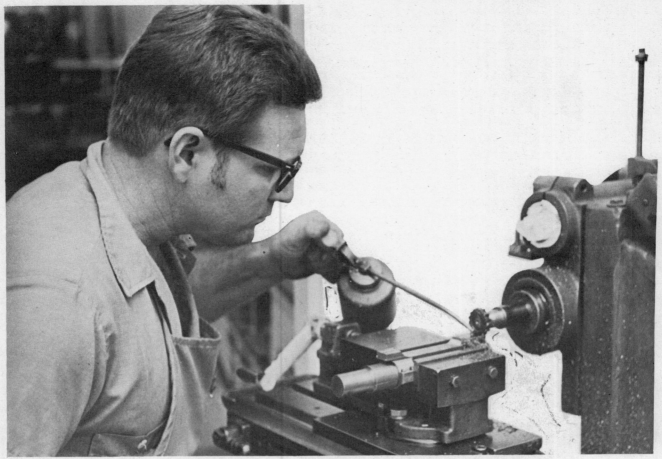

Dave Miller makes scope mounts individually, one at a time. This permits him clean design and unshakable ruggedness at the same time.

set back and gradually increase headspace.

Squaring the front of the receiver ring involves making sure that the threads run square to and concentric with the outside of the receiver to begin with. If they don't, a light cut taken off the front of the receiver will true things up. This can be done by grinding, which is the preferred method. After getting a smooth, square ring face, the barrel shoulder will bear evenly when drawn up, without stressing the barrel in one direction or another. Once in awhile, however, you find a receiver in which the threads are not concentric. In this case the receiver is set up so a piece of true, round barrel runs concentrically when threaded into this receiver and checked on a dial indicator. The piece of barrel used to indicate on is then removed and the receiver face cleaned up accordingly. If the receiver threads are not aligned square with the axis of the receiver, however, you'd best find another action.

While the action is disassembled and everything is being spotted, lapped in and squared up prior to barrel fitting and chambering, the good worker slicks up any rough spots in the rifle's operation. This is best done in moderation, the intent being only to remove burrs or rough spots, not to polish out all the tool marks. Doing so would change the basic dimensions, making the parts fit loosely, which causes problems. It doesn't hurt to polish the bolt raceways a wee bit, but only a little, since you don't want a loose bolt. For the same reason you don't ever polish a bolt body very much. Engine turning or jeweling a bolt body gets the smoothing done, dresses it up nicely, and if done right removes very little metal. You must be careful not to polish a rough cocking cam on a Mauser cocking piece too much for it is only surface hardened and it will drag on the bolt notch unless hard surfaced or welded up with a carburizing rod so it can be ground back to a suitable smooth contour. The same goes for the cocking notch of the bolt body.

Major action alterations were often undertaken 20 years ago when a gunsmith's labor was underpriced and a fellow wanted to utilize a bargain military action. Although these make good projects for the gunsmithing student or serious do-it-yourselfer, I'd discourage shooters today from spending a lot of money on converting most military actions. Expensive alterations should be limited to top quality stuff, only when re-

Here are the steps in producing the Dave Miller scope mount from a single piece of bored steel. All the steps are not shown, of course, but the course of the job is plain to see.

Besides the scope mount, this extraordinary 338 1909 Argentine Mauser action has special metalsmithing features: The integral rib is one; the barrel band is custom; the front sight and single standing rear sight are all going with the work. The wood is California English.

quired. A good example of the extensive work which people used to do, which makes little sense today, is the M1917 U.S. Enfield. The Enfield was and is a very serviceable, strong action, well suited to any standard or large centerfire cartridge. But unless you just happen to like the beast, it hardly makes sense to do all the work. With the money invested by the time you get done, you probably could have bought a "good" action, like a pre-war Mauser or pre-1964 Winchester Model 70.

In the 1950s U.S. Enfields fed more gunsmiths than all the other military actions put together. It's easy to see why gunsmiths either *loved* U.S. Enfields for keeping the wolf away from the door, or they *hated* them for all the work they were. The receiver bridge must be machined away and contour ground to accommodate either a receiver sight or scope; the classier gunsmiths also removed a lot of the metal on the left rear of the receiver behind the hinge pin housing, creating a Mauser-style bolt stop, welding up the slot and grinding it to a smooth contour. The bolt stop spring was then reduced somewhat, since they were always stronger than necessary, and the ejector replaced with

State of the Art: Metalsmithing

(Below left) This Mauser action was lengthened by welding by Phil Fischer, the Portland, Oregon, smith. Apart from making side rails, bolt and striker longer, Fischer put in a Model 70 type safety and a new bolt handle. The trigger guard-floorplate assembly were custom made, not original.

(Below right) This Polish Mauser action has been shortened to accept the 250 Savage cartridge exactly. Note that this one also has the Model 70 safety, the new bolt handle and a custom-made magazine and trigger guard assembly.

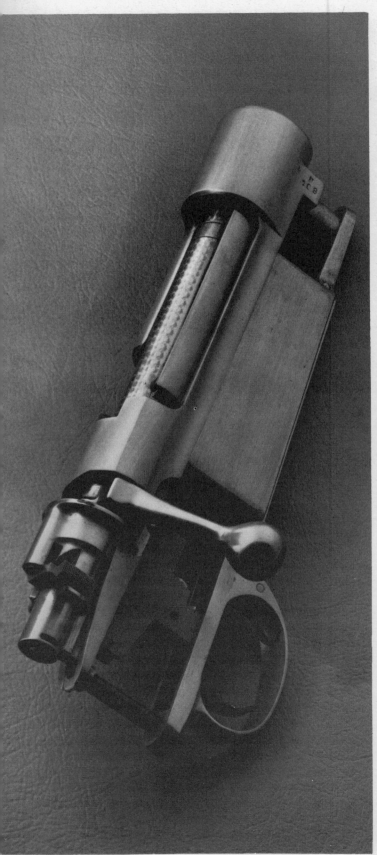

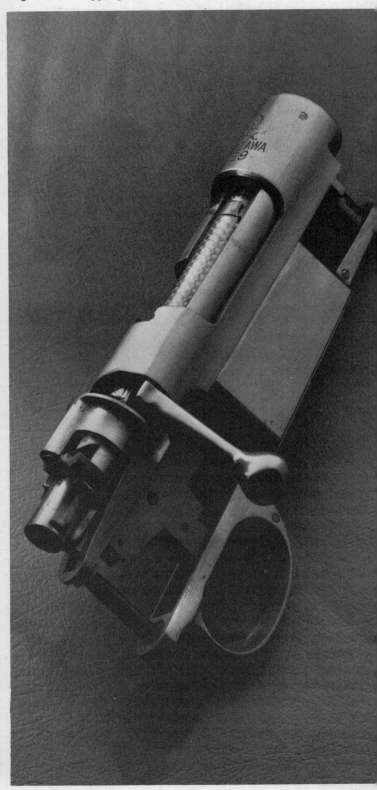

The neat thing about this Model 70 in 375 Holland & Holland Magnum, built by Dave Miller and Curt Crum, is some fine metal work perhaps helped by the ivory inlay as well as the panels in the 5-panel bolt knob. The trigger guard in this example is a Blackburn trigger guard.

This older Sako rifle has its bolt handle reshaped and checkered. and a lot of subtle snaping went on in and around the trigger guard to bring the metal work up to the standards of the New Zealand walnut stock.

This somewhat unusual blind magazine job is on a Stephen Billeb full-stock rifle, and has some not-often-seen touches like a diamond-shaped inlay in the belly of the stock. The metal-work includes the sculptured butter knife bolt handle, the special trigger guard, and this job was done at a time when one obtained a Biesen skeleton grip cap by machining a solid Biesen grip cap.

This checkered Model 70 bolt handle by Pete Grisel is a solid little job of work. Bolt checkering is an option that can be taken quite far—from one panel to five—which makes a considerable difference in the complexity and cost.

One minor quibble fine gun fanciers have with the Ruger No. 1 is its safety button and the operation thereof. Pete Grisel does this job on No. 1s to improve matters. Among other things a roller is installed at the safety engagement point.

one from a Remington Model 30. Then you had the job of converting the bolt to cock-on-opening, using a Remington 720 cocking piece, mainspring and firing pin, and welding up, hard surfacing, and regrinding the cam on the bolt notch. The bolt sleeve and firing pin were then altered to fit the modified bolt. To get rid of the "belly" under the action, the magazine was shortened and the trigger guard straightened. Straightening an Enfield guard is probably the hardest welding job to do perfectly; at least I think so. The guard also was often streamlined and hinged, if desired. This covered only the basic action work, not bolt face alteration, or modifying the action rails or feed ramp for magnum-size cartridges. It doesn't take much imagination to figure out what all the action work would cost at today's prices, and spending it on an M1917 would not be good economics.

For building a custom rifle, the pre-war German, Czech, or Polish Mausers, F N Mausers, the Interarms Mark X and pre-1964 Winchester Model 70 are the only good choices, as they are all "controlled round" types.

Pre-war M1903 Springfields (not rough 03 A3s) are also OK. Little needs to be done to these actions for them to look good and work well.

A good method used to dress up the military Mauser (which was popularized by Roy Dunlap) is to replace the military Mauser trigger guard and magazine with a milled one from an '03 Springfield. These guards may still be available to NRA members as parts from the DCM or available to anyone from one of the major parts-supply houses. Using the Springfield guard simply requires reducing the magazine lip to fit the Mauser receiver and occasionally heating and bending the last ¾-inch of the receiver tang down a wee bit to accommodate the angle of the rear guard screw without affecting the fit of the bolt sleeve in the runway. Then the trigger is bent to the rear about 5/16-inch. An alternative method which is no more work is to grind and file out the swivel hole in the original Mauser guard, contour the guard bow, weld up the holes for the lock screws, and recut the counterbores for the heads of the guard screws. When using the original Mauser guard for

Metalsmithing by Don Klein made a great deal of difference in the problems involved with stocking this BSA Martini-International rimfire rifle. The operating lever has been reshaped, bent, and even checkered. The lines resulting from the work permit quite a handsome stock seen elsewhere in this book in its entirety. Metalsmith George Hoenig made the trap grip cap shown.

longer cartridges like the 30-06 or 270, the magazine box must be lengthened by filing and the feed ramp of the receiver blended smoothly with the magazine box so cartridges will feed easily without hanging up.

When converting actions to shorter cartridges, as in converting a 30-06 length Winchester Model 70 to 308 Winchester, or converting a military Mauser to a shorter round like the 22-250, you'll probably want to have cartridge guides installed to position the rounds in the magazine and keep them from moving forward under recoil. These are usually thin beveled or rounded strips of metal soldered vertically inside the magazine

box just ahead of the shoulder of the cartridge. The magazine follower must then be relieved to clear the guides, of course.

If building a belted magnum caliber rifle, there are a variety of modifications required besides opening up the bolt face. With the current availability of factory-made long actions for the Roman candle rounds like the 375 H & H or 8mm Remington Magnum, it isn't a good idea to put these on standard actions. You risk removing too much metal behind the lug seat, and it will set back. Stick to short magnums like the 7mm Remington

Magnum or 338 Winchester in standard-length actions. Even for these, it will still be necessary to alter the action rails for the fatter rounds to feed right. They must move upward without being crowded inward before being stripped from the magazine by the bolt. Sometimes it is also necessary to enlarge the opening between the tops of the rails, but this can get tricky and shouldn't be done unless necessary, and then cautiously.

Action shortening is an expensive job which calls for a skillful welder. This type of work used to be fairly common, but with the more ready availability of factory short actions today, it is rarely done. It requires a lot of work and in cost rivals a custom-made action. Still, if you desire a high-grade featherweight sporter for a short cartridge like the 308 Winchester, 250-3000 or 7mm-08 using a controlled round action, this is a viable, high-class option. The short action reduces weight by removing excess length from the receiver and bolt and makes the whole rifle somewhat more compact. The shorter bolt stroke holds a lot of the appeal. This is an involved job, but not an impossible one. When done right, the result is both pleasing and impressive.

When shortening an action, the receiver is cut in two

Here is a Model 70 bolt handle checkering job that rather broke down on the side nearest the viewer where the pyramids are broken by some false strokes. This is quite serviceable, but definitely not first class.

with a power hacksaw just ahead of the receiver bridge, where the thumbcut is on the left receiver wall of a Mauser, for instance. The front cut is made as much as you wish to have the action shortened, minus the width of the saw cut. The receiver is held in a mandrel which aligns the two halves after they are cut apart. The cut edges must be square and meet perfectly when placed together, and then the outer edges beveled for the weld. The receiver ring and bridge are packed in wet asbestos to keep them from overheating. After joining the pieces at two or three points, the mandrel is removed, their alignment checked and, if OK, the receiver is turned lightly onto an old barrel and the outside weld completed. Then the receiver mandrel is removed, the ring repacked and the inside walls of the receiver done. The inside surfaces are milled out so the unaltered bolt will slide in all the way without binding, and the exterior surfaces machined back to their original contour. Properly done, the strength of the receiver is unaffected by this operation.

Next the bolt is shortened, by scribing an index mark first for alignment, then cutting it ahead of the bolt handle, ahead of the safety lug or rib. The two pieces are fit into the receiver with the front half locked and

State of the Art: Metalsmithing

This handsome little rifle is a metalsmithing tour-de-force, although it has no major outline or contour changes. This total job is by Bob Snapp of Snapp's Gunshop and includes a change to 357 Magnum caliber, cleaning and slimming the barrel somewhat cleanly polishing the action and lever. That is all on the outside—on the inside, the action is considerably refined, with new cartridges guides and the like, so that handling the new cartridge is faultless.

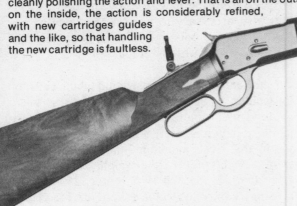

Of course, if you really wanted to, there's nothing stopping you from getting a skillful fellow to take *two* actions, and with the appropriate cutting and welding, make you an extra long action in the same way, applying the same techniques in reverse. This way you could take two standard '98 actions and end up with a 250 Savage length and a 375 Magnum length action if you wanted. Such work would be extremely expensive at

held tight against the lug recesses, and with correct clearance allowed for the safety lugs. The rear part of the bolt body is shortened in a lathe until the correct length is established, then the bolt bevel cut to the inside edges for the weld. Both parts of the bolt are held in V blocks, and the locking lugs protected with wet asbestos and the pieces joined. Steel is added to build up the weld above the bolt surface, the welder being careful to blend in the edges. The excess metal is turned off in a lathe and the bolt's alignment checked, and the bolt straightened if necessary. When the bolt is then tried in the action, it should fit tight and require some effort to go all the way forward, as the polishing and machining needed to clean everything up will finish the job. If it still remains tight after polishing, then more straightening is necessary.

After the above work is done, the receiver runways are cleaned up, the receiver squared and the cartridge shoulder recesses in the magazine opening ground farther forward, if necessary. The action is now ready for test-firing. There should be no lug setback after proofing when a used action is shortened, and only minimal initial setback with a new one.

After test-firing, the trigger guard is fitted by cutting and shortening it just ahead of the rear wall. The sides of the rear wall are then reduced to the width of the sidewalls. The sidewalls are sprung out over them so the two pieces can be attached to the receiver to again assume their correct position. The insides of the sidewalls are marked along the edge of the rear wall and then removed so they can be cut off. The shortened pieces are placed back onto the receiver to align them while they are tack welded together, then removed and the joining completed. The follower and spring are replaced, and the floorplate shortened, usually while converting it to a hinged type. The firing pin is also cut in the middle and rewelded, cleaned up, and the extractor shortened. The inside of the bolt is cleaned up with drills or reamers and polished with emery cloth.

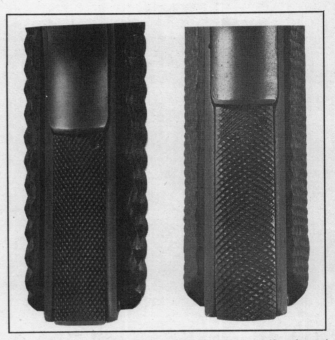

(Left) A good job of metal checkering should have uniformity and be cleanly cut, as this 1911 mainspring housing has been. (Note the exaggerated checkering job on the wood grips, which is a custom feature of another sort.) (Right) The amateur setting about checkering is more likely to wind up with a job like this, which is functional, but not handsome at all.

today's prices, for sure, and you'd have to consider that for all that time and money, you may be better off looking at other options. You have some really classy options available to you once you get above the three-digit price range, and what's a few bucks more to some folks to go first cabin, provided you've got the bucks?

In the case of a magnum Mauser action, you indeed have an alternative to lengthening a standard action, since there is a fellow who builds them from scratch, the receivers, bolts, everything. This fellow is named Fred Wells and his Prescott, Arizona, machine shop creates some of the most unusual examples of the custom metalsmith's skill. Wells' actions are made in the short length for small cartridges like the 250-3000, in the standard large ring size, as well as the magnum size, and he makes them either right- or left-handed. He makes his own trigger guards with hinged floorplates patterned after those on original Mausers, and he's very much into half-ribs, express sights, integral scope mounts, and a lot of other practical and exotic items. All it takes is money, though not a whole wheelbarrow full. About

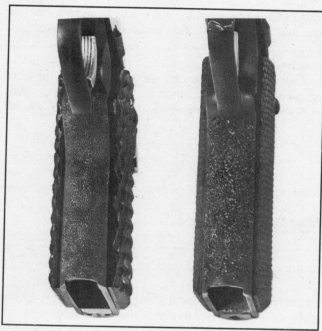

(Left) Fine stippling, here on the front strap of a Model 1911 Colt takes more time, but is more pleasing to the eye, and the grip it furnishes is as firm as coarser jobs.
(Right) This is a well-done example of rough stippling. The rough work, as seen here, is not generally carried out to the edges as fine work might be.

$1,600 will get you a complete made-from-scratch action, and complete rifles are roughly three times that figure for openers.

Though you may not want to go that route and buy a complete custom-made action, many people feel it is well worth the money to get some real quality accessories. Adding a long cocking piece or a pear-shaped bolt handle which is custom-made to copy a pre-war Mauser sporter is a nice touch and makes the "ordinary" military or commercial action look special. There are a number of people who specialize in this and do it up nice—hinged floorplates are another custom

item which really change the character of the rifle and are functional too. To my eye the most pleasing hinged floorplate is the original Mauser type with the plate hinged forward and the release in the form of a tab inside the guard bow. Burgess, Blackburn and Wells make this type, as do some others, though mine is on a pre-WW I Mauser sporting action which was born that way. The basic design of this type of guard and floorplate assembly is practically a standard item, though different craftsmen handle the hinge and the release differently. Other designs which are popular and look good when properly done are those following the Newton or Winchester Model 70 pattern.

Triggers are another thing which deserve careful consideration, since they affect safety and reliability. One of the first things most people do when sporterizing a military rifle, or converting a standard action, is replace the trigger. Most often they complain about the poor trigger pull of a military trigger, or they feel they need an adjustable one. Depending on the need, this is usually OK, but on a hunting rifle, I don't feel there's a thing wrong with a good Mauser or Springfield trigger. However, many people find the double-pull objectionable. One thing to watch out for is unsafe conversion of double-pull triggers to single-stage. The double-pull is a safety feature, and whenever you remove it you increase the risk of accidental discharge. Usually when Mauser triggers are converted, the lobe on the front of the trigger which contacts the sear bottom and prevents forward movement of the trigger is built up by welding or brazing. The tip of this lobe is made longer so that it can be drilled and tapped to take a 6-48 screw used for adjustment. This is adjusted to hold the trigger nearly to the second pull position, but works only with a tightly-fitted cocking piece and bolt. The sear spring is often shortened a coil or two as well. What you *must* watch out for, though, is that you have enough tension for positive spring return. Sear engagement must not be reduced to the point that the sear is easily jarred off.

There are two checks you should perform. Take a steel scale and, with the rifle cocked and the safety off, look for excessive play in the cocking piece. If you can raise it up enough so it falls off, you've got problems. Also, try striking the receiver bridge smartly with a rawhide or plastic mallet when the rifle is cocked and see if the striker falls. If it fails either of these tests, don't accept the job. The cocking piece on a Mauser should not be worked on since it is only surface hardened, and it will wear quickly if stoned more than slightly. If the pull on a Springfield or Mauser military trigger is too light, or if the cocking piece has been stoned on, rounding it, the top of the trigger should be dressed down to let the sear move higher in the receiver.

The quick fix for most of these problems is to junk the military trigger and replace it with an adjustable unit. Provided nobody has done the rock-a-bye baby with a stone on your cocking piece (rounding and ruining it), this may be the best course anyway. Even with good adjustable triggers, however, I don't like a very light pull on a hunting rifle, about 3 pounds is right. Some varmint rifles can safely be made lighter, and those usually used for bench rest shooting almost always are.

Generally, though, on a hunting rifle I'd stick to a simple trigger design, since you have fewer screws to loosen or parts to get out of adjustment. Even on target and silhouette rifles I get skeptical of adjustable triggers, since they foul up once in awhile and you have to inspect them periodically. The original triggers on Winchester Model 70 rifles are very difficult to improve upon. For '98 Mauser rifles the Sako trigger mechanism will work well with very little effort and is a sound design. For hunting rifles, pick a simple trigger and leave your Canjar set for targets.

When replacing the trigger mechanism, you might also exchange the safety for one having a sliding thumb lever. These should block the sear positively, and some will block the trigger as well. Still better, though, are the low-wing safeties like the Buehler which permit the original parts to function as intended, actually engaging and holding the cocking piece and firing pin, and retracting them slightly. Just make sure, whichever type you choose, that it works correctly; then use it, but don't rely on it.

These are the basics of action work, and they can go a long way toward making the heart of your rifle perform to its full potential.

C.E. Harris

Barrels

ALL RIFLE barrels are not alike and don't ever let anybody kid you about it. The choice of a barrel for your custom rifle is every bit as important as the action. A good, properly selected barrel will give thousands of rounds of accurate service; the wrong barrel, even of highest quality, can result in less than complete satisfaction.

The first requirement is that of *barrel quality:* how well the barrel is made, the finish and uniformity of the tube itself, and the care with which it is handled afterwards. You must also be concerned with *barrel suitability* to the specific job—caliber, length, weight, twist, bore and groove dimensions, and metal itself. Stainless steel, for instance, is favored for target barrels, but it is less abrasion resistant than chromemoly and is blued only with difficulty. Consequently, chrome-moly steel is favored for hunting rifles.

Most sporting rifle barrels today are button rifled or hammer forged. Both processes make good barrels, but just because a barrel is button rifled or hammer forged doesn't mean it is good. Thirty years ago, almost all rifle barrels were made by cut rifling, either by cutting the grooves one or two at a time to the desired depth; or by broaching wherein a long rod with progressive stepped cutters is passed through the bore, cutting all the grooves at once. Broaching is still widely used today in production work, especially with centerfire revolver and 22 rimfire barrels.

Factory barrels are often hammer forged and can be quite good, as are the barrels on recent Winchester Model 70 target rifles, for example. In this process the bore is drilled and reamed somewhat oversize and the rifling is formed by inserting a mandrel into the barrel and hammering the barrel down around it. The blank starts out shorter and fatter than it is when finished, but if the drill and ream is well done and the percentage reduction in the forging machine isn't too great, barrels made this way can be quite smooth and accurate.

Hammer forged barrels in general, some say, can't take a lot of exterior machining, but there is some difference of opinion on this. Some people say they can be worked on, but only slowly and carefully, as with

This Al Lind Model 70 in 30-06 weighs just 7¼ pounds, not least because of its slimly contoured Titus barrel. No alloy parts were used to achieve the weight, but there were a few important decisions. The weight of the Lind 30-06 was also kept down by choice of blank, which is Turkish Circassian, and through the use of the blind magazine technique. Thus, with the right choice of barrel and stock wood and design, the goal of fewer ounces is reached.

any quality barrel, to minimize relieving any built-up stresses in the hammered blank. Others feel any exterior machining is bad, since the parts cut on will stress relieve and the interior bore dimensions might change. Since the diameter is reduced most at the muzzle, any bore enlargement induced by the machining would cause a taper going the wrong way. I don't know how much truth there is in this, but I know several people who had hammer forged barrels put on target rifles which shot well at first, then pooped out after only a few thousand rounds, when they should have been at the peak of their shooting accuracy. I'd suggest not using a hammer forged barrel unless you are content with its dimensions the way it comes off the machine, doing nothing more than shortening or polishing it.

Most high quality rifle barrels today are made by button rifling. The four top makers of button rifled barrels today are Hart, McMillan, Shilen and Douglas. You can't really get hurt dealing with any of these makers, as they all make quality stuff. In button rifling a bar is drilled and reamed (the better ones are also lapped) before forcing a carbide plug through the bore, which has the rifling in relief upon it. Quality of the bore finish and dimensions depend primarily on how smooth and uniform the hole is before the button is forced through, but the size of the hole and hardness of the steel affect the amount of pressure needed to drive the button, the flow of the metal around it and the uniformity of the finished barrel.

Better makers all lap the reamed blanks before rifling them, regardless of whether they button or cut. Lapping insures that the tops of the lands will be smooth, without tool marks running across the direction of bullet travel, and also helps reach uniform bore dimensions by cutting down high spots, before pressing or cutting the grooves, so the tool meets uniform resistance over the whole stroke.

The importance of a smooth drill and ream can't be overemphasized. Any tool marks left in the bore before the button is forced through will still be there afterwards. A good friend of mine bought a 308 Winchester silhouette rifle of a popular make which fouled badly. When carefully cleaned with JB paste or Corbin cleaner, it would put the first group under an inch at 100 yards with handloaded 168 Sierras, but within 20 shots you couldn't keep it within 3 inches. Cleaning it well restored accuracy for a few rounds, then it opened up again. The barrel looked OK to the naked eye, but looking inside it with a Kollmorgen borescope, we saw that deep circumferential tool marks went all the way around—the remains of a bad reaming job. It looked like someone had taken a file, annealed it and tried to roll the grooves out. When he returned the rifle to the factory, though, they cleaned it and it shot within their "normal specifications." They wouldn't replace the tube. This hacked off my friend, who later spent $150 rebarreling it. He now has a very accurate, competitive rifle, but is soured on that manufacturer's products. His experience isn't all that unusual. The caveat, therefore, is to buy only top quality. Deal only with name makers who have a reputation to protect, and who will stand by their product. These fellows usually inspect by air gauge for dimensions and optically for finish, and it's rare to have a bad barrel get by their inspection. On the very rare occasions when one does, they'll make good on it.

Every bit as important as getting a good barrel is getting good work, since even the best barrel will shoot poorly if installed carelessly. Most "bad" barrels I've seen were actually quite good ones which had been botched by quick and dirty contouring, which warped them, poor chambers and the like. You should expect to spend as much on contouring, fitting and chambering as

used to rifle them are very expensive to make. If you want anything out of the ordinary, like special bore and groove dimensions, a different number of lands and grooves, a specific rifling form, or odd twist, you better find a fellow who cut-rifles, rather than buttons. You can get almost anything reasonable in a cut-rifled barrel.

A friend once got a real buy on a large lot of 140-gr. 7mm bullets because they were undersize—.281-inch. In standard barrels, they were useless as either 270 or 7mm bullets, but that didn't bother him a bit. He was trying to decide between a 270 Winchester or a 280 Remington anyway, so he split the difference and with 5,000 bullets in hand, he got a 10-inch twist barrel made to use them up. He had the somewhat oversized barrel chambered to 270 Winchester. It so happened the stan-

This David Dunlop near-miniature lightweight offers a particularly interesting barrel. Note the shape of the barrel reinforced ahead of the action and the quick-tapering short octagon styling of the tube.

you did for the barrel. There's almost no way you can expect to get a good installation on a bolt-action for less than $60-75 above barrel cost these days. By the time a fellow squares the action up, laps the lugs in, profiles the barrel and cuts a good concentric chamber, he's barely making anything at that. The fellow charging less is probably cutting corners. But don't trust price alone. Unless you know the fellow doing the work, ask what comes with the job. If the extra action work needed to do it up right isn't included in the basic price, and he wants to charge extra for it, look elsewhere. If he doesn't routinely square up and spot in every action he does, his attitude is a little slapdash, which is just what you don't want.

Although there is no real difference in the inherent accuracy of a button rifled or cut rifled barrel, comparing best quality in each case, there are certain advantages of cut barrels over buttoned ones in some applications. Button rifled barrels are made only in popular calibers and rates of twist because the carbide buttons

dard reamer cut a large enough neck to give a nice snug chamber with adequate radial clearance to utilize those oversized (for a 270) bullets. The bore diameter of the barrel is normal for 270, but the grooves are deep, .2805-inch diameter. The rifle actually gives very good hunting accuracy with factory 270 loads, and is so marked, so nobody using it in the future will get into any trouble. The beauty of the whole thing was that this job cost him no more than if he'd bought an ordinary 270 barrel made by the same fellow. He used standard reamers, headspace gauges and loading dies to take advantage of a lifetime supply of hunting bullets he got for 3¢ apiece. This is a fine example of one advantage to getting a cut-rifled barrel, since he couldn't have done it otherwise.

There are other interesting examples. Another friend in Pennsylvania has a 22-250 which is a bit unusual, in that it has an 8-inch twist, rather than the 14-inch twist which is standard in this caliber. Theoretically, the faster twist wouldn't be as accurate with the lighter bullets, but don't try to argue the point since you'll never convince him. I've shot this rifle and can tell you it's as accurate as any 22-250 I've ever used. I once shot a half-dozen 5-shot groups in succession at 200 yards. I started with 45-gr. bullets at nearly 4,000 f.p.s., then followed successively with 52-gr. and 63-gr. bullets, and finished up with some special long boat-tail 68-gr. hand-swaged jobs—you could cover those individual groups with a single target paster. As long as the bullets are good and the jacket strong enough for the twist and velocity, such a barrel can shoot very well.

I have found that faster twist barrels are particularly impressive on varmints, since the bullets blow up better. I once also did a lot of shooting with M16 rifles having a 9-inch twist instead of the standard 12-inch twist, which was very interesting. Even with standard service ammunition, they shot far better than the 12-inch twist rifles, and these were ordinary military barrels, not specially made and chambered. Going the other way, if you try to shoot GI 5.56mm ammunition in

heavy soft points at Hornet velocities kill turkeys better than FMJ slugs, but the 12-inch twist provides more explosive expansion with 45-gr. bullets on chucks. For nearly any 22 centerfire rifle from the Hornet to the Swift a 12-inch twist is the best choice. The 14-inch twist is OK with bullets not over 55 grs., but it is marginal with 55-gr. boat-tails. The 14-inch twist, however, is preferred for bench rest shooting with the 52- to 53-gr. bullets and is best for that specialized purpose.

In the 6mm calibers the same generalizations hold true, with the faster twists such as 9-inch or 10-inch being best for general use. The 12-inch twist is OK for bullets up to about 90 grs., and will usually give satisfactory hunting accuracy with blunt 100-gr. bullets such as the 100-gr. Hornady roundnose for deer hunting in the 243 Winchester or 6mm Remington. The 14-inch twist is a specialized one for bench rest shooting or varmint hunting with 6mm bullets not over 75 grs. In 25 caliber rifles such as the 250-3000, 257 Roberts or 25-06 the 10-inch twist is the best all around choice if you use

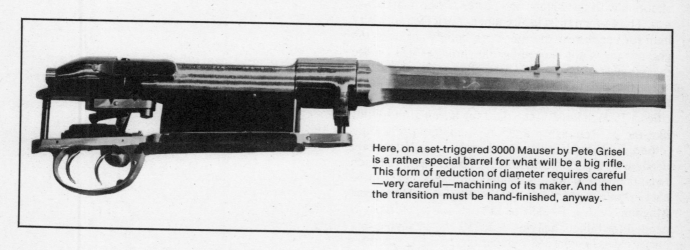

Here, on a set-triggered 3000 Mauser by Pete Grisel is a rather special barrel for what will be a big rifle. This form of reduction of diameter requires careful —very careful—machining of its maker. And then the transition must be hand-finished, anyway.

a 14-inch twist it seldom does well, the group sizes being roughly twice as large as in a 12-inch twist, even though the slow twist barrel may shoot flatbased 55-gr. bullets or 52-gr. match bullets splendidly. If you are unsure, always pick more twist rather than less.

Some suggestions on twist are in order, since getting a barrel with a twist which is inadequate for the bullets you wish to shoot is disappointing. In the tiny 17 caliber, a 10-inch twist is about it, but in the 22 centerfires you will run into several options, so some thought is required. For instance, in the 22 Hornet, a 16-inch twist is traditional because the first Hornet rifles were made from rechambered 22 rimfire barrels. However, a 14-inch twist is far better, since it permits use of heavier bullets up to 55 grs. with fine accurcy. I know of one 22 Hornet turkey rifle made with a 12-inch twist which lets the owner load 63-gr. and 70-gr. .224-inch bullets, which he feels give just enough expansion at about 2200 f.p.s. for clean kills without tearing up much meat. He prefers this combination because the

the rifle for both varmints and deer-sized game. If you plan on using your 25 only for varmints, a 12-inch twist is alright, but you may not get very good results with 100-gr. pointed bullets or the longer 117-gr. or 120-gr. spitzers. Blunt 100-gr. bullets like those used in 250 Savage factory loads will usually give satisfactory hunting accurcy in a 12-inch twist, though.

In the 6.5mm most readily available barrels are 9-inch twist, though in cases smaller than the 6.5 Remington Magnum or 6.5-06 this might not be enough for stabilizing the longer 140-gr. boat-tail or 160-gr. roundnose bullets. The 6.5x54 Mannlicher and 6.5x55 rifles had very quick twists of about 7½-8 inches. If you want to shoot bullets heavier than 140 grs. in 6.5 cases smaller than the '06 you should seek a fast twist, such as 8 inches.

In the 270 Winchester the 10-inch twist is standard and best though with 130-gr. or lighter bullets a 12-inch twist will do. In the 7mm calibers a 9-inch twist is pretty much standard, but in cases of smaller capacity than the

280 Remington, or with bullets heavier than 160 grs. a faster twist such as 8 inches is sometimes preferred.

In popular 30 caliber cartridges the 10-inch twist is suitable for all bullets, but for rifles shot exclusively with bullets not heavier than the 168-gr. boat-tail, a 12-inch twist is noticeably more accurate. Some match shooters, wishing to have a good compromise twist which shoots the 168s well for 200- and 300-yard rapid-fire but still has enough spin to stabilize the 190s well at 600 yards, have gone to an 11-inch twist. This has proven so successful that some of the big military teams have had 11-inch twist barrels made for their M14 rifles. Although bullets as heavy as 190 grs. aren't shot in service rifles, bullets up to the 180-gr. Sierra Matchking or the 185 Lapua can be used in them without problems, and the 11-inch twist is about ideal. The 10-inch twist is still favored in 30 calibers for long-range 1,000-yard shooting with the 200-gr. and newer 220-gr. match bullets. The 14-inch twist in 30 caliber is strictly a specialty item for bench rest shooting with bullets not over 168 grs. at ranges not exceeding 200 yards, as it is on the ragged edge of instability.

Getting into the medium bores, a 10-inch twist in the 8mm and 338 calibers is about all you see. In 35 caliber rifles a 16-inch twist is standard for Remington rounds like the 35 Remington and 350 Remington Magnum, although when pointed bullets heavier than 250 grs. are used, as in the 358 Winchester or 35 Whelen, a 14-inch twist is about minimum. Bullets up to 300 grs. can be shot in large capacity 35s like the Whelen or 358 Norma Magnum with a 14-inch twist, but a 12-inch twist is needed for bullets heavier than 250 grs. in smaller capacity cases like the 358 Winchester. In the 375 calibers a 12-inch twist is standard for the 375 H&H and the new 375 Winchester cartridges, and is the best all-around choice. A 14-inch twist works fine for a 375 Magnum, except sometimes with long heavy bullets like the 300-gr. Sierra boat-tail in sub-freezing weather.

Generally, a faster twist improves bullet stability and, at least theoretically would reduce disturbance of the bullet in encountering minor obstructions like grass or twigs. Some feel it helps penetration of "solids" and expansion of soft points too. So for hunting rifles in general the "faster is better" rule of thumb for twist still holds true.

For the large bores over 40 caliber, adequate twist is also important. In the 45-70 for instance, a lot of rifles have relatively slow twists. These all work suitably for bullets up to 405 grs. depending on make and style. But don't make the mistake of using a slow-twist barrel for building a 458 Winchester, since it needs a twist of around 14 inches to stabilize the long, heavy 500-gr. bullets. This is particularly important in rifles used for African hunting. A slow twist might work fine on the

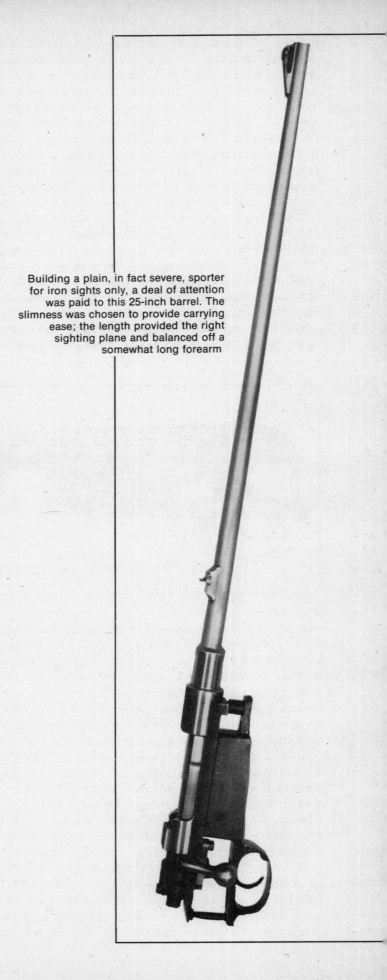

Building a plain, in fact severe, sporter for iron sights only, a deal of attention was paid to this 25-inch barrel. The slimness was chosen to provide carrying ease; the length provided the right sighting plane and balanced off a somewhat long forearm

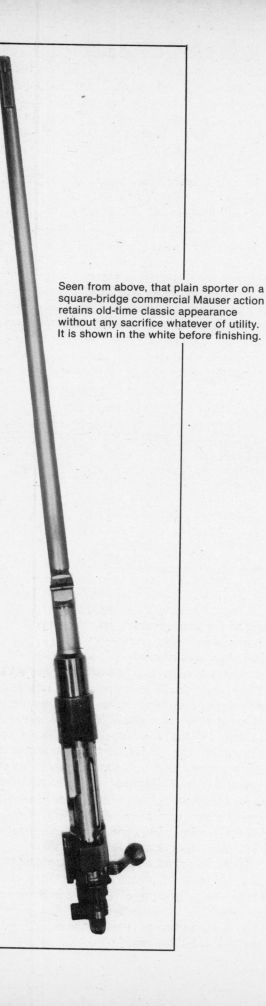

Seen from above, that plain sporter on a square-bridge commercial Mauser action retains old-time classic appearance without any sacrifice whatever of utility. It is shown in the white before finishing.

light soft points used for North American game, but it could have disastrous consequences if a fellow tried to use it with 500-gr. solids. The longer, heavier bullet might not be adequately stabilized to give the required penetration under extreme conditions, like a frontal brain shot on elephant. Selecting the proper twist, therefore, can have urgency as well as importance.

Most people have their own preferences for caliber and fall into two general categories: wildcat lovers and those who prefer standardized cartridges. The wildcat lover doesn't necessarily like anything the factories provide. Showing up at a hunting camp with the same caliber rifle everyone else has just doesn't suit him. Realistically, there are good arguments in favor of some wildcats, since you can get characteristics not available in factory cartridges. Many of the better wildcats like the 22-250, 257 Roberts, 25-06, and 7mm-08 have been standardized. There are some wildcats remaining which have a certain appeal since they do their job very well. For instance, the 35 Whelen is a favorite of mine. It is sufficiently more powerful than the 30-06 to make a big difference on large animals, but it permits a lighter carrying and recoiling rifle than a 338 or 375. Moreover, it enables the Yankee in me to use my plentiful supply of 30-06 brass. Although other cartridges might be more glamorous, I have chosen the 35 Whelen as my basic all-around big game rifle and have been happy with it.

Overall, standard factory cartridges are best for most purposes, since you have standardized chamber specifications, headspace gauges, and loading data available. There are few unknowns to reckon with. You don't have to worry about losing your ammo and not being able to replace it when your reloading room is 3,000 miles away. Cartridges like the 30-06, 270 Winchester, 7mm Remington Magnum, 300 Winchester Magnum, 338 Winchester Magnum, 375 H&H Magnum, and 458 Winchester are standard throughout the world and can be obtained anywhere. Depending on the game you hunt, any of these are excellent choices.

For a lightweight hunting rifle on a short action, the 243 Winchester, 6mm Remington, 7mm-08, 308 Winchester and 358 Winchester are best choices. For long actions my preferences would lean toward the 25-06, 270 Winchester, 280 Remington (or 7mm Express Remington which is really the same round), and the 30-06.

In realistic terms there is no significant difference in the game killing ability of 270 Winchester, 280 Remington or 30-06 rifles on deer-sized game. On smaller game like varmints or antelope the 25 or the 6mm cartridges will do the job neater, but on game larger than deer you should have something bigger. Similarly, while there's little difference between the 270, 7mm or 30 calibers on deer, the 30 caliber rifles (with the exception of the 7mm Remington Magnum with proper bullets) have a definite advantage on anything bigger. Most experienced hunters consider the 30-06 with good 180-gr. bullets about minimum for elk, which is why they sell a lot of 7mm, 300, and 338 Magnums. For animals over 500 pounds the medium bores have a distinct advantage over the 30s, though the 30-06, 7mm, or 30 caliber Magnums with correctly constructed bullets will handle anything on this continent. For most big game hunting the 30 caliber standard which Americans have judged other cartridges against is still valid. The somewhat smaller 270 and 7mm rounds will shoot a little flatter, but won't have as much punch on the big stuff. The bigger rounds don't shoot as flat, but thump more on both ends and are superior on large animals when you need to hit hard. Probably the most popular calibers overall are the 270 Winchester, 7mm Remington Magnum, 30-06 and 338 Winchester. Which one you choose for your all-around big game rifle depends entirely on what game you hunt most and which school of thought you subscribe to.

Once you have determined the proper barrel for the

when finished to 20 inches. A standard sporter barrel in 30 caliber would generally be .625-inch at the muzzle, 24 inches long and weigh 3 pounds. You could make a very light 358 on this contour, though it would be whippy. The minimum contour barrel for a 375, however, is .650-inch at the muzzle, or a #4 contour, whereas a 458 requires a #5 contour which is .70-inch at the muzzle.

Heavy sporter barrels for calibers like the 7mm Remington Magnum or 300 Winchester should be .65-inch at the muzzle and at least 24 inches long, as otherwise you give up some of the inherent advantages of the larger case. This contour is also best for 35 caliber rounds like the 358 Winchester or 35 Whelen. Varmint and silhouette style barrels generally start at what is called a #5 contour, being typically .70-inch at the muzzle, 24 inches long and weighing 4 pounds or more in 30 caliber. Target barrels are usually a straight taper from shoulder to muzzle and can be loosely classified as those 5 pounds and over at 24 inches and .80-inch at the muzzle. Bull barrels are the big heavy jobs over 6

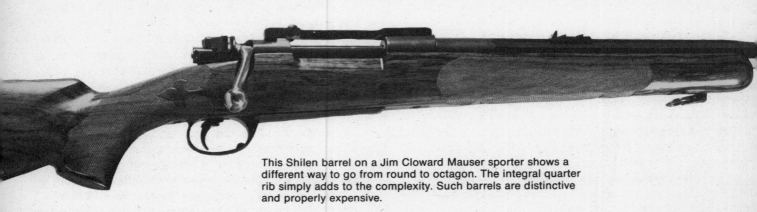

This Shilen barrel on a Jim Cloward Mauser sporter shows a different way to go from round to octagon. The integral quarter rib simply adds to the complexity. Such barrels are distinctive and properly expensive.

caliber of your choice, then you should give some thought to its length and contour. Rifles used primarily for woods hunting at short range don't give up much when shortened to convenient carrying length, but the hotter, large-capacity cartridges don't realize their full potential when the tube is too short. A 7mm Remington Magnum with a 22-inch barrel is hardly any different in performance from a 24-inch 280 Remington. When you are unlikely to shoot over 200 yards, and where fast handling is a prime requirement, a barrel as short as 20 inches is OK, but for general use in open country I'd prefer a barrel length of 22 inches or more for 30-06 class cartridges and 24 inches for belted magnums to permit obtaining their full potential. Barrels longer than 26 inches, except on single shots like the Ruger No. 1, are somewhat awkward. Weight, length and contour of the barrel are dependent upon caliber, since even a minimum weight 375 barrel must be physically larger than a 22 caliber. Featherweight or lightweight sporters not over 30 caliber can have barrels as small as .55-inch at the muzzle, weighing as little as 2½ pounds

pounds which have muzzles over .875-inch.

Custom barrel work gives you a lot of options other than the plain, round barrel. If you start with a full blank and don't mind paying for the extra machine work, you can have such things as integral half-ribs for open sights, integral recoil lugs (a good idea for the heavy recoiling cartridges like the 375 Magnum), integral front sight ramp, or sling swivel stud on the barrel (another good option for the hard kickers). Octagon barrels are usually machined from an oversized round blank, and done right they will still shoot well. The really elegant way to do things on classic style big-bore rifles is to do it all and have half-round, half-octagon with integral half-rib for express sights, integral recoil lug, barrel swivel stud and front sight ramp. Doing all of this costs, however. On varmint rifles you can get into custom work too and you can even have a big, light barrel by fluting it. This gives the rigidity of a large barrel without the weight. Tom Seitz is the master at this. So overall, there's practically no limit to what the skilled craftsman can do, it just takes work (and cash).

Even muzzleloader barrels have their complexities, as this full view of a completely accoutered Sharon barrel demonstrates. The modern barrel looks a great deal simpler; its problems are more subtle.

Aside from a barrel's length, weight, caliber and whether you want it round, octagon, or some of each, you must consider the details of its contour. Most think target barrels should be heavy, hunting barrels light and silhouette or varmint barrels somewhere in between, but it's more complicated than that. Target barrels are often a straight taper, since they can be heavy and there's no real disadvantage in making them so. Hunting rifle barrels, however, aren't wanted too heavy, so a straight taper barrel has more meat in it than is desired. Therefore, the barrels of lightweight hunting rifles are only as big as they must be at the breech end, then they taper rapidly to a smaller diameter forward of the chamber reinforce and then more gradually from there forward.

There are safety limits as to how small you can make the reinforce at the chamber end. Most sporter barrels are amply strong, but it's wise not to fudge on the contours too much. About the smallest dimensioned barrel you can use safely in calibers like the 243 Winchester or 308 Winchester is like the one which was once used on the Winchester Model 70 Featherweight. It was 1.137 inches at the shoulder, for a ⅜-inch distance, then it had a short radius down to a .97-inch diameter at 1½ inches from the breech. It then tapered down to .78-inch at 5½ inches from the breech face, and was a straight taper from there to .535-inch at the muzzle. This is a whippy barrel which weighs only 2 pounds in 308 Winchester. For longer cartridges like the 30-06 or 270, this basic contour must be changed somewhat, leaving a longer shoulder over the chamber for ⅝-inch and then turning a radius down to .95-inch diameter ahead of the shoulder. The barrel may then be tapered somewhat more sharply to .75-inch at 6 inches from the breech and straight tapered to .525-inch at the muzzle, and at 22 inches it will weigh within an ounce or two of the original Model 70 Featherweight barrel. For

mountain rifles this is about as small as you should go. Actually, though, a heavier barrel will probably shoot more consistently.

When transitioning from the reinforce over the chamber to the smaller tapered portion forward, a gentle taper or large radius down to the smaller diameter looks much better than a radical reduction of diameter. I'm not a fancier of very light, whippy barrels, since I like my rifles accurate and I've seen very few accurate rifles with tiny, buggy whip barrels on them. I'd be inclined to try to take as much weight off as I could elsewhere before turning a lot off the barrel. You can usually reduce weight a lot by hollowing out the stock, going to a blind magazine, and in other ways. I can tolerate a 7- or 7½-pound rifle quite easily in rough terrain, and I've toted my share of 8½-pounders, though that's as heavy as I'd want to carry out of choice unless it was a real shoulder bumper. In the heavier calibers you need more weight to dampen recoil.

Some people feel the force of gravity is perpetual, and that of recoil brief, so will tolerate a light, heavy-caliber rifle. This might work OK if you don't plan on shooting the rifle much, but I shoot my using guns a lot and after having used a 7½-pound 375 Magnum a bit, and an 8-pound 458, I decided to make my 35 Whelen, an 8-pound rifle so I could shoot it as much as I want to. Consequently, it's enjoyable to shoot, I use it a lot and I shoot it well. I never found its weight objectionable afield, though I haven't climbed any 10,000-foot mountains with it yet, so I could change my tune. For a fellow in reasonable physical shape I don't feel up to 8 pounds is too much. When you get puffing a bit after a long climb and have to settle down to shoot, you'll find a 7½- or 8-pound rifle holds a lot steadier than a 6-pound one.

C.E. Harris

Sights and Mounts

A GOOD LOOKING rifle which functions well is no use unless you can hit what you aim at. Scope sights are standard equipment today, so when building a fine custom gun you should give considerable thought to how that scope is mounted. Standard mounts from the big volume makers like Leupold, Redfield, Weaver and others will do the job just fine, and there are other options available in custom mounts which offer features you can't get in the standard items.

To get one thing straight, custom scope mounts aren't necessarily any better than the standards in terms of accuracy, workmanship, suitability or durability. For serious hunting and some target work, a Redfield Junior or Leupold STD mount is hard to beat. For

convinced this is a good idea. Having the scope mounted over the irons blocks much of the visual area around the sights, and you have trouble picking up, or following, a moving target. Also, it places the scope so high you cannot mount the gun naturally and find the scope.

The only reason the high scope, low irons system works at all is that those who use them hunt under carefully controlled conditions and seldom if ever jump an animal from its bed and bust it on the run. Their style of hunting is more practiced and deliberate, the scope being carried separately, perhaps even mounted only after a hunter has been placed on his stand. Then he waits, picks a suitable animal, usually has time to get

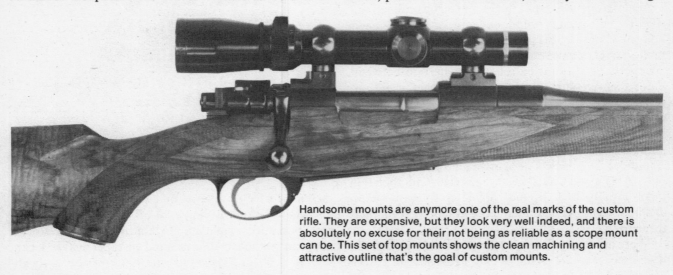

Handsome mounts are anymore one of the real marks of the custom rifle. They are expensive, but they look very well indeed, and there is absolutely no excuse for their not being as reliable as a scope mount can be. This set of top mounts shows the clean machining and attractive outline that's the goal of custom mounts.

lightweight mountain rifles the standard Weaver top detachable mounts are very light and serviceable. A few people don't like their looks, but you can't fault how they work. Many bench rest shooters I see use them, since the Weaver mounts do as good a job of hanging a scope on a rifle as any, and their light weight means more metal can be put into a barrel within weight class limitations.

Suppose you wish to have access to either scope sights or irons on a hunting rifle? There are several schools of thought on this. The European thinking is to put the irons low, and the scope high, often so you can see the open sights underneath the scope, or at best so a claw mount can be used. This means the stock must be of compromise dimensions and doesn't really work well with either. Scandinavians don't care for high scopes, and usually mount theirs low over the bore, as Americans do. Although some U.S. hunters are going to see-through mounts in woodsy country, I'm not at all

into a comfortable position, and . . . bang. U.S. hunters who take their shots as they come should have their scopes down as low as possible. You should be able to get a full field naturally as you mount the gun. This means the scope, mount system and stock dimensions must be compatible with one another.

Another answer to the instant access to scope or irons is the swing-over mount. The idea seems good in principle: You can remove or swing the scope over to use the irons, then swing it back and lock it down to use the scope. The best of both worlds, you say? My experience with these mounts is that if you lock down the scope and leave it alone, it will do fine. Then you can jerk the scope off and use the pre-zeroed irons if you need to. But you should check the scope zero afterwards. If you constantly swing the scope back and forth, the zero will wander. The military did a great deal of experimenting with swing-over mounts on the M1 rifle. They rejected the concept in favor of an offset detachable mount.

Of the swing-over mounts, the only one I have used a great deal is the Pachmayr Lo-Swing. I knew a fellow who had one on a Winchester Model 70 and swore by it. He was an experienced hunter and killed all sorts of stuff with that rig. I figured he never shot the rifle on paper, though, after I shot it enough to satisfy my curiosity. I fired a 10-shot group at 200 yards, either dismounting the scope and replacing it, or swinging it over and back between each shot. The group was about five times what the rifle was capable of. If you consider a basketball sized group at 200 yards decent hunting

shooter who has used such a mount, pick his brains and, if possible, shoot the rifle before making a firm decision on any new mount.

The next option for the iron-scope sight arrangement is the quick detachable mount. These come as top mounts, or side mounts. The top mount is most commonly used in Europe, being the Mauser or claw mount design. Top mounts aren't very common in the U.S., but they make a very secure arrangement in which the scope can be removed and replaced quickly, without loss of zero. The bases don't obstruct the iron sight plane. The drawback with most claw mount systems is

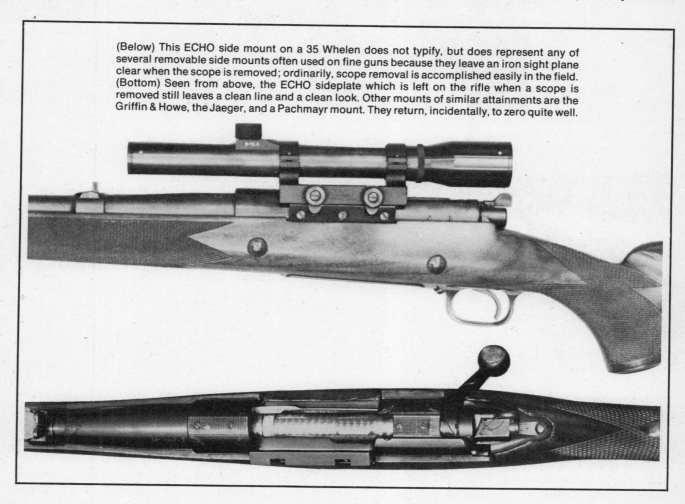

(Below) This ECHO side mount on a 35 Whelen does not typify, but does represent any of several removable side mounts often used on fine guns because they leave an iron sight plane clear when the scope is removed; ordinarily, scope removal is accomplished easily in the field. (Bottom) Seen from above, the ECHO sideplate which is left on the rifle when a scope is removed still leaves a clean line and a clean look. Other mounts of similar attainments are the Griffin & Howe, the Jaeger, and a Pachmayr mount. They return, incidentally, to zero quite well.

accuracy—it's certainly better than many people can shoot at that range—then these mounts might suit you. As for me, I like to know where that first shot is going every time I pick up the rifle. In all fairness, though, I should point out, this occurred some years ago, and the Pachmayr folks tell me the mount is improved now. It might be, but without having shot one, I can't say for sure. The best use for a swing-over mount would be for a powerful rifle used at close range on big game, like a 375 or 458 Magnum. Minute-of-buffalo-shoulder out to 200 yards is all you require in such a rig. Serious riflemen, however, would be well advised to seek out a

that they place the scope high, in European fashion, though I have seen some newly-made claw mounts installed by Paul Jaeger of Jenkintown, PA, which were lower, according to U.S. practice. Claw mounts, the associated rings and the labor which goes into fitting them, are expensive, but they make a very sturdy, convenient, repeatable platform on which to mount a scope on a hunting rifle. If I could get the job done right, they would be my choice for an accurate, rough-duty, do-everything rifle, though that's probably only because I'm envious of Ken Warner's new Remington 700 30-06. It has a fiberglass stock and uses claw mounts to

State of the Art: Sights and Mounts

Some custom rifles, like this BSA Martini rimfire gun demand a custom mount because they are not ordinarily scoped with hunting scopes as this example is.

The Dave Miller mount is seen elsewhere in these pages. It is shown here to point out that it is precisely manufactured to match its receiver contour which can be clearly seen here.

anchor the scope and supplement the irons. It's a highly practical rig.

There are few other top mounts which are really suitable for instant iron sight access, since U.S. makers feel the scope is the primary sight system (which I feel it should be) and the irons are seldom used at all, being there only for backup.

Some standard U.S. top mounts lend themselves to quick removal of the scope, and easy reinstallation with little or no change in zero. The Ruger top mount system is probably the best of these. I've used Ruger rings a great deal on both rifles and on handguns (yes, they work there too) and I've found that you can take them off and reinstall them without any loss of zero. I've shot several series of groups at 200 yards, taking off the scope and reinstalling it after every shot, and the combined 10 shots remained within the 7-inch ten ring of the military SR target. This may not sound impressive to you, until I mention this was on a customized Ruger 357 Magnum revolver. My Ruger 77 rifle will do as well or

better when shot the same way. The trick to repeatability of zero is to snug up the rings on the integral bases of the receiver snugly. You don't need to wring them off—as snug as you can manage by hand using a coin as a tool is enough.

The Weaver standard top mount bases don't have the "class" of Ruger rings or claw mounts, but they will usually come back to zero too, or darned close, if you snug the rings down uniformly on the bases. I use a coin here also. Leupold and Redfield rings have the potential for quick removal, but instant return to zero is a bit tricky, since the windage screws must be returned to the same position to center the rear ring precisely; otherwise, the windage zero goes to pot. The new Pilkington conversion for Redfield or Leupold rings might be the answer here. While I haven't tried it yet, it looks interesting and should have possibilities.

Quick-detachable side mounts have been used successfully for a long time. The Griffin & Howe double-lever mount is the best of these. The G&H mounts were widely used in sporting rifles before WW II and saw extensive use on M1 sniper rifles during WW II and later in Korea. I'm told a few rifles with G&H mounts were used by Marine snipers in the early years of the Vietnam fighting. Any scope mount which can hold up under military service warrants serious consideration for a hunting rifle.

Although the G&H side mount hasn't been made for a long time, they can sometimes be found secondhand (at handsome prices). I have known guys to buy rifles to get the G&H mount. I would too if it was a good rifle. Custom metalsmiths have occasionally made G&H-type mounts from scratch. The Griffin & Howe side mount is an excellent choice in this role and is probably one of the best if you can get one. Faithful copies, such as the Lan-Dav mount which was available for a few years in the 1970s, are also excellent. Fred Wells and several other custom metalsmiths make their own side mounts which also follow the G&H basic design.

The Jaeger side mount resembles the G&H somewhat in appearance and works about the same way, but has rings of black-anodized aluminum and a blued steel base. I've never used this mount, but a friend has one on a Kurt Jaeger (Mainz, Germany) customized, double-heat-treated '03 Springfield, which he likes a great deal. I haven't shot the rifle, but I've watched him shoot it, removing the scope and using the irons, then replacing the scope and shooting again, and the arrangement seems to work fine. The Jaeger side mount appears to be a readily available substitute for the G&H mount. Two versions are available, a standard mount with one locking lever, and a "magnum" mount with

double levers. Of the two, I'd be inclined to pick the latter.

Another mount which used to be available was the E.C. Herkner "Echo" side mount. This mount used light alloy rings and a steel base, with knurled knobs instead of levers. I have one of these which has worked fine for me, though after writing about it once I got letters from folks saying how lucky I was. Theirs apparently weren't worth a hoot. I think many of the problems experienced with side mounts are caused by poor mounting jobs, combined with carelessness in replacing the scope. I've heard similar complaints occasionally with other side mounts, such as the Jaeger, but have never been able to nail them down to my satisfaction. The G&H mounts seem to be uniformly good, since they leave no room for error in replacing the scope. The Jaeger mount should work the same way if properly installed and used.

Undoubtedly, some shooters reading this will ask, "Why do you place so much emphasis on having iron sights?" A scope is vastly superior to irons, even for people with good eyes, but there are times when having irons available makes a difference. If your scope fogs, or if you fall and drop a rifle on the scope and break it (both of which have happened to me), auxiliary iron sights can enable you to keep hunting. For a lot of woods hunting irons are completely adequate, and a young shooter with good eyes can shoot well even with open sights.

Of course, a lot of people can't shoot open sights and never will. If you don't have eagle eyes, there is hope for you yet. The receiver sight is one answer. There are

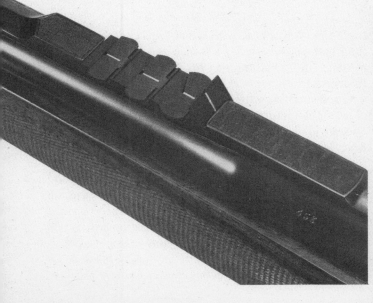

Much-favored for heavy rifles, this one a 458, is the British-style "parade" of open sights, often mounted, as are these, in a quarter-rib. The sights are British-style, but the installation is on a Jaeger rifle.

This Model 70 in 35 Whelen has a standing bar plus one leaf, and a rather special front sight as back-up irons. The rig belongs to Ed Harris, who got lucky in his early zeroing of this sight, which suits the ballistics of this particular 35 Whelen very well indeed.

State of the Art: Sights and Mounts

many shooters whose eyes aren't as young as they used to be, and they may as well sight along a naked barrel as try to use an open sight. A peep sight, however, will generally work OK for them. One such fellow I know carefully zeroes the receiver sight, sets the movable indicator on the elevation slide and adjusts the knob covers to reflect a mechanical zero when he's got his 200-yard setting on. Then he turns down the little stop screw on the elevation slide. This way he can remove the elevation slide and carry it in his hunting kit in a safe place. If he wishes to use the irons, or if he dings the scope, the scope pivots off the Redfield Junior base, and the slide of the Lyman 48 goes in, and returns to

standard mass produced open sights aren't very suitable for alternate or backup use on a custom rifle, as they look awful and usually work the same way. The best open sights are fixed, usually custom-made, and filed into zero for a chosen load at a useful range. When set up right, these are very good. I know a half-dozen shooters who make a game out of shooting the metal silhouette chickens at 200 meters with open-sighted rifles just for kicks. They have a ball and do better than the average hunter does with a scope. These are ordinary hunting rifles, but carefully zeroed. The guys are all good shots, so don't shoot your scope against them unless you have shot the critters before, since they average 50 percent or better most of the time. Granted, this would get only laughs at a silhouette match, but the shooting they do would surely get deer-sized game out

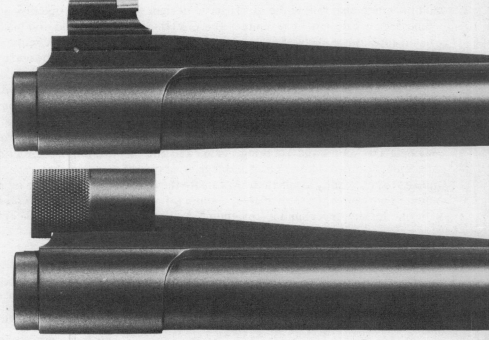

Special front sights can be obtained and made, as is this barrel band ramp from Dave Miller of Tucson, AZ. It is considered something extra for there to be a slick hood furnished for such a front sight.

zero. Of course, he's added an extra stop screw out on the arm of the elevation slide, giving him an extra point of reference against the receiver. This also protects the sight arm from bending if it receives a blow. This system works well if you are used to using a peep sight.

Another idea, which is the only way for a serious scope lover/iron sight hater, is to carry an extra pre-zeroed scope in its own rings. On hunts far away from home where weight or space requirements don't permit you to take an extra rifle, this is a smart way to go. Ideally both scopes should be exactly alike, and should be identified in some way, though they don't have to be.

Auxiliary open sights make sense for most people, since they are always there and there's little fooling around with them. Unfortunately, it takes a bit of work to get a good reliable open sight arrangement. The

there, and any sights with which you can keep better than half your shots on a 8-inch target at 200 meters offhand isn't a bad hunting rig. It would sure keep the freezer full.

Good shooting with open sights depends on getting a clear sight picture and having a perfect zero for the chosen load. There are no quick and easy methods here. It takes work in shooting, filing, measuring, and a few simple calculations before you get where you want to be. While I've known fellows who could do a good job by cut and try, a deliberate approach gets the job done better and more easily. Start by finding the style of open sight leaf and front sight combination which will give you a clear sight picture. If your eyesight doesn't permit this, don't waste any time fooling around, go with an extra pre-zeroed scope, or an auxiliary receiver sight. There's no use having open sights on there for window dressing if you can't use them. If you can see good open sights OK, or *think* you can, given the right combination, do some experimenting. Most custom open sights come blank, and there's a reason. Before doing anything to the rear sight, determine how big the bead must be. Try the sight picture with no notch at all in the standing bar, just centering the bead on top. Most likely you will find the bead that works best is a polished white metal $1/16$-inch bead with an angled face which reflects the light to you. This works better in dim woods than a plain bead. An alternative is to have an extra large bead that folds down into the ramp and then pulls up for dark lighting conditions when the standard small one isn't big enough to see clearly. Westley Richards has this arrangement on their heavy caliber double

Iron sights for installation in a quarter rib or other sight base look like this in the white. They are customarily filed to zero before finishing, at which time any inlays on the face or the leaves, together with engraved range markings and the like are accomplished. This set is from London Guns.

This is a view looking down at a Westley Richards sight and ramp. The key thing here is that the user may, at his option, select between a standard small gold bead and a very large wide night bead, either available instantly. The night sight folds up out of the ramp and over the gold bead and, since it is designed for coarse shooting, furnishes an adequate zero just like that.

rifles, the standing bead being $1/16$-inch angled white metal, and the folding bead being a huge $1/8$-inch porcelain inlaid dish. These were originally intended for night shooting—hence the name, "Westley Richard's Folding Nite Sight."

If you have trouble finding the center of the bar when you throw up the rifle, you need a reference point for the bead. Unless using the British system of an inlaid white metal reference line, start with a *small* U-shaped notch. Enlarge the notch as necessary until you can see the bead clearly and get a good sight picture. The horizontal bar and U notch is about standard on most European guns and may work just fine for you. You shouldn't need a deep U notch, but it should permit a good bit of light around the edges of the bead. If the U notch obscures too much of the target, you might prefer the broad, shallow V notch used in British "express" sights. This is easily made by machining the sides of the U notch to just clean up on the bottom. The angle of the notch depends on how much you need to clearly define the center of the standing bar. A variation of the V cut is simply to take a 1-inch radius cutter and mill the top of the standing bar. This is most useful for machining a precise amount from the sight in making adjustments, which we'll get into a bit later.

The above experimentation with notch and bead configuration to obtain the best sight picture should be done in the rough before you have taken much of the excess metal off the sight because you will need to leave enough room for machining or filing the sight to zero it. Ideally, the line of sight with the irons should be as low as the comb height of the stock will permit to enable you to mount the rifle naturally and find the sights. You may want to start with a collimator to rough-align the sights, but if you do, make sure to leave some extra height in the standing bar for final elevation adjustment since it is easier to file or machine the rear bar down than to make a new, lower bead sight. Shooting should start with front and rear sights centered on their bases.

I start firing from a sitting position at a 2-inch bull from 25 yards, taking a close hold. If you can't shoot steady from the sitting position, shoot from the bench, but DON'T rest the fore-end on the bags, simply use the front bag to steady your arm and hold the rifle as if you were shooting from the shoulder. If you rest the fore-end, you will probably get a different point of impact. Fire three shots, then carefully measure the distance from the group center to point-of-hold. To determine precisely how much adjustment is needed to center the sight, apply the formula:

$$X = \frac{RE}{D}$$

where X is the amount the sight must be moved (or how much is filed or machined from the sight); R is the sight radius in inches; E is the desired change in the point of impact; and D is the distance to the target in inches. The formula beats guesswork, since you minimize the risk

State of the Art: Sights and Mounts

This deceptively simple set of parts is a Continental-style claw mount. The mount itself is quite expensive; getting it mounted on any given rifle can be even more expensive; but many people are discovering that such mounts are severely practical for some rifles, something Continental hunters have known for a long time.

heavier loads. Heavier cartridges like the 375 will shoot on again at a shorter range, which varies with the rifle, but one such gun I know puts factory 270-gr. loads only slightly low at 200 yards, and only a bit high out to 100 yards, which is a useful arrangement for "quick and dirty" shooting. A 458 would probably shoot on at around 100 yards with a 25-yard zero.

Of course, once you are "on" at 25 yards, you shouldn't stop there, you should shoot the gun at succeeding distances, preferably in 50-yard increments, until you find the crossover point. Most likely, you will find you must make a minor windage correction to be centered up, once you get to 100 yards or so. That's normal, since a small error of 2 m.o.a. or so isn't obvious at close range, but will be apparent as you get out

Here is how the claw mount works, shown here on a drilling. Once in place the scope is pretty solid; by moving the knurled catch on the rear base to the rear, the rear claws are freed and the scope and rings simply tip up and off the gun, leaving a relatively clean sighting plane for the use of iron sights.

of filing too much. Windage corrections, of course, are relatively safe to make by trial and error, for if you tap too far, you just tap back, but botching the sights for elevation might mean starting over again with a new sight.

I have found, with most hunting rifles, that if the standing bar is filed in to shoot precisely to point of aim at 25 yards, it gives a good rough-duty zero for most purposes. An iron-sighted 30-06 will shoot approximately to point of aim at around 200 yards using 150-gr. loads at this setting, and only slightly low with 180-gr. or

farther. Once you have a good windage zero, you should strike a reference line on the sight and its base so that if the sight must be removed for subsequent machining you can put it back where it was. Once you find out where the standing bar shoots "on," you shouldn't stop since continuing to extend the range makes it far easier to "sight in" the remaining leaves. Using a suitably large target paper, shoot a group, or better yet, several, at each range where you would like succeeding folding leaves to be zeroed. Measure how low the group shot from the standing bar strikes from that range, apply the formula again, and you now know how much HIGHER the next leaf must be from your first "point blank" range to your "long-range" leaf. You then apply the same process again, actually firing the modified sight at the desired distance, making fine adjustments as necessary, and repeat for as many leaves as you have to zero. This ritual makes what can be a complicated job relatively simple.

While British express sights often come in "dress parade" style with several folding leaves to supplement the standing bar, you'll almost never need more than a standing bar and one extra for either a different load, or a longer range. The extra leaves going out to 300 or 400 yards might be romantic, but aren't very practical. Unless you shoot quite well, you certainly don't need an open sight leaf adjusted to shoot farther than 200 yards. I find the standard European open sight with a standing bar and single extra leaf entirely adequate. For most purposes a single fixed rear bar, suitably zeroed, is all you need.

What you'll probably want to do, though, is get a two-leaf sight, zero the standing bar with your favorite load, and leave the extra blank in case you eventually want to shoot a different load which needs more elevation. On my 35 Whelen Winchester Model 70, the standing bar of the open sight is zeroed at 100 yards for the 300-gr. Barnes bullet and 60 grs. of IMR-4350, which is my "bear bumper" for close-range shooting in thick cover. It just worked out that my general-purpose load with the 250-gr. Hornady spire point and 58 grs. of W-W 760 shoots on at 200 yards with that same standing bar, and my cast bullet deer load with the 290-gr. Hoch #359272 and 54 grs. of W-W 760 shoots to the same zero as the 300-gr. Barnes load. The second leaf is set up for a small game and plinking load with the 150-gr. Hornady 357 Magnum FMJ flatpoint and 8 grs. of Unique, with a tuft of Dacron to hold the powder against the primer, which is a nondestructive small game load at around 1100 f.p.s. I also have a cast bullet load which

shoots to that second leaf sight. My 30-06 Mauser has its standing bar filed in to hit an 8-inch sighting gong at 200 meters with 150-gr. Federal factory cartridges or my handloads with the 150-gr. Hornady spire point and 52 grs. of IMR 4064 in Federal cases. The 180-gr. Federal Premium Nosler shoots a bit low at 200 yards with that leaf, so the second leaf is set up for that load at 200 meters. My cast bullet plinking load of 28 grs. of RL-7 and the RCBS 30-180FN will shoot close enough to the second leaf for 100-yard plinking. The interesting thing about the Mauser is the open sights are the only sights. It works well with any of the loads I want to shoot, and it's a very friendly gun to carry, since it is light and trim, without having all the extra optical gear hanging on it. It's not a long-range rig, certainly, but a handy, practical rifle.

How you mount the open sights on the rifle depends on the style of rifle and how much you want to spend. The British style express sights look best on a half-rib, since it otherwise takes a large base to accommodate them, which just doesn't look right. A half-rib, though, is good for things other than as a platform for open sights, since you can also make a scope base out of it. The half-rib of the Ruger No. 1 single shot is a good example. You can use a Ruger half-rib and put custom open sights on it, or you can have a custom metalsmith make a rib from scratch for you. Ruger rings work well on a half-rib, though I've also seen European claw mounts and Sako-style bases incorporated into them. The smaller European type open sight with only one or two leaves which fold down close to the sight base look acceptable on a half-rib too, but they don't require one. They will work about anywhere a dovetailed rear sight will go, such as on a barrel band on the old Winchester Model 70 or Remington 721, or a small soldered-on base, or right on the barrel.

There are lots of options on sights and mounts, you just have to decide what's best and get it done right.

C.E. Harris

Rifle Furniture

ACCESSORIES or "furniture" on a gunstock add contrast or protection to the original wood, and can affect its character and utility significantly. Many such items are purely for show, but many are functional.

The butt of a custom stock will usually be covered, but there are a few cases when it should be left bare. The plain checkered butt is often seen on some European shotguns with the exposed end grain being only

sealed, finished and checkered. While this arrangement is elegant, it is also delicate and is suitable only for pampered guns, since a sharp blow on the unprotected butt will at least cause an unsightly ding and could break a piece off the toe. People using guns with checkered butts afield, protect them with some type of leather "boot." Unless sharply and coarsely checkered, the plain butt is somewhat slippery against the shoulder.

State of the Art: Rifle Furniture

Most wood butts on custom shotguns are not deeply checkered, since the diamonds on end grain would be very weak and easily damaged. Landed gentry might make good use of a checkered butt on formal, organized hunts, but the average hunter's shotgun or rifle butt requires and deserves more protection than the plain butt provides.

The next step after no buttplate is a wooden one. Contrasting hardwood, such as rosewood, is sometimes used. Horn buttplates fall into much the same category as those from exotic woods. Both are handsome, but less durable than metal. Horn looks great, but it can't take a lot of abuse. The inherent weaknesses of horn or wood buttplates are their splitting through drying out (checking) or being broken from impacts. They should not be chosen for rough duty use, but will give good service if given some care in handling.

A wood or horn buttplate is made easily to fit any stock, in any size contour or shape desired. If made of dense wood, such as rosewood or ebony, it is every bit as heavy as a recoil pad, unless hollowed out. Hollowing out a wood pad makes it lighter, but also weakens it. Wood or horn used in the plate must be well sealed to prevent checking. A glued joint seals the butt's end grain well, but when the finish on the plate itself wears, it is liable to drying out, splitting or other damage.

The skeleton metal buttplate provides a frame inletted into the edges of the butt. These provide a useful degree of protection and look far better than any ordinary steel, horn, or synthetic buttplate. It takes a good craftsman to install a skeleton buttplate with no visible gaps between wood and metal. The skeleton butt is one of the most elegant ways to go.

An alternative to the skeleton butt, probably more common on shotguns than on rifles, are steel heel and toe plates. These are caps shaped to fit the top and bottom of the butt, leaving the sides open. With either the skeleton butt or heel and toe plates, the metal surface should blend smoothly with the wood. When inletted these are fitted so some wood protrudes above the metal, and both surfaces are filed and sanded down

together until they blend smoothly, the metal pieces being removed while the wood is finished and checkered. The metal parts are then blued or case-hardened in colors before the final installation.

Full metal buttplates are the best for general use on most custom rifles. They are good looking, reasonably lightweight (compared to thick rubber recoil pads) and

This skeleton buttplate by Pete Grisel is tasteful and different. More usual in the skeleton plate is the use of four small screws. This three-screw design is distinctive. It also exposes more wood than many skeleton butts.

This is the Paul Jaeger style of skeleton butt, left plain here, in order to provide a frame for the checkering.

extremely serviceable, giving good protection to the end grain of the stock. However, while the steel buttplate is a standard item, few of those readily available really shape up into a first class job for a high-grade custom rifle. The best checkered steel buttplates are those by Al Biesen, Tom Blackburn, Fred Wells and other custom metalsmiths, though some of the mass-produced ones sold by Brownell's, such as those by Albright Products are quite good and reasonably priced. The relative quality of the finished rifle should be your guide.

A really top smith doing much of your work for you will probably want to use his own buttplate on a rifle, though if you are building yours using readily available accessories, the better mass produced plates are suitable. The buttplate must have enough metal around its checkered border to permit clean edges, though you trim the butt to fit the plate and not the reverse.

Of the mass-produced steel buttplates the Albrights with the trap turn me on. These are quite well made, and while they aren't exactly inexpensive, they cost a whole lot less than custom-made. A trap buttplate is an interesting piece of gear. Some people use the trap door to provide access to a few extra cartridges stored away in the butt, while others use them to stash a small pocket knife, matches, compass, fish line, hooks, or other survival gear. A knowledgeable hunter I know uses the trap in his rather deluxe 358 Winchester Remington 600 to store a take-apart cleaning rod. This is an intelligent idea, if you can think of times, as I can, when you wished you had a cleaning rod in the woods to clear a stuck case or obstruction, instead of walking miles back to a camp for one.

I have only one rifle with a trap buttplate, and as of this writing there is still no hole under the trap. If I ever make up my mind what I'd like to store in it, I have that option available and until I have the need, I'll leave the stock alone, being content with its good looks. Everyone who picks up the rifle admires the trap butt, but nobody has thought to open it and remark that nothing was inside. Interesting? If the snob in you wants something different, go ahead and get the trap butt, but don't worry about the hole. You can use and still enjoy the buttplate, which is entirely serviceable, and you have all your storage trap options open for an educated choice after you have used the rifle a while. That makes a lot of sense.

Some steel buttplates are smooth, but most are

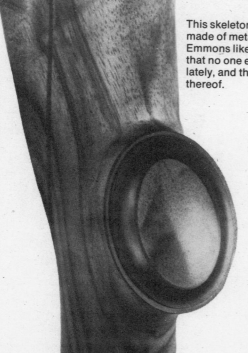

Hubert Hecht makes this trap butt which includes a recoil pad. This is a very deluxe accessory, although the user would probably not store fired cartridge cases in his own rifle. As can be seen, the trap spring-loads the cartridges and pumps them up when opened.

This skeleton grip cap is not made of metal, but ebony. Bob Emmons likes to do things that no one else has done lately, and this is a fine example thereof.

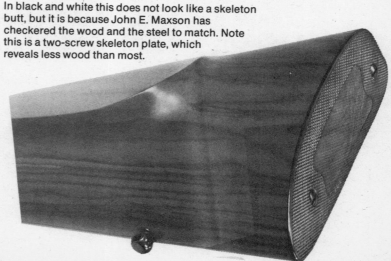

In black and white this does not look like a skeleton butt, but it is because John E. Maxson has checkered the wood and the steel to match. Note this is a two-screw skeleton plate, which reveals less wood than most.

grooved or checkered. The purpose of checkering on a buttplate is to keep the butt on your shoulder during recoil and subsequent operation of the action. A smooth buttplate is supposedly less likely to snag on clothing or hang in your armpit when you mount the gun. This argument doesn't really hold water upon close examination. If any buttplate or pad hangs up when you mount the gun, it usually isn't the fault of the buttplate. The gun is telling you that the stock is too long. If the butt hangs up only once in a while, shortening it ⅛-inch will usually be enough. The only real purpose for a smooth buttplate or pad that I can see is for an upland bird gun, an ISU Skeet gun, or some snap-shooting rifles for shots taken from a low-gun position, where the gun must be mounted quickly. Smooth steel buttplates were traditional on rifles years ago, and they were also curved so as to hold the butt against the shoulder. The buttplate's shape served the same func-tion as checkering in keeping the stock from being jar-red off the shoulder during recoil, flipping the bolt or working the lever.

Most people choose recoil pads (rather than horn, wood, or steel buttplates) for rifles having substantial recoil, for target rifles which will be shot a great deal, or for hunting guns which will see rough use. A good rubber pad is useful if properly installed and if you buy a good one. Some thin, solid pads, called ''rifle pads'' are not recoil pads at all, but are simply soft rubber buttplates. These are very useful on hunting rifles. They make little noise when set upon rocks, yet they protect the butt, are not easily damaged, and they stay put on the shoulder. Most rubber pads are somewhat heavier than a steel buttplate, and not quite as good looking, but they are relatively inexpensive and func-tional. I loathe white-line spacers, but many pads have them. Fortunately, there are some good plain pads available such as the Pachmayr Old English. The smooth Pachmayr Presentation pad is another fine choice for a classic style stock.

This is the Westley Richards trap grip cap mentioned in the text. It is shown open here; when closed, it is very handsome and has been left plain because it is so handsome.

Another John Maxson skeleton plate, this one on the pistol grip. Again, the wood and steel are checkered together to match. The effect is subdued, but striking.

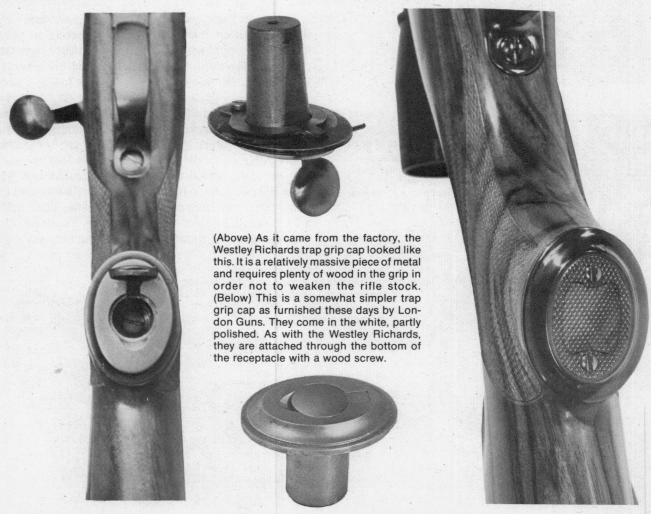

(Above) As it came from the factory, the Westley Richards trap grip cap looked like this. It is a relatively massive piece of metal and requires plenty of wood in the grip in order not to weaken the rifle stock. (Below) This is a somewhat simpler trap grip cap as furnished these days by London Guns. They come in the white, partly polished. As with the Westley Richards, they are attached through the bottom of the receptacle with a wood screw.

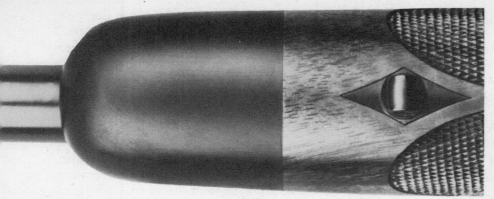

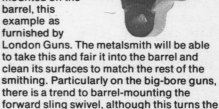

This is a sling swivel base to be mounted on the barrel, this example as furnished by London Guns. The metalsmith will be able to take this and fair it into the barrel and clean its surfaces to match the rest of the smithing. Particularly on the big-bore guns, there is a trend to barrel-mounting the forward sling swivel, although this turns the sling into a carrying strap only.

Here is, on a Paul Jaeger rifle, an extremely nice handling of a small piece of rifle furniture—the sling swivel. The little diamond inlay of wood matches the forearm tip, and complements the checkering pattern very nicely. Touches like these throughout distinguish the truly fine rifle.

While some so-called solid pads indeed are vented, most have a hollow cavity formed into them to give the pad more cushioning effect. Those which are solid rubber aren't really recoil pads but are rubber buttplates. A lot of shooters feel a need to put a recoil pad on any hard recoiling rifle, but this isn't always necessary if the stock is well shaped. I've shot several lightweight 375s and one 458 Magnum with steel buttplates, and didn't find them at all objectionable because the stocks fit. Just spare me from the steel carbine buttplates of the 45-70 trap-doors or 58 caliber rifle-muskets firing the 500-gr. bullets and heavy blackpowder loads like I shot as a youth. These stop being fun after a very few rounds.

Recoil pads or rubber buttplates must fit flat against the end grain of the stock. Most have screws but gluing is the better way. You seal the end grain and positively hold the plate *flat* against the stock. The end grain of the stock must be trued perfectly and the plate also must be perfectly flat, or you cannot get a good fit. The screws are used to hold and position the pad.

Although most people installing pads on hunting rifles don't worry about the screw holes showing, they are unsightly on a high-grade custom gun. On utility guns the holes can be hidden pretty well by using a razor to slice entry holes for the screws and greasing screws and screwdriver well to avoid tearing up the rubber. After the screws are snug, clean a smooth pad with a little 400 grit and water, or textured pads with a rag and lacquer thinner so the marks don't show. Some pads, like those used by Griffin & Howe, and some English makers, have matching removable rubber plugs for the screw holes. These are dressed flush with the pad face, and are almost invisible once cleaned to blend them in.

Fore-end tips and grip caps are traditional furniture on most custom stocks. Their original purpose was to seal and protect the end grain of the stock, but this is often forgotten in recognition of their obvious cosmetic role. Tips are made of contrasting wood or horn. Hard rubber or plastic is used only for inexpensive sporters.

Buffalo horn was once common, though it tends to check or crack badly. I've seen very few old custom guns with horn buttplates, fore-end tips or grip caps which weren't cracked. Ebony is often used for this and works well, though ebony blocks used for making tips and caps should be coated with paraffin and sealed with linseed oil during shaping if they must be left unfinished for more than a short time. Other woods used for this purpose are cocobolo, rosewood, lignum vitae and desert ironwood. These are more often used on modern style stocks than on classics, though rosewood goes well with almost any wood and is attractive on either type of stock. Rosewood isn't subject to checking as much as ebony or horn.

Grip caps are intended to prevent the exposed corner of the grip from breaking or chipping if it receives a sharp blow, though its purpose is now generally cosmetic. When iron sights were used exclusively, British gunmakers, Westley-Richards in particular, used a trap in the grip cap to store an extra "caterpillar" front sight element with a very large bead used for night shooting. I have one of these which carries an extra front sight for a rifle I own, but there is little need for a grip cap of this type generally. It might not be a bad idea on some rifles, such as the Ruger No. 1 or 77 with factory iron sights, as the Ruger front sights are of caterpillar type and could easily be replaced afield. If you desire a large or luminous bead for low-light-level shooting in those first (or last) few minutes of legal shooting time, that might provide an answer. For rifles on which irons are the sole sighting equipment, an extra front sight could be a useful accessory in case one gets lost or damaged.

Wood or horn grip caps are suitable for most needs, since the grip cap is seldom exposed to impact, as is a buttplate. Therefore, materials which aren't great choices for buttplates still make good grip caps.

Although wood or horn is attractive and functional, metal grip caps are more popular. The best looking mass-produced grip caps I've seen are those in cast steel used on the Ruger No. 1. These are well shaped, about the right size, and are as elegant as the handmades costing many times more. I'm not sure if they are readily available as parts or not, but if not, some enterprising outfit should copy these and have them cast for sale to the trade.

Custom metalsmiths make steel grip caps from scratch. These are quite handsome and usually somewhat expensive. A few fellows make the British style trap grip caps. The real British trap grip cap is expensive, and unless you must have the real thing, you can probably get one made here for less money. I bought a Westley-Richards trap grip cap and two front sights for 35 pounds Sterling in 1972. As I remember, the grip cap was 20 pounds, or about $36, then, I think. Today the price would be much higher. The custom metalsmith set up to do these could make a good looking one rather easily, though it very likely wouldn't have the cap and the receptacle for the trap all machined integral from one piece of steel, as mine was.

Another type of trap is for cartridges. Fajen makes one to be fitted to the toe of the butt and will hold several rounds. Some European break-open rifles or combination guns have the same arrangement. This works alright with fairly slim-profiled cartridges, such as the 22 Savage 25-35, or 9.3x72R, used in European guns, but fatter American sized cartridges require a thicker stock. In that case, the trap throws the proportions of the stock off, and on a light rifle, the balance might be affected too.

If you have sling swivels put on your custom rifle, I'd suggest you have either quick-detachable swivel studs, or flush-mounted swivel bases such as Pachmayr's. European-style QD swivels are standard items these days and are a popular and serviceable alternative. However, the flush-mounted swivel base makes a much more attractive arrangement if the sling is to be used only occasionally.

Heavy recoiling rifles shouldn't have the front sling swivel on the fore-end of the stock, lest the hand be struck by the swivel or stud in recoil. In rifles heavier than the 338 Winchester, it's usually better to have the front swivel attached to the barrel slightly ahead of the fore-end. Sometimes the swivel stud is attached by a band; or the stud can be made integral with, or silver-soldered to, the barrel. That's a neater job.

When you start to think of rifle furniture for what it can do for you, rather than what it looks like, you are well on the way toward making intelligent choices. Stock accessories should look good, but they are more than what meets the eye.

C.E. Harris

STATE OF THE ART
Doubles

THERE HAS not yet developed quite the scope for the creation of the custom double shotgun in the United States that there is for rifles. Part of the reason for that is that double-barrel shotguns are only now in full comeback for field use and that there is a healthy industry in Europe supplying the demand for specially constructed shotguns. Roy Vail used to bring in British actions and barrels and stock them to suit American tastes, and an example of his work may be seen in the NRA Firearms Museum. The guns he made were handsome and truly custom doubles.

There is, of course, now a great deal of restocking done of existing double barrels. With the growth of collector interest in original factory guns of Parker, L.C. Smith, Lefever, and Winchester make, some impetus in this direction was lost. It seems silly to reduce the value of a shotgun by adding several hundred dollars of cost to it, but that is what restocking such factory models might have done.

Today, the overseas contract and contact exploits the custom potential in this direction. The gunmakers of England, of course, and of Belgium, France, Germany, Austria, Spain and Italy, all of whom have large home markets, still spend some efforts in working toward the U.S. market. Indeed, some—notably, at the moment, Renato Gamba and Daniele Perazzi—make it a major effort.

We ought to note here that much double gun emphasis is on fine guns rather than custom guns. The fully bespoke gun, from any of the countries cited, is the exception rather than the rule. A heavy proportion of the total of production is made to order in the sense that the customer may specify the stock dimensions and, to some degree, embellishments, but they are not "bespoke" guns.

There are several sales operations in the United States with manufacturing arrangements abroad who concentrate completely on furnishing shotguns of standard pattern made to order. Hunting World of New York, Orvis of Manchester, Vermont, and Robert A. Painter of Austin, Texas, are three of these. The Orvis guns are made in Spain, so are the Hunting World guns;

FIG. 73.—THE SHOOTER IS RECEIVING INTO HIS LEFT HAND THE GUN HIS ASSISTANT HAS LOADED, AND IS ABOUT TO HAND HIM THE GUN JUST FIRED (SEE FIG. 72).

N.B.—I have drawn the shooter facing round more than would be usual in order to plainly show the action of changing guns in a grouse shelter.

This is the situation for which the British game gun was evolved—birds driven to a line of guns in butts. The guns were often used in pairs; a loader helped to keep them hot; the shooting had to be quick.

Painter specializes in Chapuis guns from France. Prices range from as low as approximately $1,200 retail for the plainest Chapuis from Painter through $2,000 to $3,000, depending on features, for Orvis guns to the $5,000 and quite deluxe Hunting World guns. In the case of Orvis, there is also a shooting school, and one may be fitted by shooting if he can get to the Orvis facility.

The grand custom gun of double persuasion, of course, has one of several names on it and no others. Those names are, today, for new guns, Holland & Holland, Purdey, and Boss. One may still attend the showroom and shooting grounds of such a British name in or near London, have a consultation and perhaps a shooting session with a try gun, place his order and be certain that when the gun arrives, it will have been built for him to the measurements they made, starting from scratch. The stock dimensions will begin at the post of the top snap, the weight and balance will be as specified, as will be boring, embellishment, and furniture. The operative word is *when,* of course. It takes at least several years at present writing to accomplish this task. Why it takes so long is shrouded in the grand mystery of British gunmaking. Less mysterious is the price—upwards of $20,000, sometimes a long way upwards. At the moment, there is a rather special Purdey gun for sale in the United States which I have handled. It is rather grand and the asking price is $75,000, and whoever buys it, of course, is not getting a bespoke gun.

Gun Digest readers will be familiar with the firm of Armi Famars. This Italian specialist in double-barrel shotguns has established itself over the last decades as one of the very finest makers for fine doubles in the world. There are those, indeed, who claim that no one in the world, anywhere, can put together a best gun as

The hot corner is the dream of every shotgunner, although it comes to us in America on doves or maybe pheasants. With the right gun, the one that both fits and shoots, a gunner could put a lot of birds down in a situation like this.

Armi Famars does. This is particularly true, it is felt, in the matter of embellishment. Singlehanded, if the activities of a whole firm can be called that, Famars has brought back to prominence the *bulino* style of engraving, called sometimes in the United States *banknote* engraving. Through their efforts, the grand scenes—battles of the Napoleon wars, fierce eagles on lonely crags, the classical allegories and legends—are once again to be found gracing arms of high quality.

Famars guns are not surface alone. They are made with the utmost refinement and integrity. There are only so many shops in the world equipped and able to undertake the making of, for instance, a four-barreled gun with grace and Famars is one of them.

The European contract is often fulfilled through a U.S. agent who's prepared, with language and other

State of the Art: Doubles

The fine double has almost always been the result of careful handwork. For instance, hand-struck barrels are part of the bag of tricks that produces splendid balance. (Malin & Son photo)

There are a few other ways to get a custom gun. One can, in the higher grades, order a Browning to suit, and Winchester still builds Model 21 shotguns, and each they build is built-to-order. There are other special-order situations available from all the importers of major European brands. Japanese gunmakers, by and large, seem to tend to their knitting and build only guns to standard pattern.

The European connection apart, then, in order to have a custom shotgun, one must first own a gun. If it is a good enough gun, it can, with the help of U.S. artisans, become a custom gun. There are two kinds, as it works out—restored guns and reworked guns.

Taking up the restoration first: The wide and intense

This is not a discussion about the ordering of a gun, but this is what such a discussion often looks like. All the trappings are here —stocks to look at, fine gun cases, and total interest. (Malin & Son photograph)

skills, to deal with the intricacies of ordering so personal an artifact as a shotgun in a foreign language and a foreign country. Unfortunately, importers and agents are businessmen in a difficult business and one of the results of the difficulty is that they change. One of the most important things to discover, no doubt, for people who wish to order a foreign shotgun is how long the agent with whom they are dealing has had his arrangement with the makers overseas.

These very uncertainties are what makes a business possible for Orvis and Hunting World and other prominent purveyors of tailored, rather than built-to-order, guns. Dealing with a known entity on this end, that has the size and the capital to produce results on the other end, is comforting to a fellow investing $1,500 to $5,000.

interest in Parker shotguns as collectible objects came early enough that stocks of Parker parts and experienced Parker craftsmen were still available. Around the Parker mystique, a small industry has sprung up. The chief name in the industry is that of Larry Delgreco.

The intense interest in Parkers came along so quickly and so many of the guns disappeared into collections, and so many Parker guns had been actually used, some of them hard-used, that it soon devolved that someone who wanted to shoot a nice Parker had to get a rough gun wherever he could and have it restored.

The net result is that one can take a veritable shambles of a Parker—or an L. C. Smith or a Lefever or any of the other grand names of American double

This 20-gauge Lefever has been virtually rebuilt by J.J. Jenkins, including recoloring; engraved by Pedini; stocked in Russian Circassian by Philip D. Letiecq. It weighs 5½ pounds; its barrels have been rechoked; it is done up completely to suit.

suitable doubles if requested. Interestingly, they offer both "replacement" stocks of what they call "field" style, and often, also offer stocks for the same guns of different styles, some of which may appeal to you. In any event, within relatively narrow margins, such restocking with semi-inletted stocks does permit some fitting of the gun to the shooter.

In the reworking of a good grade double we find the stock work and *le tout ensemble* can come right up to the mark of the fine rifles made today in the United States. When a stockmaker who knows what he's doing takes on the chore of fitting up, for example, a continental sidelock double, or perhaps a turn-of-the-century British best gun by a name now gone, and these, incidentally, are jobs that many of the stockmakers delight in as a change from their regular run of work, they seem to get a bit in their teeth and they do it all. It is interesting to see how they can meld an American idea of looks and proportion to metalwork built along an entirely different scheme, perhaps three quarters of a century gone.

The metalsmiths, too, can busy themselves with old shotguns. They get into the locks, and into the trigger manufacture—to the appropriate place and wind up, some months and many dollars later, with a gun that looks as though it had just come out of the box from Meriden, Connecticut.

When the repolished, refitted, reblued, restocked and recolored gun is complete, it is a true restoration. The work, standard as it is, is known to the expert collectors, but there is a curious condition. In most all other collectibles, extensive restoration except for the pure gems, affects the price adversely. It does not seem to do so with Parker shotguns. There is another advantage, of course, in the restored American double—it can be made to order, with stock dimensions and balances to suit.

All restoration is not complete refabrication, of course. Many guns which appear distinctly scruffy at first glance need only tender, loving and knowing care. Dents are raised and repaired, checkering recut, stocks refinished; barrels are carefully restruck when necessary and polished before bluing; the whole making them not a new gun, but a gun which looks as if it had the care of generations.

It is not necessary, of course, to go to the acknowledged masters. Refurbishing of guns is a standard practice and indeed the mainstay of many general gunsmithing shops. Of late years, the major makers of semi-inletted stocks have managed to put their machinery to work to produce stocks for virtually any double ever available in any quantity in the United States. The same firms are prepared to do the work of restocking of

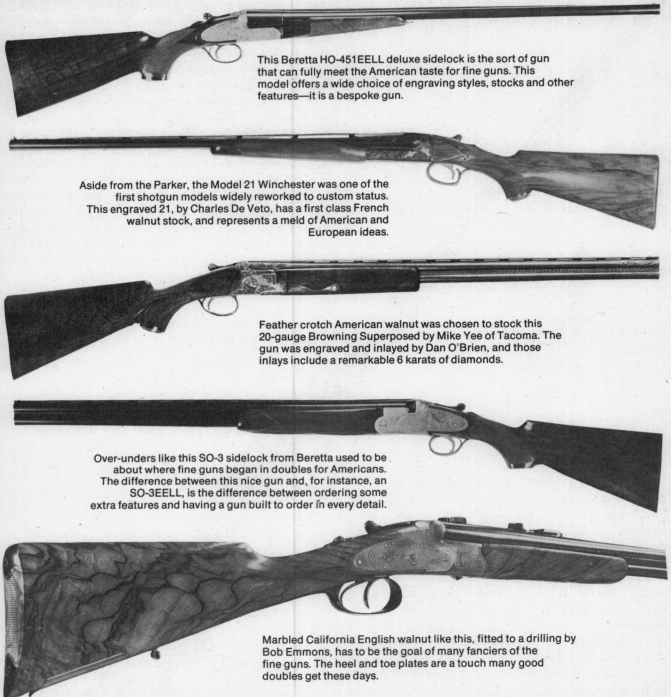

This Beretta HO-451EELL deluxe sidelock is the sort of gun that can fully meet the American taste for fine guns. This model offers a wide choice of engraving styles, stocks and other features—it is a bespoke gun.

Aside from the Parker, the Model 21 Winchester was one of the first shotgun models widely reworked to custom status. This engraved 21, by Charles De Veto, has a first class French walnut stock, and represents a meld of American and European ideas.

Feather crotch American walnut was chosen to stock this 20-gauge Browning Superposed by Mike Yee of Tacoma. The gun was engraved and inlayed by Dan O'Brien, and those inlays include a remarkable 6 karats of diamonds.

Over-unders like this SO-3 sidelock from Beretta used to be about where fine guns began in doubles for Americans. The difference between this nice gun and, for instance, an SO-3EELL, is the difference between ordering some extra features and having a gun built to order in every detail.

Marbled California English walnut like this, fitted to a drilling by Bob Emmons, has to be the goal of many fanciers of the fine guns. The heel and toe plates are a touch many good doubles get these days.

guards and top snaps; they clean and polish once more the old and faded metal of the action, and find someone to color them once again. When there is old engraving, now worn, it is possible to find the artists to touch it up once again. They, too, can take a shambles and restore it to order.

What we speak of here is not restoration, but rebuilding, reworking. It seems ridiculous to think that someone could take a fine old shotgun and rebuild it to a "classic," but that is what we are saying here. It was, of course, a classic. In its new form, it becomes a new classic—still functional, still a cleanly designed tool for the slaying of passing birds, but with a look that fits it to hang beside the other fine work of today without drawing attention to itself by difference, only by excellence.

This work, at best levels, is not cheap, either. For older shotgun barrels, for instance, common methods of hot caustic bluing will not work. Because of the soldered joints along the ribs and between the barrels, the more expensive and hard to find bluing systems such as old-time rust bluing must be used. Often, in an old shotgun gone "off the face" or loosened up in its principal joint, metalwork which is not major surgery but is time-consuming must be undertaken. There are

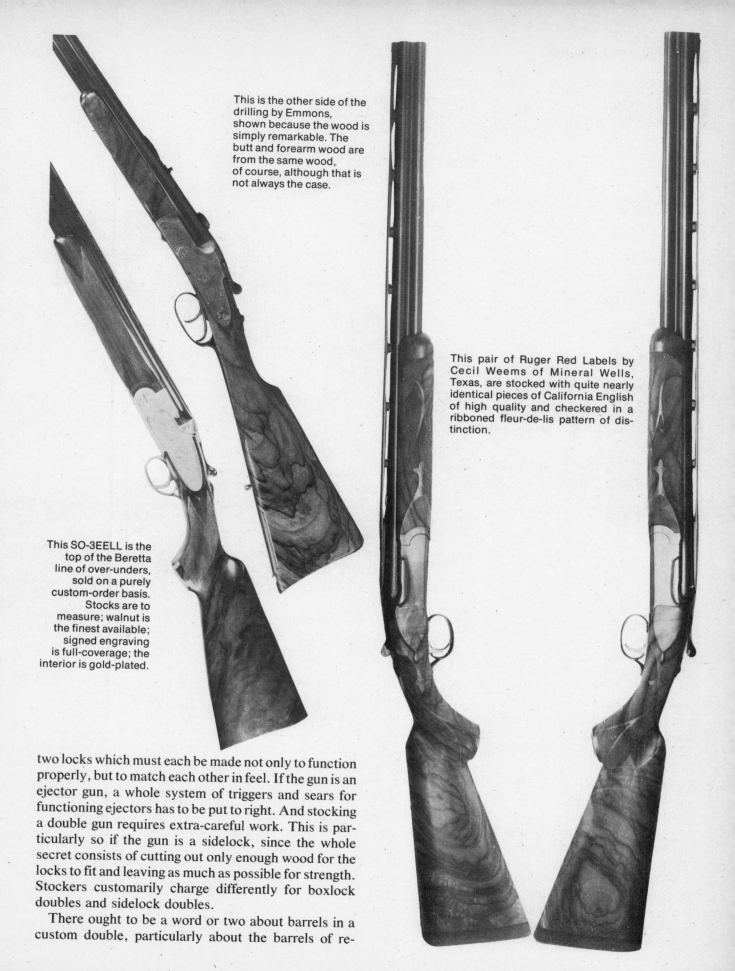

This is the other side of the drilling by Emmons, shown because the wood is simply remarkable. The butt and forearm wood are from the same wood, of course, although that is not always the case.

This SO-3EELL is the top of the Beretta line of over-unders, sold on a purely custom-order basis. Stocks are to measure; walnut is the finest available; signed engraving is full-coverage; the interior is gold-plated.

This pair of Ruger Red Labels by Cecil Weems of Mineral Wells, Texas, are stocked with quite nearly identical pieces of California English of high quality and checkered in a ribboned fleur-de-lis pattern of distinction.

two locks which must each be made not only to function properly, but to match each other in feel. If the gun is an ejector gun, a whole system of triggers and sears for functioning ejectors has to be put to right. And stocking a double gun requires extra-careful work. This is particularly so if the gun is a sidelock, since the whole secret consists of cutting out only enough wood for the locks to fit and leaving as much as possible for strength. Stockers customarily charge differently for boxlock doubles and sidelock doubles.

There ought to be a word or two about barrels in a custom double, particularly about the barrels of re-

Another Charles De Veto job, this Fox Sterlingworth 12, with its butt of burled American walnut was upgraded with almost everything, for instance, a single trigger.

This DHE Parker was stocked in French walnut and given an AHE checkering pattern. The Parker and the Winchester 21 led the way prior to WW II in custom doubles for Americans.

Forearms are always a problem in rebuilding double guns for American use, since in America a more hand-filling piece of wood up front is usually desired. This is a Bob Emmons solution on a drilling. In this case, the German character of the original was held on to, while more beef remained.

worked and restored guns. We are taking it for granted here that responsible artisans will be working on the gun, so that there will be little if any question of safety in the finished product. Many fine old guns have Damascus barrels, for which there is a sure cure in the ammunition to be used and another sure cure of a more permanent nature. That aside, however, we are principally talking about new chokes, possibly new chambers, and often a new barrel length.

Taking the last first, a great many older guns were made with longer barrels than either fashionable or required today. In the case of very, very good barrels, which were originally struck to obtain the proper balance, even at 30 inches, the question of barrel length is not so important. In rebalancing an old gun, however, it is often very advantageous to shorten barrels. Anything down to about 25 inches is possible, but the length ought to be decided before a stocker does the designing. There is nothing particularly complicated about shortening a set of shotgun barrels; there is some finish work to be done to fill in gaps, customarily and ordinar-

ily done with careful soldering. At the time this is going on, any dent removal operations can be accomplished, and then it is time for working on the interior of the barrel.

It might well be, of course, that no choke at all is the best choke, particularly for a lightweight bird gun. However, few shooters are that sophisticated and most want some choke. Shortening the barrels, of course, makes them cylinder bores, at least usually. Some guns are choked with a long parallel section and a modest shortening does not remove that choke. In the main, however, if you take 2 inches or so off a set of barrels, you are left with two cylinder bores.

Into those bores, a canny fellow can cut new chokes. With selected ammunition, it ought to be possible to attain a modified choke in one barrel. The best thing is probably to tell the mechanic involved what sort of performance you want with what sort of load and get his comments and his agreement that he can achieve that sort of performance.

In many guns, there is the question of chamber depth.

Starting with a customer's Perazzi shotgun, Paul Jaeger, Inc., did a total job of embellishment to order. The foliate scroll on fore-end iron, receiver and barrels surrounds game scenes all around; here a flushing pheasant.

Fine gunmakers rarely neglect the top of the gun, since the shooter sees it so much. This is the top snap and breech of an Ambassador Executive gun by Renato Gamba.

On the left side of the Jaeger Perazzi it is the ruffed grouse enshrined. More than most such jobs, this Perazzi's left and right sides are near mirror-images in the scrollwork.

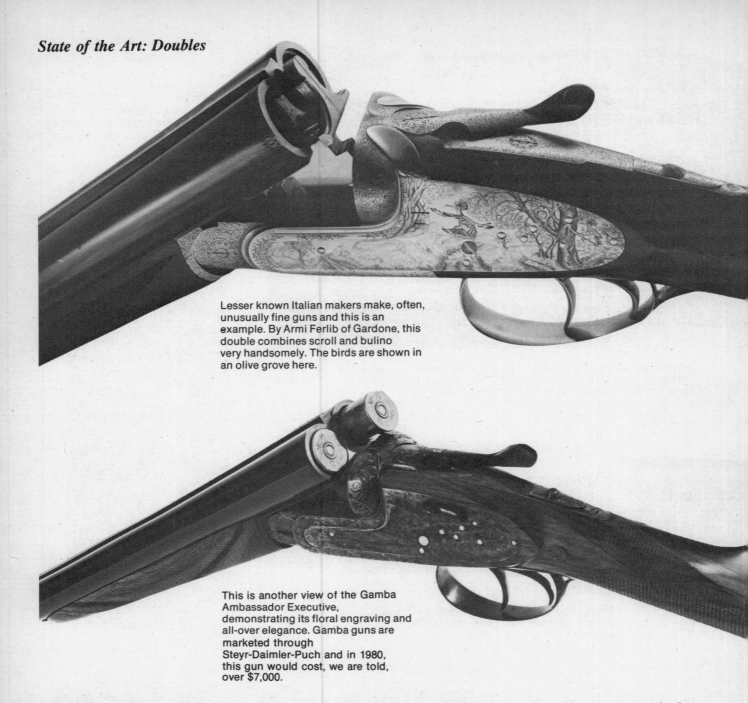

Lesser known Italian makers make, often, unusually fine guns and this is an example. By Armi Ferlib of Gardone, this double combines scroll and bulino very handsomely. The birds are shown in an olive grove here.

This is another view of the Gamba Ambassador Executive, demonstrating its floral engraving and all-over elegance. Gamba guns are marketed through Steyr-Daimler-Puch and in 1980, this gun would cost, we are told, over $7,000.

In the event the gun at hand was not built with 2¾-inch chambers, or 3-inch chambers for 410s, some considering has to be done. In a lightweight foreign gun, it is not always wise simply to get the chambers deepened. Some careful measuring is in order to be sure that the necessary cuts will not create a very thin wall in the tube. Again, a good mechanic is the best guide here. It helps, of course, if he has some experience with double guns. Many guns have been provided with deeper chambers with no ill effects whatever. It is unlikely that one can or should rise to magnum chambers in a re-worked gun. Far better to begin with a magnum gun.

There are a number of other niceties, most of them fairly standard operations in the gun trade. Mildly pitted barrels may be restored to smoothness through reaming and polishing operations. Any particular thinking and wish and desire so far as the shape of a forcing cone and the like can be handled during this segment of the job.

Often a barrel technician will have his own techniques for delivering patterns. Some shortened barrels will include all the work on the forcing cone, and perhaps even the creation of an oversize bore. The methods are empirical; a good man almost always makes them work.

It might be worth it at this point to tell something about how guns are regulated in one European factory. The goal here is to achieve with the right barrel the widest possible pattern at about 12 yards and with the other barrel to get that same size pattern at 24 yards, or thereabouts. The technicians first bore and ream the chokes to what is normal to get the kind of performance they seek. They then shoot the gun. If both barrels perform as required, that is the end of it. If more work is needed, the next step is to lengthen and make more gradual the forcing cone. The gun is reshot at this point, and for the most part, the desired performance has been reached. In the event it has not, the next step is to grind in a recessed choke in whichever barrel is not up to standard, and this will always get the job done.

Think about that for a minute. What we are saying is that a well-respected European double gun producer does not say in advance how he will choke his barrels. He simply says that they will perform at a given level. And, if you line up the barrels of several of his guns and look through them, it is the usual case to see that nearly every barrel is bored differently.

There is one other thing: No one who involves himself with the barrels of double guns, particularly older double guns, is the least bit dismayed by ribs coming loose. It is a standard job to resolder. It costs extra money, of course, but one ought not complain.

Ribs, meaning ventilated ribs, are sometimes added to double guns. A fellow who is accustomed to an elevated sighting plane can hardly do without it. The jobs are all routine for people like Simmons. However, any such work ought to be accomplished before the stock is designed and finished.

Reworked, rebuilt or restored double guns can and do become the full equal of the very finest specimens of factory guns. We have not mentioned the embellishment of engraving and inlaying herein, but almost any double gun offers a considerable scope in this direction. The sky is literally the limit.

The custom shotgun offers its user, properly done, a re-refinement of every satisfaction to be found in the custom rifle. To the extent that a properly fitted shotgun quite actively helps its user to shoot better, there might well be more satisfaction in the custom shotgun than in the rifle. Many think so.   *Ken Warner*

Other Shotguns

THERE IS, save perhaps in embellishment, no place like the United States to get first-class work done on other than double-barrel shotguns. When it comes to understanding and dealing with the intricacies of the various repeating mechanisms, American gunsmiths have the edge on the world. This is so despite the fact that a great many excellent repeating shotguns are now made overseas. One should remember in this regard that the principal market for repeating shotguns made overseas is the United States.

There have always been high-grade repeaters in American gun company catalogs. Such a giant production facility as Remington, for instance, has almost always offered special selection for wood, special combinations of features, and even engraving of one form or another from their custom shop. Standard designs in pump guns and autoloaders can be, to the degree permitted by their general plan, dimensioned to order right from the factory.

There are good reasons, sound reasons, why American shooters who can afford anything will still prefer the repeater and when a more deluxe example is wished, go for the special-order magazine gun. Among those reasons: long familiarity; entirely adequate shooting capability; and even—regardless of what some think—a solid belief that the repeater is the better gun. Such shooters have already accepted the general structure of a repeater, its characteristic balance and handling quality, and its undeniably machine-age looks. Certainly this writer is not going to argue with them.

That does not mean that one can start with, for instance, a Browning Auto-Five and sufficiently alter its contours to make it sleek. What can be done is to somewhat alter its handling by careful balancing, to select wood that entirely complements a finish, and to make the metal as slick and clean as its designer originally intended by introducing the handwork, the sophisticated handwork, that the factories no longer can apply.

Then, of course, with a suitable checkering pattern and a considerable expanse of engraving, one can make something quite special of what is actually a utilitarian object.

In general, repeaters simply do not offer the scope for changing their handling characteristics that is offered by most double guns. If one wants a lightweight shotgun in a repeater, one must, willy-nilly, commence with a lightweight model. The amount of weight that can be saved by barrel-shortening, for instance, is quite limited. One cannot simply chop away the metal of the receiver to suit himself, and a considerable effort to lighten a standard repeater by using lightweight wood is bound to generate an amount of forward balance few would consider ideal. On the other hand, the fellow who

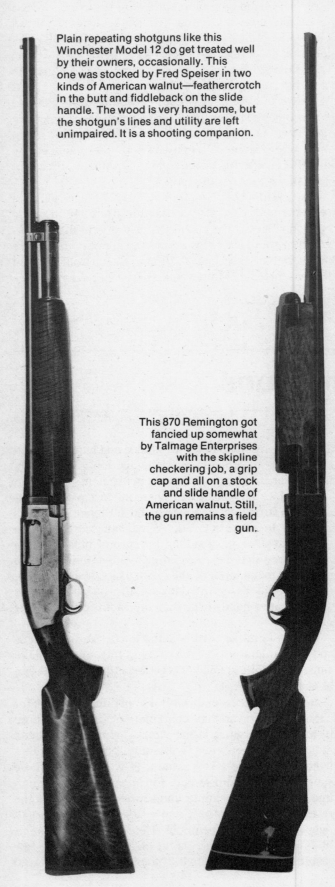

Plain repeating shotguns like this Winchester Model 12 do get treated well by their owners, occasionally. This one was stocked by Fred Speiser in two kinds of American walnut—feathercrotch in the butt and fiddleback on the slide handle. The wood is very handsome, but the shotgun's lines and utility are left unimpaired. It is a shooting companion.

This 870 Remington got fancied up somewhat by Talmage Enterprises with the skipline checkering job, a grip cap and all on a stock and slide handle of American walnut. Still, the gun remains a field gun.

is willing to accept an increase in over-all weight and does a careful job of selecting wood, can greatly improve the balance of a repeating shotgun. Happily, a bonus that comes with this is the chance to use highly figured wood of the very densest character and a bonus that comes with *that* is that such wood permits a checkering artist full rein to his talents.

Thus, the repeater owner can deliver to his special gun all the care in choosing wood, all of the embellishment choice, and an equal expectation of satisfaction that any other custom gun can deliver to anyone. And there are some things that can be done in the matter of boring and sighting and accessories.

Taking barrels first, the repeater owner, except those who own solid-frame guns, can relatively economically have a set of matched-for-length barrels in varying chokes. He can be sure that every one of his barrels is properly headspaced, and bored and polished for the kinds of loads he likes to shoot. There are, of course, adjustable choke devices, but they are rarely as neat a solution for a gun you are going to spend some money on as separate barrels are.

There are ribs to be had, and on a custom gun where barrel lengths are chosen strictly to suit the owner, the independent shotgun rib maker, again like Simmons, can fit up a rib to suit the barrels in hand, whatever their lengths. While he is at it, the builder of a repeating shotgun can suit himself in the matter of sighting. He can have the beads of his choice up front; if he has chosen a rib, he can get a middle bead to suit; he can even scope his shotgun, which is not the worst idea in the world, whatever it does to the lines and balance. When it is not possible for sighting arrangements and the stocking to be carried on simultaneously, it is best if all sights are installed and the stock then fitted. The choice of a rib, for instance, as a sighting plane, changes stock dimensions to accommodate it, or should.

In the matter of barrel length, the repeater user should not be too quick to make up his mind. Someone who has an entirely happy experience at a given barrel length who sees no reason to change shouldn't change, of course, but those with an open mind, or a slight yen to try a nonstandard barrel length should consider the matter further. I myself have used, quite happily and as successfully as I could expect, a Remington 870 slide-action 12-gauge with three barrels, all 20 inches long, for nearly 20 years. Other experiences with relatively short barrel lengths have been uniformly good. Therefore, I take it as established that a shooter may have the barrel of his repeater at any length he wishes down to 20 inches. He will hardly realize any disadvantage whatever and will achieve some advantages in the matter of balance, and handiness.

I speak from some considerable experience. Those three 20-inch barrels have, used in their turn, all done the job, from doves to turkeys. The gun balances a little farther back than most 870s; it is a great deal handier in

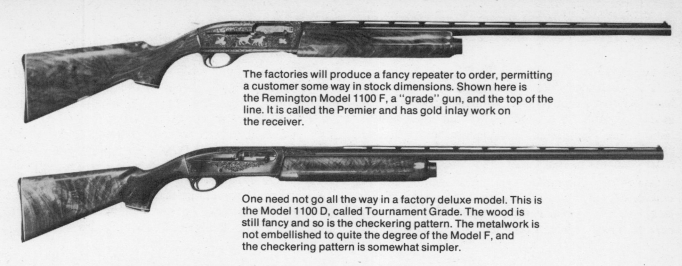

The factories will produce a fancy repeater to order, permitting a customer some way in stock dimensions. Shown here is the Remington Model 1100 F, a "grade" gun, and the top of the line. It is called the Premier and has gold inlay work on the receiver.

One need not go all the way in a factory deluxe model. This is the Model 1100 D, called Tournament Grade. The wood is still fancy and so is the checkering pattern. The metalwork is not embellished to quite the degree of the Model F, and the checkering pattern is somewhat simpler.

All F Remingtons or Premier grades do not have gold inlay. This is the straight engraved Premier Model 1100 displaying all the fancy touches of any other extra-priced gun.

the field; it breaks down into a short package and will pack suitably in a standard dufflebag.

What are the barrels in terms of choke and fixtures? Well, the basic barrel is a slug barrel, with rifle sights, and it shoots slugs well. I took a long barrel and had it Poly-Choked at 20 inches as the utility barrel for this gun and it works out; the third barrel is a full choke barrel, and there is a little story to that. Actually, this is one of those things that happens to gun writers occasionally. A good friend at Remington heard me talking about how well I liked short barrels for much shooting with repeaters and found a sample barrel made up in preparation for a military contract long ago and simply gave it to me. It is as tight-shooting and hard-hitting as virtually any full choke barrel I ever used.

Along this line, it is not necessary to buy barrels at the length you want anymore. Many gunsmiths have or can get choking tools for single-barrel guns which will permit them to put a full choke by swaging into any length barrel. They can, indeed, put any other choke into a cut-off barrel as well. Since some factories, to one degree or other, swage chokes in their barrels, this cannot be called an inferior way to go about the job.

From this writer's point of view, one of the big advantages of the single-barreled gun, whether it is a repeater or not, is the fact that these tools have made it possible to have, conveniently, any length barrel with any degree of choke needed or wanted. There are numerous other possibilities in the custom shotgun line beyond standard field guns for game shooting, which is what we have been discussing heretofore, or competition guns, which we will discuss elsewhere.

As with rifles, people occasionally find a need for extra lightweight arms, which can be accomplished by shortening one or another lightweight repeater and stocking it with specially selected wood. Provided one starts at under 7 pounds, he might well get a standard gun down below 6 pounds, which is about as far as one wants to take a 12-gauge, or indeed, a 20-gauge with heavy loads.

It is also possible to heavy up and ruggedize a standard repeater for emergency use or other tough duty. Parkerizing, black chroming, a set of fitted spare parts, the shortest possible barrel (18 inches), coupled with, depending on the model, one or another of the available folding stocks, could net out at a rugged and powerful firearm which would pack, with a supply of shells, in a space not much larger than two shoe boxes.

Then, there is the all-out self-defense gun, characterized by police down South as the "whippet gun." As I have seen them, most whippets are 20-gauge pump guns, usually utilizing the small ringed slide handle and a minimum buttstock, possibly even a mere pistol grip. The rules for civilian ownership of short shotguns are that the gun must have a barrel 18 inches long, and that the gun with barrel mounted must be 26 inches over-all.

It is quite simple, using today's models, to get a 27-inch whippet together. Such a gun has the disadvantage that it is purely and simply a trouble gun; it has the advantage that it is a damned good trouble gun. Each of us should make up his own mind in this regard, but you may take it as true that one does not, without a great deal of practice, reach much wingshooting success with a shotgun that has no buttstock. The whippet is, however, very handy.

It goes without saying that any single-barrel gun may have its bore tailored to suit a given load or a given style of use in the matter of chokes, forcing cones and the like. As has been noted, the single-barrel is an easier chore to work on for the gunsmith, and there are many tools available for the jobs.

That brings the good news that, stocking and engraving excepted, most of the work on repeating shotguns costs less than getting similar jobs on double-barrels. That might be classified as another benefit of

reliance on the repeating system. Of course, it is a general advantage and not a specific advantage of the repeater that a damaged barrel is not a total disaster. One can simply order another barrel from the factory and drop it in place. It is also, because of these factors, much easier to find reasonably competent people to work on magazine guns.

Obviously, it is not necessary for a fellow with an affection for a standard repeating shotgun to simply resign himself to the ordinary in a firearm. He can, at possibly less expense than with most other kinds of firearms, create something distinctive, something that doubtless suits him even better than the standard, and something that looks good.

Ken Warner

STATE OF THE ART

Revolvers

AMERICANS have a fascination with handguns unmatched by any other people in the world, probably because handguns are a part of our heritage and played an important part in settling this country. While the revolver originated as a fighting tool, it soon became a food gatherer and personal defense implement of the common man and gentry alike. The frontiersmen of the

post Civil War period relied on a rifle for serious hunting and the shotgun when he anticipated a fight, but the revolver was the personal sidearm which was always with him. Consequently, it became a general-purpose tool, used to kill small game for the pot, and occasionally larger animals such as deer or hogs, as well as being the instant response weapon of need. As our country

Here is an example of a very personal revolver because it is not something out of the factory catalogs. This began as a standard square-butted stainless Ruger Security Six. Its owner, Ed Harris, prefers the round-butt mode and simply altered the grip metal to fit a set of Ruger round butt grips.

One of the benefits of the round-butting of a Ruger Security Six intended for use with hot loads is that it can then be fitted with the Pachmayr neoprene grips that go a long way toward making heavy-recoiling rounds comfortable.

This gun, which appeared on the cover of the 35th edition of *Gun Digest,* is a truly personal revolver. Harris started with a Model 1917 Smith & Wesson, had an extra 45 Colt cylinder fitted, and added some touches like inlaid sights, matting on the top strap and the like. The gun has worn a variety of grips. It is shown with Harris' standard carrying rig.

There has been for years a minor league hue and cry for a big double action revolver in 45 Colt. Smith & Wesson has heard the crowd and is now delivering the Model 25 in 45 Colt shown here. Big-bore buffs like it really well.

became more urbanized, the revolver became a defensive tool of the householder. It was depended upon less for daily chores, as its use for home defense and later for recreation use increased. This trend continues to this day.

Few modern shooters, besides lawmen or those who work in remote areas, use the revolver as a daily tool as did the frontiersman, so most of us are interested in working and defense guns as recreational items. The hunter, backpacker and survivalist want reliable, compact, useful guns which could fill the pot and serve for defense in a pinch. The urban dweller wants a dependable, safe, personal weapon which handles instinctively and can be relied upon in an emergency when he can't wait for the police to arrive. In these troubled times,

defense seems to be an overwhelming motivation for people to own handguns. Personally, I feel the average homeowner who is not a shooting enthusiast has no business keeping a handgun around the house, unless he fully intends to learn how to use it well, and practices frequently. Otherwise, if a person wants a simple firearm which can be operated by any member of the family with minimal instruction, a break-open single shot or double barrel shotgun with open chokes and short barrels would be the best choice.

If you are reading this book, however, it could be assumed you are an active shooter or have an interest in becoming one. In that case some comments on personal handguns are in order. Few are anything more than altered factory guns. There are very few entirely

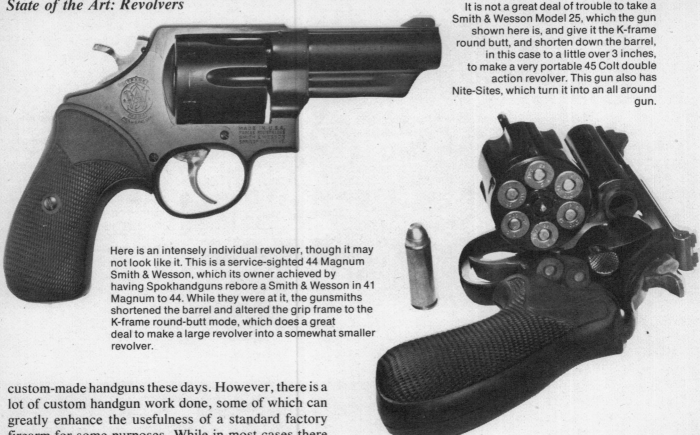

It is not a great deal of trouble to take a Smith & Wesson Model 25, which the gun shown here is, and give it the K-frame round butt, and shorten down the barrel, in this case to a little over 3 inches, to make a very portable 45 Colt double action revolver. This gun also has Nite-Sites, which turn it into an all around gun.

Here is an intensely individual revolver, though it may not look like it. This is a service-sighted 44 Magnum Smith & Wesson, which its owner achieved by having Spokhandguns rebore a Smith & Wesson in 41 Magnum to 44. While they were at it, the gunsmiths shortened the barrel and altered the grip frame to the K-frame round-butt mode, which does a great deal to make a large revolver into a somewhat smaller revolver.

In a search for the relatively unusual, it has been possible to have a K-frame Smith, in this case a Model 13 heavy barrel 357 altered to 5-shot 44 Special. Spokhandguns did the work, using the original barrel bored out, and manufacturing a special cylinder, and retiming the mechanism. Such work is expensive, but many feel the resulting gun is worth it.

custom-made handguns these days. However, there is a lot of custom handgun work done, some of which can greatly enhance the usefulness of a standard factory firearm for some purposes. While in most cases there isn't anything wrong with using an out-of-the-box factory revolver, many can benefit from a little careful tinkering which makes the gun work more smoothly and reliably, shoot more accurately, or handle better.

Customizing a factory revolver often starts as a result of initial test-firing. Quite often when I examine a new gun, I find little things that bother me, a hitch in the DA trigger pull, fixed sights which don't shoot where I point them, or minor mechanical bobbles which are easily fixed. Most often, you will simply want to smooth up the action of the gun and little else. Action jobs are a standard item and encompass all the little things which are done to make new guns work smoothly, like old guns. Years ago new revolvers never needed action jobs, since they were lavished with tender loving care. The new S&W double action you pick up today, however, isn't anywhere near as smooth as those of 20 years ago, or even 10. There are fewer skilled hands around, and handwork is something most makers try to avoid these days, because it costs money. Colt and some other makers offer action jobs as extra-cost options on new guns, making it a "custom shop" item. Such a job gives optimum fit of the working parts, while smoothing all points of metal-to-metal contact. There are also many custom gunsmiths who do action work, and they are all busy these days.

There are two types of action jobs, the full-house competition-tune and the duty/hunting-tune. The competition guns are smoothed up and the DA pull light-

(Above and right) This gun takes the K-frame Smith about as far as it is ever going to go and in fact there aren't going to be any more like this one. This is a 45 Colt on the K-frame, an alteration which Spokhandguns no longer believes is a good idea. There just isn't quite enough room for the fat 45 Colt cartridge in the available space.

ened as much as possible, which often means hammer energy is about minimum for reliability. Some competition guns are tuned so fine that if you change brands of ammo or primers, you risk misfires. In competition guns it's relatively common to shorten the strain screw only slightly to lighten the DA pull. This has the effect of also reducing mainspring tension and hammer energy. The S&W rebound spring may be shortened a coil or two also. Shortening the rebound spring is normally used to reduce the single action pull, but has an effect on the initial DA takeup as well. If the strain screw of an S&W is backed off or shortened, it may misfire with hard primers, such as those used in +P service and 357 Magnum ammunition. If the rebound spring is shorter than 15 coils, the trigger may not return positively when the gun is cycled rapidly double action. Competition guns can be tuned to the ragged edge for maximum smoothness, since if the gun fouls up, it costs the shooter only a match, not his life.

Duty guns are a different matter, and so are home defense and hunting guns. Functional reliability is *the* prime requirement of both. Nothing you do to a hunting or service gun in hopes of improving its handling or accuracy should impair reliability. If it does, it's a bad idea. Action jobs on hunting and duty guns usually consist of smoothing the contact surfaces only. The S&W rebound spring might be cut up to one coil, one-third at a time. Further shortening is seldom advised. The strain screw and mainspring should be kept at their full tension. In function testing a service gun you should shoot it double action as well as single action, since the hammer fall is slightly shorter in the DA mode. A gun might function fine when cocked single action, but mis-

(Below) From left to right: The 3-inch 25-5 Smith in 45 Colt; the 3½-inch 44 Magnum rechambered in a Model 58 Smith; the one-of-a-kind 45 Colt 5-shot 4-inch Model 64 Smith; the 5-shot 4-inch barrel 44 Special on a Model 13. All guns are round-butted to take the Pachmayr Signature Compact stocks. The K-frame guns are less bulky, obviously.

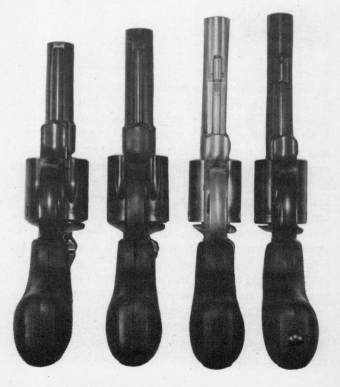

fire occasionally when fired DA. I routinely test 38-357 revolvers with either Federal factory +P or magnum ammunition, which has a "hard" primer, or handloads using the Federal 200 small *rifle* primer. If it will set these off 100 percent of the time (I usually shoot a box single action and a box double action), the gun is OK. If I get a single misfire, I get suspicious. You should also check the hammer for push-off when cocked for single action firing. If you can push the hammer off full cock with your thumb with less than about 30 pounds of pressure (use a bathroom scale), the job was botched.

Most of the smoothing of the DA trigger pull on S&W revolvers is accomplished by freeing the cylinder on the yoke, and insuring proper fitting of the thumbpiece and bolt. The cylinder stop is also deburred so it moves up

Another single action engraved by Bill Johns is a little less usual, but has its own charm even though the engraving pattern is not fully realized.

and down freely without binding; the trigger is stoned so it will return easily; and the rebound slide deburred and smoothed. The hammer seat on top of the rebound slide is broken slightly with a stone to aid trigger recovery, and the back corner of the rebound seat on the hammer might also be broken slightly. It shouldn't be necessary to polish everything inside an S&W revolver. Doing so accomplishes little else but removing the case-hardening. A skilled revolversmith can make these minor adjustments in a few minutes, since it involves little other than making sure the parts function as designed.

When doing revolver trigger jobs, the rule is that you never work on the hammer, only the trigger. If the hammer pushes off, it means the single action sear of the trigger is losing engagement. Provided the hammer notch has not been cut on, this is a relatively simple repair job, requiring some careful stone work on the

trigger sear. However, this isn't the sort of thing you should attempt yourself. I've seen skilled gunsmiths at the S&W factory do this freehand, but very few others can. Usually a jig is used to keep the proper angle on the engagement surface of the trigger. At worst, you end up replacing the hammer, or trigger, or both.

For an action job on a used gun, a pistolsmith worth his salt will tear everything down and give it a complete inspection, replacing worn parts and making any minor repairs necessary. This is important, since timing, trigger rebound, cylinder locking, endshake, cylinder gap, and forcing cone condition affect the overall reliability and accuracy of the revolver. Some of the things done to smooth up the action in general tuning require that the revolver be mechanically correct to start with. Otherwise you are wasting time and money.

Pistolsmiths who do a decent action job on a Colt revolver charge more than their counterparts who slick up S&W's or Rugers. It is puzzling to those who don't know why that they can get an action job on an S&W for about $35, but that it costs $85-100 on a Colt Python. The reason is that S&W, Ruger, and Dan Wesson action jobs entail careful stoning, polishing and perhaps a bit of cautious coil spring clipping, and little else. The Colt action job is mostly a "spring" job, but with leaf springs you just can't clip away. You can't even bend them much to get any effect without annealing the "elbow," adjusting the bend and reheat-treating. Once you bend a leaf spring past its elastic limit, you've damaged it irreparably. That's why a Colt action job is expensive work. Flat springs used in current Colt revolvers are stamped and don't lend themselves as easily to alteration as a forged one. Occasionally you see guns which have been customized by putting old-style springs in them and altering them, but these aren't readily available and don't often fit right in current production guns. Top revolver mechanics make new springs from scratch. This isn't cheap or an easy job, but it gets the desired results. That's the essential difference. Other parts, such as the bolt, are also critical in the Colt, and a complete action job usually involves extensive rework or remanufacture of it. I'm not sure if any revolver mechanic actually makes new bolts, but for the amount of work which goes into altering these in some jobs, it probably wouldn't be that much more work. Given the amount of time that takes, it's easier to understand why an S&W action job costs only $35 and a Colt rework $100.

A worn hand or ratchet is the culprit in most off-timing of S&W revolvers; in the Colts it is usually the bolt which locks the cylinder. In worn guns, the bolt will usually work adequately single action, but may not if the hammer is cocked slowly, particularly if there is any drag on the cylinder from a high primer or thick cartridge rim. You check for this by placing light thumb pressure on the cylinder while you "milk" the hammer back slowly. Timing in Colt double actions is corrected by limiting the travel of the bolt inside the action. Sometimes a tiny set pin is used, though it is better to replace the bolt with one having a higher hump at the pivot hole. On S&W revolvers, off-timing is corrected

duce a push-off condition from full cock.

The S&W double actions are easier to work on and more gunsmiths do a satisfactory job on these than on the Colts. The single action trigger pull is controlled mainly by the rebound spring, as was explained earlier. Timing is controlled mostly by the point of the hand. With most Smith & Wesson revolvers it shouldn't be necessary to do any stoning to adjust a single action trigger pull.

A big part of customizing a service or duty revolver is getting fixed sights to shoot where they look for a chosen load. While adjustable sights work fine for a target gun and for hunting guns which will be used with a variety of loads, any revolver subjected to rough service should have fixed sights. The problem with most factory fixed-sight guns, however, is they seldom shoot the preferred ammunition where you want them to. Zeroing fixed-sight revolvers isn't a big deal if the

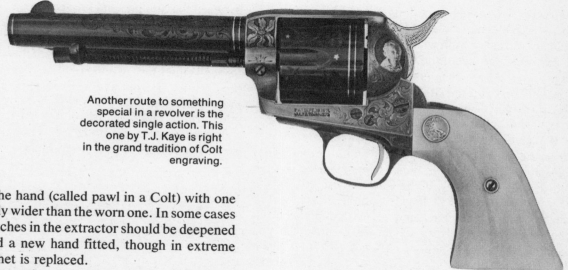

Another route to something special in a revolver is the decorated single action. This one by T.J. Kaye is right in the grand tradition of Colt engraving.

by replacing the hand (called pawl in a Colt) with one which is slightly wider than the worn one. In some cases the ratchet notches in the extractor should be deepened with a file and a new hand fitted, though in extreme cases the ratchet is replaced.

Crane alignment is another potential problem often seen in secondhand revolvers, especially if somebody has been watching too many TV detective shows and swings the cylinder shut with a snap. In S&W revolvers this is usually corrected with a special tool which is inserted through the crane, the pistolsmith taking a lead hammer and giving it a smack in the right place, and between times inserting the cylinder, checking it for wobble. Oversized center pin (ejector pin) holes in the frame are less easily fixed, and require either bushing the hole or an oversized replacement pin.

Adjusting the single action trigger pull on Colt double actions depends mostly on sear engagement and only slightly on mainspring tension. Simply burnishing or polishing the parts often helps, and stoning shouldn't be attempted to reduce the trigger pull until the gun has been disassembled, cleaned, perhaps lightly burnished, relubricated, reassembled and tried. Careful stoning to remove rough spots is usually all that is necessary. Any reduction of engagement should not be enough to in-

pistolsmith knows what he's doing. The hobbyist can usually do this himself given knowledge of the fundamentals, though he may have to reblue the gun or touch it up afterwards. The basics are the same as in adjusting fixed open sights on rifles, described elsewhere in this book, but there are some important differences.

First you should make an intelligent decision on what loads you wish to use in a fixed-sight gun. Except with very short, or very long barrels, most fixed-sight guns will shoot either high velocity, or low velocity loads close to the same point of impact, if the bullet weight is nearly the same. Bullet weight affects point of impact more than velocity, since it is mainly a factor of barrel time, though recoil enters into it also. Generally speaking, heavy bullets shoot high, and light ones low. However, in light, short barreled guns, like 357 snubbies, hot loads will shoot higher than a standard velocity load of the same bullet weight since barrel time is short with either, but there is a considerable difference in recoil. In longer barreled guns, over about 5 inches, the higher velocity load will shoot lower, just as if you switched to a lighter bullet. In medium-weight guns, having barrel lengths from about 3-5-inches, bullet weight is by far the most important factor. For most 38 Special and 357 Magnum guns, the 158-gr. bullets make the most sense for general use. This is because most factory fixed-sight guns are fairly well zeroed with them as they come from the box, and you have a variety of loads suitable for most applications. In the 44 Magnum the 240-gr. bullet makes sense for the same reasons, since you have both high velocity and low velocity loads of varied types of bullet construction.

Once you've decided what bullet weight to shoot, pick a load in the middle velocity range, or the one you expect to use most. Establish where the gun shoots to start with. On a fixed-sight duty gun, start by firing at 7 yards with a center hold. If it shoots dead-on point of hold at 7 yards for both windage and elevation, go back to 25 yards and repeat the exercise. If it is off on windage at 7 yards, a sight adjustment is necessary to insure you will be centered at longer ranges. Don't adjust elevation yet, without determining where the load strikes at 25 yards.

Windage adjustments on most revolvers are simple, since the barrel can be "tweaked" a bit in the frame, loosening or tightening it, which cants the front sight in the desired direction. If the gun consistently hits a 25-yard repair center at 25 yards on the first try out of the box, you usually have enough margin to play with, even with S&W revolvers. On the S&W, however, you can only make slight adjustments this way, the reason being that the ejector pin housing on the barrel rotates with the barrel also. Before tweaking an S&W barrel, the barrel pin must be removed. Usually the slot in the barrel pin is oversized enough that slight corrections in windage can be made without increasing the size of the notch. If the barrel pin doesn't tap back into place easily, then file only a little clearance on the side needed with a needle file. Also check and be sure that the ejector lock plunger engages correctly when the cylinder is closed normally. S&W revolvers which require more correction than can be obtained without interfering with the function of the lock plunger usually have other problems, such as an out-of-square receiver face. This can usually be corrected by lapping the front of the frame in, using a fixture made for this purpose.

While windage adjustment is mostly a trial-and-error proposition, the elevation adjustment can be done exactly and only needs a careful approach. A good shot can shoot a 10-shot group offhand to determine the center of impact, but the average shooter should fire the gun from a sandbag rest.

Since handgun groups are usually larger than rifle groups, it might require some work to determine the precise group center. Knowing the accurate placement of the group center is important if any adjustments are to be accurate. Fire at least a 10-shot group. If you *know* you fired a bad round—you jerked, or if the sights weren't aligned—disregard it and fire another. I find I get the least sighting error if I take a center hold. A 6 o'clock hold is OK for target shooting if you are always shooting at the same sized bull, but it is worthless for a field or duty gun. Not all field targets are the same size, so the revolver should be sighted to shoot "point of aim—point of impact." Instinctively hold to center of mass and when zeroed accordingly, you'll hit whatever size target you aim at, rather than always being an arbitrary distance high, because of that 6 o'clock hold.

Draw a horizontal line through the lowest shot in your group, then measure the vertical distance from that line to every other shot in the group. Average these values and draw another horizontal line. The distance between the first line and the second one is the amount of elevation correction needed. At the same time, you should do a similar determination for windage, to see if a minor correction is needed there. Draw a vertical line through either the extreme right or left shot, and repeat the exercise. If your average lateral point of impact is more than about 1-inch off point of aim at 25 yards, you may wish to make a correction.

The amount the front sight must be built up (or reduced) is determined by the formula:

$$X = \frac{RE}{D}$$

where X is the amount to be added or removed from the sight; R is the sight radius; E is the desired movement in point of impact; and D is the target distance in *inches* (as are all measurements here). To move the point of impact *up*, the front sight must be made shorter. To adjust point of impact *down*, small corrections can be made by filing, or machining a light cut off the top of the notch at the top strap. For large adjustments, the front sight must be replaced with a higher one or built up by welding, after which it is filed back into shape.

Younger shooters can usually see fixed sights without much trouble, but almost anyone over 40 needs a wider rear notch than comes standard. If the gun shoots "on" for windage as it came from the box, the notch may be carefully widened the same amount on each side. But if some windage correction is needed, the formula tells how much must be removed on the side toward which you wish to move the point of impact. It is extremely rare to find a fixed-sight gun which shoots so far off it cannot be zeroed adequately by slight barrel tweaking combined with minor widening of the rear notch. It's best when making these corrections not to go the whole way without shooting the gun to reestablish point of impact at least once at an intermediate stage. This provides a check in case you made a measurement

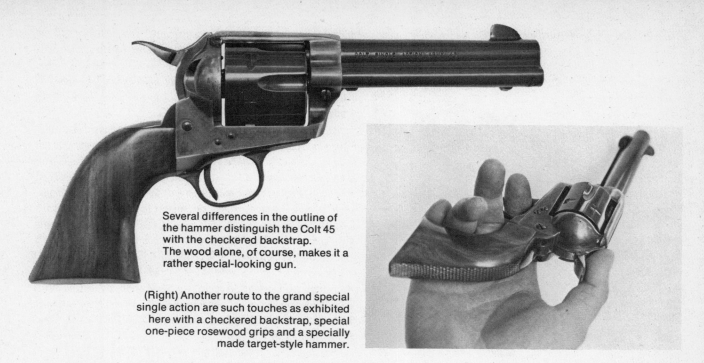

Several differences in the outline of the hammer distinguish the Colt 45 with the checkered backstrap. The wood alone, of course, makes it a rather special-looking gun.

(Right) Another route to the grand special single action are such touches as exhibited here with a checkered backstrap, special one-piece rosewood grips and a specially made target-style hammer.

or arithmetic error and may prevent taking off too much. During shooting trials you should have the sights well blacked, and you must use the same type of ammunition you did before. Recheckering or sandblasting the top strap, if needed, and blending the front sight contour back in before refinishing the gun completes the job. For obvious reasons, any zeroing of fixed-sight guns must be completed before you apply any metal finish. Most pistolsmiths who do this type of work on duty guns on any regular basis include a thorough cleaning, degreasing and dunking in the blue tank as part of the fee, any additional metal preparation being extra, of course.

We go, by the way, into such detail here because such a revolver zero is a personal thing. The man that shoots it has to zero it. The custom gunsmith can come along behind and clean up cosmetically, or even duplicate a set-up by remaking the parts, but he can't decide where they should be for you.

The fellow who likes to experiment with different loads, or who must be able to adjust his sights for different ranges, as in metallic silhouette competition, needs good adjustable sights. The factory adjustable sights which come on Colt, S&W, Ruger or Dan Wesson guns are usually entirely serviceable, but some target shooters prefer to replace them with a Micro, Behlart, Clark, Elliason, or other replacement unit. It is common practice on PPC revolvers to install a full-length rib having new sights on it, giving a broad, matted sighting plane. These work suitably for competition, but are a bit gaudy and awkward for a field gun.

On several of my own guns I've gone the opposite way. On most field guns I recognize the obvious utility of fixed sights, but I like the convenience of adjustable sights, since I do more load experimenting than the average guy. My approach is to disassemble the sight thoroughly and degrease it. Once reassembled, I zero the gun carefully, and when satisfied it's right, I apply a drop of high impact epoxy to each of the adjustment screws. This insures they will stay put through any normal punishment. Should I ever need to adjust the sight again, I simply heat it with a match until the epoxy softens, then I adjust it. Once the epoxy cools, it is usually rigid again. This system has worked for me on several guns. I still prefer fixed sights on most field guns, but some of my favorite pieces weren't born that way, so this gives me the best of both worlds.

Front sights are often altered to make them more visible, or to provide a reference mark for elevating the front sight a bit above the rear notch for long-range shooting. Although it has become fashionable to use colored plastic inserts for this, as can be done using the kit from Bullshooter Supply, I still prefer metal inlays, since they look better and are less likely to get knocked out. Gold is expensive these days, but a little gold wire will go a long way toward inlaying a reference point on your front sight or outlining a rear notch. White-outline rear notches are standard on some S&W sights. Omega and others make them available for the Colt and Ruger revolvers.

For the police officer, however, the only way to go on a serious duty piece is Nite Site, available from Nite Site, Inc., P.O. Box O, Rosemont, MN 55068. These sights are available for most adjustable-sight or fixed-sight revolvers, but require gunsmith installation. They feature a beta-emitting isotope, Promethium 147, with a phosphor compound, which is encapsulated in clear epoxy. These sights are visible in total darkness and require no batteries, yet they don't affect the size or weight of the service revolver. Point of impact is the

The Smith & Wesson Chief Special is favored by many, but there is not all that much one can do to one without extensive gunsmithing. The net result is that a very great many Chief Specials are done up as is this by George B. Spring.

same day or night. The sight picture is a bar-dot on adjustable-sight guns or a double-dot on fixed-sight guns. I've fired these a great deal, and they really work. Most recently I fired them on a darkened range with a 3-inch barreled 44 Magnum snubby, using full loads, and despite the brilliant muzzle flash I had no trouble regaining a normal sight picture or keeping all my shots in the K5 at ranges up to 25 yards. These are the hot setup for a serious duty rig.

On some new guns, the forcing cone may be too tight, sharp edged or rough. This will affect accuracy by causing increased bullet deformation and leading. Usually this can be corrected by reaming the forcing cone slightly to remove tool marks and provide a smoother finish which scrubs less lead from the bullet. The important thing here is that the reaming must not be overdone. The factory forcing cones in S&W, Ruger and Dan Wesson guns are 18 degrees. When reaming the forcing cone, the pistolsmith will usually use a more gradual angle which permits him to clean up tool marks or other damage without enlarging its basic diameter. Brownells has an 11-degree reamer used for this in 38-44 caliber guns. This is the preferred method. If a steeper angle cone, such as 18-degrees, is run in to clean up, its major diameter might be too large. This causes exces-

sive bullet base upset, leading and inaccuracy. If an 18-degree reamer is used to recut the forcing cone, it usually requires the barrel be set back one thread. This isn't always possible with S&W revolvers because of the placement of the ejector lock plunger, though in Colts it poses no trouble.

Rebarreling is an option not often considered, but it is often worthwhile. You might want a different barrel length than is standard on that model, or to replace one that is worn-out. A friend made a Police Positive from his Colt Detective Special by installing a Police Positive 4-inch barrel on it. Another fellow has the only 3-inch S&W Bodyguard I've ever seen, made by putting a Chief's Special barrel on it. I wanted a 3½-inch barrel on my S&W 22 Kit Gun, but didn't want a Model 43 Airweight or a Model 51 22 WMR, so I got a Model 43 barrel and installed it on my Model 34. A fellow with a fascination for odd barrel lengths has plenty of options just in those the factories have put on that frame size, swapping one for another. One very useful and good shooting conversion done by Bill Davis, of Davis Company, in Sacramento, California, is called the Cougar, and uses a Colt Python barrel rethreaded onto a Ruger DA frame. Another similar conversion he does is called the Smolt, using the Python barrel on an S&W K-frame. Why the Python barrel, you ask?

Twist of the rifling can have a big effect on revolver performance, particularly with jacketed bullets. The S&W Military and Police started as a blackpowder cartridge around the turn of the century, and the 18¾-inch twist was originally intended, as far as I can tell, to reduce the problem of fouling with blackpowder. It was entirely adequate in terms of bullet stability for the full service load in the standard 5- and 6-inch barrels which were customary at the time. But when you chop back a 38 Special to 4 or 2 inches, the 18¾-inch twist might not always be quite enough to stabilize the long, heavy 158-gr. bullet. It's not unusual to see 148-gr. wadcutters tip somewhat when fired in a 4-inch barreled 38 with slow twist. The rapid growth in PPC competition in recent years has caused the current generation of revolver shooters to relearn what was known by revolver competitors back in the 1930s. While the Colt action was preferred for its easier cocking, the big argument in its favor was its 14-inch twist which gave it better accuracy. Consequently, the Colts are less often rebarreled by PPC competitors, but the S&W and Ruger guns almost always are. The 14-inch twist is most popular, though faster rifling of a 12- or 10-inch twist is often employed in custom barrels. For service use the faster twist has an advantage in improving expansion, since the greater rotation imparted to the bullet by the sharper pitch increases the hoop stress or "flywheel effect" on the bullet's surface. Often I've observed that a load which doesn't expand in a 2-inch S&W will often do so reliably in a 2-inch Colt, even though there is little or no difference in velocity. The greater bullet stability imparted by the faster twist also improves penetration of non-expanding bullets, such as Keith types, in soft targets. They tend to go straight through rather than expending their energy by yawing. Of course, the yawing bullet would probably kill better, but you have to hit your target first. The Keith bullet works best by shooting clear through game to provide a good exit and blood trail. A faster twist does this more consistently than a marginal one.

Rebarreling a revolver can be a satisfying experience. I put a 12-inch twist barrel on a 357 revolver I own, and it has proven to be a very worthwhile addition. It shoots all the normal loads I wish to shoot, wadcutters and 158-gr. loads, as well as heavy bullets up to the 200-gr. 35 Remington soft point, which I sometimes use for silhouette shooting. It isn't awfully good with bullets lighter than 140 grs., but acceptable, and with 158-gr. loads its accuracy is astounding. It's no trick to hit the rifle chickens from a rest at 200 meters using the scope sight and factory 158-gr. 357 loads.

Rebarreling isn't always the straightforward job it might seem. While original factory barrels for the same size frame can often be fitted with little work, this usually requires facing the breach to provide proper cylinder clearance and reaming the forcing cone at minimum. If the barrel doesn't snug up tight when the front sight is aligned, the barrel shoulder must be adjusted accordingly. Custom barrels made from a blank require much more work. They must be threaded, fitted, the forcing cone cut, and the front sight or rib installed. On S&W revolvers the ejector lock plunger must also be installed. Some gunsmiths simply dovetail a lug to the barrel to install the plunger, others silver-solder one on. Very few machine the lug integral with the barrel as the factories do. Still others eliminate the barrel lug altogether and instead install a yoke lock which takes its place. One form of this I've seen which works well uses a spring-loaded ball detent in the yoke which engages a matching cut in the frame when the cylinder is closed. If done right this works very well, and it's not that hard a job. Davis Company is one outfit that does it this way.

For guns which are carried a lot, particularly for law enforcement use, it might be advantageous to adapt the gun to a round-butt shape. The Ruger Speed Six or S&W K-frame models are factory-made in round-butt style, but usually only in the shorter barrel lengths for the S&W and in fixed-sight guns for the Ruger. A very useful service gun is a 4-inch barreled S&W Model 19 Combat Magnum with round butt. While the Office of Naval Intelligence got theirs made by S&W that way, you can't get one from S&W, so you have to do it as a custom job by either rebarreling a 2½-inch round-butt Model 19 with a 4-inch tube, or round-butting your 4-inch gun. I wanted a round-butt Ruger Security Six with adjustable sights. I had one gun Ruger made that way which was part of a special run, but I wanted

Sometimes the personal revolver equation is solved with a completely stock 3-inch round-butt 38. Hard to find in Smith & Wesson, one can locate a Taurus as this one is with relative ease.

another, so I made one. On a stainless steel gun round-butting is easy, since you don't have to reblue it afterwards. With blued guns you have to recontour the backstrap, groove it if you want it to look "factory," and reblue to match the original finish. Done right, you can't tell if the factory did it or somebody else.

Suppose you wanted a big 44 snubby. This is an unlikely candidate for a factory gun, but the S&W N-frame is easily round-butted to take the K-frame Pachmayr "compact" grip. This trims the gun noticeably, yet it is very manageable. The 3-inch barreled 44 Magnum I mentioned earlier was done this way, and while I wouldn't want to shoot 100 full loads at once out of sheer joy, with practice a skilled shot would be able to use it very well. Most often, such a gun is used with milder loads like Remington's "medium velocity" 44 Magnum lead load. This still churns up about 900 f.p.s. in a 3-inch barrel. The round-butt grip is quite manageable if it is reasonably full, like the Pachmayr.

Round-butting guns which have a factory version on the same basic frame, such as a square butt K-frame S&W or Ruger Security Six is easy. Start by installing a set of factory wood round-butt stocks on the frame, and scribing a line around the frame edges. The frame is then filed or ground away not quite to the line. Then the

The serious shooter, even the silhouette shooter, will often go to great lengths to get a revolver that meets his needs. This 357 Ruger has been rebarreled with integral rib set up to accept Ruger rings. It may be, in the space of 5 minutes, changed from a accurate-to-200-yards silhouette gun to a quick-holsterable heavy-barreled field gun. And, of course, vice versa.

Here is how the sight-converting aspects of the heavy-barrel Ruger belonging to Ed Harris work. The milled slots on the rib are in the side of the rib and quite inconspicuous; choosing the mount placement and ring height carefully permits one to simply move the scope on and off the gun without touching existing iron sights or their zero. This system works.

flat-filed or ground surface is draw-filed round to just blend the edges to the scribe mark. Tool marks are polished out with 320 grit on stainless guns, to match the factory finish. On blued guns they should be taken down to 400 grit before rebluing. A fellow who's done this a few times can do a good job on a stainless gun in a few hours. Grooving the backstrap to match factory S&W guns takes a proper machine setup or careful handwork, and correspondingly more time and money. Overall, though, the effort is worthwhile. The only way most people can get a round-butt, adjustable-sight Ruger Security Six, for instance, is to make one. Mine is a very friendly, useful general-purpose sidearm. It's the one I carry most often outdoors if I want something bigger than a 22. Once you have one nice round-butt revolver, it's easy to want and accumulate others. Single actions can be round-butted too, though this takes

considerably more work on reshaping the grip frame and making new stocks to suit. This is usually a gunsmith job rather than a do-it-yourself project.

Another viable custom option is conversion to other calibers. For instance, if you desire a 44 Special double action today, or a 45 Colt, your options are limited, but given a good large-frame 357 Magnum and a willing gunsmith, all you need to do is make the holes bigger. The S&W N-frame 357s, 41s and 44s will all convert to 44 Special or 45 Colt just fine. Some outfits are making new 5-shot cylinders for K-frame S&W revolvers, making 5-shot 44 Specials out of them. I don't know what these would offer over a good 4-inch 357 for the size, but if you like the bigger hole better it will physically work, after a fashion.

The most sensible options are the ones which take least work, since they are the ones which usually work best. I know several Winchester collectors who sought to have modern 30 Carbine or 44 Magnum Ruger revolvers converted to 32-20 or 44-40 by rechambering extra cylinders, to avoid cobbling up their choice Model 92 rifles. You can usually get an extra revolver cylinder for rechambering more cheaply than converting the rifle. You don't hurt the revolver by adding the extra cylinder, and you won't wreck the collector value of the rifle either. A Ruger Super Blackhawk rechambers easily to 44-40 and will digest the high-speed rifle loads with no difficulty. Colt made some 45 ACP cylinders for single actions, but they aren't readily available today. The fellow wanting one for his pet thumb-buster can time a 38 Special, 357 Magnum, or 44 Special cylinder to his 45 Colt and have it rechambered.

More unusual revolver conversions are those which don't use standard cartridges. I have seen one 25-20 Colt Army Special revolver which in all likelihood was "born that way," but the owner of a 25-20 rifle wanting a companion handgun could do it several ways. I heard of one such gun made from an S&W Model 14 which a guy rebarreled with a Douglas blank, and fitted a K22, 22 Long Rifle cylinder, which he had rechambered. He shoots only standard velocity loads and the gun works fine. A fellow wanting to shoot more authoritative '92 Winchester style loads could have somebody like Snapp's Gun Shop jazz up a cylinder and rebarrel a Ruger Blackhawk, as he has been known to do occasionally. Other conversions of this nature done years ago were taking K22 revolvers out to the 224 Harvey Kay-Chuk, a shortened 22 Hornet, or Colt single actions out to 22 Hornet, or 218 Bee.

Going more modern, it would be entirely practical to take the extra, seldom-used 9mm auxiliary cylinders for Ruger convertible Blackhawk revolvers and rechamber them to Winchester's new 9mm Magnum. I'm not sure such a conversion would offer any advantage over a 357 Magnum, but if you already had a Thompson/Center Contender barrel for this caliber, a wheelgun for it wouldn't be a bad idea. The same idea could probably be applied to Ruger's 45 Colt/45 ACP Blackhawk convertible, taking the 45 ACP cylinder out to 45 Winchester Magnum. This idea doesn't appeal to me. I don't think the 45 Magnum will do anything the 45 Colt in the Ruger won't. The 45 ACP cylinder makes too much sense as a general-purpose, practice, plinking and fun gun to do anything but leave it alone.

Part of the appeal of a custom revolver is a sense of pride in the ownership of something which is, for your purposes, better than the factory product. It shouldn't only feel and shoot better, it should have a look about it as well. After all, half the fun of having a classy custom gun is its being noticed. If your gun looks just like the other 16 K-38s on the line, why bother?

Maybe you don't care about being noticed, you just want a gun that works, and one that you can shoot well. That's fine, but not all folks are as easily pleased. If you

want your revolver to look special, as well as work special, there's no reason not to have it that way. Some of the custom options, such as metal checkering a revolver top strap to prevent glare, metal sight inlays, or a hump-backed hammer for easier single action cocking, are all functional, yet they are distinctive and enhance a gun's appearance as well. Other embellishments, like engraving, make a gun look nice, but they don't help you shoot it any better. A very highly decorated gun usually won't get used much at all, but people shoot fancy guns, and not all are Texan millionaires. I know a retired North Carolina sheriff who always has a factory engraved S&W Model 27 with him, which he uses often, though he takes loving care of it. Careful use of a fine gun won't hurt it a bit. If you like pretty guns, but feel bad about not using them, go ahead and enjoy them. Just be sensible.

Blue finish is standard on new factory guns, but a lot of folks don't seem to like it on their customized revolvers. I guess they think a custom gun should have a different finish which makes it stand out in a crowd. For a lot of purposes, a blue finish is still pretty good. It's certainly the least expensive option in most cases, and there are a lot of different ways it can be done. Most factory guns do not receive a high polish, but are usually polished to about the equivalent of 320 grit. A high polish blue like the factory S&W Model 29 would probably be equal to a 600 grit polish. A high polish blue shows every fingerprint. A low polish doesn't reflect as much light afield to spook game. A less reflective, or nonreflective finish is useful on hunting and duty sidearms. One very good way to achieve this is to glass bead blast the surface before bluing. This gives a soft matte surface which is very attractive, yet doesn't shine. A fine sandblast gets somewhat the same effect, but is more harsh. The one advantage of sandblasting over bead blasting is its more porous surface which gives a better adhesion of preservatives for field use.

Also good for field use are platings or coatings which protect the steel from corrosion. Industrial hard chrome applied after sandblasting or bead blasting is one method. Armoloy is one name for a process of this type, but other companies do the same thing, though they cannot use the name. Nickel plating was used years ago to protect guns in moist climates, and it works fine as long as the plating remains intact. Its main disadvantage is its high shine. If you wish satin nickel, you bead blast beforehand. There are also chemical nickel coatings, which can all be lumped under the term "electroless nickel." These processes are all nearly the same, the differences being mainly in the metal preparation before the nickel is applied, which gives the resulting finish its distinctive appearance. As a result Nitex does not look quite the same as SimGard, and so on, but chemically they are the same.

If you don't like a bright finish, you should consider "black chrome," Teflon S or Parkerizing. Black chrome is good if well done, but on much industrial chrome applied on firearms, the film is not of uniform thickness in crevices or around corners, and I've seen many botched jobs. Very few places do good gun work in black chrome. Teflon S isn't particularly attractive to look at but is a very satisfactory, durable finish. When in the service, I had a 45 automatic which was Teflon S treated and I carried, used and abused it for a year in a sandy, salt-water environment. It held up fine. I shot the gun a lot, and eventually sold it, but I liked the finish. Teflon is a good choice for guns used in cold weather or salt-water environments, since it requires no additional lubrication to freeze or pick up grit. In very cold weather, bare skin won't stick to it.

Parkerizing has been used on U.S. military weapons since about 1930, and has proven very satisfactory. Unfortunately, there are very few places which aren't already swamped with industrial orders who do a good job at this. The ones who do it for industry will seldom do individual guns for customers. Davis Company in Sacramento, California, is one outfit who does decent Parkerizing, I'm told, but I haven't seen any samples of this work. The bluing and satin nickel plating done by Davis is top notch. But if considering dealing with any company you haven't heard of before, beware. A fellow I know wanted a gun Parkerized and sent it out to a firm advertising Parkerizing in *The Shotgun News*. When the gun came back, the bore was Parkerized inside as well, and the gun had not been properly cleaned and degreased before treating. It was gray in some places and blue in others. The firm had sent the gun back to him disassembled, but the package was damaged in transit and some parts lost. The gun could not be made to work even when the parts were replaced. The fly-by-night outfit took his money and disappeared from the face of the earth. Numerous attempts through the Postal Inspector's office, the Better Business Bureau, and the State Attorney General's office didn't get his money back. Finally he returned the wreckage to the original manufacturer and they sold him the needed parts at cost and repaired the gun. Total cost for repairs was $80, but this included a replacement barrel, since his original one was pitted beyond salvage. His case isn't unusual, I'm told. He's lucky, he got his gun back.

The moral is, custom handguns can satisfy, but you have to know what you want, how to get there and who can do the work right. Finding the right man to do the right job isn't always easy, but given the right combination of ingenuity a skilled pistolsmith can make almost anything reasonable work, as long as it's a possibility and not a pipedream.

C. E. Harris

STATE OF THE ART — Autoloaders

ALTHOUGH the revolver is used most by police and hunters in the U.S., the automatic pistol is the primary target, military and service handgun throughout the world. With the exception of the NRA-style police revolver and metal silhouette, the semi-automatic is the dominant handgun used in target shooting. The semi-auto is also the principal military and police handgun everywhere, except perhaps in the U.S.

Many years ago revolver fanciers scoffed at the semi-auto, saying it was too fragile and unreliable. Those arguments don't hold water at all today. The same arguments are now directed toward the revolver, which most armies and non-U.S. police agencies in the world view as an anachronism left over from the last century. In fact, the U.S. military is actively seeking new semi-automatic pistols to replace the various 38 Special revolvers bought for interim use since WW II. Revolvers were said to lack stopping power (sound familiar?) and had poor reliability and maintainability compared to the semi-automatic pistol. Although the eventual replacement of the M1911A1 45 pistol seems certain, it will probably remain standard until all revolvers are withdrawn from service and enough new 9mm handguns are produced to start replacing 45s in inventory.

The motivation for these trials wasn't that the M1911A1 is an unsatisfactory handgun, but that the 38 revolvers used as alternatives weren't. The problem is that there are no longer sufficient inventories of 45 pistols to satisfy projected needs. That's why the services got hooked into buying revolvers as a short-term solution in the first place. Faced with the prospect of having to buy more pistols instead of repairing existing ones, the military is looking at the alternatives in 9mm handguns which could provide improved handling characteristics and performance. A major criticism of the 45 cartridge which first surfaced during the Korean conflict, and which is again in the limelight, is that it lacks adequate penetration of body armor. The 9mm is judged superior in this respect, especially with new

Collectors of Lugers and Mausers often have personal autoloaders out of their collection, and at the upper levels, these might well be restored guns rather than originals, as are these guns which have gone through the shop of J.J. Jenkins.

ammunition which is being developed. Another factor favoring the 9mm is the fact that it is NATO standard for all members of the alliance *except* the U.S. Adopting a 9mm handgun would enhance interoperability with our NATO allies.

Although the 45 is as sacred to Americans as apple pie, the 9mm Luger cartridge has been around since 1904 and is the most used military and police pistol cartridge in the world. The arguments are likely to be continued and heated, but the fact is that *both* cartridges are good ones. They are nearly comparable in performance. Their kinetic energy is virtually identical, and with proper bullets, so is their killing power. If you need the greater momentum of the 45 for pushing the IPSC pendulum or knocking over silhouettes, use it. But if you want a lighter recoiling, flatter shooting, better penetrating handgun for military service, the 9mm is a good choice.

This discussion of the 45 and 9mm cartridges is in order, because they are the two dominant service pistol cartridges, and they illustrate the basic schools of thought regarding service pistols: the big slow bullet vs. the light fast bullet. I'm not going to tell you which to use, but I simply wish to cover the options on how to get the best out of each.

Custom autoloaders, like custom revolvers, fall into two basic categories, hunting or service guns, and target guns. The IPSC combat guns fall into an area which overlaps somewhat into both categories. The same admonition holds true with automatics as with revolvers: Service guns shouldn't be tinkered to death in hopes of getting the last bit of gilt-edged accuracy, since you risk malfunctions at a crucial time. Within the constraints imposed by functional reliability, however, the semi-auto shooter has a great deal more he can do to the gun to make it suit him. Unlike the revolver shooter, most of the common gunsmithing jobs done to a semi-automatic pistol are to enhance reliability and do not detract from it. Most of the "standard" combat modifications, such as magazine adjustment, ramp polishing to smooth the feed cycle, and adjustment of the chamber throat to permit easy closure of the slide with semi-wadcutter ammunition, all contribute to smoother, more reliable functioning. Unless you do some of those jobs, most pistols would be limited to FMJ "ball" ammunition, unless you sacrificed reliability. A few out-of-the-box semi-autos will feed semi-wadcutter or hollow point loads, but not all do. Therefore, you must function test your gun with the ammunition you are likely to use, and test every magazine, to determine the extent of customizing which is necessary to fill your needs.

The only modifications which are likely to get you into trouble on a duty pistol are the ones which get beyond the realm of functional changes, those accurizing steps which reduce clearances between parts, making the gun fit tighter. Accurizing in moderation isn't bad, but for duty or hunting guns you should stop short of a full-house Camp Perry style bull's-eye gun. For serious service use a lot of professionals don't go as far as the typical IPSC competitor. IPSC is supposed to simulate combat, but it is still a sport, just as NRA police revolver matches are. The guns and holsters are specialized for competition more than for military or police service. Somewhere between the two extremes of full-house competition and loose, right out of the armorer's cage, falls the compromise gun which will suit most people best.

A good rule of thumb in working on any hunting or duty pistol is to ask yourself three questions: Is it safe? Is it reliable? Is it accurate enough? Safety must be your first consideration, then reliability. Anything further you do which compromises the first two considerations is a bad idea. Before going out and spending $300 on custom work, you should decide just what you need done. This should always start by a serious, careful shooting session, not just a day's plinking.

Shoot at least 20 rounds with *each* magazine. Number each one distinctly and keep track of the

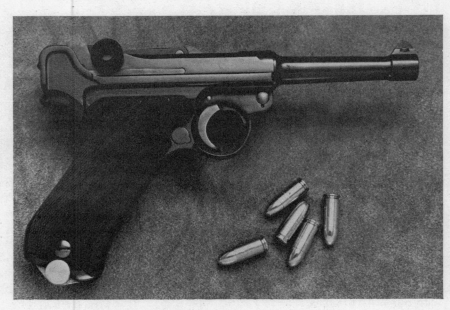

Even close up, the cleanly restored Luger, this one a 9mm, exhibits all of the clean lines and forthright machining that are part of the Luger's tremendous appeal to many autoloader fans.

A surprising number of Model 1911 Colts are given the deluxe treatment, as in this Martin Rabeno engraving job in large scroll. The size and scope of this work is entirely in keeping with the character of the gun; certainly such work when done to order makes an autoloader personal indeed.

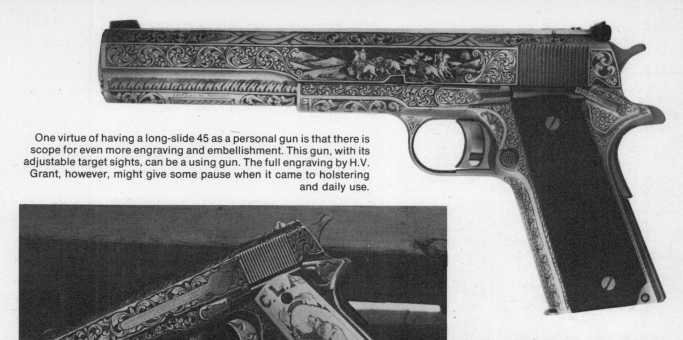

One virtue of having a long-slide 45 as a personal gun is that there is scope for even more engraving and embellishment. This gun, with its adjustable target sights, can be a using gun. The full engraving by H.V. Grant, however, might give some pause when it came to holstering and daily use.

Another bold Government Model, this one embellished in areas not usually worked on, such as the trigger itself and the beading around the trigger guard. Certainly, with the primitive style stock embellishment, and the very large monogram, all accomplished by Wayne Reno, this gun is the apple of its owner's eyes.

number and type of malfunctions which occur, if any. Start with ball ammo, and if it works satisfactorily, then try SWC or JHP styles. Make sure to test all types of ammo in every magazine. Any magazine which gives persistent trouble must be fixed or junked. After this initial exercise, you can pretty well tell what modifications are needed.

Unless your gun comes from the box with a good trigger pull, this is one of the first things you'll wish to have a gunsmith adjust. For service pistols it usually isn't a very good idea to try for a trigger pull lighter than 4 pounds. Although a well set-up trigger lighter than this will last for awhile, it gives little margin for wear. On a wadcutter gun a pull should last, but it requires other modifications besides the basic trigger job. The standard hammer on the Colt Government Model has higher hooks on the full cock notch than are necessary for safe sear engagement. Cutting these hooks down reduces a lot of the trigger and sear movement needed to fire the gun. Usually, the hammer is held in a jig, and the tops of the hooks cut down with a flat India stone against a feeler gauge held tightly into the full cock notch. Although guns used only with light loaded wadcutter ammunition for target work might be safely cut down to .016-inch, the normally accepted minimum for National Match "hardball" guns is .018-inch. It's a good idea on service guns to not go below .020-inch, since this still permits a good trigger pull when everything else is right, and it gives an extra margin of safety.

If the hammer hooks are cut down too much, it is easier for the sear to be jarred off the full cock notch during the operating cycle. The hammer has considerable override beyond full cock when the slide recoils over it. With heavy loads, the jarring of the closing slide, perhaps aggravated by a heavier than standard recoil spring, and considerable override of the hammer, can cause the hammer to gain enough velocity on the rebound that it will jump the notch, causing automatic fire. It's a good idea when getting a trigger job to have the hammer nose shortened somewhat also. This reduces the override of the hammer to just slightly greater than that needed to assume full cock reliably.

The shape of the sear nose has a great influence on the trigger pull, and it is important that it bear evenly in the hammer notch. Different pistolsmiths occasionally have their own ideas how the sear nose should be shaped, but all do this in a fixture, so it can be done quickly, and uniformly each time.

While discussing service modifications, I should mention the Colt Gold Cup. The Gold Cup National Match 45 is basically a target pistol rather than a duty gun, but it does well with service ammunition too and isn't a bad choice for service use, IPSC or NRA competition. If the gun is to be used exclusively with hardball ammunition, it's a good idea to replace the recoil spring with a 16-pound load type. The Gold Cup doesn't require a heavier spring to shoot service loads for occasional use, but the gun will last longer if a regular GI spring is used. The standard Gold Cup spring is a bit lighter, probably about 14 pounds, to permit reliable functioning with wadcutter ammunition. The Gold Cup frame or slide are of the same material and hardness as the Government Model. There is no difference. However, the lighter spring permits greater recoil velocity of the slide with hardball ammunition, and long use of service loads will increase wear, compared to wadcutter loads. Using the standard GI spring or a 16- to 18-pound Wolff model will help the gun last longer.

Another thing you should consider on the Gold Cup if you will use service ammunition exclusively is to have the trigger set up to GI National Match specs, with .018-inch minimum depth on the hammer hooks, and a 4-pound pull. A lot of IPSC shooters simply remove the sear depressor and put a heavier recoil spring, firing pin retracting spring and mainspring in the Gold Cup, but I don't want to suggest this. I've seen some guns "double" after long use, given this treatment. The Gold Cup hammer has the hooks of the half-cock notch cut away except for a small area in the middle, so as to help avoid the half-cock notch damaging the sear if the hammer follows down. The sear depressor also aids in this, much like the "fly" on a muzzleloader lock, but it also helps to keep the sear firmly in the full cock notch. If you take that depressor out, you should install a regular service hammer and sear and adjust the trigger to serv-

Rudd Arms has this prototype in work as an experimental model. Very often the desire for a distinctive personal gun will take the auto fan toward the really unusual, which this gun is. (Walther Rickell photo)

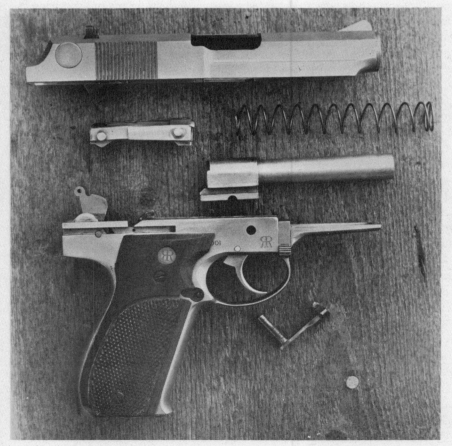

Broken down, this prototype Rudd 45 reveals an ecclectic technical background in the mode of barrel-mounting, and with its separate breechblock.

ice specs. Doing anything else is asking for trouble eventually. Don't tell me how many rounds you've shot through yours without trouble, because I've seen enough of these guns double fire to be very cautious about it. These precautions cost little, but give you a bit of added assurance in safety and reliability. Very few people can tell the difference between a clean breaking 4-pound pull and a clean breaking 3½-pound pull. A lighter trigger isn't likely to make the poor shot shoot any better. If he can't control a 4-pound trigger he's got problems anyway. A good shot won't be handicapped by a good service trigger. A good consistent trigger pull requires that the hammer and sear pins fit snug in the receiver. If they don't, it may be necessary to peen the holes slightly or make oversized pins.

Other parts of the trigger job include polishing the stirrup of the trigger so it will slide easily in the gun frame, and building up its rear surface to reduce the initial take-up needed for it to contact the sear. Everything else is flat polished except for the top of the disconnector. The sides of the trigger stirrup may be built up or peened to take up any excess side or vertical play of the trigger in the frame. Many shooters prefer the "long" National Match type trigger. The shorter military one fits persons with short fingers better. Custom triggers are available which have a set screw to reduce over-travel. These are sometimes used on combat competition guns and are almost always used on bull's-eye guns. They aren't necessary on a service gun. If you do have a trigger stop on a service gun, adjust it carefully and insure you have it backed off a bit more than necessary. Then stake or epoxy it in place so it can't loosen.

Once the trigger has been worked over to suit you, your gunsmith should work on other functional modifications. The most important of these are those which affect feeding. The feed ramp in the frame should be polished to form a smooth blend with the barrel ramp. This involves removing tool marks only and doesn't change the angle of the ramp. The radius of the feed ramp is usually increased to provide better feeding with blunt-nosed, hollow point or semi-wadcutter ammunition. This is a good idea, and most pistolsmiths do it as a standard procedure. The Colt Gold Cup and some of the newer semi-autos such as the Vega 45 and Browning BDA come with a wide enough feed ramp ready to accommodate most factory loads and handloads. The Mark IV Series 70 Government Model needs only a little work here. It's usually suitable, except for polishing. The face of the slide should also be polished so the cartridge slides easily up under the extractor. The Colt M1911, the Browning M1935, and the good Colt copies all feature a "controlled round" feed cycle. The round is stripped from the magazine and fed up under the extractor, where it is held until struck by the ejector after it is extracted. The main difference between wadcutter guns and hardball guns is the timing of the release of the cartridge from the feed lips, so it rises under the extractor. The round-nose bullet can be fed into the chamber at a slight angle. If it hits the barrel hood, it will bounce down into the chamber. The hollow point or semi-wadcutter cannot, however, since its flat nose or square shoulder will hang up. Therefore, wadcutter magazines have their lips relieved so the round is released about ½-inch (in a 45, somewhat less for a 9mm) from the rear of the magazine box so it will jump up under the extractor and be shoved straight into the chamber. When the pistol is set up right, the magazines are in good shape, and the feed ramp/barrel junction smooth, it is possible to feed empty cases through a gun manually with the recoil spring removed. Not all gunsmiths can do it this well, but those who can don't mind showing off a little.

The feeding cycle is somewhat different on the S&W Model 39 and 59, the Beretta 92, SIG P220/P225, H&K P9S, Walter P38, P1, P5, and the Star BKM or BKS pistols. In these or others like them, the cartridge is stripped from the magazine and forced ahead of the extractor, which must snap over the rim at the last moment as the breech locks. This last motion of the extractor adds to the effort needed to lock the slide. The feeding relationship is such that magazine function and slide velocity are critical when trying to attain reliable feeding. The gun might bobble occasionally if it is extremely dirty or if fired in an unusual attitude, such as inverted. The better designed pistols like the Benelli, Beretta 92, Walther P5 and SIG P220/P225 will usually feed alright inverted with service ammunition, but they don't necessarily like short-nosed rounds like the Winchester Silvertip.

Some unknowing shooters who have blindly replaced springs and tinkered with M1911-type pistols have changed the timing of the mechanism so it no longer works as a controlled round feed, but on the "snap-over" principle. Usually such guns work adequately, but they are more reliable if a gunsmith adjusts the spring rates and magazine configuration to retain the controlled round feature designed into the gun. Another potential problem with the Colt automatics, and to a lesser extent with the Browning Hi-Power, is the extractor. A common complaint with recent production pistols is that they throw brass straight up, hitting the shooter in the face. Brass is often dented as well. Most often the approach taken to this is to enlarge the magazine port and bevel its rear edge, like the Gold Cup. This is needed with light wadcutter loads, but is entirely unnecessary with service ammunition if a gunsmith really understands how the gun works. The problem is related to the shape of the extractor hook. If the bevel on the extractor isn't cleaned up to give some relief on the lower front edge, the case will be driven off the extractor at 3 o'clock and strike the inside of the slide under the ejection port. The closing slide then kicks the case up, or may even close upon it. If the bevel is cleaned up to the front edge just on the bottom one-third of the extractor hook, the ejector will drive the case out in the 2 o'clock position, so it can exit the gun without striking the slide. A lot of money spent on "porting" M1911-type pistols could be saved if more people recognized this minor detail.

Another useful modification for the service pistol is "throating" the barrel for semi-wadcutter lead ammunition. Ordinarily, the 45 chamber has an abrupt origin of the rifling, intended for jacketed ammunition. When handloaded lead bullets are used, it is necessary to seat the bullet so about .015-inch of the wadcutter shoulder is exposed above the case mouth. This provides a means of reducing end play of the round in the chamber, to compensate for the reduction of shoulder diameter induced by crimping the bullet. Most lead bullets require at least some crimp to avoid their being pushed deeper into the case when they strike the feed ramp. Although a taper crimp does this without affecting headspace, some of the lead shoulder still must protrude into the lead. This increases the effort needed to close and lock the slide. "Throating" the barrel then, is reaming the rifling origin slightly to advance the forcing cone enough to permit free chambering of lead semi-wadcutter rounds. Usually this will incur a slight penalty in velocity, since it increases free bullet travel. However, the amount of velocity lost is small enough to be insignificant. It has the effect of lowering pressures somewhat too, so many IPSC competitors simply increase the load enough to qualify Major Caliber, which they can do in the 45 ACP with no trouble.

Once the trigger pull and feeding cycles are adjusted, the only remaining required modification for the service gun is getting sights which suit you. Fixed sights are best for most field use, particularly so with the automatic pistol since they are jarred around more than on a revolver. A good fixed-sight zero at 50 yards will satisfy most requirements.

If you prefer adjustable sights, be careful to get rugged ones. The S&W rear sight is popular, but requires a rigid installation to be completely suitable on heavy recoiling guns like the 45 auto. I've also found that with heavy loads the adjusting screws may "walk" unless fixed with Loc-Tite or epoxy. The Elliason sight used on the Colt Gold Cup makes a neat, rugged installation. The S&W sight will work OK if the tang is shortened, anchored with a suitable, larger socket-head screw and if the rear leaf is adequately protected. The best installations I've seen are those by Davis Co. which place the rear sight down into the original rear sight dovetail. The tang is bobbed off so it doesn't extend into the hood cut of the slide. Getting the sight down low, and rounding off the corners, is also a wise idea. Then you don't need a high sight to get a decent zero, and there's nothing to

snag holsters or clothing. The Elliason sight can also be installed this way, and I've seen the Micro replacement sights for Colt or Ruger revolvers done similarly. Some pistolsmiths such as Behlert make their own sights which work OK. Personally, though, I prefer carefully adjusted, fixed sights for all handguns except competition guns.

Micro makes high profile fixed sights, or you can have the popular King-Tappan fixed sights installed. The GI National Match fixed sights can be cut down into good service sights. These, however, are a bit higher than needed for holster use, though they are alright for competition. A compromise is to start off with the Micro or King-Tappan sights and round off all the sharp corners and widen the rear sight notch only if necessary to get a good sight picture. If the sight picture suits you, you must then adjust the sights to hit where you aim. If you plan on doing any accuracy work to the gun, sight adjustment must be done first, since lug locking, tight bushings, or elimination of the vertical play in the barrel will affect the elevation zero as well.

Start by shooting your preferred load at 25 yards, but move the rear sight for windage only, unless point of impact is so low you might drop shots off the paper at 50 yards. Following the formula and instructions in the custom revolver section, calculate the mean group center, and determine how much the rear sight must be drifted in one direction or another to obtain windage zero. Make a small index mark on the sight, measure the appropriate distance on the slide, and lightly make another one there, double checking the measurement with a vernier caliper. Drift the sight until the two marks line up, then test-fire again. If the gun is shooting close to point of aim at 25 yards, then go to 50 yards and repeat the exercise. You may have to make another slight correction at 50 yards to get things centered up for windage. Most likely you will need some elevation adjustment as well. Measure the mean group center from point of aim again and calculate the correction needed for windage and elevation.

If windage is off so much that the rear sight must be drifted noticeably off center, the front sight is probably canted or not square with the slide. One alternative method is to install an over-width, high, front sight. Center the rear sight in the notch, then machine the required amount off the sides of the front sight to obtain windage zero, and also machine the needed amount off its top to raise the point of impact for the required elevation. This is probably the best way, though if you wish to use a factory front and rear sight set, there usually isn't enough meat in the front sight to let you go this route. The King-Tappan is an exception here. With most front sight sets, at 50 yards you will probably need to raise the point of impact slightly. This is done by reducing the height of the front sight. Some pistolsmiths measure the height of the sight with a depth mike and slip a filing jig over the muzzle end of the slide, which permits filing small amounts off the sight while keeping it square. Large corrections, though, are usually done in the milling machine. Once the front sight height is established, the blade may be reshaped to undercut it for target work, or provide serrated ramp for holster use, etc.

Worthwhile additions are sight inlays which enable them to be seen clearly against dark backgrounds, like the IPSC silhouette. The King-Tappan sights come with an enamel paint on them, but it may have been filed so much during zeroing that it no longer looks right. In this case, it's usually better to have your gunsmith dress off the rear face of the front blade and start over. Groove the face with a fine checkering file, then install a white metal inlay which can be polished or burnished to reflect light. A method I have seen used is to drill and

angle so if the drill exits, it will do so on the dovetail portion, rather than where it will be visible. The insert is trimmed to .140-inch and epoxied in. In daylight the conventional sight picture is used, under low light conditions the front dot is centered over the rear dot. It is important that this type of insert be installed *after* the fixed sights have been properly zeroed and reblued, if necessary. The required NRC label must also be placed under a grip panel. If the gun must be refinished later, the sight is warmed slightly with a match or lighter so as to soften the epoxy, then the front sight element pushed out from the muzzle. The rear sight insert can be removed by heating the sight slightly, then snagging the red plastic polycarbonate capsule gently with a pin, and pulling the insert out.

Besides the usual trigger, feeding and sight jobs,

Another sort of personal autoloader as a serious using gun is this Browning 22 with a Davis Gun Shop base for Ruger rings. Such an outfit properly handled is a tackdriver and can fulfill an equal role as a fun plinker and on small game for the pot.

tap the sight for a stainless steel screw, which is silver soldered into the hole and cut off not quite flush. The slide is dunked in the blue tank and the inlay polished afterwards. Soft stainless steel or gold wire is used to inlay the rear sight.

For police duty pistols, a better idea would be to use luminescent inserts, such as those sold by Nite Site, Inc. These can be installed in the semi-automatic pistols with no trouble. A No. 47 drill is run lengthwise from the muzzle and through the center of the sight, .049-inch from its top surface, or deeper if required to obtain a minimum sight "chamber" length of .140-inch. The insert is epoxied in, allowed to harden, then the excess plastic is trimmed off the front of the sight. On the rear sight, the No. 47 drill is run in only .160-inch, just below the rear sight notch, and downward at a slight

there are other functional modifications which are useful for the custom autoloader used as a personal defense or trail gun. Replacement stainless steel springs are wise on service guns and aren't a bad idea for hunting guns either. Bar-Sto and Wolff make these for the Colt Government Model, as well as for other pistols. Stainless steel barrels are a very good idea for service guns, since they reduce the risk of bore rusting in rainy or salt-water environments. Contrary to popular opinion, stainless steel barrels are not immune from after-rusting from corrosive primed ammunition or salt water. They are damaged less easily than ordinary steels, but if neglected they will pit, though not as badly. The Bar-Sto stainless barrel and collet bushing is a good idea for the lightweight Colt Commander pistol. The alloy frame guns are not easily accurized, and then only partway, since the frame rails cannot be peened to lower and tighten the slide onto the frame as a steel one can. The Bar-Sto service replacement barrel will drop into most guns without any modification, and it amounts to an instant accuracy job. The collet bushing is a great improvement over the typical loose, GI type. The Bar-Sto barrel has higher lugs to remove most of the vertical play in the barrel lockup, and a bit longer hood, which reduces end play. The link hole spacing is slightly greater than a regular GI barrel. All this provides a drop-in barrel with a half-accuracy-job built into it. The 38 Super Bar-Sto barrels are essential in customizing guns of this caliber if you wish to get any reasonable accuracy. This is because the Colt barrel headspaces on the semi-rim, rather than on the case mouth, as is the 45 ACP. A replacement barrel is the only easy way to do this.

While these barrels aren't cheap, they are worth the money. A full-house target barrel is also offered by them, for gunsmith installation, but the standard grade barrel will shoot as well as anything but what the serious bull's-eye competitor will need. A light alloy frame Colt Commander I used to own is a good example of what mere parts replacement can do. As my gun came from the box, it would not do better than about 4- to 5-inch groups from a machine rest at 25 yards with National Match hardball loads, and not much better with wadcutters or handloads with the 185-gr. Sierra JHC. After installing the Bar-Sto springs, barrel, collet bushing and recoil buffer the gun would do about as well at 50 yards

as it used to do at 25. The barrel and bushing accomplished most of it. The springs, and buffer were mostly for long-term durability. Aside from these drop-in parts, I did little to the gun besides putting on high profile fixed sights, filled in to a 50-yard zero with ball ammunition, a trigger job, and adding a set of Pachmayr stocks. It made a darned fine holster gun. The guy who owns it now is quite pleased with it.

There are a lot of other modifications seen on IPSC competition guns which are occasionally used on duty pistols, though you must judge for yourself whether you really need them. The squared, checkered trigger guard is useful if you use the two-hand hold and want to wrap the fingers of the off hand around the guard for support. If you don't use this grip, though, you don't need the squared guard and it's only eyewash. Ambidextrous safeties are something else which gets a lot of attention. They are fine if you get a good one, but most people never shoot with the off hand, so don't need them. They are more a competition option. Deactivated grip safeties are something I don't care for, but there are those who feel the grip safety might interfere with getting off a shot in an emergency. I feel you should always have a firm grip on the gun, and if you do, the grip safety will give you no trouble. What you may wish to do is have a gunsmith adjust the grip safety so that any reasonable pressure will depress it, but so that it still functions as intended. This is more prudent than removing a safety device designed into the gun.

A lot of competition shooters like to extend the thumb safety tab so it is easier to release. The only thing which bothers me is that if it's large enough to release really easy, and you also have a blocked off or deac-

In yet another approach, many turn to the Detonics 45 as the personal gun they live with. Its flat, if thick, package delivering the power of the full 45 Auto has a great deal of appeal to those who feel a serious need for a constant self-defense companion.

tivated grip safety, the thumb safety might get brushed off afield while carrying the gun around in the holster. The thought of having a cocked, unlocked, ready-to-go pistol pointed down my leg isn't comforting. A proper holster thumb strap fitting between the slide and hammer is some insurance, sure, but a lot of them fit loosely enough that the hammer could simply push them aside and fire the gun. I know of it happening. Always remember the three criteria: safety, reliability, accuracy. Then think about what you are doing before you do it. Unless you really have trouble reaching the safety, leave it alone, except to be sure it works as intended.

For competition-only guns, it makes sense to go farther with customizing. You may need accurizing to get the last bit of gilt-edged accuracy from your gun. Slide fit really isn't critical for service gun accuracy, so it's a good idea to let the slide stay loose to give dirt clearance for feeding. By far the most important factor in pistol accuracy is the lockup of the barrel so as to eliminate end play and vertical play. The best way to eliminate vertical play in the Colt is by lug locking, so the barrel locking lugs are cammed into full engagement with the slide by the underlugs bearing against the slide stop. The link is loose and serves only to disengage the locking lugs from the barrel during rearward travel of the slide. Link locking is an expedient used on 45 service guns. It was once used for target guns years ago. The long link has a greater spacing between the link pin hole and the slide stop hole which forces the barrel upward. The link, however, must be fitted to the individual gun, and is subject to wear, so it must be replaced periodically. Link locking is seldom used in match guns today, lug locking or shroud locking being the preferred methods.

Shroud locking is achieved by fitting the barrel hood tightly to the slide recess and fitting a plunger which exerts pressure on the barrel hood in a forward and upward direction to force it into engagement. This works very well if properly done and can be applied to many semi-automatics besides the Colt Government Model, such as the Browning Hi-Power, Star or Llama pistols. This is an easy way to achieve a rigid lockup.

Some modifications done to semi-auto pistols amount to redesign of the gun to fit an entirely different role. Examples are compacting or "chop jobs" such as the Devel or ASP, 45 Bobcat conversions, or shortened slides on the Browning Hi-Power. Other rebuilds include the various double action conversions of the Colt Government Model and Commander pistols, or the Browning Hi-Power. The caveat on all these major alterations is that they are expensive, and if they don't work perfectly, they aren't really good ideas. I've shot a lot of these extensively customized guns, most by the top makers, and only one in ten was 100 percent reliable on the first go-round. In general, the greater the amount of modification, the more likely you are to have troubles. If you stick within the framework for which the

piece was intended, and simply make it work more smoothly and accurately, you are money ahead.

It takes a master craftsman to make a complete redesign of a handgun work. I've seen lots more of these jobs that didn't work than those that did. Unless you know the man's work, or can put it in writing that if it doesn't function perfectly, you'll expect him to fix it or eat it, stay away from him. Before spending a lot of money on some pie-in-the-sky custom job, try to shoot similar guns. Double action conversions sound neat, but have you ever used a DA auto? You may find it impossible to hit anything with the first shot. Some double action automatics have such a heavy trigger pull that experienced DA revolver shooters have trouble using them. It's very hard to get off the first shot with any accuracy if the DA pull is much heavier than 10 pounds. A lot of DA conversions, though, and many factory DA autos, have trigger pulls of as much as 12-14 pounds for that first shot.

Most Bobcat or chop jobs have all kinds of potential for functioning problems. Once you shorten the barrel and lighten the slide, you change the functioning characteristics of the gun considerably. The inherent problem is that the lighter slide recoils faster, and the magazine may not have time to catch up. It becomes a very interesting problem in mechanics to get the spring rates and the mass of the recoiling parts adjusted so you get everything to work right. It's not a simple matter of chopping everything down to fit. The best gunsmiths have done their homework, or made enough mistakes to have them all corrected by now, or so you hope. Very few of these guns, however, will give 100 percent reliability with more than a few types of ammunition.

Velocity loss in short barrels is something else to consider. When you shoot a cartridge like the 45 ACP hardball load, you get about 850 f.p.s. in a 5-inch barrel. Going from the Government Model to the Commander you lose only about 50 f.p.s. But in stepping down further to a Detonics or Semmerling, you lose a lot of energy, compared to the full-sized pistol, since that hardball bullet is loafing downrange at only 700 f.p.s. You won't do much better using hollow points in short barreled guns, since most of these are designed to expand only at full service velocities. Most of the 45 and 9mm loads I've tested in barrels as short as 3½ inches didn't expand reliably, if at all. You have to expect to give up some performance to get the compactness. The sad thing with most of these "chop jobs" is that you usually must spend a lot of money to get very little weight or size reduction. By now you've realized I'm prejudiced against these, and it's true, but it's based on experience. If you need full-sized performance, get a full-sized gun, unless you can find a factory-made one of the size you want, in the caliber you need. Fortunately, these are now more common than they used to be, and have been around long enough so that the bugs are out and the guns work.

There's a lot to say for compact pistols in some applications. A light semi-auto is handy on the trail, or as a backup piece for the police officer. Some of the small autos like the Star BKS or PD pistols are quite reliable and compact. Some people feel you gain enough in size and weight reduction to justify what you give up in ballistic performance. The Detonics and Star PD pistols are inherently accurate, if you can hold well with them.

For most trail use, though, a light 22 pistol is still the best choice, though some advocates of the 32 and 380 use them for small game hunting. An accurate pocket pistol in 22 LR, 32 ACP, or 380 ACP is about the most satisfying handgun a fellow could own. Now that good expanding ammunition such as the Winchester Silvertip HP is available in the 32 ACP and 380 ACP, it makes a lot more sense to carry one of these for trail use if you like. They hit sufficiently harder than a 22 to make a big difference on larger small game animals such as woodchucks. There's no disputing the fact that for defense they are far superior to a 22. If you keep one for defense, it would make sense to carry it afield to get accustomed to using it. The modifications useful in a pocket pistol are the same basic feeding and slicking up motions done on the service guns. Some locked-breech 380 pistols like the Llama lend themselves to accurizing like the M1911, but in miniature. I know one fellow who has a gun set up this way, and it's surprisingly accurate. Most pocket centerfires will shoot accurately enough out to 50 feet or so for small game, and they only require sight adjustment, or adding adjustable sights, such as the MMC, to make decent trail guns.

There are few real pocket automatics today, though, since none have been imported since 1968 and the U.S. makers don't produce any quality ones anymore. The fellow having a 1903 Colt, or M1922 Browning, Walther PPK or Remington 51 had better hold onto it. The current generation of pocket autos, such as the Walther PPK/S or PP, and the Astra Constable can usually be slicked up and tinkered with to make them reasonably accurate and reliable. However, I wouldn't swap my pre-war Colt Woodsman 22 for one.

The compact, accurate 22 automatic is the ultimate trail pistol, in my opinion. There are few light 22 pistols, however. It is possible to customize some of them to get them down to about 2 pounds which is getting into the trail gun category. Some people aren't bothered by my arbitrary weight limits, and feel enough weight for steady holding is highly desirable. The inherent accuracy of a 22 target pistol enables the good shot to do some amazing things with a scope sighted handgun. However, a scoped 22 pistol is hardly more convenient than a rifle. Still, it is smaller than a rifle, and shoots more like a rifle than a pocket pistol. I've seen and fired one customized Hi-Standard, which was written up in *American Rifleman* awhile back, which had an extra detachable 16½-inch rifle barrel with stock lug attached. The stock was attached to the barrel, and couldn't be used with the shorter 4½-inch tube. This prevented the little gun from violating the law. Although this rig weighs as much as a Remington Nylon 66, it takes apart cute and is more accurate than most ordinary 22 rifles. One-inch 10-shot groups at 25 yards were easy.

There's almost no limit to what an imaginative gunsmith can do to a good automatic pistol. Just make sure you get it done right, so it's safe, and so it works all the time. If the fellow can do that for you, I'll bet it's reasonably accurate, too.
            C.E. Harris

STATE OF THE ART
Hunting Handguns

ALTHOUGH handgun hunting is popularly thought of as a recent development, it isn't really. Handgun hunting as a *sport* is relatively new. Handgun hunting is not. Handgun hunters today use the short gun as a matter of choice, not necessity. They use it to increase the challenge and satisfaction of the hunt, by forcing themselves to get close and shoot well. The handgunner must be more of a hunter, a better stalker, and also a better shooter to collect his game. The rationale is the same as that used by blackpowder buffs and archers who use primitive weapons.

Early handgun hunters rarely shot the short gun for sport, but because the handgun was the available tool. Soldiers discharged after the Civil War would have gladly used a shotgun or rifle to forage game on the long trip home, but most felt lucky to have any kind of a gun at all. The frontiersman of that age was limited in what he could carry on horseback, and gladly used his handgun to shoot camp meat when possible in order to save his meager supply of heavy, precious and expensive rifle ammunition for more important targets like big game, outlaws or Indians. The revolver was something

Carol Jones can and does shoot a Thompson/Center in 375 JDJ, a hot wildcat, aided by the fitting of a Juenke brake. Such long-barreled handguns deliver rifle velocities to the chronograph under a wide range of conditions.

the westerner could always have with him. Movies and TV westerns depict the handgun as primarily a weapon, but it was also the humane horse killer, cattle slaughterer and food gatherer. Game killed with the revolver usually wasn't the act of deliberate handgun hunting, in the sense we know today. More often, a fellow happened to have a handgun with him when a deer or other animal came by, and there was a need for fresh meat. In the Old West, the handgun was typically the weapon of opportunity, while the rifle or shotgun was the one of planned deliberation.

Handgunners in the old days were handicapped by not having the powerful, accurate pistols, revolvers and good ammunition we enjoy today. In blackpowder days, the typical small game handgun was probably a 32-20, firing a 100-gr. lead bullet at about 900 f.p.s. compared to 1300 f.p.s. for the same round from a rifle. Big game handguns as we now know them didn't exist. Ammunition catalogs before 1900 sometimes cited the effectiveness of large-bore revolvers like the 45 Colt or 44-40 for deer or black bear. Their energy is low by today's standards, but in skilled hands, cartridges equivalent to those blackpowder loads can do the job at ranges under 25 yards. However, you wouldn't recommend them for big game today, since there are far more effective cartridges available.

Even the best handgun hunting rounds today are no match for a modern high-powered rifle. The 44 Magnum fired from a handgun compares closely with the 44-40 blackpowder load when fired from a rifle. Even the more powerful rifle rounds shot in the T/C Contender, such as the 30-30 Winchester or 35 Remington, lose about 200 f.p.s. compared to the same cartridge fired in a rifle. The 30-30 Contender compares closely to the old Super-X load for the 32-40 Winchester, and the 35 Remington is roughly equivalent to the 351 Winchester Self-Loading round. Neither of these are any great shakes as rifle cartridges. As for the smaller varmint cartridges, the 222 Remington is an excellent round for the Contender pistol, but gives velocities virtually equal to 22 Hornet handloads with the same weight bullet in a rifle.

If you accept the inherent limitations of the short barrel and apply them to practical hunting ranges, you aren't that bad off. The 35 Remington Contender will hit just as hard at 50 yards as the 35 Remington rifle will at about 150. The relative comparison is reasonably close for other cartridges like the 30-30 or 222 Remington. When you consider that most handgun hunting takes place at short ranges, the handgun hunter doesn't really give up that much. The important thing is that he must be able to shoot well at his shorter effective range and make his shots count. Provided a fellow can make good hits on game and doesn't exceed his or the gun's limitations, the handgun is a very challenging and entirely sporting alternative.

Most hunting handguns are only slightly modified factory guns. The only real custom hunting pistols are limited production ones like the single shot Merrill, and some questionable, over-powered hand cannons. Regardless of what you choose, however, getting the correct handgun stocks which give you a comfortable, secure grip are very important. Even in light calibers where recoil isn't a factor, a consistent grip is essential for accuracy. In the heavier magnums the right grips are

State of the Art: Hunting Handguns

essential to prevent injury, as well as to insure comfort and control. The original grip used with early T/C Contender pistols was downright painful when firing full loads in the 44 Magnum. The standard grip on the Merrill pistol is little better. Current Contender stocks, however, have been improved immensely, and T/C got the message from shooters and is now putting Herrett's stocks on all their pistols. Herrett's stocks on the T/C make even the 35 Remington manageable. I wouldn't have enjoyed firing such a load with the early, first-issue Contender stocks.

For revolvers, the heftier stocks like Herrett's Jordan Trooper or Shooting Master provide a good balance of comfort and control. If the stock is too bulky, you may have problems maintaining a consistent grip,

adequate, but other times you need something better. You have options, so use them.

It is necessary to distinguish between handguns carried as auxiliary equipment, and those carried as the primary hunting firearm, to the exclusion of others. An author whose name I can't remember now wrote in *American Rifleman* some time ago describing a *hunter's* handgun as a companion carried on outdoor trips when you didn't expect to need a firearm, but simply wanted one along. It might be used for snakes, recreational shooting, or finishing off a wounded big game animal without spoiling a trophy. The *hunting* handgun, he said, is the one which you have chosen to use *instead* of a rifle or shotgun. You use it out of choice and have no other gun with you. It is your primary firearm used in hunting. This is the best distinction of the purposes I've ever read.

Although most emphasis on handgun hunting in the

When it is available widely, experts believe Ruger's Redhawk will be one of the most-sought hunting handguns. Of course, there being none really available, the customizing details are yet to come, something to look forward to.

though too small a stock is uncomfortable in a heavy recoiling gun. A compromise is needed. Sharp checkering isn't a good idea on heavy recoiling guns either, since the hand takes a beating from it. I have often taken sandpaper to knock the tops off diamonds on S&W target grips used on the heavier calibers. For most handguns a smooth, but not slick, finish is best. In some cases you need a grip which is "sticky" when your hands are wet. An inexpensive and serviceable alternative is the Pachmayr Signature grip. These work fine for most revolvers. I don't care for them—though others do—on the Contender, because they don't seem solid enough. The "give" they have feels alright on a revolver.

On a handgun you use a lot for serious hunting, it's worth the money to get good stocks. Getting handgun stocks which fit right is just as important as having a rifle stock that fits. Many times the standard article is

shooting press is related to big game, most handgun hunting is probably for small game and varmints. This makes sense, since varmint hunting is something you can enjoy year-round, and it helps you become more proficient by the time deer season rolls around. Serious handgun hunters should spend a lot of time afield practicing their outdoor skills, as well as their shooting. Small game or varmint hunting is one of the best ways to accomplish this.

Ideally, you would want to use the same handgun for small game or varmints that you would use for big game, so the techniques you learn, the "muscle memory," is directly applicable to your final objective in the fall. With this in mind, you may wish to use lighter, frangible bullets in your magnum handgun. In sparsely settled country, using a 44 Magnum on rockchucks, for instance, is less of a problem. The best solution is a swap-barrel arrangement like the Merrill Sportsman or T/C Contender, which lets you have several barrels of different calibers to fit the same receiver. You can then use a 22 Long Rifle or 22 Hornet for edible small game, and a 44 Magnum or 30 Herrett for deer. Yet, the gun always feels the same.

Of course, you will probably enjoy using one of your

other handguns for small game hunting, and there's nothing wrong with that either. I know several avid handgun hunters who hunt nothing but small game and varmints, and they have more fun than almost anybody. They most often use scoped 22 target pistols, usually the S&W Model 41 or Hi-Standard Victor. Both are fine target pistol shots. Either of them can head-shoot a squirrel from an improvised rest at 50 yards about as easily as I can with a rifle. They don't feel the least bit handicapped. They shoot well enough to make most rifle squirrel hunters feel downright inadequate. One of these guys also owns a T/C Contender which he shoots in either 22 Long Rifle, 22 WMR or 22 Hornet, depending upon his mood that day. If, when testing loads, he finds anything that gives him a 5-shot group as large as 2 inches at 50 yards, he forgets it and goes on to something else. People who don't appreciate that a good customized handgun is a precision instrument

targets at relatively long, unknown ranges. They are best for relatively large targets not exceeding about 50 yards. On small game they are best not over about 25 yards.

Getting a good sighting arrangement usually means a scope sight. Thank goodness this is easier today than it once was. Handgun hunters can thank the handgun silhouette folks for prompting the scope manufacturers to design rugged instruments which will handle the recoil of today's heavy loads, while providing good optical quality and repeatable adjustments. The handgun scopes we have today are excellent and are a far cry from those even a few years ago.

The most important factor in scope mounts for handguns is that they be solid enough to stay put, without loosening or shifting under recoil. Most scopes will hold zero if installed and left alone, but there are no readily available handgun mounts which are quick detachable

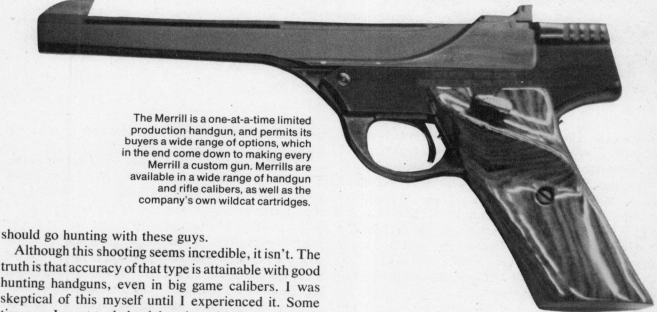

The Merrill is a one-at-a-time limited production handgun, and permits its buyers a wide range of options, which in the end come down to making every Merrill a custom gun. Merrills are available in a wide range of handgun and rifle calibers, as well as the company's own wildcat cartridges.

should go hunting with these guys.

Although this shooting seems incredible, it isn't. The truth is that accuracy of that type is attainable with good hunting handguns, even in big game calibers. I was skeptical of this myself until I experienced it. Some time ago I went rockchuck hunting with Steve Herrett, who is certainly one of the nicest people and greatest handgun hunters ever. I felt a little sheepish when I showed up with a 22 Hornet rifle. When Steve started hitting them surer and out farther than I could with the little rifle in the wind, he remarked, "Put that *toy* back in the truck and go get yourself a *real* gun." I swapped the little Sako for a T/C Contender in 30 Herrett and have been hooked ever since. I was amazed what it would do. Within a few days I was almost holding my own with Steve, busting the chucks solidly out to around 150 yards, and getting occasional ones farther. Steve feels any load in his 30 which shoots as large as 3 inches at 100 yards is "bad." His best ones will do about half that on a good day.

The most important thing in getting the potential out of a hunting handgun is having sights you can see. Good target iron sights are OK for a lot of hunting, but they aren't really suitable for low light conditions or on small

and permit the shooter to remove the scope or replace it easily without loss of zero. This means that the handgunner must carry the scope attached to the gun whenever afield. This presents obvious problems in protecting the scope from damage and in holstering.

The best holster style for hunting handguns is a shoulder holster, though holsters that accommodate scoped handguns are few and far between. The best I've seen are those sold by Thompson/Center for the Contender pistol. Though made especially for the T/C, they will also accommodate some large-frame revolvers. When so used they may require the safety strap be placed through the trigger guard rather than behind it, which I don't like. A longer strap is better and safer. George Lawrence Co. makes a hip holster for the T/C Contender or other scoped handguns, though it leaves the scope exposed. It is then prone to pick up dirt, grass and lint. The T/C shoulder holster covers the scope so it

139

State of the Art: Hunting Handguns

Here is a very custom Thompson/Center fitted with very standard stocks. The stocks are Pachmayr's neoprene grip and fore-end, but the barrel here is a Mag-na-ported 45-70. The gun belongs to Hal Swiggett, who uses it for what it is made for—hunting.

Thompson/Center Contender is far out in the forefront of the special hunting handgun. This standard model with special stocks, scoped, typifies the early breed. Guns like this one gave rise to later, more evolved T/Cs.

is protected. The market is ripe for a good holster maker to provide a shoulder holster for hunters which will accommodate a variety of handguns with scope sights.

The handiest arrangement on scope mounting I have seen was thought up by a hunting buddy of mine who doubles as a part-time gunsmith. I was rebarreling my Ruger Security Six 357 Magnum anyway for use as a combination PPC and silhouette gun and decided it should be scoped to make it a multi-purpose firearm. Chuck agreed, and upon deliberate examination of the situation proposed an ambitious, but ingenious solution. Since the barrel was to be machined from a blank anyway, we'd machine integral scope bases on it. I wanted quick-detachable rings which would return to zero and provide a clean sight plane for the irons when the scope was detached. I had used Ruger rings on several of my rifles and had confidence in them, so bases for the Ruger rigs were machined into the barrel's integral rib. The machining job itself isn't all that difficult, though it requires a milling machine. The mounting sytem works like a charm. Since then, I've seen him use the same arrangement on a Browning Challenger 22 pistol, a Ruger Mark I and a Bo-Mar ribbed 45 match gun. As for repeatability of zero, the outfit is outstanding. I have fired several 10-shot groups at 200 meters, taking off and replacing the scope between every shot, which were inside the 7-inch 10-ring of the military SR target. Any time you can take a 6-inch barreled 357 Magnum out of the holster, mount the scope in about 30 seconds and hit one of the rifle chickens off the sandbags on demand at 200 meters, you can't

complain. It's not bad on woodchucks out to about 100 yards either.

This job is strictly custom work, but I have hopes this type of option may someday become an over-the-counter thing. I've shown my revolver to several major manufacturers and custom gunsmiths, who viewed it with more than idle curiosity. In the meantime, a solid mount (which you should leave alone) and a reliable scope sight is probably the best arrangement. While the more powerful 4x scopes are popular for silhouette shooting, those more than about 2½x are awfully hard to use in any position but sitting or prone. I have used the 4x Leupold for shooting chucks from a rest, and it works fine there, but the field of view is small, and its hard to hold steady offhand. I prefer the Leupold 2x, Redfield 1½x, or the T/C 2½x for most hunting, though the higher power scopes would be better for varmint hunting at longer ranges. Many silhouette scopes have short eye relief which isn't well suited for use from a variety of field positions. For this reason the Leupold and Redfield scopes seem better suited for general hunting use for me than the T/C scopes.

Aside from the target 22s for varmint shooting, there are few suitable semi-automatic pistols for hunting. Shooters occasionally use accurized 45s and such for varmints, but there are no readily available big game autoloaders. The Automag pistol was an interesting concept, but never really got off the ground, due to functioning and production problems. It is no longer made. The Wildey automatic pistol might get a better shot at success than the Automag, but only time will tell. Neither the 9mm Magnum nor 45 Winchester Magnum cartridges seem to offer anything to the hunter he can't get with the 357 Magnum, 44 Magnum, or 45 Colt, loaded in a strong pistol like the Contender. I'm not convinced the semi-auto pistol offers any real advantage for hunting over the revolver. Some hunters might try to use fire-power as a substitute for shot placement, which couldn't do much but give handgun hunting a sour image. I confess to being a traditionalist, and I suppose we'll have to accept the semi-auto hunting pistol when it comes, but it isn't here yet.

You can make significant improvements in performance by upgrading barrel quality or providing longer barrels for increased sight radius with iron sights. Longer barrels also give higher velocities. Long barrel 22 pistols are particularly pleasant, being more quiet and quite accurate. They also hold steadier. Barrels much longer than about 8 inches are awkward to carry afield, except on the T/C Contender, but even there I prefer the shorter 10-inch barrel to the Super 14. The standard 10-inch barrel Contender seems to shoot every bit as well as the long barrel gun, is a lot handier to carry, and gives up very little in striking energy.

Generally, though, there isn't a lot of need to rebarrel if your present gun suits you and is accurate. If you have a long barreled silhouette revolver, it might work for hunting, but a very long barreled handgun is little more convenient to carry than a rifle, unless you can find a way to holster it. Most often, you rebarrel a gun in the course of conversion to another caliber. You might, for instance, want a long barreled 22 pistol. A chunk of 22 target rifle barrel fits up easily to a Hi-Standard semi-auto pistol frame, and gives you a heavy tube as

long as you want it. The Ruger semi-auto has the same potential for only a little more work. I've seen one 6-inch barrel Ruger Bearcat which was customized by a fellow a few years back. It shot great and was a nice handling little gun. Other possibilities for rebarreling are almost endless, putting 4- or 5-inch custom barrels on small frame 38 revolvers to make small, steady holding, accurate, possibly adjustable-sighted centerfire kit guns; converting large frame 357 or 41 Magnums to 44 Special or 45 Colts, etc.

Some rebarreling and cartridge conversions don't make sense, however. There is a whole cult of shooters who want to see how big a cartridge they can fire in a handgun. The Remington XP100 and the T/C Contender are popular candidates for such conversions, but you also see them on the Merrill single shot and in custom-made over-sized revolvers of Paul Bunyan proportions. Personally, I think anybody who feels he needs anything larger than what is already offered by the factories is either a glutton for punishment, or has some kind of machismo complex. I've shot the 44 Magnum in revolvers and in the T/C a great deal. I'm no stranger to recoil, and while I don't relish it with pleasure like some people, I'm less sensitive than a lot of shooters. I don't find shooting a custom 3-inch barrel 44 Magnum snubby, with full-house loads, or the Contender in 35 Remington with factory 200-gr. loads a great deal of fun, but I've done both and didn't shoot all that badly. But while I'd use either of those arms for their chosen purposes, I feel anybody who needs more than that, or thinks he does, ought to be carrying a rifle.

Not long ago I saw a fellow who had a 35 Remington Super 14 that somebody rechambered to 358 Winches-

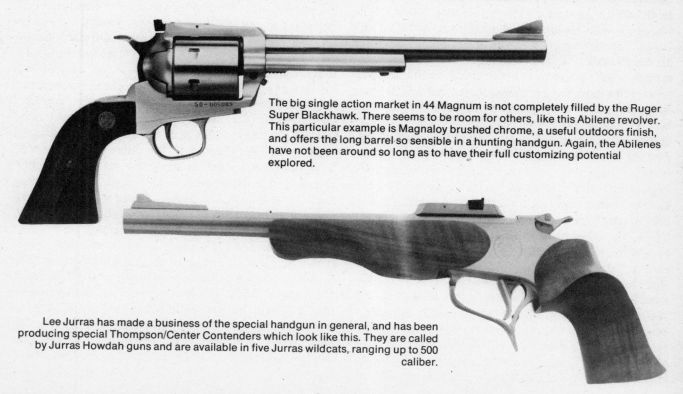

The big single action market in 44 Magnum is not completely filled by the Ruger Super Blackhawk. There seems to be room for others, like this Abilene revolver. This particular example is Magnaloy brushed chrome, a useful outdoors finish, and offers the long barrel so sensible in a hunting handgun. Again, the Abilenes have not been around so long as to have their full customizing potential explored.

Lee Jurras has made a business of the special handgun in general, and has been producing special Thompson/Center Contenders which look like this. They are called by Jurras Howdah guns and are available in five Jurras wildcats, ranging up to 500 caliber.

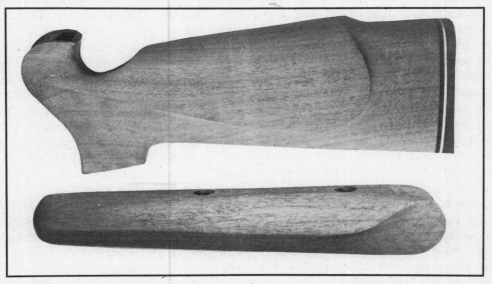

(Above and below) From Marshal, one can get this outfit which will make a legal rifle out of a Thompson/Center handgun, provided a long enough barrel is in place. The result is, users say, a very handy, very lightweight, usable carbine which can be put together in a wide range of calibers suitable for hunting.

ter. Neither T/C nor I recommend this one at all, as it really isn't a good idea. The Contender action works very well with rounds developing up to about 45,000 c.u.p. The 358 Winchester, however, usually operates at over 50,000 c.u.p. The Contender is a robust gun, and probably isn't going to come unglued on the first pop with such a load, but exceeding its normal design limits isn't smart. You might get away with it for awhile, but how long is anybody's guess.

Pressure is expressed in copper units which are roughly equivalent to pounds per square inch. But the number of units isn't the only thing, since every bit as important is the number of square inches you've got. Lee Jurras has concocted a series of rounds in 375, 460 and 500 calibers based on a shortened 465 N.E. case. These are claimed to be the world's most powerful handguns, the 375 Jurras throwing a 285-gr. bullet at over 1,700 f.p.s. and the 500 Jurras lobbing a 400-gr. slug at almost 1200 f.p.s. The head diameter of the Jurras case is .570-inch, and averages about 2 inches long, depending on caliber. The 500 Jurras case swallows a 44 Magnum round with ease. With the obvious increase in chamber area, it doesn't take much imagination to realize that the Contender wasn't intended to handle a round that large, even though its pressures (hopefully) aren't even close to those of the smaller ones ordinarily chambered in it. These over-sized cartridges are more of a stunt than a practical option.

Other experimenters are making 45-70 barrels and creating other exotic oversized wildcats for the single shots. This seems kind of pointless to me. In the 45-70, for instance, it's hard to utilize the entire powder capacity in rifles, except with a strong-actioned gun like the Ruger No. 3. Then you have something more akin to a 458 Winchester. Some of the new cartridges being used in the XP100, such as the 7mm Remington BR have promising potential since that gun is incredibly strong, and standardized chamber data and loads will soon become available, as they have for the 30 Herrett and 357 Herrett. But some of the wildcats which must be loaded by guess and by God are scary.

The whole point of custom work is to get something better than you can get as a standard item. You must first make sure it will do what you expect of it, then go get it done right. Spending money on a hare-brained idea is a waste, but a brainstorm can develop into a good project if you give it time and planning. How you go about it, and how far you go with it, is up to you. For hunting, whatever you do to get that first shot in there is worth it.

C. E. Harris

Embellishment

FIRST on the list of the extra things that people want to do to fine guns is engrave them. In fact, a lot of people want to engrave guns that aren't fine guns, as an inspection of a number of "The Art of the Engraver" pages from *Gun Digest* over the years will reveal.

Whole books, of course, have been written about engraving and not covered the subject. This is because there are, in the first place, many levels of engraving, both in terms of mechanical ability and artistic talent. Then, there are styles of engraving, meaning how individual lines are cut in the metal, ranging from heavy work to work so light you can see it only with the aid of good illumination; and there are schools of engraving—

meaning that the Germans have their classic style, as do the British, and the American factories, and so on. And then, there is the combination of engraving in steel with inlaid metals, with plating and other coloring, and even, so help me, in combination with gems and precious stones set into the steel. Because of this complexity we will here try to confine the discussion to the kind of engraving more or less easily available to Americans who are having fine or special guns created for themselves or as gifts.

I say as gifts because one of the classic American presentations is an engraved handgun. That has meant, in the past, a Colt or a Smith & Wesson or a Browning.

This matched pair of rifles by Jerry Fisher, with Burgess metalwork and John Warren engraving are elegant at a distance and richly so close-up. The full and matching coverage of the engraving is not so profuse as to keep the rifle from coming through. Both are short Mauser actions; one is a 22-250, the other a 243. They're owned by Bud McCollum and were built for him.

This is John Warren engraving on a pair of short Mauser actions, built to match by Jerry Fisher. The full-covering scroll and inlay work—the animals are gold—is worthy of the rifles, which may be one of the very best matched pairs ever built.

State of the Art: Embellishment

Indeed, Browning made quite a thing of engraved specimens as a standard offering in the catalog. Regardless, police officers, military people, and sportsmen who have been of service to one or another kind of sporting organization have long had their services commemorated by the creation of a special gun just for them. No less a personage than Samuel Colt may have begun it. Certainly, part of his sales technique was the presentation of embellished Colts to personages of importance; this gave rise, it seems, to people ordering Colts embellished, sometimes to a great degree, sometimes only lightly, for presentation to valued friends.

Generally, such guns then and since, are engraved with cut foliate and scroll designs in a variety of coverages, beginning with the frame of the handgun, down the sides and over the top. Next, trigger guard and backstrap could be added to the coverage, then a portion of the barrel at the rear, and then perhaps at the front, and from that point a fully engraved gun was possible by simply filling in the available space. Such guns were often further decorated by furnishing them with extra special stocks of fine hardwood, pearl, or, especially, ivory, either smooth or carved.

Once engraved, the gun might be blued, or plated in silver or gold, or sometimes even a mixture of bluing and plating. In this case, the result is always showy. In fact, the combination of plating and bluing is by itself so striking that some skip the engraving for a fancy gun without much cost or effort.

The engraved handgun is, to a large degree, the genesis of all engraved guns in American thinking. The factories offer them decorated in standard patterns, identified ordinarily with alpha denominations: A, B, C and so on. Over the latter half of the 19th century it was possible for firms of engravers to exist, at least in part, doing work for the firearms industry to fill these wishes on the part of the eventual customers.

It is not that long guns were left out, not at all. All the major factories offered embellished arms at greater cost; eventually, in the case of the shotgun makers, this evolved into catalog offerings of increasingly fancy guns, with extra quality wood and extra quality treat-

The embellishment of fine firearms is accomplished by hands and hand tools, driven by intense concentration, the work shaped by a sense of style and design and the mastery of technique. This is a Malin & Son worker.

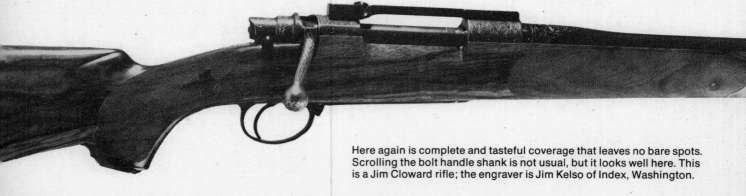

Here again is complete and tasteful coverage that leaves no bare spots. Scrolling the bolt handle shank is not usual, but it looks well here. This is a Jim Cloward rifle; the engraver is Jim Kelso of Index, Washington.

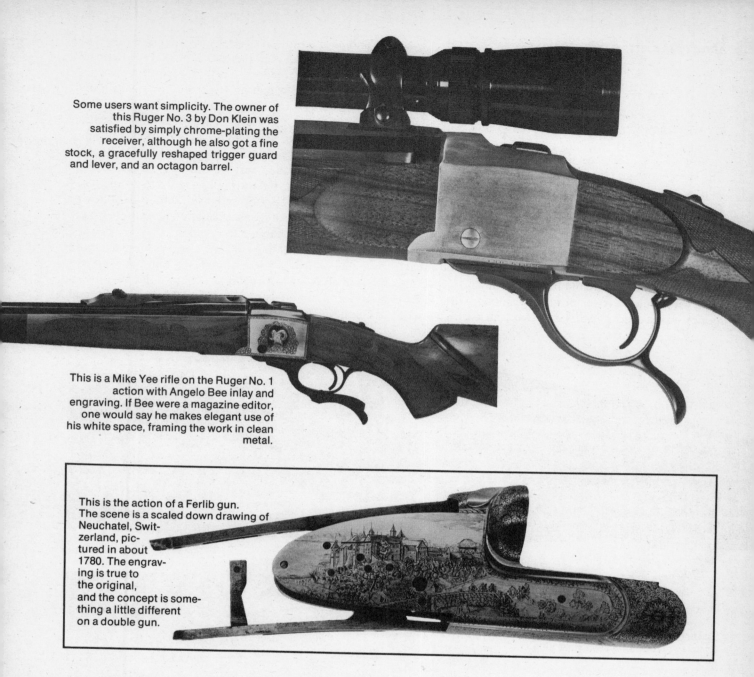

Some users want simplicity. The owner of this Ruger No. 3 by Don Klein was satisfied by simply chrome-plating the receiver, although he also got a fine stock, a gracefully reshaped trigger guard and lever, and an octagon barrel.

This is a Mike Yee rifle on the Ruger No. 1 action with Angelo Bee inlay and engraving. If Bee were a magazine editor, one would say he makes elegant use of his white space, framing the work in clean metal.

This is the action of a Ferlib gun. The scene is a scaled down drawing of Neuchatel, Switzerland, pictured in about 1780. The engraving is true to the original, and the concept is something a little different on a double gun.

ment of that wood, together with engraving, and engraving in fancy modes, culminating in guns at the very top, sold at what were then astronomical prices, called "excelsior" or the like.

They all did it, to all guns. It is not terribly unusual to find, for example, an engraved and original Remington Model 8 autoloading rifle; Marlin lever-action hunting rifles done up very fancily may be seen, now most of them collected together at gun shows each year; certainly Winchester was not backward in its prettying up of virtually every model they ever made.

For the most part, all of this American engraving, done by and for the factories, is just that—American engraving. Most of it is, by the highest standards of the art, relatively routine, but hardly any of it is unattractive. There seems to be, or to have been, a certain lustiness of approach to decorating their guns, or the guns they sold that—to my eyes, at least—carries what I know to be relatively rudimentary technique sometimes to excellence, nonetheless.

These days, except for our handguns, and one must admit that, whether or not the fact is based on fact, handguns are very American, we have grown far more sophisticated in our demands of the embellishers when it comes to our fine guns. People these days presume to have opinions—properly—whether or not Purdey's new scrollwork is up to the old standards. Many, these days, have come to know that the bulk of German engraving is the routine application of a surface finish by journeymen. Certainly, those who can describe, contract for, and acquire a best-quality American-fashioned sporting firearm are more and more happy

State of the Art: Embellishment

with the artistry of the stockmaker and the metal finisher alone unless they can have the very best engraving. Engraving of a routine nature is simply avoided by such people.

Now, it is time, let us say, to have a gun engraved. The stock work and the metal finishing is complete and, as it is, suits. There is something between $1,000 and $5,000 invested, thus far. It is now time to consider the matter very carefully. It could also have been time to consider the matter *before* the whole project started and arrange, in the same fashion, as one should now.

Given that one has seen engraving of a character that suits, then the man who did that engraving is the one to start with. Send a letter of inquiry, along with a little money on the order of a dollar or two, and ask for a price list and photographs if available. Sometimes this effort is better carried out on the telephone, which depends, of course, on the freedom to call during normal business hours. Regardless, one must get in touch with a man who does engraving known to be satisfactory.

From thereon, the whole matter becomes a question of finding the man who can do a good enough job in a time frame that is acceptable at a price that can be met. The very best choice may be too busy; the next best might be available, but too high priced; a third might not be interested in the job; and so it will go until somewhere among the dozens of engravers and engraving shops, a suitable bargain is struck.

What do you tell them? Well, if you say you want full coverage on a given sort of gun, without gold, the engraver will want to know if you want a fine scroll or a large scroll, if you want scenes and if so what sort, and ask in detail just how much of the gun you wish to be

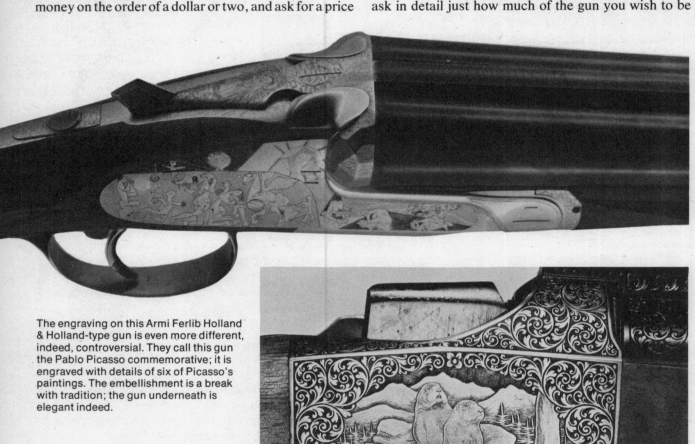

The engraving on this Armi Ferlib Holland & Holland-type gun is even more different, indeed, controversial. They call this gun the Pablo Picasso commemorative; it is engraved with details of six of Picasso's paintings. The embellishment is a break with tradition; the gun underneath is elegant indeed.

This is the work of Claus Willig, accomplished in deep scroll with a light touch for the scene. The rest of the gun is heavily embellished, as one can see.

covered. Once he knows that, he then can price the job. It is advisable to be seated when opening a quotation letter from an engraver. The contents are often shocking. One can be bolstered in his fortitude by the fact that the finished first-class gun, with a finished first-class engraving job, is worth some increment above the cost when once they are all put together. That is, in broad general terms, a $3,000 gun with a $1,500 engraving job, in the hand and all complete, probably has a value much closer to $6,000 than $4,500.

When it comes right down to it, mystery and art though it is, engraving, to an engraver, is a job of work. He knows how long it takes to do the various sorts of chores involved and he has a price for his labor and he simply adds it all up to reach a total. Gold inlays are, for instance, simply so many dollars each, depending, of course, on whether they are small or medium or large. Areas of scroll or arabesque or foliage are charged virtually by the square inch. Scenes are a little more problematical, depending on the particular skill and talent level of the engraver. Still, an average scene will cost a given amount of money.

Why aren't you reading prices here? Well, in the first place, every engraver is individual about his pricing; in the second place, engravers sometimes need work more badly than they do other times and they strike bargains; the inflation we are in seems to affect such labor-intensive high grade efforts as engraving even more strongly than it does the price of meat at the supermarket. There is, in short, no telling where prices will go by the time this volume has been printed and delivered to you and you have purchased it and taken it home and read it. It seems, therefore, far better to explain what is in the other man's mind and the problems he has to solve than to try to give real dollar guidelines.

It may be, and this is said with some trepidation because it has been thought before, that it is going to get

Perhaps typical of the kind of things that suit hunting rifles is this trigger guard and floorplate from Paul Jaeger. The game scene surrounded by scroll seems to suit any hunting rifle.

Full coverage, again, is very expensive and very handsome. The gold running sheep on this floorplate, which is on a Jaeger rifle, is a particularly striking composition.

This is a different sort of embellishment although it is cut engraving. This bolder, less-schooled, job is a Bortmess Gun Co. Sako hunting rifle. The coverage is full but much of that is stippling in the background. Cut deep and executed with a flair, such an approach has its own charm.

This Famars Jorena smallbore shotgun is graced with a different sort of scroll Famars can do and a bulino game scene of considerable dictinction.

From pistol grip cap to the front of the trigger guard, this Heide Hiptmayer engraving is all of a piece. That is, the embellishment flows properly from one point to the other, even though this is not full coverage engraving.

easier and easier to embellish fine guns in the future. To that end, a fellow named Ken Hurst is, in Virginia, some months into an experiment which, if it works, will absolutely make firearms embellishment easier. Hurst, an engraver himself, is in the process of discovering that American art students, treated fairly, can be taught to do firearms engraving of all kinds. On page 151 we show pictures—something like rubbings—from bulino work that Hurst's student craftsmen are producing after only a few months of trial. It is quite creditable.

Hurst is not running a school, as such. What he wants to do is offer fine work, reasonably priced and delivered on a reasonable schedule. He is in the process of discovering that he can offer speeded-up apprenticeships. As soon as his workers are good enough, he puts them to work and pays them at a fair hourly rate.

How can he do it? Well, he is discovering that there is an untold amount of embellishment work out there. He gets six to 12 jobs in a week from one gunshop in North Carolina. They are working on Winchester 22 rifles, American shotguns, revolvers, and even high-grade foreign guns. They do a great deal of work with

Another Bortmess Sako, cut boldly with an interesting use of a receiver surface to provide a sort of small painting.

This is the front end of a Bortmess Sako rifle, cut lavishly in large scroll with much use of stippling for a background and the use of the relatively square-shaped receiver surface to create a small "painting."

Shown in the white, is a classic pistol grip cap as furnished by Paul Jaeger. People have preferences in the scroll and design of such caps, but any well done concentric design seems to grace a gun, when well polished and blued.

Bold and isolated banknote scrolls provide more than the ordinary surface interest in this all-of-a-piece combination, an optional treatment on the Famars smallbore.

Ruger shotguns. Hurst is very high on the future of such activity. He can and does seek out bulk jobs—250 handguns, perhaps, for an importer who wishes to catalog them; he has risen to offering a standard embellishment for the Ruger Over-Under; he thinks that his young artists, working under close supervision to a standard they can understand, are learning how at a rate even he finds hard to believe.

"If they are right for it, they really enjoy the work," he says. "And on the bigger jobs I cannot control them. We are working to a quote of so many hours, of course, but I find them in here late, making sure the job is good by putting in extra time. I frankly don't know whether they have decided to work slower to make it better, or whether they are doing something extra, and I suspect it is a little of both."

If the work is good enough and it all goes as Hurst now sees it might, this will be a breakthrough in fine guns. Part of the problem in buying engraving is that most American engravers are teaching themselves or have taught themselves, and engravers trained abroad come from a school and a situation designed as much to limit the number of engravers as to provide the service.

Whether or not it is meant to do just that, the several-years apprenticeship does do it.

For now, however, it is necessary to review the "Art of the Engraver" pages that appeared and appear in *Gun Digest* every year to find the spirit and approach one likes, and then seek out that artist. When the artist is very good, the delays are likely to be considerable unless the job is both extensive and expensive.

In general, engravers differentiate themselves or the jobs by whether they are light scroll work, deep-cut work, or something inbetween. There are engravers who work with a *bulino* style creating the entire effect in a scene with a very thin point, in the style of banknotes. How an engraver works definitely has an effect on the price. Some techniques are simply faster than others and, at the bottom of it all, an engraver is covering so many square inches of metal with a pattern. He is entitled to a good wage for his time; the total paid for any given number of square inches depends on their difficulty.

How to judge quality? That is the eternal question throughout the whole series of operations which are involved in creating a custom gun. Virtually all Ameri-

State of the Art: Embellishment

This is the very British-looking bottom of the Fausto Massi gun made in Brescia stocked by Maurice Ottmar. Massi furnished the engraving, in which the scroll is only slightly larger than what is thought of as typical British scrollwork. In a gun cabinet, this would catch the eye.

cans carry with them at all times splendid examples of formal engraving. These are to be found on American currency. Just take bills of several denominations out of your pocket and look at them. It is better to work with clean money, but all money is nicely engraved here. You will find, in the corners, interesting scroll work, and often there will be foliate engraving surrounding scenes and some of the numbers; the edges of the whole pattern demonstrate how gracefully borders can be marked out. Understand, this is not, except for some small details, the kind of engraving one finds on guns, but it is very good engraving and an eye used to it in detail will be able to look at engraving on a gun and reach some sort of judgment.

One must look at the arcs, which should be portions of true circles; leaves should get smaller, not larger as tendrils of foliate engraving spread across the gun; there certainly should never be any coarse stippled background; the pattern must grow within the space it occupies and not be jammed in. It is an unfortunate tendency among some beginning engravers to make a little bit of effort go a long way by providing small elements and large amounts of background. That ought to be avoided.

That is not to say that the character of some guns does not sort itself out very nicely with coarse en-

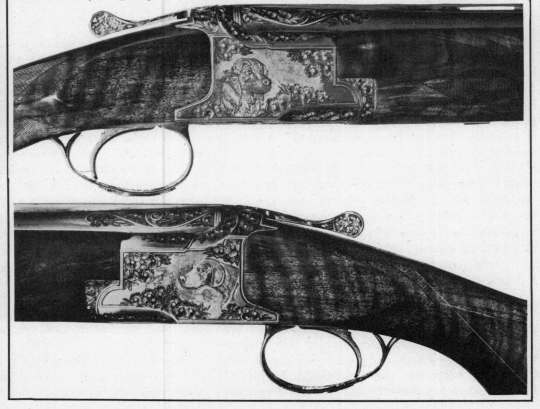

This Browning Superposed 20 stocked by Mike Yee has been engraved by Dan O'Brien, very likely with portraits of the owner's dogs framed by worked foliage. The choice of floral patterns was dictated: There are six karats of diamonds inlaid into this gun. On the left side O'Brien's confidence on his touch can be seen by comparing two sides—each is a separate composition, but they go well together.

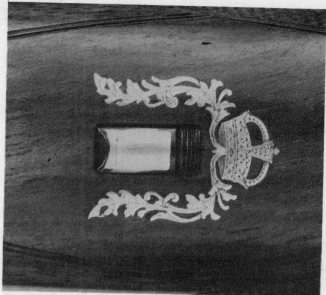

Occasionally, one finds metal inlaid in wood in pleasing pattern. This is a detail from a Famars Jorena shotgun, and appears on the fore-end around the fore-end latch.

These muggy looking illustrations of a small squirrel and a goose are actually made from pieces of scotchtape which have been pressed over inked surfaces on a gun. This bulino work was produced by Jack Jones and Bill Schackelford who, respectively, have exactly 5 months and 2 months working experience at the Ken Hurst Firearms Engraving Co. in Lynchburg, Virginia.

graving—large scrolls, dashingly executed, deeply cut, as an example. We cannot all love the fine and delicate and elegant guns; some of us like gutsier things. Real artists among the engravers can adapt the character of their work in this way to suit either the owner or the gun at hand.

Personally, for instance, I have long felt that fine scroll, let us say done in rosettes as on English shotguns, is simply out of place on a Colt single action handgun. I have seen perfectly charming six-guns decorated with representations of cattle brands; but cattle brands, one must admit, would be simply awful on a sidelock shotgun. It is both characteristic these days, and a good plan, for a bolt-action hunting rifle to be embellished with scroll and leaf patterns, coupled with animated scenes, often of animals themselves, sometimes done up in gold. Hunting rifles don't ordinarily get arabasque patterns, and possibly should not. Neither are they the right place for large bold scroll, it seems. In the fine hunting rifle, of bolt-action design, some understatement seems to suit the general character of a hunting rifle best. That goes even when there is gold inlaying to be done. A little bit of gold goes a long way on a hunting rifle, where twice that amount might look good on a double-barrel shotgun.

The way to achieve your own opinions in these matters is to look critically at a large number—or as large a number as you can lay hands on—of engraved firearms. There is no substitute for that and one ought not try for any shortcuts.

There is more to embellishing a gun than engraving, of course.

There is etching. This work, in which designs are worked in steel by the action of acid, has become increasingly more sophisticated over the past years. It is often used at the factory for standard embellishments, both here and abroad. It is a relatively inexpensive way to get quite complex decoration accomplished. There is, at the moment, a considerable vogue for etching on high-grade knives and it could be expected that some guns will be etched to order on a custom basis from time to time.

As it happens, I own an etched Model 98 Mauser action, a Spanish version. I got the action from the U.S. representative of La Coruna Arsenal, as a matter of

Some people have guns made to suit a rather lighthearted approach to life, and this shotgun receiver from R. D. Wallace is an example. Pan and his companion are prancing on the side of a Winchester Model 24 "camp gun." The big scrolls and hidden grotesques virtually cover this short shotgun and probably give its owner great joy.

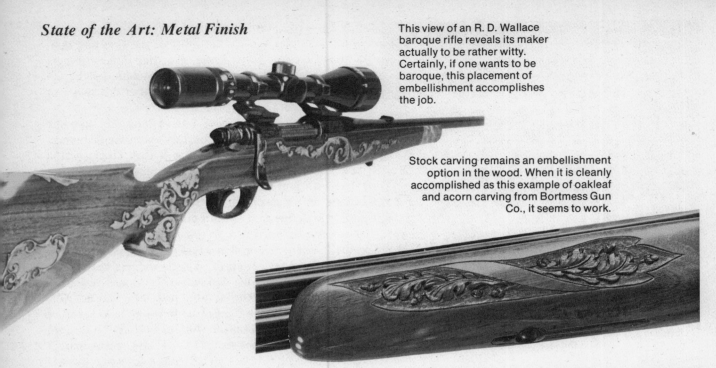

This view of an R. D. Wallace baroque rifle reveals its maker actually to be rather witty. Certainly, if one wants to be baroque, this placement of embellishment accomplishes the job.

Stock carving remains an embellishment option in the wood. When it is cleanly accomplished as this example of oakleaf and acorn carving from Bortmess Gun Co., it seems to work.

fact. It is etched in a scroll pattern and, while no one would ever mistake it for engraving, the job is not unattractive.

One hears, from time to time, that engravers occasionally etch a pattern and then touch it up by cutting. However often it may be used, that particular combination of techniques, is not yet fully accepted among those who buy good guns.

Occasionally, guns, either plain or fancy, are plated in precious metals, but plating alone is not a fine finish for a fine gun. Now, a plated *interior* is a very nice touch. Many fine shotguns have plated lockwork, in fact gold-plated lockwork, to guard them against rust. That is a very classy way to keep the inside of a gun saved from moisture.

Apart from checkering, one sometimes finds excellent guns with carved stocks. This is particularly popular in Germany. Apart from scrolls and other kinds of line work, including the carving of foliage, particularly oak leaves, one occasionally will find scenes carved in panels on the buttstock. And occasionally fine workers will embellish with carving what must be called the "corners" of a buttstock—the space immediately behind the pistol grip, the heel and the toe, and maybe a little space around a cheekpiece if one is present.

In general, the fine gun fanciers don't think much of carving. Well done, it is all right for those who like it, the feeling runs, but it is not the style these days. My own view is that someone who is willing to spend a great deal of money to have a gun that suits him and who likes carving may as well get it. Even more than checkering, however, he should buy only the best. Carving that looks absolutely splendid on a piece of furniture is ordinarily far too gross for something as small as a gunstock.

It all boils down to this: The best embellishment for a firearm is lots of first-class engraving, done to a relatively conservative taste. It is important that the concepts for any scenes relate either to the history of the owner or the potential use of the gun. Really good engraving always pays for itself by adding more than its cost to the value of the gun.

Ken Warner

STATE OF THE ART

Metal Finish

ALTHOUGH many muzzle-loading guns in days gone by were left bright, they didn't stay that way for long. The rigors of normal wear, combined with the effects of blackpowder residue soon turned the bright polished gun into a dingy, grayish brown, unless it was painstakingly cared for. Rust, fouling and the weather have always been enemies of the gun owner, but metal finishes make the job of protecting guns somewhat less difficult today than it was years ago.

Our most popular firearms finishes—browning, bluing, and blacking—are nothing more than "controlled rust" processes. Browning of muzzleloaders is nothing more than a fine rust. It has been said of browning that, "The hard part isn't getting the color, it's stopping the action . . ." The same can be said of other controlled rust processes, such as cold-rust blue. If the cold-rust process is rushed the steel will pit, and the bluing must be started all over again.

While most traditional finishes are oxidizing proc-

When you go to the trouble of having someone checker the bolt knob, stock a rifle to your taste, choose a special caliber—do all the things that make a custom rifle —the only thing to do is also get the deluxe rust blue treatment, which gleams softly and, more than other blues, stays goodlooking even after it wears as the rifle grows old with you.

esses, others involve protective coatings applied to the steel which protect it from moisture, abrasion or corrosive agents. These include the various plating processes such as hard chrome, nickel, (which can be applied in several ways), Teflon, and chemical treatments such as Parkerizing. Each has its own peculiar characteristics and certain advantages for some purposes. But they may have disadvantages for others. Picking the right finish for a certain job can be important and isn't always a matter of just picking what "looks" best.

The blue steel finish is every bit as traditional on modern guns as the brown finish is to muzzleloaders. However, there are several methods which can be used to achieve it. The one used depends mostly upon the result desired. While most new factory guns are blued by the hot black oxide process, this cannot be used on old double-barrel shotguns or combination guns with soft-soldered barrels. These guns are done by the cold rust process. The cold rust blue is preferred for many high-grade custom guns, even when you don't have to worry about the soft-soldered parts, because it gives a nicer finish which is more durable than the usual black oxide, hot-dip blue.

Metal preparation governs the final quality of the blue job to a marked degree. The best chemicals can't produce a fine finish on a poorly prepared surface. The steel used in the firearm will also affect the type and quality of finish, since some modern steels with high nickel or chrome content will not take a traditional cold rust blue. Most stainless steels won't respond to the hot black oxide process, though there are means to black some types of stainless, such as 410 or 416 which are often used in gun barrels. The Heatbath Corporation has a process for bluing stainless steel, and several gunsmiths specialize in this work. These methods sometimes involve treatment of the steel in various acids, and then staining with organic dyes, while other lower-alloy stainless steels can be blued in an ordinary hot-dip tank using virtually the same process used for ordinary steels, but with different chemicals. Often

153

these chemicals can be used with chrome-moly and similar steels as well.

Most custom rifles start in-the-white, and stripping the old finish won't be necessary. Guns which have been finished should be stripped by pickling in hydrochloric acid. This reduces a lot of the polishing time required and gets all the old finish out of the corners, making heavy polishing unnecessary to clean them. This is a big help in keeping all the corners sharp and contours true. An acid etch thoroughly cleans the steel surface so it will take any type of finish better. The stripped parts are first degreased in the detergent and rinsed in boiling water. Then they are dipped for a minute or two in a 25 percent solution of hydrochloric acid, and rinsed in hot soda water and dried. Then they can be polished as required.

Tight contours inside trigger guards, etc., are done on flexible shaft attachments with various shaped felt balls.

If you are using an old action, which has pits, or deep scratches in it, you should resist the urge to mash it against a buffing wheel. My 30-06 Mauser was built on an old action which had been used a great deal. There were many scratches and minor pits from long use. I knew that to clean this up by hand would take long hours of work, which I wasn't prepared to pay for. But given a handful of fine carborundum stones in various shapes, and a can of honing oil, I worked on the action in my spare time. I cleaned it up, keeping the contours right, working evenings while watching TV. I had it done beautifully in a few weeks. All the gunsmith had to do was degrease it and wire brush it a bit before bluing. This is one place where you can save yourself a lot of money. If you do your own metal preparation, you must be slow and careful, and do it right, or the final job won't

Perhaps, your taste is for a little more gleam as revealed on this Sako considerably worked over by Al Lind. Even so, at such levels, rust blue is the way to go. You get the extra shine from extra polish.

Ordinary polishing is usually a power equipment job, but a top job on a custom gun usually requires some careful hand work to keep all the contours just right. Barrels are polished lengthwise to avoid any ripples in the surface. Any lathe marks are removed by draw-filing, then the barrels are struck again with 220 grit to remove the file marks, and the process repeated with finer grits, down to 600 if a high polish is desired. Careful power buffing can be done, but the slapdash worker may apply the barrel across the wheel, causing ripples. When looking across the surface of the polished barrel, the lines should appear smooth. Cloth polishing wheels charged with 200 grit are often used for general polishing, while 400 or finer will provide a higher polish. Over-polishing, however, is something to avoid, since it removes metal. Flat surfaces are never polished on a wheel, but on a belt polisher with a flat backing plate.

have that professional touch.

Hand polishing is much preferred on a custom gun, but it takes time, and therefore costs money. There is no disputing the fact, though, that a good hand polishing job looks a lot better than a power-buffed one. To do a good hand polishing job on a bolt-action rifle will probably take 4-5 hours. Fine single-cut files are used to draw-file any rough spots having pits or tool marks on the receiver and barrel. Following up the draw-filing with 200 grit will clean up the file marks and reveal any defects which need more work. It's alright at this stage to gently cross-polish the rounded contours of the barrel and receiver, which will instantly reveal flaws such as scratches or depressions in the metal, which need going over again.

Following cross-polishing, the surfaces are flat polished using strips of 280 grit wrapped around a flat file or strip of wood, turning them as needed to cover the curves. Polishing is alternated between crosswise and lengthwise until all toolmarks or draw-filing scratches are removed. This should be done with care to keep all sharp edges square, giving the final polish in a lengthwise direction with finer grits until the final degree of polish is obtained, 400 grit being adequate if the surface is to be bead blasted, though 600 grit, perhaps followed by crocus cloth if needed, if you want a mirror polish. Final inspection should be done outdoors in full sunlight, to reveal any flaws. If the polishing is good, having a dull sheen all over, the metal is ready for final degreasing in Oakite or detergent and bluing.

The high polish blue is often used today, but it doesn't have the elegant look of a fine cold rust job. The high polish blue looks alright on the rack, but shows every fingerprint and is easily damaged. Personally, I think a shiny gun looks cheap. You may come to expect

beaded barrel provide a nice contrast on a hunting rifle, though on a gun made more for show, you might wish a bead blasted receiver and wire brushed barrel, giving a classier touch.

A durable finish on hunting rifles which will receive hard use is simply to sandblast and blue. This gives much the appearance of Parkerizing, and provides a porous surface which holds oil or other preservative treatments better for wet weather use, etc. However, sandblasting or even bead blasting should never be used on points of metal-to-metal contact, as they impede smooth operation. You would never bead blast a bolt body for instance. You should also avoid blasting the interior parts of the action.

A cold rust blue finish usually requires about four days to apply. The cleaned degreased parts are swabbed, the rust carded off with wire brushes or with degreased steel wool, and the metal boiled in clean water between applications to limit the rusting action. The

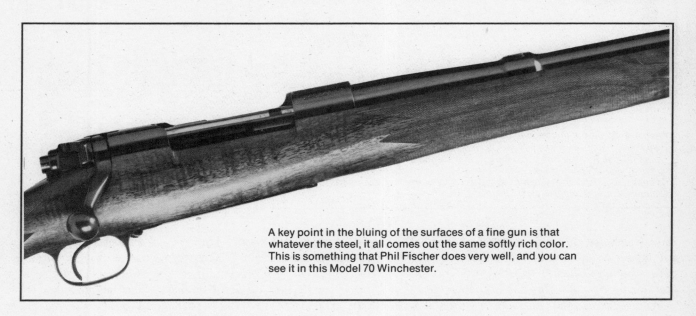

A key point in the bluing of the surfaces of a fine gun is that whatever the steel, it all comes out the same softly rich color. This is something that Phil Fischer does very well, and you can see it in this Model 70 Winchester.

it on a Weatherby, but it is obviously out of place on a fine classic rifle or shotgun. However, even if you wish to achieve the soft, subdued blue finish, you should always take the metal to a good polish first. Then instead of bluing it right away, the final touches in metal preparation come into play which make a great blue job different. Old-time classic gunsmiths often wire brushed the polished surface, using a power wheel with a .005-inch wire. This is one way to obtain the "satin" blue. Another method often used today is glass bead blasting. When done before using fresh good quality black oxide chemicals, it gives an appearance which takes a trained eye to distinguish from a cold rust job. Glass beading doesn't give the severe dullness of sandblasting. However, the *fine* sandblast finish is useful to impart contrast and to dull the sheen on sighting surfaces. A lightly sandblasted receiver and glass

first coat achieves a dull gray color, and each successive application darkens it more. The bluing solution is wiped on with a lint-free cotton cloth, which is replaced after each use. The bores are plugged with long birch or maple plugs, which serve as handles during the process.

It is important to remove the plugs and wipe the bores clean before and after each boiling, since no oil can be used. After the last coating the parts are boiled for 20 minutes in clean water to stop the rusting action, then the last of the rust carded off and the surface well oiled. The old-timers used linseed oil for this, but today water-displacing polarized oils are preferred.

The black oxide process can achieve a dark finish in a day and has largely replaced the cold rust process for production work. It uses a heated chemical bath into which the cleaned metal is submerged at about 300 degrees Fahrenheit, generally for about 10-20 minutes,

Here is a hunting rifle by R. Cubriel which is complemented in severe simplicity by a matte blue of barrel and receiver that is still rich, but is less reflective than most blues, which makes considerable sense for a serious hunting rifle.

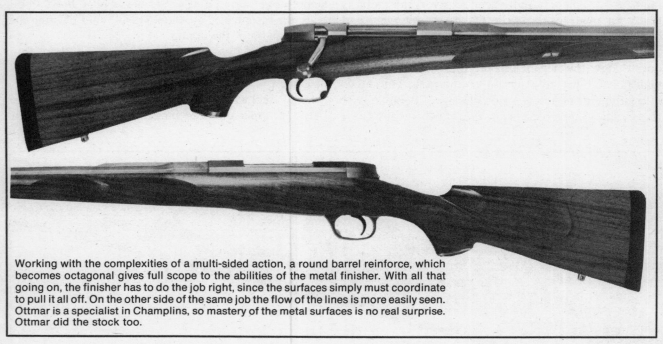

Working with the complexities of a multi-sided action, a round barrel reinforce, which becomes octagonal gives full scope to the abilities of the metal finisher. With all that going on, the finisher has to do the job right, since the surfaces simply must coordinate to pull it all off. On the other side of the same job the flow of the lines is more easily seen. Ottmar is a specialist in Champlins, so mastery of the metal surfaces is no real surprise. Ottmar did the stock too.

though some steels require more time. The bath attacks soft solder or aluminum, so it cannot be used on those parts, though silver, copper or brass are not affected, and inlaid or bead sights can be immersed safely.

Heat bluing is used occasionally on small parts, such as springs or pins, and is done simply by heating the part in an open flame or oven until it reaches a blue color. Another method which is also satisfactory for small parts is to heat them to about 700-800 degrees Fahrenheit and quench them in oil. A different heat blue process was once used by Smith & Wesson in which the polished parts were heated in an oven for 1-3 hours while being agitated in a powdered bluing mixture.

Parkerizing is a general term used for phosphate coatings applied to steel. This finish is a dull, nonreflective gray-green, and is widely used on U.S. military arms. Though it isn't a particularly good looking finish, it is very abrasion and rust resistant and is a good choice for service arms or hunting rifles which require a non-shiny, durable finish. It is applied by boiling the degreased, sandblasted parts in a solution of phosphoric acid, containing dissolved iron filings or manganese

dioxide and water. The original Parkerizing process dates from about 1910. A formula given by Dunlap in his book, *Gunsmithing,* is 61 grains of phosphoric acid (density 1.5) and 22 grs. of manganese dioxide added to enough distilled water to make 1 quart. Degreased metal parts are boiled for 1-1½ hours, or until the solution has been reduced to one-third its volume. They are then rinsed in cold water, then again in hot water, dried in sawdust, and again heated until water dropped on the surface is immediately thrown off. The parts are then dipped in linseed oil, and drained and heated again to dry the oil.

There are other phosphate treatments for steel similar to Parkerizing, which give similar results. Bonderizing is a trade name for one such finish, widely used in the automotive industry. Another is Du-Lite Phosteel. In England and Europe the trade name Fermangan is sometimes used to describe a phosphate-type process, almost identical to Parkerizing, which is used by FN on military arms. Colors of these finishes vary from light gray-green to black, but it takes an expert to distinguish one from another. As with bluing, it is essential the bores be protected during any of these treat-

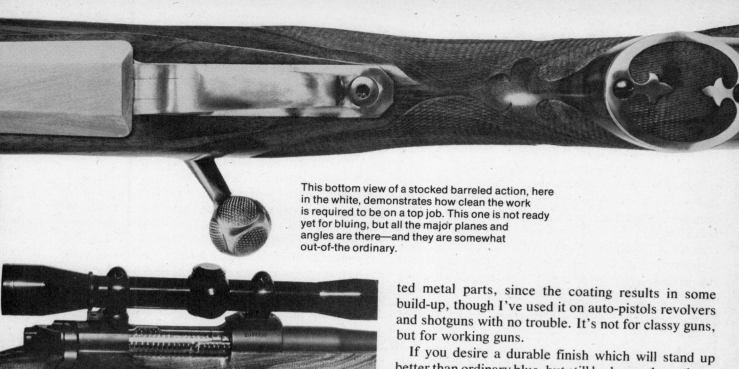

This bottom view of a stocked barreled action, here in the white, demonstrates how clean the work is required to be on a top job. This one is not ready yet for bluing, but all the major planes and angles are there—and they are somewhat out-of-the ordinary.

One of the difficulties in finishing the metal surfaces of a rifle is the problem of the scope. The surfaces of the scope are not normally matchable. In this photograph of a Stephen Billeb Model 70, there is not much coordination between the basic metal surfaces of the rifle and the scope rings and the scope itself so far as the finish is concerned. However, by bringing the scope rings close to to the scope finish, Billeb has made the two different surface elements live together.

ments. Neoprene plugs are generally used in production work.

Parkerizing should not be used on parts fitted to very close tolerances, nor should it be used for those on which you desire smooth operation, since the porous surface increases friction, even when lubricated. It is best confined to exterior surfaces only, although the finish can be removed on small points of contact by careful stoning or polishing, which will give smoother operation. However, this also reduces the effectiveness of rust protection in areas where the finish is removed. The best candidates for Parkerizing are semi-automatic rifles, pistols, shotguns, and the barreled receivers and other exterior parts of hunting rifles which will be used in a harsh outdoor environment.

An alternative to Parkerizing for rough duty guns is Teflon S. This is a dull, highly rust resistant finish which is self-lubricating. Its main disadvantage is that it feels slippery to the touch, though it is excellent for cold weather applications, since it requires no other lubrication, and skin won't stick to it in sub-zero conditions. It provides better protection from salt-water exposure than Parkerizing. It isn't really suitable for closely fit-

ted metal parts, since the coating results in some build-up, though I've used it on auto-pistols revolvers and shotguns with no trouble. It's not for classy guns, but for working guns.

If you desire a durable finish which will stand up better than ordinary blue, but still looks good, you have few options, but there are some. Black chrome is a common name for a popular finish which is just what the name describes. It can be either dull or shiny, depending upon the surface treatment on the metal. It looks best over a glass beaded surface, since if applied over a high polish, it looks more like plastic or paint than metal. It can also be applied over a sandblasted surface and looks somewhat like Parkerizing with a "shine." Regardless of the process used, chrome plating for firearms should be bonded directly to a properly prepared steel surface.

Black chrome, and the various kinds of industrial, hard chrome, require preparation by removal of some metal in a process called electro-polishing, before plating back up to size. The thickness of chrome deposited is limited to a few thousandths of an inch in any case, usually .001-inch or less. Most decorative chrome, as on automobile bumpers, is only a flash plating, of a few ten-thousandths of an inch. To be effective on firearms (inside the bore, etc.) the film must be thick enough to prevent flaking from thermal cracking and the stresses of firing. The chrome film in military M16 rifle barrels is about .0005-inch thick, whereas that in M14 rifle barrels is about .0007-inch thick. In 50 caliber or 20mm barrels it is usually several times that much. Chrome-lined bores are less prone to foul if the chrome is applied on a smooth surface. However, if the bore is rough to start with, full chrome lining does more harm than good. I once experimented with some 9-inch twist M16 rifle barrels which showed promise, but they metal fouled badly, despite the chrome lining. Examination showed the bores were quite rough in places. I never got those barrels to shoot well until the chrome was stripped out so they could be lapped to remove the tight spots and the worst of the tool marks. Although they were then somewhat oversize, about .225-inch groove diameter, they shot extremely well with flat-based bullets having a long bearing length, such as the 60-gr. Hornady HP, provided you used a fairly stiff load with a moderately fast burning powder, such as 3031.

Hard chrome finishes are sold under various names. Armoloy is a trade name for one brand of hard chroming, though the same process by another name is probably just as good. As with black chrome, the surface preparation of the steel is what gives the final finish its character. If you want a bright finish, apply it over a high mirror polish. If you want a soft luster, glass bead the surface after polishing. If you want something

There are also chemical nickel finishes, done without electro-plating. These finishes are lumped under the general term "electroless nickel," but there are several trade names for the same basic finish, depending upon who does the work. Simmons Gun Specialties calls their version of it SimGard, then there are other brand names such as Nitex. They are all basically the same thing. Electroless nickel when applied to a brushed or grit polished surface has much the appearance of stainless steel. For this reason it is often used on ordinary alloy steel parts used in customizing stainless guns. For instance, if you wanted a 3-inch heavy barrel Model 60 S&W, you could use a 3-inch Model 36 barrel and have it SimGarded or Nitexed, and install it on the stainless frame, and it would be a pretty good match. You can tell the difference upon close examination, but from 3 feet

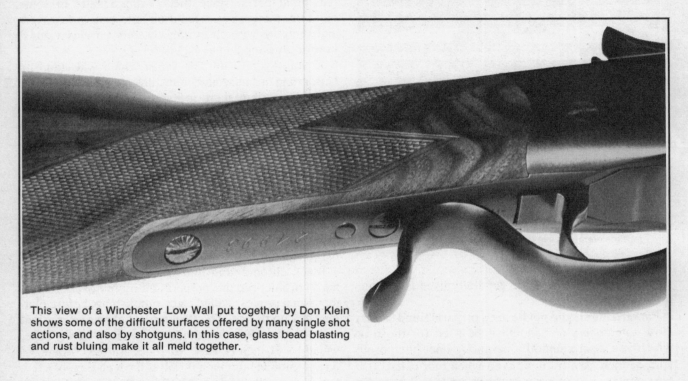

This view of a Winchester Low Wall put together by Don Klein shows some of the difficult surfaces offered by many single shot actions, and also by shotguns. In this case, glass bead blasting and rust bluing make it all meld together.

which looks like Armoloy, sandblast it.

Nickel plating is another area where there is a lot of duplication under various trade names. Most nickel plating is done by electro-plating, and it may be applied either directly to a clean polished surface, for bright nickel, or to a bead- or sand-blasted surface, to provide a satin finish. Nickel plating was once very popular for use in wet climates or near large bodies of water. It provided a good deal of protection from rust; however, it is less often used now, with the ready availability of stainless steel guns. Certainly, a good nickel plate is probably at least as resistant to corrosion from saltwater exposure on the exterior as stainless steel. Nickel plating is also a good protective finish for Dural or other aluminum alloys. Satin nickel makes a good finish to cover the frames of pistols or revolvers since it is more abrasion resistant than ordinary black anodizing.

away most people could never tell.

Aluminum parts are blacked by a process called hard anodizing, which forms a layer of black aluminum oxide on the metal surface. On most gun parts this coating isn't very thick, and it will eventually wear off, though while it lasts it is quite good. Anodizing can be made any color, since the oxide itself is a gray color, and can be stained with a dye. Anodizing can be done either to a highly polished or glass-beaded surface. It isn't a really good idea to sandblast aluminum parts, unless done with fine grit and very low pressure since the material is softer than steel and easily damaged. Most ordinary anodizing, such as that used on scope rings and alloy handgun frames, isn't all that durable, so when the finish wears through, it is often better to go ahead and have it refinished with satin nickel. This provides a nice contrast with blued steel parts.

There are tough, hard anodized coatings, such as Martin Hardcote, which are file hard and extemely durable, though they cannot be used on parts which must be held to close tolerances, since the coating itself is .002- to .003-inch thick. Examples of aluminum parts treated with Martin Hardcote are the upper and lower receivers of AR-15 and M16 rifles. Kollmorgen Optical Company used it to finish the tubes of their Bearcub line of scopes back in the 1950s. I have one which is nearly 30 years old and has been used a great deal, and the finish looks like it was put on yesterday. There are few firms, however, who can do a good job of this on firearms.

There are times when a gunsmith may want to blacken non-ferrous metals, such as silver-solder (to hide the joint) or to black brass or copper front sights as are often used on old Savage 99 and some current Remington rifles. Silver is easily blackened with silver nitrate solution. Copper is blackened effectively by dipping in nitric acid, and then heating to dull red. There are other chemical processes used to blacken brass or nickel, which are given in standard texts such as Dunlap's *Gunsmithing*.

Case-hardening is often thought of as a decorative metal finish, since we associate it with the pleasing colors of Colt Single Action revolver frames, Winchester 1873 rifles, or fine double shotguns. Actually, the colors are a by-product of heat treatment. In the old days gun frames were usually made of low alloy steel, or malleable iron, and case-hardening was a process by which the physical properties of the steel could be improved somewhat. The hard layer of carburized material imparted to the color-hardened surface is usually only about .005-inch thick. Though less colorful, deep carburizing might penetrate twice as far. It just isn't as pretty.

Although the carburizing effect of case-hardening is a predictable thing, getting colors is less so. There are few fellows who do a really superb job of color case-hardening today. The carbonizing substance is usually charred bone dust. Metal parts to be color-hardened must be very well polished, but not buffed, since this tends to smear closed the pores of the steel. The polished parts are cleaned thoroughly by boiling in lye, or pickling in acid, then handled only with clean cotton gloves thereafter. The parts are packed in a cast iron or welded mild steel box with loose fitting lid. In doing so, the pieces are placed on and covered in a layer of charred bone about ¾-inch thick and then heated to 1400 degrees Fahrenheit for 2-4 hours. Afterwards, they are quenched in clean, soft water. The quench tank is about 1½ feet deep with a wire mesh screen about 8 inches below the surface. An air tank blows bubbles through the water as the work is dumped, which gives the desired mottled finish. When the work is cool, it is dried in sawdust and oiled or lacquered. Certain chemi-cal salts are used occasionally to deepeen the colors. The colors are highly variable depending upon the heat of the parts when quenched, the type of steel used, etc.

Although color case-hardening is mostly decorative, other carburizing treatments give deeper penetration into the steel which can give a marked improvement in wear resistance. Kasenit is one compound which is widely used to induce a deep surface hardening on about anything from malleable iron to tool steel. The steel part is heated cherry red and dipped in Kasenit, which melts and forms a coating over the part. The steel is heated again to bright red, which burns off some of the coating, driving carbon into the steel surface, and then quenched in clean, cold water. This type of process doesn't impart the brilliant colors often sought in color-hardening, usually dull color or no color, but gives greater penetration of the hardness into the steel. Most color-hardening, however, is more color than hardening. You should therefore decide whether appearance or wear resistance is more important to you. You can't always have both. In many cases a good carburizing treatment is better on old shotgun receivers, which can be left natural, or blued as desired. Cyanide can also be used to color-harden steel, though this is a risky business, since it requires dealing with one of the deadliest substances known. Those doing it must exercise proper safeguards.

Some European shotgun or combination gun receivers are left bright polished or gray finished. This involves polishing the metal and pickling in acids which tends to passivate the steel and make it less susceptible to rusting. A good gray finish will retain its character for years. Another "natural" finish which is much misunderstood is the so-called "coined" finish. This description is usually a misnomer. It describes a die stamped finish left on the steel from being pressed by a highly polished surface under considerable pressure. When applied to anything other than small stamped parts which are left natural and not polished before bluing, the term really isn't accurate. Current Winchester Model 70 receivers might be erroneously described as a coined finish, but they aren't. They are forged. The surface of the forging is left alone and receives little or no additional polishing before it goes into the blue tank. This is what some people mean by a coined finish.

There is a lot of mystery and magic associated with metal finishes, but there needn't be. There are no secret formulas or magic qualities. The best finish for your particular job depends on whether you need good looks, protection only, or some of each. Then you have to consider the options and decide the best way to go. Depending on how you approach it, getting a top job can be either the easiest or the hardest part of the problem. The easiest and *cheapest* way out is seldom the best way, so think carefully about your wants and needs, then go do it right.

C.E. Harris

Wood Finish

THE CHOICES seem wider than ever before, but they really aren't. Certainly, there are more sophisticated chemicals now with which to treat wood surfaces, but at the same time those who would use and admire those surfaces have grown more selective in their taste and so we are back to some form of oil finish or some form of synthetic.

Some artisans would have it that the choice is between finish *in* the wood and finish *on* the wood. Most finishes, truth to tell, are a little bit of both. Regardless, anyone will agree that it is the care and method of application of any of the finishes that makes the difference. Any of the formulae properly followed up will produce a finish that is handsome to the eye and durable to the touch and wind and weather. The differences are much less apparent than are the similarities.

Given the all-out treatment of this very deluxe sporter by R. H. Devereaux, with its extensive engraving, including the scope mounts; its unique barrel form; its handsome wood, one has no choice. One cannot stint on finishing the wood, including a checkering application in design sympathy with the rest of the rifle, and the very best of wood surfaces.

We may as well dispose of such things as "French polish" and lacquer, those things which are often called "piano" finishes. They are all best achieved by applying a very thin layer on a very smooth surface. It follows that their serviceability depends on the finish never being broken, nor worn—something that is hardly possible with a gun handled regularly. Some practitioners still try for the high polish and bright finish, but these sorts of wood finishes are not in the mainstream today.

The so-called oil finish is probably the most desired way to top off the surface of the wood, as it has been for at least a couple of generations. Wood is a porous material, and in order for its surface to be smooth, pores must be filled. About half the problems of the finisher are involved with this filling. Almost anything that will in fact fill the pores and stay there will work out as a basis for an oil finish. Some gunstock finishers borrow material from the furniture industry, using one or another form of inert clays in suspension in oil, forced into the wood by the pressure of a cloth and the hand; others rely on the raw oil, applied in many, many coats, scrubbed away when dry, over a long period of time; others, and likely the majority, mix oil with high-quality varnish, and with a carrier such as mineral spirits to get the finish down into the wood, and then scrub it all away from the surface of the wood. Some, among them Phil

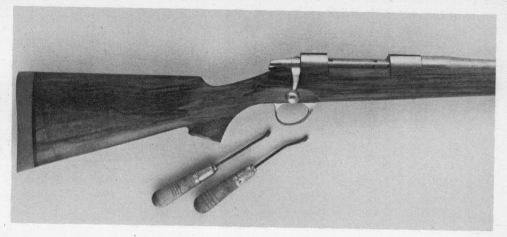

This is when it happens, under ideal circumstances: The metal work is in the white, but the shape is all there. This job is by Reggie Cubriel, on a severely handsome sporting rifle.

Good men suit their designs to the job at hand. This and the butt stock below are both by Pete Grisel. This one is on a Model 52B Winchester. Note the cheekpieces and the checkering treatment below the cheekpieces are approximately the same on both guns, but with different effect because of the different wood.

This Grisel stock is a Husqvarna sporter, showing fleur-de-lis accomplished on a piece of tiger striped walnut.

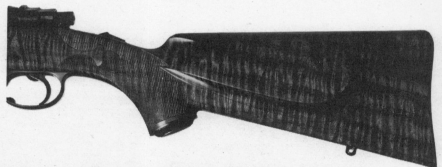

Pilkington whose seminar on the subject is reviewed elsewhere in this volume, apply their mixed finish and rub it into the wood with sandpaper in successively finer grits. This creates, on the surface, a mixture of sanding grit, wood particles, and the oils and varnish of the mixture and serves to pack this mixture rather rapidly into the pores of the wood.

To a degree, it is knowing when to stop. These days, in the best work, there is no stopping until the surface of the wood is glass-like—that is, utterly smooth, with no wrinkles or dimpling. There will be no raw spots and no extra-shiny spots—the surface is the same all over.

There are claims made for one or the other of such efforts, mostly revolving around whether or not the wood is darkened, or remains its original color once finished, and to what degree either of these conditions prevail. With the class of wood used these days in the best custom guns, it would seem ideal if the final finish did not much alter the character of the wood. In the old days, red dyes and reddish oils provided a characteristic almost mahogany color to many fine gunstocks.

That is no longer a desirable direction, except for the fellow who wishes to recreate a piece with the character of the past.

There is much mystery here, but it is a mystery of technique, not of chemistry. Many top gunmakers simply use Tru-Oil, or GB-Lin-Speed or other packaged materials with brand names. Most likely they simply follow the directions on the package, adding whatever stunts they have acquired through experience.

That is hard to believe, but that is the way it is. Getting a fine stock finished to look like a fine stock finish is more a question of preparation than it is of application. The stock must be brought to its final shape, must be successively sanded with finer grits of paper until all marks disappear, must have its grain raised and the resulting splinters eliminated, and then its grain raised again and then the splinters eliminated, and so on until, before a drop of finish is applied, the wood has a hard, dense and utterly smooth surface. It is at that point that you can start to do something about the finish.

State of the Art: Wood Finish

There is yet another point to be made. Fine guns are made with fine wood, and that wood bears no more relationship to the soft and open-pored black walnut often furnished as semi-inletted stock blanks than it does to the handle of the average shovel. This is not to say that black walnut does not make a perfectly excellent gun handle, or that it does not have its own virtues in plenty. However, when compared to a properly prepared blank of French or Bastogne or English walnut, black walnut hardly presents the same sort of surface. And the point in saying this is that a great deal of experience finishing the large-pored American walnuts does not necessarily prepare a fellow for finishing the wood on a fine gunstock. It is a different ball game entirely, based strictly on the character of the wood itself.

So there are two things that greatly affect the problem of finishing a gun stock that have nothing to do with the finish materials—the quality and character of the wood and the quality and character of the preparation of the surface of the wood. Getting all that just right makes the final finishing relative child's play.

Reality sometimes strikes different people in differ-

The plain checkered butt remains an entirely acceptable finish detail on a good custom gun. In the field, such butt-end treatment is relatively fragile, but careful riflemen and shotgunners use them anyway.

This is the Grisel Model 52 again, and the quite full coverage of the forearm is still graceful, particularly in the matching contours of the ends of the pattern and their relationship to the pistol grip pattern of similar line.

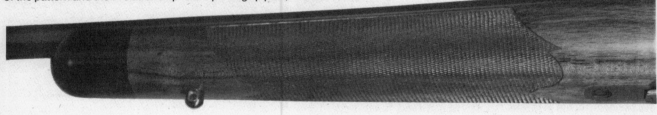

This is a Kleinguenther custom stock's forearm treatment. It is well cut checkering in a difficult pattern and is certainly full coverage for a good grasping surface.

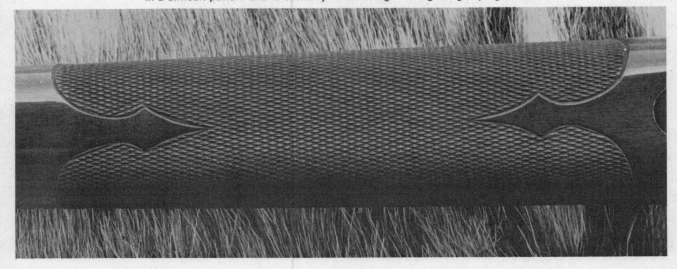

The grip and how it is shaped and finished makes a great deal of difference in a custom rifle. It is from this point, indeed, that the rest of the stock takes its lines of departure. This Don Bartlett checkering at 20 lpi on a bigbore rifle stands up well to magnification. The key here is simplicity and execution.

Here, in a quite-close pistol grip, are shown other ways to make the transition from checkering to butt in one direction, extending lines, and to flow upward into the action in the other direction.

ent ways, and some makers and first-class artisans prefer to go with the chemically more modern finish applied over the surface of the wood. In short, we're talking about fiberglass and epoxy finishes, along with polyurethanes and who knows what else? Some of the major manufacturers in the firearms industry prepare their gunstocks this way: They shape them and sand them to fair smoothness, and then apply, often by spraying, a coat of self-curing chemicals, such as epoxies. When the epoxies dry, they are rubbed out and another coat is applied and rubbed out, and then a final coat is applied very carefully. The result is an exceedingly durable finish which does not appreciably change the character of the wood. It is, however, indubitably on the surface. And it is shiny until made otherwise by careful rubbing. The average among us can't always distinguish at first glance which way a gunstock has

been finished, but the knowledgeable always can.

Certainly there are good reasons for using epoxies and their ilk on gunstocks. The materials are not quite impervious to defeat from the elements, but they are very stout against wind and water. They are easier, and what is more important, take less time to apply than other sorts of finishes, which at their best are relatively laborious tasks. The look of a good piece of wood with a nicely-applied transparent coat of epoxy with, perhaps, the high shine just lightly knocked off with rubbing compound is certainly adequate. There is little doubt that such finishes are closer to being impervious to water than other more traditional sorts. The new chemistry certainly serves the gun owner.

It's strange to put it this way, but the next thing—the way most people do it—to accomplish after having finished the stock is to scratch it all up, but this time in

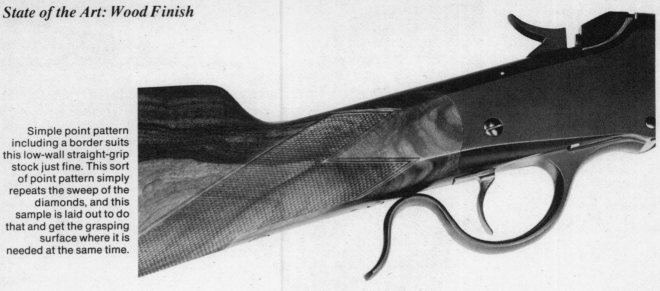

Simple point pattern including a border suits this low-wall straight-grip stock just fine. This sort of point pattern simply repeats the sweep of the diamonds, and this sample is laid out to do that and get the grasping surface where it is needed at the same time.

the regular pattern most often called checkering. This is not true, by the way, for those makers who opt for the epoxy finish. Epoxies are very rough on checkering tools and are applied afterwards, or should be. Regardless of when it is accomplished, most fine guns are checkered.

Checkering takes, in detail, many forms, but essentially is created by a series of parallel rows of V-grooves, overlaid at an angle with another series of V-grooves, the angles chosen to leave between the grooves, pyramids of wood in diamond shapes, sometimes with the diamonds in proportion of one-to-three for width and length. Each checkerer, however, makes his own choice in this matter, fudging off one way or another depending on either the work at hand or his personal taste.

Checkering is a labor-intensive endeavor. It is also immensely demanding, since virtually any mistake among the ordered rows of pyramids, is clear from as far away as across the room. Therefore, checkering costs a lot of money, all things considered.

There have been and are immensely creative checkering patterns, involving little islands of wood in the form of fleur-de-lis, sometimes ribbons through the pattern in graceful curves, and very often tackling the very difficult problem of checkering over the top and bottom of the pistol grip. That is difficult because it is impossible. That is, you cannot with straight lines go all the way around an irregular cone and come out as even-looking as most masters can accomplish. What they do is cheat the line at crucial points, but they do it so cleverly the cheating is hard to find.

With all the elaboration possible, a number of afficionados still prefer the plain point patterns, wherein the basic diamond shape is the principal form of the checkering, repeated at the ends in what is almost a

This is the grip of a Kleinguenther K15, specially stocked by Kleinguenther. The robust diamonds suit the shape here; the transition from the action area back into the checkering and from the checkering back into the buttstock flows very nicely.

This pistol grip area from Paul Jaeger demonstrates about all the complexity a grip area can stand, but does it very well. Key points: fleurs in both directions with the shape repeated in a checkering patch behind the grip; ribbons to tie it all together; a ribboned-off checkering section over the top of the grip; the whole quite handsome.

very large-scale rendering of saw-teeth. The whole question of patterns being a matter of personal taste, we can step aside at this point, having noted that some patterns are practically the personal property of some stockmakers.

The purpose of checkering, most of us think, is to provide a grasping surface for the hand. In fine guns, that is a moot question. Certainly, the "stickiness" of any checkering of finer degree than 28 lines per inch, is just not there. The checkerer by the art of his effort succeeds, really, in substituting a barely perceptible bumpiness for the slick finish of the untouched wood. As we get down to 24-line and even coarser checkering, we do get a tactile sensation which is functional. Coarse checkering, well carried out, with sharp and pointed diamonds on very hard wood can in fact be painful to the bare hand on a gun which recoils appreciably.

At any rate, coarse checkering is in general disdained by makers of fine guns. They regard their checkering more as embellishment than as a practical aid to the grasp, and therefore the finer it is and the more intricate the pattern, the better the work is. There are limits, of course. Some perfectly handsome wood of elegant grain and coloration, is very difficult to checker at, say, 32 lines per inch. I am told that some handsome Claro walnut, however suitable otherwise, is just not possible when it comes to terribly fine checkering.

No matter the niceties of pattern or the number of lines per inch, checkering is well done when the grain of the gunstock may be clearly seen through it. That is, the expanse of grooved wood is smooth enough in execution that the checkering does not constitute, visually, a panel laid upon the wood, but rather appears to be in the wood. It is a phenomenon not often perceived in factory guns, but which is awfully easy to get used to in fine guns.

This is another, but different, Jaeger solution to the pistol grip area. The fleurs are smaller; the curves deeper; the need for a transition in the butt-stock area was eliminated by using a fillet treatment behind the grip. Lines—almost "grind lines"—in the stock above the trigger lead to the pistol grip area.

State of the Art: Wood Finish

There have been in the past, of course, other ways to handle the problem. Even today, to achieve a particular design goal, a stockmaker may stain a checkering panel to achieve a contrast which suits him. Even so, beneath the stain, the grain should appear.

There is also the question of the border of any checkering pattern. In production work, and on some fine guns of European make as a standard way of doing things, panels of checkering are given borders. That is, the edges are all chiseled away with a different sort of tool to achieve a uniformity of edge. This too is a technique held in disdain by the modern fine gunmaker. The mark of the fine craftsman in these matters is the borderless checkering pattern. It is not, of course, borderless visually. It all comes to a stop along a line. That line, however, is formed simply by the checkering coming to a stop. And that is the secret and the pride of the craftsman.

Naturally, in the work of the less-than-best craftsman, an excellently executed border on a routine checkering pattern is probably more to be desired than a somewhat sloppy borderless edge. This would be particularly true in the case of working guns where the checkering pattern is actually provided as a grasping surface rather than as an embellishment of the wood.

It is perhaps easier to judge checkering than any other of the features of a good gun. We have already mentioned borders and borderless jobs. In the case of the borderless jobs, there ought be no runovers, no places where the checkering tool has advanced outside the pattern and nicked the adjacent wood. On the mechanical side still, the diamonds should be pointed up, and the flats of the pyramids, should be smooth and clean, top to bottom. The lines should run on, regularly, from one side to the other. It is hardly possible and not even desirable that all the lines be parallel, but they should certainly appear parallel. Occasionally, a checkerer will go over the top or around the bottom of a pistol grip, but the shape defeats him and he must permit a seam in the pattern. Personally, I think a modest attempt to hide this seam by making it somewhat irregular is legitimate—after all, there are limits of accomplishment.

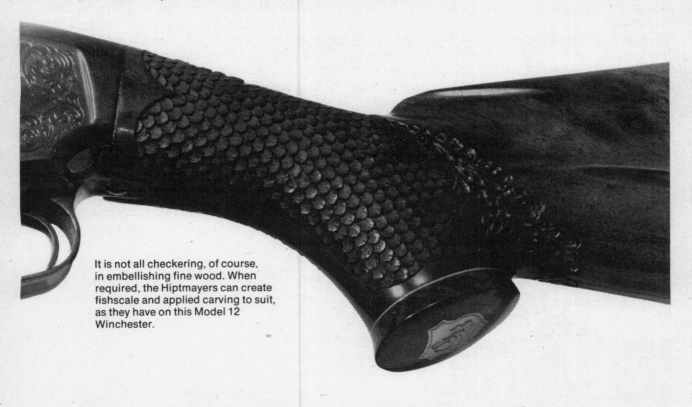

It is not all checkering, of course, in embellishing fine wood. When required, the Hiptmayers can create fishscale and applied carving to suit, as they have on this Model 12 Winchester.

This is the fore-end of the Hiptmayer Model 12, where the fishscale checkering and carved motif is repeated. However, this fishscale runs in the opposite direction to that on the pistol grip, which makes sense in a pump shotgun.

It is in the broader pictures that most checkering stands or falls. The mechanical aspects are available to any man of accomplishment with his hands. It is the art of making the whole pattern fit the whole gun that really makes checkering patterns succeed. Some of the factors include the total coverage allowed and how it is distributed between the pistol grip and the fore-end; the shapes of the panels and how they relate to the shape of the stock itself and to the metal above it; the fitness of the chosen sort of pattern, whether a point pattern or something more elaborate and curved, when considered together with the sort of grain the stock's wood offers.

In considering these matters, perhaps the most important thing is the length of the checkering pattern on the fore-end, related to the amount of fore-end available ahead of the receiver ring, and the way the panels on the pistol grip blend into the buttstock behind. Nothing spells "skimp" quicker than a checkering pattern inadequate in size. If one must err, one ought err on the side of generosity in checkering patterns. However, it is not necessary to err. The eye of a man who understands what he is doing will ordinarily provide approximately the right size patterns for the job at hand.

There are patterns other than straight checkering, of course, and there are diamond designs other than pointed. There is a certain vogue for what is called "French" checkering, which means that the pattern is interrupted regularly to provide large flat-topped diamond-shaped insets, so to speak, of wood in the pattern, and on some guns that looks good. Some like the so-called English or flat-topped diamonds, diamonds not brought to a point. The problem with this, despite its functionality, is that diamonds not brought to a point must be even more regularly cut than those which are pointed. All those little flat places must be precisely regular in order not to be disturbing to the eye.

Occasionally, some of the masters in wood choose to border their checkering or embellish it with a modest amount of carving. For some, this is almost a style note, a particular fashion they have set for themselves and which amounts to a trademark. Ordinarily, those men do this style of thing very well indeed and ought to be left to do so. Carving beyond this is more properly an embellishment of the whole gun and is treated elsewhere. There are such things as fish-scale checkering, and other offbeat modes of providing handsome roughened surfaces, but they are not in the mainstream.

There they are—the marks of the final treatment of the wood of a fine gun. They include a finish which is in the wood or appears to be in the wood, smooth as glass but not glittering, hiding nothing of the beauty of the wood from the viewer. Embellished or furnished, depending on how you look at it, with checkering of the right pattern, properly executed, or finished as is the rest of the stock, such a job of finishing is expensive and time-consuming, but chances are that you do not have a fine gun unless you have it.

Ken Warner

Buying Wood

MONEY spent on wood for a gun is hardly ever lost. There are times and places when it is a far better investment to spend more money than less, and certainly the prettier wood that you get will be before your eyes constantly while you own the gun and you will enjoy it. The money—well, money goes, it seems—regardless.

This does not mean that you go out and just look for high-priced wood to build a gun. What it means is that you should look for the wood that really suits you and, if you can possibly stand it, pay the price.

There is, of course, a lot more to it than that. Part of the problem is patience and its brother impatience. If you must have fine wood right now and are certain the wood must go under the knife soon, there is no way around it. You must pay what is bound to be the highest price, because you must find a dry stick of wood, ready to go right now. All the people who cut it and bought it and dried it and cared for it have to be paid out of the final price you will pay.

There are other ways. A number of smart cookies, for example, are buying wood, even green wood, well in advance. If it is good wood, there is hardly any way to lose money on it and, if you are not in a hurry, you can calmly and confidently air-dry that wood on your own premises. If you can afford to buy it, see that it is going along all right for the first 30 days or so, and then turn it every few months over the course of several years. You would have to have it in a very difficult place indeed to get into trouble.

Wood in the blank is forgiving of almost everything but speed. Most of the tricks involved in drying wood properly without running into shakes, splits, and warps is involved with drying the wood fast. If you don't need speed, you can avoid almost all the problems, the experts tell me.

There is another route and that depends on whether

State of the Art: Buying Wood

or not the man who is going to build your rifle already has suitable wood. He won't sell it too cheaply, mind you, but he is hardly likely to hang you up to dry, either.

Then, of course, there are the many sources for fine hardwood known to people with rural connections. Exceedingly fine and handsome grain characteristics are not the norm in the kind of walnut, for instance, once used to frame barns and other farm buildings, but warmth and stability are definitely there in any piece of wood that has spent a century getting dry. There are other rural sources—old lumber yards, for instance, the really old ones, often once dealt in hardwoods and may have the odd plank or two around. For these sources, you have to get well out of the mainstream, of course, and they can be hardly counted on.

The most reliable source is always the fellow who is in the business. His business depends on having wood around to sell, a steady supply of it, and to a considerable degree on customer satisfaction. The big commercial fellows, like Reinhart Fajen whose business is primarily semi-inletted stocks, offer catalogs that

There is no fancier of fine guns who would not be thrilled by this display of wood by Pachmayr Gun Works, whose fine guns are also in the picture. Pachmayr is reported to have a great deal of such wood and if that is so, the firm is to be envied. Such a collection to shop from would be a boon to anyone building a custom gun.

Here are two blanks and the sort of gun that can become of them. Both the California English walnut and the Ruger rifle are Bill Dowtin's. Wood with such grain and texture is called, among other things, exhibition grade.

provide pretty complete descriptions of the wood they have for sale. With a little extrapolation, their prices can be translated into estimates of the prices of other kinds of woods you are offered.

It is time to note that the basic wood for fine gunstocks is walnut in one of its many persuasions. Other kinds of woods are useful and attractive and will be discussed later, but here we are discussing walnut. Further, we are, in the main, discussing some kind of walnut other than American or black walnut. I personally see no ironclad reason why it is so, but it is a fact that the bulk of fine guns, the really first-class works, in the United States are accomplished with what everybody thinks of as higher grades of walnut—English, Claro, so-called Circassian, French, Bastogne and the like.

The people who do the work claim that these are just simply better woods. They are harder, and stronger for their weights, and they take checkering and embellishment better, and as a matter of style, the delicious grain patterns of these foreign walnuts are more popular,

more classic. In the 1981 edition of *Gun Digest,* Stuart Williams goes at great length into the subject of walnut, and his article is worth reading.

Assuming that you have located one or several merchants of the sort of walnut stock blanks you want, the thing to do is to get to where the walnut is and look at it. Establish some sort of relationship with the man, mostly by telling him straight up what you want, both immediately and in the future. If you are interested in acquiring green blanks for slow air drying, tell him so. A lot of merchants like to sell green wood. They like it because they can turn their money around quicker than by having to dry it, and the buyer of green wood assumes what little risk there is that a given stick won't dry properly.

On that subject, I had a conversation with a stockmaker who specializes in furnishing the wood for the stocks he makes and has built that part of his business to where he also furnishes the wood to a lot of other stockmakers' use for extra-fine guns. He dries his own wood at home in a relatively elaborate setup, but he has

This dark dense French walnut, worked up by Don Klein, shows the character that even a working gun can get from special wood. The grain and color makes even such a flat surface as this buttstock interesting to the eye.

The wood in the rifle stock is Bastogne fiddleback walnut; the stock blank is California English. Dowtin, who specializes in furnishing wood as well creating such rifle stocks, is the source of both of these.

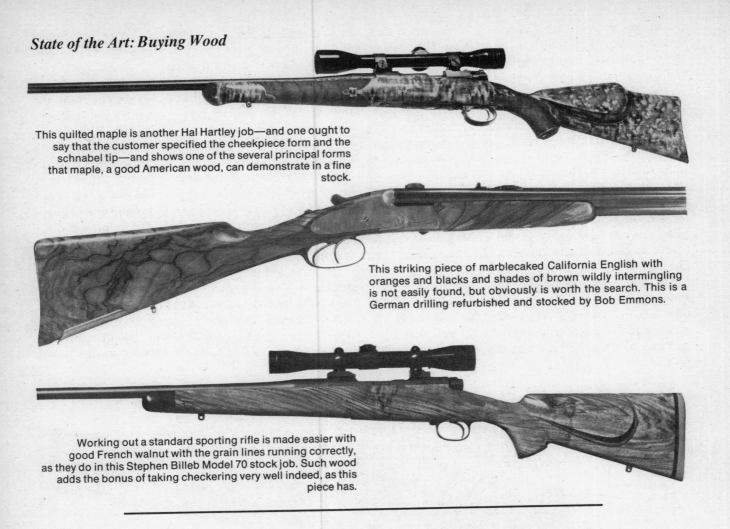

This quilted maple is another Hal Hartley job—and one ought to say that the customer specified the cheekpiece form and the schnabel tip—and shows one of the several principal forms that maple, a good American wood, can demonstrate in a fine stock.

This striking piece of marblecaked California English with oranges and blacks and shades of brown wildly intermingling is not easily found, but obviously is worth the search. This is a German drilling refurbished and stocked by Bob Emmons.

Working out a standard sporting rifle is made easier with good French walnut with the grain lines running correctly, as they do in this Stephen Billeb Model 70 stock job. Such wood adds the bonus of taking checkering very well indeed, as this piece has.

that setup because he wants to speed the process, so far as he can with safety, because he has a lot of money tied up in wood. Nevertheless, he tells me he has never lost a blank. He pays, by the way, not less than $200 even for a wholly green stick of walnut. He buys only good wood.

When you get to a supply of good blanks you can really look at, try not to lose your heart immediately. There are certain things about a rifle blank that are absolute requirements, regardless of its beauty, its dryness and its character. It must, for instance, be of a certain size. If it is not long enough or it is not wide enough, it is simply not long enough or wide enough. A shotgun blank, and that means one intended for a gun that is going to be built with a fore-end and a buttstock from the same piece of wood, may be smaller, of course. Do not fall in love with any piece of wood that isn't big enough.

When faced with perhaps a dozen blanks, blanks you can look at because one side has been planed and oiled or finished, you will find it easy to make a choice if you are going to make a choice right then and there. That is, if it is straight grain you are looking for, a number of the blanks will disqualify themselves, and the reverse is

true, of course, if what you want is marblecake, and there is any marblecake there. Given that there are three blanks that are possible, the first thing to do is to look at both sides of each blank. That will instantly tell you which are the higher priced blanks, because the ones with the grain figure on both sides are more expensive. Selecting one of the three, you must then put your chosen project up against it mentally. You have to picture the gunstock cut out of this stick of wood in front of you. Where does the grain flow, will it get in the right place, and if it is all there when you have trimmed it away for the gunstock is it going to look right for the kind of gun you want? Now, often you will find that the purveyor will have outlined a stock shape on the side of the blank to help show you how it will work out. It wouldn't hurt to measure that outline to make sure that it is full-size.

One ought to be very selective at this point to ensure that the grain of the wood, no matter how fancy, does run properly up through the grip and along the forearm, without dipping down as it goes. Classically, if the grain does not run, in the forearm, quite parallel to the barrel, it ought to run up toward the barrel. Again classically, any figure in the buttstock ought to settle down when it

This Vic Olson-stocked rifle exhibits the straightforward practical character that has its own beauty, obtained from straight grain pattern and some color contrast. Many of the buyers of custom guns who intend a rifle to be used and shot a great deal prefer such wood for those rifles.

Here is Oregon black walnut done up by H.L. "Pete" Grisel. The rifle is a Model 70 in 220 Swift with all the trimmings, and the whole ensemble shows that carefully chosen American black walnut can hold its head up in any company.

This is Ed Harris' pet squirrel gun and plinker 22, done up on a Savage Mark 10 target rifle barreled action. The nicely figured wood is cherry. Work is by Wayne Schwartz.

gets to the pistol grip area and commence its run to the end of the stock up front. No matter how attractive the piece of wood is, if it will not work up into a stock that fulfills these criteria for structural strength, do not buy the wood.

In this time of inflation, there is no telling where wood prices will go. Therefore, there can be no real guidelines set up for those just beginning to think about putting together fine guns. Already, as this is written in 1980, people pay $500 routinely for exhibition grade walnut in one or another of the species. They are paying $1,000 for exceptional blanks, and for those once-in-a-lifetime sticks, the sky is apparently the limit—or at least $2,000 is a limit. That is, I repeat, for a wood blank only.

That ought not be dismaying, even for a beginner. There are, if not plenty, at least a reasonable number of entirely adequate blanks, both for figure and strength, to be found. Prices for these, depending on the individual source and the state of the market and the economy, can be purchased for as low as $200 or up to $500 in the higher ranges in this class of wood. What you get in sound English, French or Bastogne walnut in this grade is functionally as good as any wood that is ever put into

a gunstock, with all the working qualities it takes for excellent checkering, taking a good finish, plus a bit of color and figure.

Still, one has to think of the investment. If one is to pay $500 or some additional increment thereof for the work to be done on the piece of wood, one probably ought to bite the bullet and spend some money on the wood, also. If investment is not a factor, of course, and one is building a working tool, having chosen to have it as a very best tool in every sense of the word, then the sound but plainer blanks make a great deal of sense.

There are other woods besides the fine walnuts, of course, and the first of these is American black walnut. It has what some believe are deficiencies as earlier noted, but that does not mean that exceedingly handsome and sound gunstocks cannot be built from American walnut. The grain and figure of American walnut works out somewhat differently than that in the fine walnuts. In the excellent grades, called often "AAA" or some such, a blank will show approximately the same figure on both sides, there are featherings and shadings of tone and flares of the lines of the grain. The colors of American walnut do not show the wide range of the other walnuts, tending rather more toward the

The above pair of rifles show the forthright appeal of maple, particularly maple done up by Hal Hartley as these were. The rifles were made as a pair in Weatherby calibers, and they are so close in appearance that it probably was smart to have the checkering patterns differ just a little between them.

French walnut can be flawed, and Charles DeVeto, who did the job, says that this piece had many defects that had to be worked around. Obviously, the job succeeded.

Some fanciers and some artisans prefer that the stock blank not distract from the workmanship and choose utterly high quality, but quite plain wood for their stocks. This Phil Fischer Model 70 is an example of such preference. The wood, in this case, is American black walnut, a particularly hard and dense sample.

dark side of the color spectrum. It should be noted that stockmakers have long dealt with American walnut and know how to handle its peculiarities when it comes to creating checkering patterns that will work. And finishes that take full advantage on American walnut's warmth are part of every maker's repertoire.

There are certain guns, particularly repeating rifles and shotguns, which actually look more "right" with American walnut than with the other walnuts. At least, so it seems to this reporter. Since so many of us use repeaters that are not bolt-actions, in the case of rifles, and slide-action and autoloading shotguns for much of our shooting, stocking these, what might be called working guns, in American walnut is certainly appropriate.

Fine, which means very highly figured, American walnut is getting scarce, too. However, it does not carry quite the price tag that the other walnuts carry and a truly fine blank can be found under $200, and for $100, American walnut blanks can be found that far exceed

most factory wood.

The same rules apply in buying. Try to see a lot of it and try not to settle for anything but the stick which will make you happy as you live with it for a long time. The grain flow through the stock still should be up through the pistol grip and along the forearm.

There are more sources for American walnut than for the other woods, and a great deal of such walnut is available as semi-inletted stocks, of which we will say something below. Often, the sources for the semi-inletted stocks will also sell in the blank, but of course their costs are largely already in the blank and one ought to be able to buy equivalent walnut cheaper elsewhere. On the other hand, the nationally advertised firms with catalogs and the like are very convenient sources.

There are other woods, of course. I recently heard of a quite handsome gunstock made of an exceptional piece of elm, so doubtless anything is possible. Recently, I acquired a rifle stocked with stained maple and I find the effect so intriguing I'm having a couple of

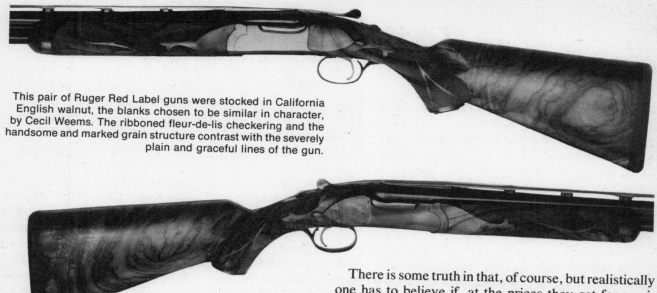

This pair of Ruger Red Label guns were stocked in California English walnut, the blanks chosen to be similar in character, by Cecil Weems. The ribboned fleur-de-lis checkering and the handsome and marked grain structure contrast with the severely plain and graceful lines of the gun.

guns stocked in a matching battery.

In this book you will see photographed a most handsome cherry wood stock, which shows excellent figure. Maple, of course, is second to walnut in general and has been for many decades. Myrtle in its myriad patterns is another favored, and for heavy guns, mesquite is not *often* used, because it is not easy to find, but it has a special character of its own. Almost all of the tropical hardwoods have been tried for gunstocks. I remember an exhibition rifle, put together by Winslow Arms in its heyday, made of one magnificent piece of cocobolo. Since the rifle was got up in the extreme style that some Winslow rifles had, the result was certainly a most striking firearm.

For any of these, the buyer has to be his own guide. There are plenty of texts which compare the various woods technically with walnut, which is the acknowledged standard for gunstocks.

Probably there are hundreds and thousands of semi-inletted stocks sold and used happily for every first-cabin from-the-block stock in the United States. Such an important source of satisfaction cannot be ignored. The people in that business know what they are doing, they are serving a public that wants their services, and while the resultant guns are seldom classic, they are for the most part handsome and functional. It would be easy to simply turn away and say those are not truly custom gunstocks, so they ought not to be recognized. It would not, however, be realistic, and there are some things to say about semi-inletted stocks.

At a time when I had something to do with the technical staff of the *American Rifleman*, the old-timers there would chuckle and say, as one writer has said here in this book, "Yes, a semi-inletted stock has 90 percent of the easy work finished."

There is some truth in that, of course, but realistically one has to believe if, at the prices they get for semi-inletted stocks, one can purchase 90 percent of any of the work done, it is not a bad deal. One can, with regular wood working tools, and just a few special scrapers and the like, set the metal parts of his gun into a commercial semi-inletted stock, and then finish the job at least to factory standards. He can equally, one has to point out, botch it completely and still wind up with a using gun that suits him.

In looking over the market in semi-inletted stocks, there is no substitute for research with the catalogs and price lists that all purveyors will furnish. One must remember that the written descriptions and statements in the catalogs have two purposes—one to inform the reader, the other to sell the gunstocks. Be sure to look at the pictures to be sure you understand the words.

Apart from the giants in the semi-inlet business, like Fajen, Bishop, Herter's, there are others who have sales points of their own to make. The smaller firms do not offer the wide selections in stock styles and wood choices, nor do they permit the purchase of a semi-inletted stock to suit almost any gun ever made. However, they often have their own styles for the guns they do fit, and, in some cases, work a little closer to the bone than the bigger firms. This has an advantage and a disadvantage. The advantage is that the style of the finished gunstock may wind up a little cleaner; the disadvantage is that there is less room to work with in the matter of dimensions. A shooter who takes a standard factory arm and restocks it himself with wood that he likes better in a style that appeals to him does not have, of course, a custom rifle. He has a restocked factory rifle, which some people call semi-custom. For tens of thousands of shooters, that is enough, of course.

In closing, let me repeat what was said virtually at the outset: Money spent on fine wood is never wasted. The price is forgotten eventually and the wood continues to satisfy for generations.

Ken Warner

To Buy the Work

THERE are more ways to buy work on fine custom guns than there are kinds of work to be done, but the standard way is with the checkbook. That is, one decides what the work ought to be, one orders it and when it is finished, one pays for it.

That all sounds good, but it is never that simple. *Never* is a big word, so perhaps it does happen sometimes, but I personally have never heard of such a deal. There are always complications.

The principal one is time. It almost always takes lots longer than calculated at the beginning. From the day an action is shipped to the metalsmith and the wood to the stockmaker, the system starts to break down, it seems. When, for example, either of the gentlemen

absolutely assures them of that much work and more, and there is little point, they feel, in trying to broaden what is, at base, a one-man, one-job-at-a-time kind of business.

It is this factor more than any other that is going to give rise to a whole new class of first-class artisans. The masters just aren't going to be accepting work, and those who want the work anyway are going to have to go to someone else or do without. Since no American citizen who wants a gun is going to do without, there are simply going to be more artisans doing this work. With standards set high, as they have been, there is little doubt in this reporter's mind that the workers in the field can rise to this potentially profitable occasion.

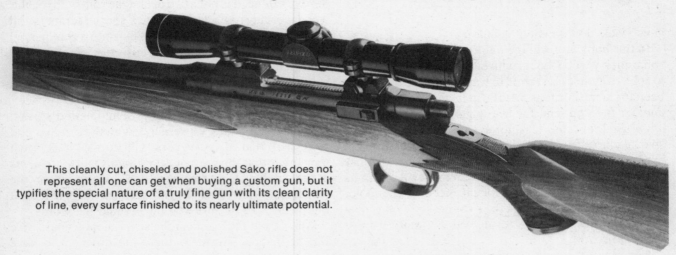

This cleanly cut, chiseled and polished Sako rifle does not represent all one can get when buying a custom gun, but it typifies the special nature of a truly fine gun with its clean clarity of line, every surface finished to its nearly ultimate potential.

involved gets ill or hurt, there is a delay. Domestic situations, wholly out of the control of either the would-be gun owner or the artisan, sometimes cause delays. Parts go astray, wood does not behave as it ought to, other jobs—we are telling the truth as we know it here—simply must be stuck into the pipeline out of turn. It all adds up. It all adds up, sometimes, to 2 years beyond the original deadline. Sometimes, it never happens. As this is written, one prominent metalworker, at least, has a large number of "sometime" jobs stacked up, I hear. The betting is they'll not get done.

In part such circumstances are economic. When one has agreed in the past to "sometime" do a job for $300 for which one now gets $900, it gets less and less easy to find time to do such a job. For some artisans, the problem has resolved itself quite simply: They no longer accept work from anyone who is not an old customer. They know they can accomplish only so many jobs a year, and their list of satisfied customers

As time goes on, and the qualities of fine guns are known to more and more people, it will be possible to judge the work at hand without knowing who did it. It is at that point that the new masters of the trade will be able to make their marks.

Doing business in the field of fine guns begins with research. That is, a wide variety of sources must be consulted, catalogs obtained, prices compared, well before one is ready to order the work. One must first know what he wants, and what he is willing to pay for it.

Prices and time being what they are, it is probably as well at the beginning to have a fallback position in terms of the amount of work one wants accomplished. One could, for instance, do without the hand-built scope mounts at the beginning.

The main thing one has to do is talk. Talk to everyone and anyone who knows anything about the kind of guns involved or about the artisans or the field in general. There are only a very few of the top workers who will pass any negative comments about other people in the field, but everybody always knows when a given artisan is not delivering, or has suffered the quality of his work to slide, which can happen for any number of reasons, some of them legitimate or nearly so. To stay out of trouble, one must keep his ears tuned for hints in these directions.

This is all sounding rather negative, and to the extent that this book will be read by people who never tried to get a fine gun together, that tone is taken to keep them from being surprised when things don't go just right. It is difficult to explain, but artisans in the firearms field, the fine craftsmen, are as "artistic" as fine artists and others are reputed to be. In fact, I have had many occasions to use commercial artists and have known many fine artists and have never found one nearly so difficult about deliveries or special demands as the average craftsmen in the gun business. It has something to do with the character, the general character, of the sort of men who are interested in guns enough to spend full-time with them.

Understand, please, that when it is all finished and it is done to specifications, and it is the best work of everybody concerned, the result is glorious. It is a satisfaction that lasts and lasts and lasts, an artifact that can be put to use and remain beautiful and functional. The joy of a fine rifle or a super shotgun is like that first day with a new driver's license and a new car. The best part is that you can never repeat that teenage day when the world was yours on your first wheels, but you can repeat the experience of a new fine gun any time your pocketbook will let you.

The reason for all the research and the worry and the gossiping is that the buyer is contracting for work to be performed to his specifications. He must, therefore, first understand the specifications himself, and then he must be sure that his contractor understands the specifications in the same way, and then he must be sure that he understands the price he must pay for the work. As with any contract, delivery dates or, in this case, potential or intended delivery dates, are part of the deal.

For instance, the stockmaker fits the stock to metal in the white so that he may sand adjacent surfaces and get them fitted properly, if for no other reason. Many stockmakers, therefore, include bluing the finished gun in their price. Some, however, do not. In such cases, the metalsmith may include bluing, but he will blue only after the stock work is finished. Sometimes, indeed, both worthy gentlemen will wash their hands of the bluing and it is necessary then to engage a third party.

The matter of dimensions ought to be carefully considered. There seems to me to be little point in spending time and energy and money to construct a fine gun without fitting that gun rather precisely to its potential user, even if the gun might never be fired. You might have to use it sometime, and when you do you ought to experience the whole sensation, not just part of it.

It will be recognized that much of the process in-volves decisions, indeed, most of them are decisions about the gun you will get. The cartridge to be used, the twist rate in the barrel, the final weight of the gun, one's personal desires about barrel length and contour, details in terms of buttplates and grip caps, checkering patterns and sights and accessories, the shape of the bolt handle and the curve of a trigger—all these are for the buyer to decide. All these are part of the contract, which is not necessarily a legal document, but is somewhere on paper so all concerned know what they are working at.

Some artisans are more businesslike than others and have standardized order forms on which all this can appear; others rely on letters and notes. Whichever, the client—and anyone making these kinds of orders becomes a client—ought to have copies for his own files. One cannot expect complete satisfaction with a sloppily described job, and one takes his chances in any matter where he has an opinion that is left to the artisan to decide. I am not saying that an artisan left alone wouldn't build a prettier gun than the client could describe; what I am saying is that if the client wants it to be his gun in every detail, he must specify every detail. Where he does not so specify, and it is left to the worker, one can expect occasional minor dissatisfaction.

Prices should be firm prices. It is not good business to have it otherwise. Dealing at the very top there is an advantage in simply paying the asked price, without dickering—one can subsequently morally demand full effort from his contractor. On the other hand, as with any business deal, a certain amount of negotiating is probably normal to the business. That works both ways, of course—the worker might be negotiating up and the buyer might be negotiating down, but a bargain can be struck in this way as in any other situation.

In these inflationary times, workers quoting prices for future jobs do have problems that everyone ought to recognize. There is no easy way around this problem. It is probably wise to discuss this angle directly with the contractor. When he sets a price, he ought to be asked specifically if that will be the price when the job is delivered. It would be nice to have it in writing, but that is unrealistic. When there is uncertainty about a future price, it is probably better to have the man set a price, a higher price, that he is sure he will be happy with at the time the job is delivered, than to leave that to be negotiated at the end.

As business people, workers in the fine gun field vary all over the lot. There are those who quote high and deliver for less money; there are those who quote low and negotiate the price upward later; there are some who state a price and stick to it; and there are probably other variations. A friend of mine recently noted that, in regard to a certain operation, he several times successively told one worker that he would spend up to a given amount on a certain job. Three of those jobs were delivered and all were at the full or maximum price under the arrangement. And on one of them, the worker wanted additional money, citing inflation as the problem.

Again, we are sounding negative here, so once again I will say that there are probably no finer bunch of people than those in the gun field generally, and among the fine artisans in particular. However, it is a complete process, this fine gun business, and there are many ways for misunderstandings to arise. It is quite possible for two men of good will to believe they have an agreement when they have none at all. That is the circumstance, above all of the circumstances, to avoid. That is why things should be down on paper and the buyer ought to do his level best in advance to be sure he understands how the contractor he is dealing with wants to do business and then arrange to deal that way. It simply will not work to try to force one's personal business approach on craftsmen.

The more interesting the job, the quicker it will get done, by the way. If a fellow were to deliver to a stockmaker the finest piece of wood the stockmaker ever saw, he could expect the stock to be finished right on schedule, because it is hard for a craftsman to keep his hands off a special piece of work. That goes for metalsmithing that is beyond the routine, as well.

There are also many forms of barter going on in the gun business. Clients who can offer good hunting, automobiles, fine wood, desirable rifle actions and the like in place of money, or as boot, often find takers among the good workers. The craftsmen, indeed, trade among themselves, work for work.

Bartering generally, when honestly carried out, benefits both parties more than cash transactions. Each

gets more. And a good, happy swap puts the two closer. It becomes a more personal deal. Some fine friendships, in fact, have developed this way. The resulting guns are not better made, because top people only do top work, but they seem to mean more to both craftsman and owner.

It is also possible to stretch out the making of a fine gun. It is best to begin with the metalwork, and get that right. The owner can then use the rifle in a utility stock, or a cut-down factory stock, until the right piece of wood comes along, and then have the piece stocked, the metalwork being refinished. Then, at a later time, the piece can be engraved. This approach spreads the various costs over several years.

It's nothing new. Many a fine rifle has been reworked and refinished, rebarreled and restocked, during two or three decades of ownership. This was particularly so over the 1930s to the 1950s as scopes replaced iron sights in general use, requiring changes in the guns.

Finally, one must mention travel time. All the metal, for instance, must get from where it is to the metalsmith. Once done, it must go to the client for approval, and then to the stockmaker. The wood and various pieces of furniture have to get there, too. Then, when he is finished, the whole must be delivered to the owner.

Since all these respective destinations may be 1,000 to 1,500 miles apart, it is no accident that clients who have the funds to travel or can easily arrange their business travel for stopovers often can expedite their jobs. Dealing face-to-face is always best.

It can be an agonizing business, this management of the production of a fine gun. It is nothing like nor as simple as ordinary business deals. To a degree, the buyer is a direct participant in the work. Perhaps that is part of the satisfaction. It might well be and no one realizes it because there is so much satisfaction in a fine gun, successfully built to order.   *Ken Warner*

Match Rifles

RIFLES FOR various types of competition are specialized items not suitable for much else but their game. Most target shooters use factory-made rifles, but a lot of modification goes on within the framework of the rules. Serious competitors take the modifications as far as the rule book allows in search of that last competitive edge. Most are simply accurized and tuned versions of standard guns, but you see many which are virtually rebuilt, with new stocks and barrels to the same basic configurations. There are also a few one-of-a-kind

custom guns made especially for competition, and once somebody wins a major championship with one of these referee's nightmares, a lot of copies begin to show up.

High-power rifle competition sponsored by the NRA is done with three types of rifles, the NRA Match Rifle, the Service Rifle, and the long-range "bullgun." The NRA Match Rifle is a repeating rifle with iron sights, and not less than a 3-pound trigger pull. There is no weight limit as such, the limiting factor being how much the shooter can hold steady offhand. Most NRA Match

This is the all-out Anschutz Model 1413 rifle designed for the international smallbore competitor. It looks complicated and it is because it has virtually every refinement permitted under the rules and required by the level of competition in this demanding precision sport.

Rifles weigh about 13 pounds, though a big man might manage a rifle weighing as much as 16 pounds. Few over-the-course shooters use rifles weighing less than about 12 pounds. Most NRA Match Rifles are bolt-actions, such as the Winchester Model 70 or Remington 40X, which can be reloaded for the rapid-fire stages using a stripper clip inserted into guides machined into the receiver bridge. Standard Model 70 sporting actions are often modified by having clip slots cut into them, and Remington 700 actions are often used with a custom-made sight base on the receiver bridge with charging slots machined into it. Occasionally you see shooters using semi-automatic match rifles using the Springfield Armory M1A action with a heavy barrel and target stock. These rifles can be competitive with the bolt-action rifles, but they are temperamental and far more expensive to build.

NRA Match Rifles once had to be either 30-06 or 308 Winchester, but there is no caliber restriction today, provided the rifle meets the other rule book requirements. Most rifles today shoot the 308 Winchester cartridge, however, and the 308 outnumbers all the others combined. The 30-06 is still used successfully by a few, and if you use your over-the-course rifle for 1,000-yard matches as well, instead of having a separate magnum bullgun for those events, the 30-06 has a slight edge over the 308 for that purpose. However, for National Match Course shooting only, the 308 has an advantage since it has somewhat less recoil, and it seems to be more easily loaded to its full accuracy potential. Although the 30-06 is still a fine cartridge, it is somewhat less efficient in less than maximum loads than the 308 Winchester. The larger powder capacity of the 30-06 is an advantage for long-range shooting, since it permits large enough charges of slow-burning powders to drive the heavier 190-gr. or 200-gr. match bullets fast enough to provide a significant reduction in wind drift when compared to the 308. There is a trade off, small though it is. If you have a good 06 there's no reason not to use it, but most competitors prefer the 308 for its lighter recoil, lesser consumption of increasingly expensive powder, slightly better barrel life, and slightly better accuracy with the mild loads of moderately fast powders (such as IMR-

4895) which are typically used.

Most veteran Match Rifle shooters prefer the pre-1964 Winchester Model 70, though the recent Model 70 target rifle is used successfully and is just as slick a rifle for rapid fire as the older one, thanks to the anti-bind device on the bolt. The 4-groove, hammer forged Ultra Match barrels used on recent production rifles had a good reputation for accuracy, though sales of the Model 70 target were slow, and it was discontinued in 1980. It's a shame, since the Model 70 target was, and is, a fine target rifle. Though the Model 70 was king, the Remington 40X has a very strong following, which will undoubtedly increase now. Many Remington 700 rifles are converted also and work very well, and southpaws often use the Savage 110 or 112 with good results. The only Springfields or Mausers seen are those used by old-timers.

The most important factor about a match rifle is the barrel. A serious match rifle shooter is among the few shooting enthusiasts who ever wears out a barrel by shooting it out. A well cared for barrel in 30-06 or 308 will generally last 5,000 rounds or so, but it's not unusual for top shooters to burn that many rounds in a season, so they keep extra guns for practice, or backup if their primary gun goes sour. Even the beginning competitor will shoot several thousand rounds in matches and practice a year, and will probably only get a season or two from a barrel. Proper cleaning and choice of bullets can usually extend accurate barrel life, and I know several good shooters who regularly get from 5,000 to 8,000 rounds through a barrel before it starts going sour at 600 yards. Most shooters buying a new rifle will use the factory barrel (if it performs well) until it is shot out, and then they will replace it with a custom job, usually a Hart, though you also see barrels by Shilen, Atkinson, McMillan, Obermeyer or others. Barrels are most often 12-inch twist in over-the-course guns, but you see a lot of 10-inch twist barrels also, and more recently the 11-inch twist seems to be catching on as about the ideal compromise.

Stocks are usually the factory style used on the repeating 40X or Winchester Model 70 Target, but far better are custom stocks which resemble the ISU Army

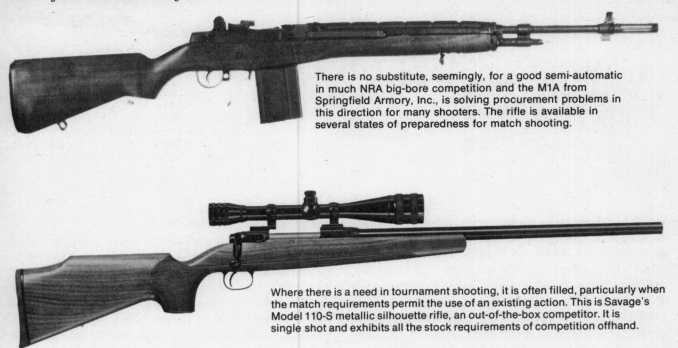

There is no substitute, seemingly, for a good semi-automatic in much NRA big-bore competition and the M1A from Springfield Armory, Inc., is solving procurement problems in this direction for many shooters. The rifle is available in several states of preparedness for match shooting.

Where there is a need in tournament shooting, it is often filled, particularly when the match requirements permit the use of an existing action. This is Savage's Model 110-S metallic silhouette rifle, an out-of-the-box competitor. It is single shot and exhibits all the stock requirements of competition offhand.

Rifle pattern used in 300-meter competition. They have a deeper fore-end and a somewhat closer grip for offhand shooting. Although these stocks aren't quite as good for prone shooting, a good shot usually has more trouble with an ill fitting stock for offhand than he does prone or sitting. The best stock designs for National Match Course work are those of the pattern developed by Roy Dunlap back in the 1950s, which are still made today by Jim Cloward and a few others. Replacement stocks are best made either of laminated wood or fiberglass, and are always glass bedded, usually using the "pillar" system. Increasingly, the high-power shooters are applying the techniques applied in bench rest shooting to their rifles and ammunition, but they are usually about 5 years behind the bench rest crowd. A few shooters try out the ideas when they first appear, and if these fellows win using a certain bedding system or technique, soon everybody will get the word. That's the way progress is made in this game.

The custom semi-automatic match rifle is a strange animal. Back in the early 1970s a few crazy fellows (I was one of them) tried to adapt the M16 or AR-15 rifles for National Match Course shooting. The rationale was that the straight stock and light recoil of the pipsqueak rounds would make the gun easy to handle in offhand and rapid fire, and that you could do OK at 600 yards by using heavier bullets and a faster twist, provided you were a good wind doper and you didn't shoot during a hurricane. All kinds of ways were found to make the mouseguns shoot, and they equaled the best boltguns. The AR-15 with a heavy Hart barrel, rigid tubular handguard and good sights, when fed good ammo, is a precision outfit. Mine would repeatedly shoot 10-shot,

200-yard groups under minute of angle, and would stay around .8 m.o.a. with the best bullets. The little gun was accurate enough to go clean easily back to 300, since the gun hardly recoiled and was almost like shooting a rimfire, but it can't buck the wind at 600. You will lose points there. You can shoot good Master scores and get your share of award points with one, but you can't win. It's that simple.

The semi-auto match rifles built using the M1A action and firing the 7.62 NATO cartridge are horses of a different color. Ray Sweet, a former armorer for the Marines, and now with the FBI, has an M1A match rifle which is astounding. A Virginia shooter, Bert Rollins, probably the top civilian service rifle shooter on the East Coast, has one also, which I presume Sweet built. I understand that Clint Fowler, another "Hardholders East" top gunner, is also building one. With serious competitors catching on to this idea of having the extra 10 seconds for holding and squeezing, but not having to operate the bolt, there are going to be a lot more of these rifles built once people start winning the big tournaments with them. I give it a few years and the boltguns will have their work cut out for them keeping up. These custom rifles are hybrids—a service rifle action, with match rifle stock, heavy barrel and good sights.

Service rifles for matches are not customized, only accurized, since the rules state that no external modifications are permitted. The allowable modifications include smoothing the function of parts, as long as the safety devices function normally, glass bedding, and heavy barrels, as long as the portion visible outside the handguards retains the original con-

This more usual, but not ordinary, rifle is Walther's Moving Target rifle. A 22 rimfire, it is set up within the rules and for the job of shooting the little hogs at 50 meters.

The old favorite on the Camp Perry firing line is the M1 Garand and Springfield Armory, Inc., has one available now. Again, the rifle is available in several states of preparedness.

tour. It is common to replace the GI match barrel with a custom replacement made on a Hart or Obermeyer blank, very often with an 11-inch twist, with the barrel being stainless steel. This usually adds 1½-2 pounds to the weight of an ordinary National Match M1, M14 or M1A rifle. Shooters say the 4-groove government rifling form outshoots the 6-groove with Lake City ammo, but that tight 6-groove barrels shoot 168-gr. Sierra bullets better. The M1 rifle is usually converted to 7.62mm NATO these days, mainly because of ammo availability, but also because the rifle seems to be more accurate in this caliber.

The long-range "bullgun" is a specialized single shot, heavy target rifle used only for 1000-yard prone shooting. It is usually chambered for the 300 Winchester Magnum, the wildcat 30-338, or 7mm Remington Magnum. Many competitors use their over-the-course guns in 308 or 30-06 for long-range matches, but the top scores today are almost always shot with the magnums. In the 30 caliber cartridges the 10-inch twist is preferred, since the usual practice is to drive heavy bullets of 190 grs., 200 grs., or 220 grs. as hard as they will go. In the 7mm Magnums a 9-inch twist is about standard, but the fellows who get custom fast-twist barrels often do better. The 8-inch twist 7mm seems to be gaining popularity.

Many 1,000-yard target guns, built in Winchester Model 70 and Remington 40X actions, are often sleeved to make them more rigid. There are also a lot of custom bench rest actions being used such as Hart, Wichita, Shilen, and occasionally some exotics like the Grunig-Elmeiger from West Germany or the Shultz & Larson from Sweden. Stocks are thick, heavy prone style, usually laminated or fiberglass, and always glass bedded. Since few competitive bullguns you could win matches with are available from the factory, most top guns are custom-made—rebarreled, custom chambered, accurized and restocked in fairly conventional configurations.

Silhouette rifles are unlike any others. While the game started with the intent of using hunting rifles that everybody owned, it has now become so specialized that anybody showing up with an "ordinary" hunting rifle with the idea of actually competing in a silhouette match would look strange indeed. Most silhouette rifles start out as factory bolt-actions, such as the Remington 700V, Savage 112V, or Ruger 77V. Such factory "varmint" rifles today are chambered in 308 Winchester and have become silhouette rifles, too. Often, however, the shooter burns a lot of rounds like his high-power rifle counterpart, and he will upgrade to a custom barrel, usually a 10-, 11- or 12-inch twist, since he shoots either 168-gr. or 190-gr. bullets like his National Match Course counterpart.

Barrels for silhouette rifles are somewhat lighter than over-the-course target barrels since the rifles must meet a 10-pound, 2-ounce weight limit with sights. Makers, twists and producers are the same, with the most common barrel being a 12-inch twist Hart stainless steel in 308 Winchester. The 280 Remington, 7mm-08 Remington, and to a far lesser extent, the 30-06 are also used. The 7mm rounds have a fairly strong following, but the 30s still lead the field.

Stocks are the most often customized part of a silhouette rifle, since barrels and actions are pretty much standardized, and vary from the conventional to

This is a match rifle of a different kind. The Cast Bullet Association shoots, obviously, cast bullets, and this is a hunter class rifle for such events. It is either a 30-30 or a 35-30, built on the Remington 788 action, restocked. It belongs to Ed Harris.

This peculiar Model 70 Winchester is or was the International Army Model. It is set up as it is set up to shoot some of the interesting center-fire team and individual matches, but saw some use in silhouette shooting also, a couple of years back.

the bizarre. The rules were nailed down a few years ago after Karen Monez almost took home a National Championship with what a few people thought was a rule bender rifle, so the number of funny guns is a lot greater now than it was before the rule change. Shooters now know how far they can go, and they do so. Before, when nothing was down on paper, few shooters strained the spirit of the rules. Now the custom silhouette stock bears little or no resemblance to what you'd expect to see out hunting. The combs are high, right up to the bore line, but not higher, as that's not permitted. The roll-over of the comb can extend above the bore line, however, as long as a rod inserted down the bore from the breech clears the stock. The grip is usually full, as deep as permitted, and nearly vertical. The buttstock may be hollowed out on the side opposite the face to save weight, and the grip might be hollowed out as well. The Fajen silhouette stock has the trigger guard as part of the stock. Deep fore-ends, as on ISU target rifles, are ruled out, but almost anything else goes. Such stocks permit the shooter to maintain a relaxed offhand position with the head erect, and they place the face high on the stock. Glass bedding, often using the pillar system, is standard procedure.

Consequently, scope mounts for silhouette rifles place the scope high, much higher than you'd ordinarily want on a hunting rifle, but this works fine since the stocks are proportioned for it. Raising the scope higher is supposed to reduce the effects of heat mirage rising from the barrel, an important factor on hot, sunny outdoor ranges when you fire a large number of rounds.

Silhouette rifles are usually tuned and adjusted like other target rifles, with special attention to careful, close, concentric chambering, recessed crowns, squared up, lapped in actions, and light pull triggers.

The triggers are often replaced with a 2-ounce bench rest trigger or a Canjar light pull unit especially designed for the sport. It's all its own ball game.

Bench rest rifles are the most advanced examples of shooting technology, as most new developments in accurate rifles originate here. Things we take for granted today, such as glass bedding, stainless steel barrels, button rifling, laminated stocks, bedding blocks, pillar bedding, action sleeves, light pull triggers, free floating barrels, the fiberglass stock, and glued-in action were all developed by bench rest shooters. Just as new developments in the space program or in auto racing filter down to the consumer, the new developments originating in bench rest shooting benefit all shooters. Bench rest shooting is largely responsible for the high quality of primers, bullets and cartridge cases we enjoy today. Without those advances, today's hunter would still be shooting 3-inch groups from his Springfield and the ½-minute varmint rifle would be a dream and not the reality it is today.

To the uninitiated, bench rest shooting seems simple, since all shooting is from a rest, but that's deceiving. Chances are, your best bragging group with your favorite varmint rifle wouldn't get much attention in this crowd. Tiny groups are the name of the game, and while you'd be surprised how large some of the groups are (even good shooters have bad days), the tiny ones hung in the "wailing wall" are unbelievable. The heavy varmint and unlimited guns routinely shoot under ⅛-inch (measured on centers), and the top dogs will shoot into the "point tens." There have been groups in the "point zero somethings" shot in registered matches. Even the light varmint rifles and sporter class rifles routinely stay under ½-minute, and ¼-minute groups in the light guns aren't unheard of, actually being common among the good gunners at the big shoots.

The bench rest crowd is fanatical about the details of fine, precision work. No bench rester would even think of building a rifle without squaring the front of the receiver, lapping the lugs in, making sure the face of the bolt is perfectly square with the receiver, and that the receiver threads are concentric and square to the bolt face. When chambering a barrel the bench rest gunsmith always makes sure the bore turns true to the outside; if not, he trues it up. Then with the barrel running true to bore center, he'll rough the chamber with a boring arrangement, and indicate the inside and outside again to be sure, before finish reaming the chamber. Chambers are usually on the tight side and are cut with special care to concentricity, usually checking the finished chamber with a dial indicator to be sure it is perfectly round and concentric to the threads, etc. If not, the barrel is set back and he tries again.

Many bench resters use what is called a tight neck chamber. This requires that a fellow really knows what he is doing, since it's very easy to get into trouble. It is used only with neck-turned or neck-reamed cases, or with those which have been carefully checked with a tubing micrometer to insure the necks will permit a minimum clearance for safe release of the bullet. Once cases are shot the first time, they need not be resized again, since the chamber is cut close enough that the natural spring-back of the brass supplies the needed tension to hold the bullet. Depending upon caliber, the neck clearance will usually be only .0010-.0015-inch. Using such a chamber with ordinary ammunition is dangerous, since it takes only a wee bit of interference to cause a dangerous and rapid increase in pressure. In extreme cases you can blow a rifle up this way, as a recent *American Rifleman* article explained. Unless you are familiar with this system, leave it to the experts. It is a specialized system which is for competition only and has no safe application in a hunting rifle.

The advantage of the tight neck chamber, though, is that it aids better concentricity of the case neck and bullet with respect to the chamber, since the case neck is not resized or subjected to deformation and misalignment by pushing the expander ball through it. Reloading is easier since there is no sizing to do, you just decap, clean the primer pocket and reprime, charge powder and seat the bullet. Bench rest shooters most often use small hand tools at the bench to reload on the line, or in a separate reloading area, between matches. In some cases a shooter may load the same case over and over until he completes his group.

Barrels for bench rest are generally stainless steel, and usually 14-inch twist regardless of whether they are 22 caliber, 6mm or 30 caliber. Hart, McMillan and Shilen are the most popular barrels. The most popular cartridges are the 222 Remington, 22 Remington BR, 22 PPC, 6x47, 6mm PPC, 6mm Remington BR, and 308 Winchester. Of course there are a variety of wildcats

also used, but the above rounds account for the bulk of the rifles.

The 14-inch twist is standard, since most of the bullets are reasonably light, 52-53 grs. in 22, 68-70 grs. in 6mm and 150-168 grs. in 30 caliber. Bench resters use the slowest twist which will give adequate stability, since this has been proven to give best accuracy, though sometimes it requires pretty hot loads. Some bench resters use what are conservatively called "maximum" loads. I know a few competitors who intentionally understate their loads so nobody will get into trouble trying to copy what they are using.

This requires some explanation. Ordinarily you would never suggest anyone intentionally load hotter than the manuals recommend, and I don't. The rifles bench resters use are very strong, and they give the brass in the cartridge case nowhere to flow under pressure, the case head being fully supported, and the firing pin opening in the bolt face being very small. Consequently, cases shot in these rifles with high pressure loads show few overt pressure signs. This doesn't make it OK. It simply means that there is no indication the load is too hot until the primers fall out. Since some top shooters don't care if the load is hot, they load to get the best accuracy and take their chances. Many use hot loads, knowing fully well they are, and as long as they group and the primers don't fall out, they use them, accepting the risks. I think this is a hazardous practice, but I'm not going to change these guys' minds saying so, 'cause they know. What I am telling you is NOT to do it.

Actions for bench rest rifles are chosen for their stiffness and rigidity. Mauser actions were used when the sport began, but you will almost never see one today. The Remington 40X isn't even as popular as it used to be, unless it is sleeved to improve its rigidity. Custom-made actions are very popular in this sport, the light aluminum actions made by Ralph Stolle being particularly prized. Other makers of custom bench rest actions are Hart, Shilen and Wichita. There are other smaller makers, but these are the important ones. If you want to get into bench rest competition, you couldn't go wrong by picking any of the above-mentioned barrels, calibers, or actions and putting them together in any order, as long as you have good work done by a top man, such as Wally Hart, Homer Culver, John Eaton, Ed Shilen and others who are well known in this specialized field.

Most bench rest rifles today are assembled on what is called a "swap-barrel" system. Very often a shooter will have a variety of barrels for the same rifle, and he can change these at the range, using a portable barrel vise, and a special action wrench which fits into the rifle receiver. The action and stock may be spun off without taking the rifle out of the stock. This permits a fellow to change his rifle from a light varmint in the morning to heavy varmint in the afternoon. Usually the only differ-

Here is the all-out AR-15 which once figured in serious attempts to make a match rifle out of the M-16. As Ed Harris says, it just didn't work at the longer ranges of U.S. centerfire rifle competition, although it was a record beater up close. This example has the tubular metal receiver, here tape-covered for grip, which adds so much to the bedding of the rifle, which in this case is a match barrel in standard issue configuration. The caliber, of course, is 223 Remington, although there were also attempts to use it as a wildcat 6mm on that same case.

ences in the barrels between weight classes will be length, as fat, heavy, stiff contours are preferred. A typical light varmint barrel will be 1.2 inches straight and 18 to 20 inches long, while the heavy varmint will be the same diameter, but 21 inches to 26 inches long, depending upon the weight of the action, stock and scope. Very often they will be of the same caliber, though some shooters may swap from a 22 BR to a 308 when the wind blows, or may have different headspaced bolts to permit changing from a 6x47 to a 308, for instance. If you do a lot of experimenting, the swap barrel system is the best way to do it, for once the action work is done, and all the dimensions are recorded for reference, it's a lot cheaper to just add another barrel to your collection than to build another complete bench rest rifle for $1,000-$2,000. You can buy a good Hart barrel and get it fitted to your swap barrel gun for a total of about $170-$200. Most guys with swap-barrel rifles have a lot of barrels to play with. As many as a dozen isn't unusual.

The most important thing about a bench rest gun besides the barrel is the stock, which is the firing platform for the gun. Bench rest shooters have just about completely abandoned the wood stock. You see few wood stocks, even laminated ones at the big shoots any more. The competitors who do use wood are self-conscious enough about them and fill and paint them so they look like fiberglass, since they wouldn't want to be ribbed by their buddies. For pure accuracy there's no getting over the fact that fiberglass is superior. This is because it is completely stable, and not subject to warpage, and it is lightweight, permitting more weight to be put into the barrel, where shooters would rather have it.

Fiberglass stocks are always either fiberglass or epoxy bedded, usually with the pillar system, in which solid columns of bedding material support the action in the stock, and prevent any compression of the stock when the action screws are tightened. Many shooters are going to glue-in systems in which the barrel and/or action, depending on the bedding system used, are actually glued into the stock. The trigger assembly is usually pinned in and can be removed for cleaning or replacement. If you ever want to remove the glued-in stock from the action, simply throw the rifle in the freezer overnight, and it will fall out with a rap or two. This is because of the different rates of shrinkage of steel and fiberglass (or epoxy). (This technique works with wood stocks too, if you ever have a problem sticking one in unintentionally.)

Cast bullet shooting is a sport which is beginning to catch on as jacketed bullets climb in price. Although blackpowder shooters and pistol shooters have cast their own bullets for years, the only practitioner of this art in rifles for a long time were single shot riflemen such as those of the American Single Shot Rifle Association. These fellows use falling block rifles and plain-based, breech-seated cast bullets of soft alloy, shot in the traditional style practiced shortly after the turn of the century. Although the barrels and scopes they use today are much better than those of the old-timers, the basic technique and equipment has changed little in almost 100 years. The only real changes are better scopes and modern made actions such as the Ruger No. 1 and Browning 78, which are seen alongside the old Stevens, Winchester High Walls and Ballards of years ago.

Recently, however, a new group of cast bullet shooters has emerged, called the Cast Bullet Association. These guys don't restrict the rifle action, but specify that fixed ammunition must be used (as opposed to separate loaded, breech-seated as practiced by the ASSRA). Most CBA shooters use bolt-actions, but a few single shots are seen. A CBA match reminds you of the early days of bench rest shooting at Johnstown, New York, back in the 1950s. The groups are small, as is the association (only about 500 members in the U.S., Canada and Australia, as this is written), but the atmosphere is cordial and friendly. Slowly the CBA is advancing the technological base of its shooters, and now it appears that serious competitors are going more toward full-fledged bench rest rifles than standard hunting or over-the-course target guns. However, a "production hunter class" which requires a standard factory rifle with few changes, is in the works. Generally, however, the CBA match rifle varies little from the bench rest rifles of a few years ago, before fiberglass stocks became common. In fact, many CBA shooters are IBS members and use their retired rifles with cast bullets. Few CBA shooters use fiberglass stocks now, but this will change shortly, since the level of accuracy they are now attaining will require the most modern bench rest techniques for shooters to remain competitive. Generally, however, the same barrels, actions, stocks and sights are used as for IBS or NBRSA matches. The only real difference is most CBA competitors use almost exclusively 30 caliber rifles, principally in the 308 Winchester, 308x47, 308x1½, or 30-30. The custom part of the CBA match rifle is in the chambering, since most shooters experiment with different configurations to optimize alignment and minimize the deformation of the bullet. A common technique used is the tight neck chamber used by bench rest shooters, though in cast bullet parlance this becomes the "CBC," which means cast bullet chamber. This is necessarily of somewhat larger diameter than a jacketed bench rest shooter's tight neck, since the bullets are larger in diameter, usually .309-.310-inch in 30 caliber. However, a lot of cast bullet shooters do quite well with standard chambers.

Competition rifles usually have a lot in common with others used for the same sport, since they are built under rules. But as long as there are rule books, there will be guys who attempt to bend the rules to get that last competitive edge. I guess that means that custom competition rifles will have a long and interesting future.

C.E. Harris

Match Handguns

COMPETITION handguns are usually modified factory pieces, but still a breed apart from working guns. They are extensively customized in an effort to get the most amount of accuracy necessary for their specialized sport. Some target handguns do overlap in their uses. For instance, you could use a PPC revolver in an NRA centerfire match, or use some NRA-style centerfire or 22 pistol in the respective ISU competitions. You could also use an ISU Standard pistol in NRA 22 rimfire matches, or an ISU Centerfire gun in NRA centerfire matches, provided the gun meets the rule book requirements for weight, trigger pull, sight radius, grip shape, etc. In many cases they do. Some bull's-eye type centerfire pistols are used for the NRA Hunter Pistol Course and are quite competitive there.

Unlike the IHMSA long-range silhouette, the NRA Hunter Pistol game uses steel targets scaled down for ranges of 25, 50, 75 and 100 meters. You don't need a magnum handgun to slam down the rams. An ordinary 45 wadcutter load works fine. The sheep is the only one you can't knock down every time with 38 wadcutters, though it will go down with almost any decent hit. The hunter pistol course appeals to the fellow who doesn't want a full-house silhouette or hunting handgun, but wants to have fun ringing the critters with a standard factory revolver or automatic. This is every bit as much a challenging game as the long-range pistol silhouette, since it's all offhand. You still must adjust the sights, and a 38 or 45 drops a long way at 100 meters. There's no real reason you can't use a 357 or 44 Magnum here, as long as it's a factory gun with a 2-pound trigger. The barrel can't be over 10 inches long, and the gun must not weigh more than 60 ounces with sights. Scope sights are permitted. This is a boon for anybody over 40, who can't see iron sights clearly.

Most target guns, however, are specialized to a particular sport. You aren't likely to see a fellow at Camp Perry with an IPSC-style combat gun, nor will you see very many ordinary 45 ACP wadcutter or "ball" guns at an IPSC shoot, though occasionally newcomers shoot with them.

Bull's-eye guns are probably the most specialized in regard to accuracy, since they don't require a lot of power. The only requirement is that the gun function safely and very precisely punch a hole of a certain size in a piece of target paper at 25 or 50 yards. The ISU courses of fire and guns are somewhat different, but there are obvious similarities to the NRA-style matches, so it's worthwhile to discuss these briefly. NRA bull's-eye competition is fired in three categories: 22 (rimfire), centerfire, and 45 caliber. All guns use the same course of fire consisting of timed-fire and rapid-fire at 25 yards, and slow-fire at 50 yards. Only the guns change. Timed-fire consists of 5-shot strings fired in 20 seconds, whereas rapid-fire does it in 10 seconds. Slow-fire gives you 1 minute per shot.

Very few revolvers are used in NRA bull's-eye competition anymore, though you see one occasionally. It used to be a three-gun match, meaning 22, centerfire (which usually meant a 38 Special or 32 S&W) and 45. Today, however, it usually ends up being a two-gun match, since most competitors use their 45 pistols for the centerfire stages as well. The top gunners found they were doing as well or better with their 45s as with the 38, so they switched over. This gave them only two guns to master.

The trend increasingly is to make the 22 gun feel just like the 45. High Standard got this going about 15 years ago with the introduction of the military grip, which had the same angle as the 45 with a flat mainspring housing. Herrett's also makes "trainer" stocks for the S&W Model 41 which achieve the same effect. Today, though, many shooters are turning to 22 conversion units like the Kart or Day, which fit onto the 45 frame. These in no way resemble the earlier Colt Ace or 22/45 conversion units which date back to the 1940s. They are accurate enough to hold the X-ring at 50 yards with good ammo. The Kart conversion is of all-steel construction, whereas the Day has a stainless steel barrel in an aluminum slide and breechbolt assembly. The Kart unit is more nicely made, somewhat more heavy and expensive. The Day unit is probably every bit as accurate and is somewhat less expensive. Both are good units and are equal in performance to most of the popular 22 target autos, such as the S&W Model 41, Hi-Standard Military Models or the Clark-accurized Ruger.

In the centerfire stages, the Colt Gold Cup 38, or various 38 Special conversions of the Colt Government Model, or the S&W Model 52 used to be most popular. About 10 years ago, however, this began to change, as shooters realized they could do just as well using the 45. You still see some shooters using the 38 for centerfire, but not in the numbers you once did. Occasionally you see a fellow using an ISU centerfire gun like the Hammerli 240 (for 38 Special) or the Walther GSP (32 S&W) in the NRA centerfire stages.

In the 45 phase, there are really two types of guns, the

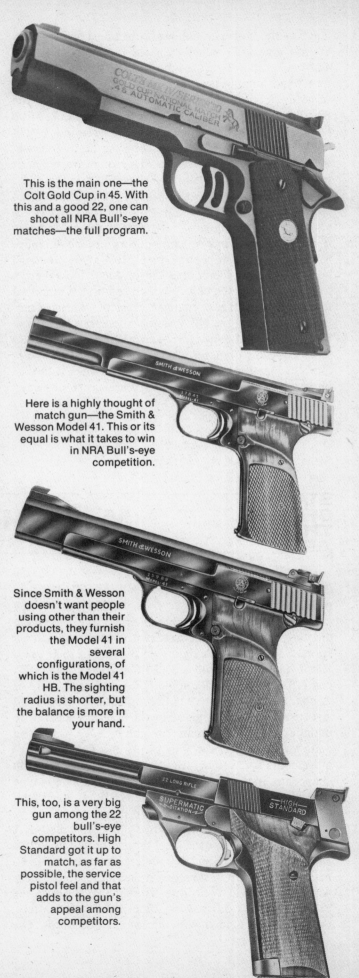

This is the main one—the Colt Gold Cup in 45. With this and a good 22, one can shoot all NRA Bull's-eye matches—the full program.

Here is a highly thought of match gun—the Smith & Wesson Model 41. This or its equal is what it takes to win in NRA Bull's-eye competition.

Since Smith & Wesson doesn't want people using other than their products, they furnish the Model 41 in several configurations, of which is the Model 41 HB. The sighting radius is shorter, but the balance is more in your hand.

This, too, is a very big gun among the 22 bull's-eye competitors. High Standard got it up to match, as far as possible, the service pistol feel and that adds to the gun's appeal among competitors.

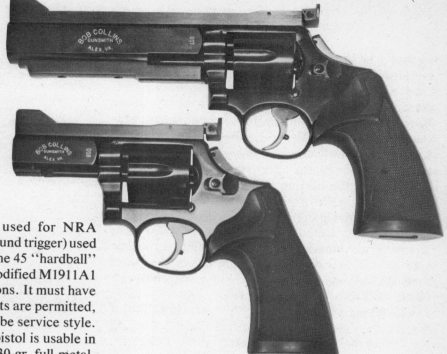

Here are a pair of Bob Collins' PPC guns—all-out efforts on the game using Smith & Wesson Model 10 revolvers rebarreled. The guns have a Collins action job, they are designed for double action only; use a unique push-off double action trigger stop with a neoprene cushion. The lower gun is a "cheater" for use, so help us, in "off-duty gun" matches.

wadcutter gun (3½-pound trigger) used for NRA matches, and the "hardball" gun (4-pound trigger) used for National Board "leg" matches. The 45 "hardball" gun is an accurized but otherwise unmodified M1911A1 pistol without any external modifications. It must have a 4-pound trigger pull. Adjustable sights are permitted, but ribs, etc., are not. The grips must be service style. The Colt Gold Cup National Match pistol is usable in this class. These guns are set up for 230-gr. full-metal-jacket service ammunition, and generally aren't used for wadcutter loads. Occasionally, a beginning shooter might use a hardball gun with a lighter recoil spring and altered magazine for wadcutter loads. Soon, however, he'll probably switch to separate wadcutter and ball guns.

Wadcutter 45 pistols are an entirely different proposition. The 45 wadcutter guns are probably the most accurate centerfire pistols going, with the possible exception of the best ISU centerfire guns. Accurizing features employed on the wadcutter gun go above and beyond what is done on service pistols or hardball guns. Because the pistol is fine tuned for light loads, it is safe to adjust the trigger pull down far lighter than you can get away with on a "ball" gun. A good pistolsmith can take a wadcutter gun down to a clean-breaking 3½-

pound pull with little difficulty. The centerfire revolver is allowed to have a 2½-pound pull under the rules, but semi-autos require the 3½-pound weight to have some margin for safety.

Most changes in the wadcutter gun are to permit reliable feeding with powder-puff loads. Ordinary service ammunition fires a 230-gr. bullet at about 850 f.p.s., whereas factory 45 wadcutter ammunition moves a 185-gr. bullet at only 775 f.p.s. Many competitors shoot handloads which are even lighter, perhaps getting only about 650 f.p.s. with a 185-gr. or 200-gr. bullet. To get the gun to function reliably with the reduced recoil impulse of target loads, the recoil spring load must be reduced to increase the recoil velocity of the slide. So it is almost equal to hardball ammunition. This requires

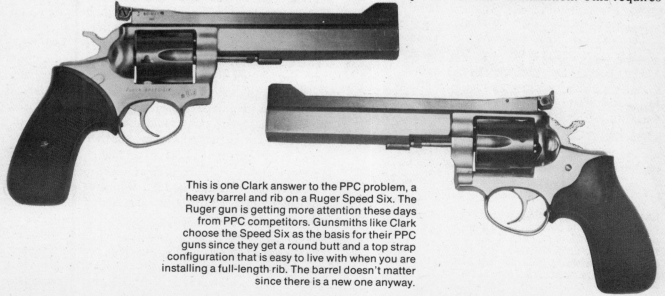

This is one Clark answer to the PPC problem, a heavy barrel and rib on a Ruger Speed Six. The Ruger gun is getting more attention these days from PPC competitors. Gunsmiths like Clark choose the Speed Six as the basis for their PPC guns since they get a round butt and a top strap configuration that is easy to live with when you are installing a full-length rib. The barrel doesn't matter since there is a new one anyway.

replacing the standard 16- to 18-pound recoil spring with one around 12-14 pounds. Typically the hammer nose is cut down to reduce override of the hammer from the full cock position, and at the same time the front face of the hammer is "scooped" away, forming a cam which reduces cocking effort. Very often the mainspring tension is reduced somewhat instead, though this must be done carefully, since it also affects cocking effort and its resistance to the moving slide, and therefore affects cyclic rate as well.

Other accurizing steps on target guns include peening the frame rails, tightening the slide, and polishing them so they work smoothly with no perceptible vertical or side play. The barrel lugs are built up, or the barrel replaced with one having oversized lugs which can be machined down to a perfect match against the slide stop, eliminating vertical play. The barrel hood is also fitted to the slide, a tight bushing fitted, and the feeding surfaces of the feed ramp and barrel polished together. Magazines are reworked for wadcutter loads by peening the feed lips in a die to provide a correct release of the round. The magazine follower is either dimpled or replaced with a rounded one to reduce the effort needed to strip the last round from the clip. This prevents the "last round jam" prevalent with wadcutter loads in standard magazines.

Aside from the extra tightening and accurizing steps, the functional modifications on target guns are much like those on IPSC combat and service guns. It's just that for a bull's-eye piece you can take the process further. Sights on the bull's-eye gun are larger to give a

In the 1981 *Gun Digest*, barrel configurations like this one in 22 target pistols were found to be more accurate, length for length, than other configurations. It is not so graceful in appearance, but such a barrel can make points.

This is a 4-inch "Smolt" as done by Bill Davis. The gun, which is a favorite among some PPC shooters combines a barrel from a Colt Python with a K-framed Smith & Wesson. Relatively inexpensively, what seems to be the right twist and a good barrel are obtained this way.

Changing the barrel seating up front on a Model 1911 to utilize this ring that offers a round bearing surface during the locking and unlocking and therefore maintains its position, shot to shot, is the latest accuracy wrinkle in custom 45's.

clear sight picture, often adding a full-length rib, such as a Bo-Mar. This gives a flat, raised sighting plane, and adds greater weight to the gun, for stability. The rib usually has a good click-adjustable sight built right into it and may have a shroud-lock accuracy tuner also. When a heavy rib is added to a gun, the recoil spring is lightened somewhat, so the gun will properly function with the heavier slide. The same procedure is usually followed with custom long slide guns like the Clark.

The main advantage of the long slide gun is increased weight and longer sight radius, but some silhouette shooters favoring the 45 have gone farther with it, using much longer barrels in efforts to get higher velocities for surer knockdown of the critters. Other modifications of the 45 which aren't needed for bull's-eye competition are usually favored for IPSC matches. These include rounding the sharp corners of sights for holster clearance, enlarged grip safety tangs, spade thumb safeties, chamfered magazine wells, and high visibility sights which can be discerned against dull backgrounds. Most of these are speed modifications to let the shooter clear

For those with an international gleam in their eye and free pistol shooting on the menu, there just isn't any viable alternative but a Hammerli. This is the latter-day Sport Pistole 120, meant for precision 50-meter shooting.

This is the Hammerli 150 Free Pistol on the Martini action. It is, by U.S. standards, a most unusual handgun, but serious competition over the years has proven that Hammerli knows how to build pistols that win.

Here is a 6-inch "Smolt" by Bill Davis. The Colt barrel at this length makes the Smith K-frame revolver hold very well, and the assembly is thought to be just a little bit better than either a Smith or a Colt at the demanding PPC shooting.

leather, find the sights, shoot and reload quickly. Since much of the IPSC shooting places more emphasis on speed than accuracy, the full bull's-eye accuracy tune isn't needed. It's much more important for the IPSC shooter that the gun work 100 percent of the time, than to shoot an X-ring group. While a Camp Perry pistol shooter would feel extremely handicapped with a 45 which groups as large as 4 inches at 50 yards, most IPSC shooters would be entirely happy with that, and could score well with it. Many guns used by top combat shooters wouldn't be any more than plain vanilla as bull's-eye pistols. That's the inherent difference in the two sports.

The NRA police pistol combat gun, however, must be accurate, since the course of fire there weighs precision over speed. A police revolver competitor whose gun won't hold 2 inches at 50 yards will usually go shopping around for another barrel or a new gunsmith, or at minimum he'll change lots of ammo. The NRA-style PPC guns shoot every bit as accurately as bull's-eye match guns. They are the most accurate revolvers

ever made. In 1981 the NRA pistol program will probably be opened up to semi-automatic pistols. This will be very interesting to see, since there has been much speculation as to whether the autoloader would have an advantage in speed, giving the shooter more time to hold and squeeze. Many of the revolver enthusiasts doubt if many semi-autos are accurate enough to shoot the 1490 scores needed to win this course of competition. While not all of the IPSC guns could, the better ones can, and any good NRA-style centerfire pistol could. I think it will prove a good race between the two types of guns.

Generally, though, in NRA police competition the 38 revolver is it, since as of this writing, there have been no matches fired for record which allowed autoloaders. Though this may change soon, we don't know which way it will go. The typical PPC revolver is a highly customized Colt Python or S&W K model, though the Ruger DA frame is being used increasingly. The factory barrels are almost always replaced with one having a 14-inch twist, or possibly faster such as 10-inch or

12-inch, since this has proven to give better accuracy with 38 Special wadcutter ammunition. The cylinders are carefully selected to give a concentric launch of the bullet into the barrel, which means checking not only the alignment of the chamber throats, but also their size. They can't be too big or too small. Most often the revolversmith will insure the chamber throats are not more than .001-inch over groove diameter, and that they are smooth and of uniform size. He will shoot the gun from a machine rest, one chamber at a time. If one or more chambers throws fliers, it might be because they are too tight, too loose or misaligned. In that case he'll have to replace the cylinder. This isn't all that unusual. Cylinder gap is adjusted to .004-.006-inch and the cylinder face and barrel squared up and fitted so there is no endshake of the cylinder. Forcing cones are usually more gradual than in factory guns, typically being an 11-degree included angle instead of 18 degrees which is standard on most revolvers. The cone is also polished smooth so there are no tool marks to scrub the bullet. Major diameter of the cone is no larger than necessary, usually not over .365-.370-inch. A proper match of chamber throat and cylinder guides the bullet straight from the cylinder into the barrel with minimal distortion. A good PPC revolver will shoot *50-round* groups with wadcutters around 3 inches at 50 yards. Many shooters will complain if individual 10-shot groups at that range go over 2 inches.

Aside from the accurizing steps, the PPC revolver has the action smoothed and lightened as much as possible within the limits of reliability. Many full-house PPC guns are double action only. Top competitors don't use the single action at all, not even at 50 yards. Most competition guns have full-length ribs with protecting ears around the front sight, and custom grips. The exception to this is the "Distinguished" gun, which is used in NRA Police "leg" matches to gain points toward the coveted Distinguished badge. This must be an out-of-the-box factory gun with 6-inch barrel, maximum, and 2-pound trigger pull, functioning in both single action and double action modes of fire. The actions can be smoothed, but little else is done to the basic revolver. These matches are fired with 158-gr. "service" ammunition and are intended to be more representative of a duty gun and ammunition. A more realistic approach is one taken by the Police Marksman Association which has a Distinguished program which uses 4-inch barreled guns. The NRA is now encouraging match sponsors to run events for the short duty-type guns also, which is an encouraging trend. Some special "belly gun" matches are held for shorter barrel guns, but some of these are customized so much they bear no relationship to the cop's off-duty piece.

The general trend is for competition guns to be

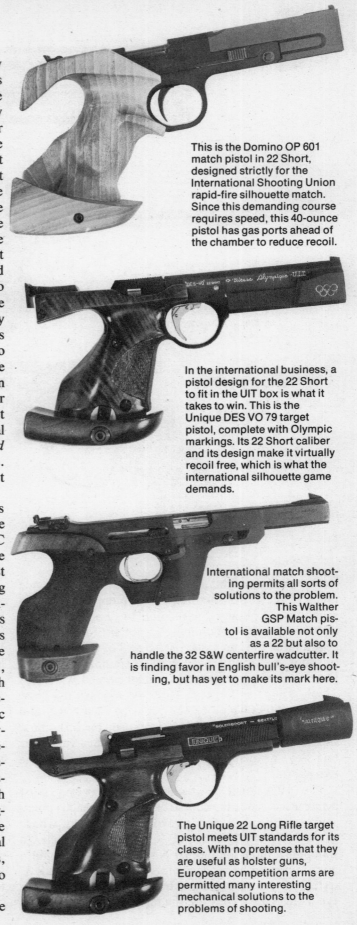

This is the Domino OP 601 match pistol in 22 Short, designed strictly for the International Shooting Union rapid-fire silhouette match. Since this demanding course requires speed, this 40-ounce pistol has gas ports ahead of the chamber to reduce recoil.

In the international business, a pistol design for the 22 Short to fit in the UIT box is what it takes to win. This is the Unique DES VO 79 target pistol, complete with Olympic markings. Its 22 Short caliber and its design make it virtually recoil free, which is what the international silhouette game demands.

International match shooting permits all sorts of solutions to the problem. This Walther GSP Match pistol is available not only as a 22 but also to handle the 32 S&W centerfire wadcutter. It is finding favor in English bull's-eye shooting, but has yet to make its mark here.

The Unique 22 Long Rifle target pistol meets UIT standards for its class. With no pretense that they are useful as holster guns, European competition arms are permitted many interesting mechanical solutions to the problems of shooting.

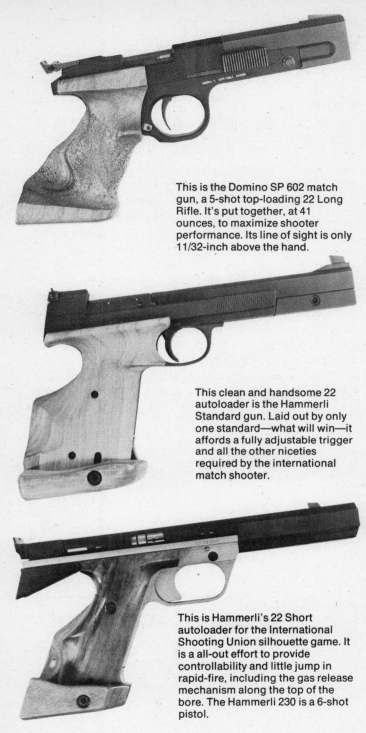

This is the Domino SP 602 match gun, a 5-shot top-loading 22 Long Rifle. It's put together, at 41 ounces, to maximize shooter performance. Its line of sight is only 11/32-inch above the hand.

This clean and handsome 22 autoloader is the Hammerli Standard gun. Laid out by only one standard—what will win—it affords a fully adjustable trigger and all the other niceties required by the international match shooter.

This is Hammerli's 22 Short autoloader for the International Shooting Union silhouette game. It is a all-out effort to provide controllability and little jump in rapid-fire, including the gas release mechanism along the top of the bore. The Hammerli 230 is a 6-shot pistol.

heavy, since weight is desired to reduce muzzle tremor and make the gun hold steady. It's not at all unusual to see NRA-style centerfire guns exceed 50 ounces. The 60-ounce rule was initiated in the Hunter Pistol course to permit almost any factory gun with 10-inch barrel to have a scope mounted, such as the long barrel Dan Wessons, T/C Contenders with 10-inch bull barrels, etc. While few IPSC guns weigh much over 40 ounces the typical bull's-eye, PPC or silhouette pistol probably approaches 50 ounces. Competition guns often crowd right up to the weight limit. The only real weight limit in

NRA bull's-eye matches is that you must be able to hold the gun up with one hand and shoot it, so its weight becomes self-limiting after a while. Most often, though, a target gun will be heavier than a holster piece. You can usually bet on it.

The IHMSA long-range silhouette guns are also quite specialized, though they fall into two general categories of "production," meaning factory guns like the Ruger or S&W 44 Magnum revolvers, and "unlimited" which includes the customized XP100s, Wichita and Weatherby bolt-action pistols. The Thompson/Center Contender is a popular silhouette gun available in a variety of calibers, both standard rounds and wildcats. The immense variety of chamberings makes this essentially a custom gun, even though it is factory-made. The standard 10-inch barrels are permitted in the "production" class, but some shooters feel the specialized wildcats in the Super 14 should be in the unlimited class. This is still up in the air as of this writing, though it would appear that the Contender is a highly accurate gun which clearly outclasses the revolvers and automatics, so it is likely to be called an "unlimited" gun.

Some accurizing work is done on the Contender, though I am told by Steve Herrett, Bob Milek, and other experienced shooters that much of the cobbling up done on some of the "mastodon killers" doesn't accomplish anything. I've shot Steve's Contenders and found they were accurate enough to head-shoot rockchucks out past 150 yards, and I'm sure I'd have no trouble hitting the rifle chickens at 200 meters from a rest. That's plenty accurate for any handgun. Some Contender shooters use what more cautious fans of this handgun call "idiot fringe" loads. The Contender is a really strong gun, and it is a credit to Warren Center's design that it hangs together with some of the loads people have been using. When I was with Herrett shooting rockchucks, he freely admitted his loads were a bit warmer than are listed by DuPont, but I also noticed I could open the gun and raise the muzzle and the empties didn't need any assist other than gravity to fall out. Obviously, there are chamber variations which affect the powder charges usable in a particular gun. I've seen Contender barrels with long freebores and some with little or none. Quite obviously the maximum load in the long-throated barrel would be excessive in the short-throated one.

Competition guns are by their very nature specialized, but they are most importantly safe, accurate and reliable, as all guns should be. The big difference between target guns and service or hunting guns is that they emphasize the ACCURACY criteria in functioning and in sighting, so you can get the most out of a gun's performance. There is often a lot of room for refinement in the factory product. Custom work helps you get the most accuracy from what started out as an "ordinary," though good, standard gun.

C.E. Harris

Skeet and Trap Guns

SATISFACTION with and the satisfactory use of a shotgun in competition is possibly more aligned with training, discipline and mental state than it is with the hardware involved, but there is, nevertheless, and for much the same reasons as with any custom gun, a great deal of interest in above-standard guns to shoot in Skeet and in trap. With a recognizable market like the tens of thousands of clay target shooters before them, most factories try to meet the market. Thus, one can buy fine, suited-to-the-job trap and Skeet guns that have to be considered above-standard by anyone, but which are nonetheless catalog items.

Still, such are extra-finish guns and worth discussing. The cream of the crop, in almost anyone's view, is the four-gun or four-barrel set in over-under persuasion. More used, of course, are sets of repeaters, and primary among these is the Remington 1100. In over-unders, the Krieghoff factory set is highly thought of, and a set of

Brownings is far more difficult to achieve, but can be seen. More often, the Brownings are used—another complication—with insert tubes, wherein the shooter uses one gun, perhaps two for all four gauges. There are those who favor the Winchester Model 12 and the 42, often owned in sets as with the others.

Particularly in trap models, since that game is fired only with the 12 bore, there are a great many more names in the field. They shoot over-unders, single-barrels, the un-single, which is half an over-under, and repeaters. Indeed, this year, Remington has introduced a slide-action single-shot trap gun. A very great many competition shotguns of all persuasions are stocked specially, often with high-grade wood, and undergo other alterations to better suit them to the task of breaking clay birds. Serious competitors are ruthless with their guns. It is not unusual to see a very expensive piece of wood, handsomely gotten up, that has been

This is a refined Model 12 Winchester trap gun stocked by Stephen Billeb. The all-out stock design provides the required dimensions quite gracefully, and the tigertail Claro stock is further embellished with a four-fleur checkering pattern on the slide handle and on the pistol grip.

This is the Holmes Supertrap 12 gauge shotgun in the straight-pull design with a Morgan adjustable recoil pad. Holmes goes all out to provide bird-busting efficiency without reference to tradition or conventionality. The guns are built one at a time.

This Ljutic Mono Gun is the adjustable barrel model, shown here with a 34-inch tube. The customers get choice of chokes, their own stock measurements, choice of pull or release trigger (release costs more) and can pay $200 to $300 more for fancy wood. The gun is well thought of.

subsequently whittled away at, possibly with a jackknife, by its owner who is seeking with his butchery to break just one more bird in a hundred. Neither, of course, is it unusual to see a big winner shooting a straight factory gun. It is as much a game of training and discipline as it is one of hardware, as we have already said.

What the competition shooter seeks beyond all else is reliability. He wants his pattern always the same, always in the same place; he wants no malfunction of the gun to disturb his concentration; he wants it to feel the same with every shot. This is at the root of all custom work on competition shotguns.

Therefore, one finds a great deal of polishing and adjusting the borings and chokes. Various forms of triggers are developed to replace factory triggers, although it has to be said that factories themselves often spend a great deal of time on triggers to make them as everlasting as possible while still being adjustable.

Naturally, almost any trap gun of almost any persuasion may have a release trigger in it. The mystique and the theory of release triggers is understood only by trapshooters and so won't be discussed here. However, the installation of a release trigger is almost a standard practice because it is widely regarded as one cure for a flinch and a great many trapshooters acquire flinches.

There are other accessories for the competition shotgun, such as adjustable recoil pads, special ribs, often ultra-high ribs, special combinations of middle and front sights and the like.

When it comes to stocks, custom stocks, most competition guns are worked over by people who specialize in claybird guns. The demands on the shooter and the gun are different from the demands in field shooting and thus are best met by the fellow who specializes. Ideal dimensions, as worked out thus far, make the competition gun a heftier beast. And weight is not a bad idea in a gun used to fire several hundred rounds a day. It remains possible for a good man to create a handsome, even if bulky, shotgun.

This is particularly so with that classiest of competition guns, the single-barrel trap gun. It remains a well-thought-of style of gun in the field as a whole. Perhaps the most objective proof is that the Ithaca Gun Company, though in dire financial straits, has decided to continue to make their single-barrel gun for trap shooters. Few of those, indeed few single-barrel trap guns made anywhere, are stocked in plain wood. The guns

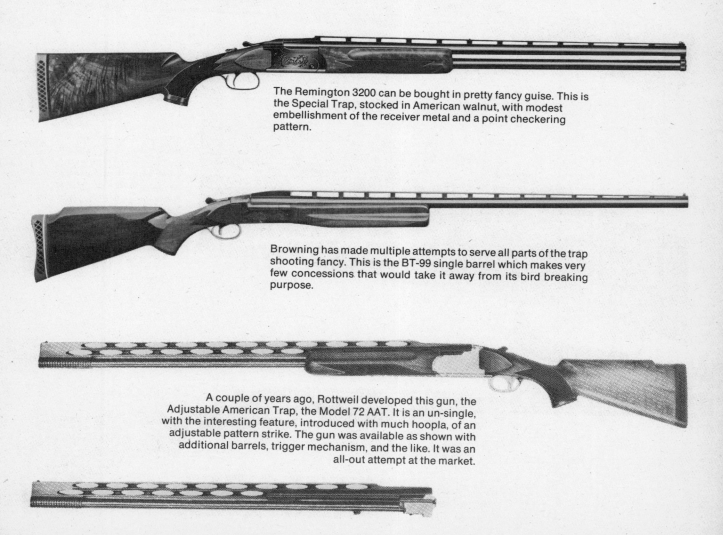

The Remington 3200 can be bought in pretty fancy guise. This is the Special Trap, stocked in American walnut, with modest embellishment of the receiver metal and a point checkering pattern.

Browning has made multiple attempts to serve all parts of the trap shooting fancy. This is the BT-99 single barrel which makes very few concessions that would take it away from its bird breaking purpose.

A couple of years ago, Rottweil developed this gun, the Adjustable American Trap, the Model 72 AAT. It is an un-single, with the interesting feature, introduced with much hoopla, of an adjustable pattern strike. The gun was available as shown with additional barrels, trigger mechanism, and the like. It was an all-out attempt at the market.

are expensive and it is a tradition that they be handsome, and as we have seen, handsome wood means a handsome gun to most people.

Apart from the outpourings of standard models in the lines of the major factories adapted to competition use, and the fine and not-quite-fine imported guns destined for clay target competition, there are numerous specialty gunsmiths in the United States who turn out guns for this market, particularly the trap market. Ljutic out in the Northwest still produces its Mono-Gun, a well thought of, highly specialized firearm made entirely in

the one relatively small shop. Down in Fayetteville, AR, Bill Holmes is busy taking an unconventional approach to see if he can design a gun, his Supertrap, that will break more targets than any other. Any number of shops conduct what must be called improving operations to make standard and not-so-standard guns break more targets.

There is the same scope, in short, in competition guns for high-grade work, embellishment, remanufacture or refurbishing to new specifications that there is in all other guns. And, just possibly, more competition shooters take advantage of the opportunity than do field shooters. Certainly, around Skeet and trap fields, the extra-special gun is no rarity.   *Ken Warner*

Browning's ST-100 over-under follows the same plan as in its other trap guns—the sighting plane, stock dimensions, and other details aim only at breaking birds.

All trapgunners are not totally committed. For these, a great many firms offer conventional shotguns, trap-stocked and trap-furnished. This is the Beretta SO-4 sidelock over-under. It has the long barrels, plain wood, and is a perfectly reliable gun.

The "grade" guns have come back somewhat in American factories. This is the Remington 3200 F Grade, which as can be seen is a considerably embellished basic gun. This particular specimen is the base gun of a 3200 4-barrel Skeet set.

Rottweil does not ignore the Skeet shooter and offers this Rottweil Olympia '72 Skeet shotgun. Rottweil pays considerable attention to special Skeet choking and the guns are used a great deal on the Continent. That explains the distinctly European styling of this gun.

PRICE AND DEMAND TRENDS

by Ken Warner and C. E. Harris

Custom Handguns

MOST customized handguns are "personal" guns for defense, trail use, or fun shooting, rather than target pieces. Target guns are important to the trade, but the personal handgun is most used, most customized, and most coveted by the serious enthusiast. A gun to carry and use a lot is more apt to be altered to suit the owner's whim.

Before WW II it was common for makers to build special-order guns with noncatalog features, though it is rare today. Bat Masterson could get Colt to make him a special 45 single action, with "easy action" and so on. Until after WW II, the S&W 357 Magnum was strictly a special-order gun. From the time it was introduced in 1935, until war production caused it to be discontinued temporarily, S&W made only about 6,000 357 Magnums. It's unlikely any factory today would even introduce a model which would sell only 1,000 pieces or so annually. (The pre-war 357s were beautiful guns. I'm fortunate enough to own one which left the factory in 1939. It was obviously a custom gun, having 6½-inch barrel, McGivern bead front sight, deep U rear notch, and a special "humpbacked" hammer for easy single action cocking. Roy Jenks, the S&W historian, was further able to elaborate that company records indicated it to be zeroed to strike center of the 25-yard Standard American target with a 6 o'clock hold using 158-gr. lead magnum cartridges. And it does.) As recently as the 1950s Smith & Wesson made target revolvers with special features, but it would be highly unusual to special order such a gun today. Anything not specified in the catalog will require custom work. Because the factories offer few options, it has created a boom for the custom gunsmiths in serving the fellows who want their personal guns a bit different. Making your guns suit you better is what custom work is all about.

Custom handgun work involves the whole gun: action work, sights and accurizing, rebarreling and/or rechambering, grips, finishes and embellishments. The cost of work on revolvers depends both on the model and what parts replacement and modification is necessary. A duty-tune on a S&W requiring no parts replacement involves only an hour or so of work on a good basic gun. It costs perhaps $25-35. If there are any parts replacements, their cost plus fitting time would add to the job. A competition-tune of the S&W takes the duty-tune just a bit farther, but not that much, and seldom costs over $50. Colts are another matter and usually require more work on altering the bolt and possibly making new springs. This runs the price of a full competition-tune to around $100, though a duty-tune leaves the springs alone and simply knocks off the rough edges, for a lot less money.

Auto pistol action work is different, but the same: making sure the safety devices function as intended, providing a good trigger pull and a smooth operating cycle. A duty-tune on a stock gun, not including any sights, accurizing or extra work, shouldn't exceed $50. Few autoloader fanciers, however, are content with a mere slicked up, stock gun. A basic IPSC combat-tune on a Colt Government Model, including good fixed sights, a trigger job and other minor action work will usually run $100-125, though if a fellow wants to go the whole course with refinishing, adjustable sights and a full accuracy job, it's not hard to run the cost of work up to $250 over the cost of the basic gun. If a great deal of handwork is spent on metal checkering, a custom safety and slide stop, and a lot of other options, you could spend $500 on custom work.

Sights are an important part of most handgun work, since a gun which works is no good if it can't hit. Fixed sights are preferred on police duty guns, but they usually require a gunsmith's touch to get them to shoot the chosen load where wanted. Adjustable sights, however, are desired for competition guns and most hunting guns, since owners often need to change sights for different loads or to adjust for various ranges.

On automatic pistols, adjustable sights are a much-wanted custom option, but the job must be done right to get a solid, durable installation. Although an S&W adjustable sight seldom gives trouble on a revolver, it can be a source of trouble if not installed properly on the autos. Adjustable sights are more likely to be jarred out of alignment in rough service, despite efforts to protect them. Fixed sights are probably better for most field use.

Accurizing is a catchall phrase which covers a lot of ground, but most often describes the work which goes a step or two beyond the ordinary duty-tune which merely makes sure the mechanism works as it should. The difference between a duty-tuned gun and a competition-tuned gun usually boils down to tolerances. A service gun must work under adverse conditions. To use a full competition-tuned gun for service purposes is a mistake because it's a malfunction waiting to happen. You must consider the purpose before buying the work.

Rebarreling and rechambering can bring much happiness, or much sorrow, depending on whether your ideas are feasible and well executed, or just pie in the sky. A good conversion which does exactly what you intend it to, is exciting, like a fast car or a well-trained horse. There are no surprises. It doesn't always happen that way, and there can be problems. The difference between a good pistolsmith and a mediocre one is the trouble he goes to in satisfying a customer. The good man has his jobs well worked out and is specialized enough that he can guarantee satisfaction on his specialty. Fred Sadowski, Ron Power, Jim Clark, and a few others fall into this category in target guns. They do good work, at top prices, but you get just what you pay for.

There are other less known smiths who will attempt jobs which amount to experimental engineering and not just ordinary gunsmithing. The more you modify the basic design of a gun and the way it functions, the more potential you have for trouble. Chop jobs on semi-autos, and double action, semi-auto pistol conversions are hard to do right, and unless you get a top man to do the work, you can expect functioning troubles. Even Seecamp can't always make his conversions work on the first try every time. You may have to be patient on the second or third go-round when a particular gun gets balky. The moral is to be sure you know what you want, and that the guy can pull it off for the price you are willing to pay.

There are trends in custom gunwork today which set good examples for the potential buyer. Revolvers are still big candidates for customizing. It seemed for a while the auto pistol was taking over, but the growth of PPC shooting and NRS Hunter's Pistol would seem to assure the revolver's survival as a competition arm, just as surely as it remains the standard duty sidearm of most police departments in the U.S. Knowledgeable revolver shooters are becoming increasingly aware of the need for action tuning to get the most out of their PPC, service and hunting guns. This is because today's handguns seldom are lavished with the loving care in production given those of a generation ago. The serious wheelgun enthusiast finds it money well spent to make his new gun feel like a slick old one. Money spent on functional tuning of revolvers and automatics is well spent if the work is done right.

Accurizing is now very much in demand since the popular target games place an increasing demand upon precision. The average shooter can probably shoot adequately with an out-of-the-box gun, but everyone wants the psychological boost of having a gun which is capable of better than he can hold. Accurizing a revolver could amount to a simple tuning of the action, polishing of the forcing cone, and adjustment of fixed sights, or it could go as far as a full PPC job with bull barrel, rib and the works. Similarly, the auto pistol job can vary from a minimal duty-tune to a bull's-eye accuracy job, or full-house IPSC tune with all the extra goodies. Since few highly competitive match guns are sold factory-ready, the 'smiths doing the custom work are assured steady employment. All this boils over into hunting and plinking guns too, for the casual shooter

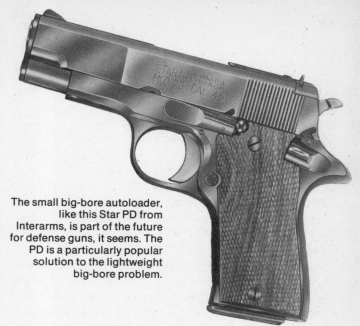

The small big-bore autoloader, like this Star PD from Interarms, is part of the future for defense guns, it seems. The PD is a particularly popular solution to the lightweight big-bore problem.

also wants something better than a standard gun. He has greater confidence in a pistol he knows is better. There is more than just snob appeal in having a first rate job done on a favorite gun. Satisfaction is found through performance as well as pride of ownership.

Rebarreling mostly aims to improve accuracy. This can provide a means of optimizing twist rate for a particular load, or to upgrade barrel quality. PPC shooters have found that the 14-inch twist gives the best accuracy with 38 Special wadcutters. Silhouette shooters have found that you need a faster twist of around 12-14 inches to stabilize bullets of 170-200 grs. adequately in the 357 Magnums at ranges out to 200 meters. Hunters have also found out these faster twists give better expansion at attainable revolver velocities than the long-standard 18¾-inch twist for the 38/357 handguns. Similarly, some 44 Magnum shooters have achieved better accuracy and expansion with 14-inch twists in their guns.

A lot of rebarreling is a part of conversion to another caliber, as in taking large frame S&W revolvers like the S&W Model up to 45 Colt or 44 Special. Usually a gunsmith will try to use an original barrel of the appropriate caliber, but as the supply of these dries up, more shooters seeking these conversions will be forced to use new barrels made from blanks. This is more expensive, but has positive tradeoffs, since the options available this way are many: extra long barrels, integral scope bases, and the like. The fresh barrel made this way will often be more accurate than the ordinary factory replacement barrel since the bore itself is smoother and more uniform. Rebarreling handguns is no longer an exotic, rarely-thought-of option. In the future, serious revolver shooters will think no more of changing barrels than big-bore rifle target shooters now do. Rebarreling is an "in" thing now and makes a lot of sense, if done for the right reasons.

Price and Demand Trends: Custom Handguns

Conversion of handguns to different, sometimes oddball calibers is on the upswing, but as more large bore revolvers become available for the 45 Colt, 44s and such, I think the trend toward these conversions will wane somewhat as alternatives become available. The same thing happened to chop jobs on semi-auto pistols. Ten years ago if you wanted a short, 30-ounce, all steel 45 ACP, you had to chop a Colt Government Model to do it. This was a considerable expense. Now you can readily buy a Detonics, and there is little good reason to chop a good Colt just to get a small 45. The 9mm enthusiast will soon have the same type of thing available to him. It will hardly seem worthwhile to spend a great deal of money chopping a S&W Model 39 or 59 to get a small 9mm once more small 9mm pistols like the Star BKS or Heckler & Koch PSP become available. If similar alternatives are available factory-made, few shooters will pay heavy money to customize something they can obtain across the counter. They may slick up the factory gun, but extensive alteration is no longer a cost-effective option.

Handgun stocks and grips are often subjects of fad and fancy, but the standards set by made-to-measure stocks, like Herrett's, will probably remain for years to come. The trend, however, is away from custom-fitted grips toward mass produced ones. Today's prices for handwork are rapidly pricing made-to-measure handgun stocks out of the market for most shooters. It's easy to spend $50 on a set of Herrett's, but they're worth it. However, the makers are adapting to the mass of shooters by making standard patterns in different sizes and shapes to accommodate almost any shooter's hand.

Although wood stocks will remain the standard for most civilian hunting and target pistols (mainly for reasons of appearance and tradition), many police departments are going to reinforced rubber stocks, such as the Pachmayr Signature grip. These are inexpensive compared to any decent wooden stock. Presentation stocks for highly embellished guns are still made mostly from fancy wood, though pearl and ivory are still seen occasionally. Few ivory grips are currently made of real ivory, though. Tropical woods are also hard to get now and seem on the way out. Walnut and synthetics seem to be the materials of choice for most handgun stocks.

Firearm finishes are also somewhat subject to fad, but the old standards will remain. A good blue finish is still the choice of shooters who can pamper their guns. Black chrome used to be fashionable, but is less so today, unless bead blasted to knock off the high shine. Bright nickel has gone the same way. Few people nickel guns now without bead blasting them, which makes a durable, subdued finish. Electroless nickel is catching on, but it's hard to say whether this will be a fad which picks up and then fades like Teflon S did 10 years ago,

or if it will become a standard. Electroless nickel has the appearance of stainless steel. Those liking stainless steel guns do it out of snob appeal, though it also gives good rust protection. It hasn't been around long enough to know if its abrasion resistance is as good as other alternatives, such as electroplated nickel. Since Sim-Gard, Nitex, and the other electroless nickel processes are applied chemically, the nickel film probably isn't as thick as can be applied by electroplating, and this might have an effect on durability.

Armoloy started as a fad and is merely a different type of industrial hard chrome, having a distinct product identity. This finish has proven very durable and has become a standard in a relatively short time. For those wanting a durable, matte finish, who don't object to the white color, it is an excellent choice. Parkerizing is probably still the best choice for those who like a dark, nonreflective finish, but it isn't particularly popular. Most custom gunmakers prefer glass beading or sandblasting before bluing, or applying black chrome. Good black chrome is better than Parkerizing, but is a lot more expensive. Of all the common finishes, bluing and Parkerizing are least expensive. Parkerizing is somewhat more expensive than an ordinary hot dip blue job, but less so than cold rust bluing. If you were to rank the finishes most often used on handguns, a good blue job on a 45 automatic might run $35, while Parkerizing of the same gun might run $40, satin nickel perhaps $45, and hard or black chrome up to $60.

Embellishments such as engraving, checkering, inlays, and other custom options will always be "in style" on custom guns, but as the cost of handwork and precious metals continues to rise, so will the cost. None of this work runs cheap if well done, though *good* engraving or other skillful handwork will usually enhance the value of a gun above the cost of the gun plus the work. The secret is to get good work at a fair price. The sky is the limit here, but with a little knowledge and prudent shopping you'll get what you pay for and then some.

The wise shopper should have some idea what he should expect to pay for certain standard services. The lists which follow are intended only as a guide. They represent average values obtained from surveying the published prices of name pistolsmiths at the time of this writing. They are only approximate, since time, local demand or trends and material costs all influence prices.

You may find that prices have gone up by the time you read this—something inevitable in these inflationary times. However, a lot of jobs are so standardized their prices don't go up that much. You may find lower prices on some jobs than are quoted here. I would caution you in that case to make sure you are getting good work, for a fellow charging less than the going rate is either barely clearing a profit, or he is cutting corners. You should be wary of paying too much for too little also. There are a few small shops outside the big cities who do very good work at a very reasonable price, but these are the exception. More likely you may find a jackleg who charges top dollar for poor work. The safest course is to seek established craftsmen with a reputation to protect. Satisfied customers are your best guide. If your club hotshot shoots a Clark long slide 45 go get your own and clean his plow. All it takes is money.

Ken Warner

APPROXIMATE PRICES FOR CUSTOM HANDGUN WORK

Revolvers

Duty-tune of DA revolvers: free up action, remove rough spots in cycle, insure reliable function (ignition and trigger/hammer return), zero for chosen duty load (fixed-sight guns) and dunk in blue tank (any additional metal prep extra) $70-100

Action work on above only (parts extra) .. $25-35
Zeroing fixed-sight revolver
  (includes blue) $45-65

Competition-tune action on S&W
  (parts extra) $35-50

Competition-tune action on Colt Python
  (including parts) $80-125

Full-house PPC conversion of S&W or Ruger DA: rebarrel with 14-inch twist Douglas, action job, rib, reblue
  (gun extra)............................ $200-275

NRA police "Distinguished" competition-tune on standard gun $90-125

Action job on Ruger Blackhawk for smooth function and crisp trigger pull $25-40

Cut barrel, crown, remount sight and reblue or nickel $90-125

Install bull barrel only (no action work), fit lug, front sight...................... $100-150

Rechamber revolver cylinder (fitting extra) .. $50-75

Convert S&W N-frame 357 to 44 Special or 45 Colt, including new 1950 or '55 barrel $150-175

Round-butt S&W K- or N-frame, or Ruger Security Six $40-65

Fit auxiliary cylinders to DA revolvers 9mm/357; 45 ACP/45 Colt; etc. $85-125

Red insert or yellow dot in existing front sight $15-20

Nite Site installation on police handguns
  (sights included) $65-75

Machine and fit bull barrel with integral ejector rod housing, integral rib, integral front sight ramp, cut for Ruger scope mount rings for dual-use iron/scope sight gun, blend to frame, and match finish of stainless or reblue entire gun $200-250

Short cylinder conversion (to wadcutter length) on S&W K model or Colt Python $250-275

32 conversion on S&W K model, Douglas barrel $250-275

Semi-Auto Pistols

Duty-tune of Colt GM or Commander (action work only, no sights or refinishing) $35-50

IPSC combat-tune (basic job on action, trigger, fixed sights, no frills) $90-110

IPSC competition-tune (sights, trigger job, refinish, action job) $200-250

Individual options:
  Micro or King-Tappan fixed sights $45-60
  S&W K sight set in dovetail $75-90
  S&W K to rear of slide, dovetail welded .. $90-110
  bevel magazine well $15-20
  checker trigger guard $20-30
  square and checker trigger guard $50-65
  pin grip safety $10-15
  stripple frontstrap $25-35
  checker frontstrap $50-65
  fit feed ramp of barrel to frame $15-20
  throat barrel for WC ammo.............. $15-20
  enlarge ejection port $15-20
  extend safety $20-30
  extend slide stop $20-30
  extended magazine release $20-30
  fit slide to remove vertical play $20-30
  install long NM trigger $25-30
  install short trigger with stop $20-25

Price and Demand Trends: Custom Handguns

trigger job on Colt GM or Commander ... $20-30

trigger job on S&W M39 or
Browning M1935 .... $25-35

Devel or ASP type conversion of
S&W M39 .... $350-400

Basic 45 accuracy job, w/o sights $90-150

Install full rib on Colt GM $45-60

Chop job or Bobcat on Colt GM or
Commander $300-400

Chop S&W Model 41 22 for field gun
conversion, 4½-inch barrel, exposed
hammer, extended slide stop, checkered
guard, S&W K sight, smooth stocks, etc.,
(gun extra)......................... $350-450

Custom 16-inch barrel with stock and lug for
Hi-Standard 22 LR pistol-carbine
conversion.......................... $150-200

Single-Shot Pistols

IHMSA package on XP100, use original
stock but glass reinforce, rebarrel, alter
extractor, install front ramp and rear sight
base, matte blue $200-250

Individual options on XP100:
Flute bolt $20-35
Alter extractor to 308 size, finger type $35-45
Open ejection port $20-25

Reinforce original stock and inlet for bull
barrel $30-35

Furnish, contour, chamber and install
Douglas premium barrel in suitable caliber
for XP100 .... $125-150

Rechamber T/C Contender barrel to suitable
cartridge $25-35

Rebarrel T/C in suitable caliber with Douglas
Premium barrel, fit underlug, extractor,
etc., from customer's barrel and reblue .. $150-175

Finishes

Service blue finish, revolver or auto $25-35
(extra for high polish with all edges sharp,
etc.) $12-15

Hard chrome $60-90
(extra for bead blast or brushed finish).... $20-30

Black chrome $70-90
(extra for bead blast or brushed finish).... $20-30

Two-tone chrome finish (black slide/white
frame)............................ $70-80

Parkerizing, revolver or auto $35-45

Teflon S, revolver or auto................. $35-45

Nickel, bright $30-35
(extra for brushed or satin finish) $10-12

Nickel, electroless (Nitex, SimGard, etc.) .. $35-50

Armoloy $50-60

PISTOLSMITHS AND THEIR SPECIALTIES:
(a sampling)

Bain & Davis
559 W. Las Tunas Dr.
San Gabriel, CA 91776

Accurizing and action work on most pistols and revolvers, specializing in 357/44 B&D conversions of large-frame revolvers and Contenders.

Behlert Custom Guns
725 Lehigh Ave.
Union, NJ 07083

Specializing in chop jobs on 45s, Hi-Powers, S&W 39s and 59s, also does PPC guns and IPSC combat.

Cake-Davis Co.
2793 Del Monte St.
West Sacramento, CA 95691

Accurizing, action and refinishing of most revolvers and autos, including blue, satin nickel, hard or black chrome and Parkerizing. Best known for Smolt or Cougar conversions of S&W or Ruger revolvers using Python barrel. Also does a variety of full-house PPC guns with Davis custom sight rig and accu-lock crane lock.

F. Bob Chow
3185 Mission St.
San Francisco, CA 94110

Best known for his excellent NRA bull's-eye guns. Chow also does IPSC and PPC guns, and custom 22 target autos.

James E. Clark
Rt. 2, Box 22A
Keithville, LA 71047

Specializes in NRA bull's-eye 45s and PPC revolvers and is best known for his excellent Clark-Ruger conversions of the Ruger Mk. I 22 for target work, and the Ruger Security Six for PPC shooting; originated long slide 45 conversion.

Devel Corp.
3441 W. Brainhard Rd.
Cleveland, OH 44122

Chop jobs on S&W 39, which are well done and also expensive.

Ken Eversull
P.O. Box 1766
Alexandria, LA 71301

Has built PPC revolvers used by National Champions and winning teams, also specializes in custom pistolsmithing tools and jigs.

Frank Glenn
5425 W. Thomas Rd.
Phoenix, AZ 85031

Specializes in full-house PPC and Distinguished revolvers, and a full line of gunsmith services.

James Hoag
8523 Canoga Ave.
Suite C
Canoga Park, CA 91301

Long slide 45 conversions, also converts S&W 41 Magnums to 44 Magnum.

King's Gun Works
1837 W. Glenoaks Rd.
Glendale, CA 91201

Makers of King-Tappan sights and white outline blades, also does accurizing and customizing of most revolvers and autos. Full refinishing services include blue, nickel, hard chrome and Parkerizing.

Mag-Na-Port Arms
30016 S. River Rd.
Mt. Clemens, MI 48045

Offers Mag-Na-Port service and refinishing, also does action work and offers general gunsmithing services for most revolvers and autos.

Maryland Gun Works
26200 Frederick Rd.
Hyattstown, MD 20734

Specializes in PPC and IPSC combat jobs, best known for his full-house PPC conversions on the Ruger Security Six; does auto pistol chop jobs.

Leroy Van Patten
612 Chenevert
Houston, TX 77003

PPC and NRA bull's-eye conversions and accuracy jobs, rib installations, refinishing in blue or Armoloy.

Power Custom
Box 1604
Independence, MO 64055

Best known for his excellent PPC guns, Ron does his conversions on both S&W's and Rugers. Offers a variety of specialized gunsmithing tools and accessories for revolver work. Also does XP100 conversions for IHMSA competition.

Fred Sadowski
4655 Washington St.
Denver, CO 80216

Full pistolsmithing services for bull's-eye, PPC, IPSC accurizing and action work on Colt, S&W, Ruger. Does a great deal of unusual custom work, anything unusual you want, write, he'll quote.

Snapp's Gunshop
6911 East Washington Rd.
Clare, MI 48617

Custom cylinders on Ruger Blackhawks, rechambering of large frame S&W's, full line of gunsmithing services, including reboring/relining. Known mostly as a rifleman's custom worker, Bob also does and enjoys good handgun work.

Spokhandguns
East 1911 Sprague
Spokane, WA 99202

Auto pistol and revolver tuning/accuracy jobs, conversion of K-frame S&W to 5-shot 44 Special, rechambering N-frame S&W's to 44 or 45, refinishing services, blue, hard or black chrome.

Swensons 45 Shop
3839 Ladera Vista
Box 606
Fallbrook, CA 92028

Full 45 auto services, IPSC customizing, accurizing, refinishing.

Custom Rifles

THERE ARE no real figures, of course, but eight or nine out of ten custom guns put together in this country are rifles, from 22s up to the big ones. Delineating trends for such a wide field can be accomplished, if at all, only in broad strokes, and that is what we are trying to do here.

At the top of the heap is the all-out custom rifle discussed in this volume at great length from many points of view. Implicit in much of the copy written has been the idea that the very top names and the very top materials are greatly in demand. That is so, but it doesn't mean that that comes anywhere near satisfying the demand. The top people are as busy as they can be, but their craft does not permit much speeding up. We are left with either a very limited supply from the very top names or there must be more top names.

Happily, the latter is what is taking place. Many lesser-known smiths, with the examples before their eyes of how well things can be done and how they should be done, are finding themselves equal to the task of rising to that level.

So, once it is established that a classic bolt-action rifle or single shot by a Fisher or a Goens is a very desirable item, we then find a price and demand trend: There is a need, now being filled, for first-class work at lower prices from those stockmakers and metalworkers who have yet to make a fully accepted national name. One cannot often buy the wood cheaper, but one can buy the work of these men cheaper, perhaps by half, than what the best-known makers get for their work. That can be an appreciable savings in a first-quality gun.

Clearly, there is a third rank below this second rank—many of these part-time workers, striving hard to

Seen close-up, custom work holds together, as the checkering of this Dave Miller-Curt Crum left-handed Model 700 shows. More than most black and white photos, this says something of the gleam of blued steel and the glow of warm wood.

(Above and right) Restrained and complete elegance such as shown in these Jerry Fisher rifles engraved by John Warren with Tom Burgess metalsmithing is the height of fine custom gunwork.

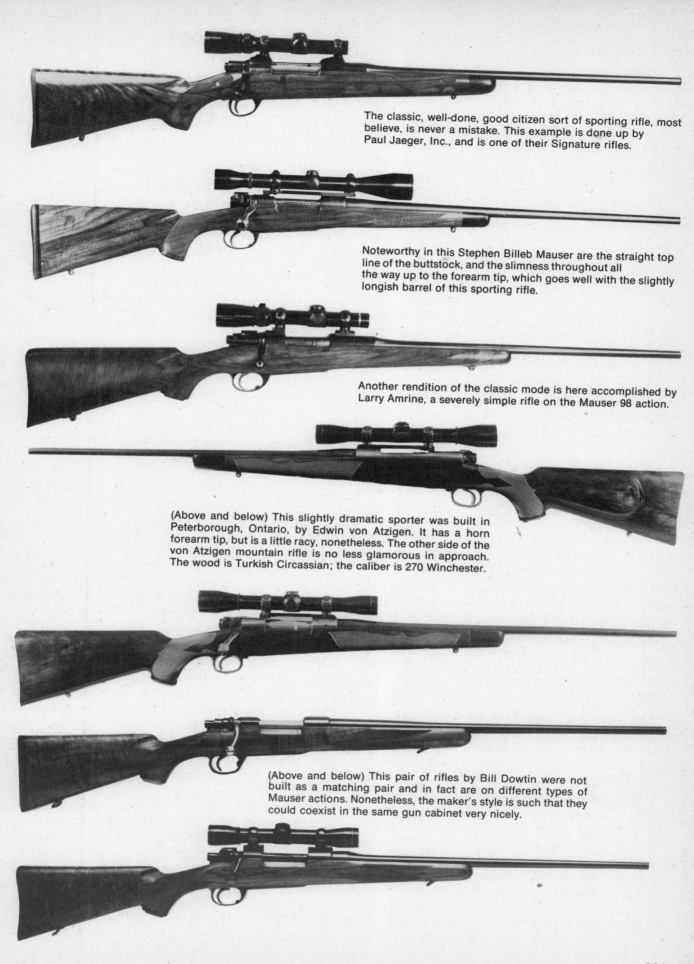

The classic, well-done, good citizen sort of sporting rifle, most believe, is never a mistake. This example is done up by Paul Jaeger, Inc., and is one of their Signature rifles.

Noteworthy in this Stephen Billeb Mauser are the straight top line of the buttstock, and the slimness throughout all the way up to the forearm tip, which goes well with the slightly longish barrel of this sporting rifle.

Another rendition of the classic mode is here accomplished by Larry Amrine, a severely simple rifle on the Mauser 98 action.

(Above and below) This slightly dramatic sporter was built in Peterborough, Ontario, by Edwin von Atzigen. It has a horn forearm tip, but is a little racy, nonetheless. The other side of the von Atzigen mountain rifle is no less glamorous in approach. The wood is Turkish Circassian; the caliber is 270 Winchester.

(Above and below) This pair of rifles by Bill Dowtin were not built as a matching pair and in fact are on different types of Mauser actions. Nonetheless, the maker's style is such that they could coexist in the same gun cabinet very nicely.

get sufficient acceptance and a sufficient market in order that they may become full-time workers. When artisans like these are destined to reach the top, their work and the guns they produce are real bargains.

Probably most of the guns which come anywhere near the true custom-built classification are built in the shops of general gunsmiths all over the country. Many of these are stocked from the block, but more are done from semi-inlets. Incidentally, it is not entirely uncommon for top names to use semi-inlets, although these are always stocks cut to their patterns on very precise machinery. There is a minor industry in furnishing such stock duplicating machinery, and the principal people furnishing this machinery are themselves fine stockmakers. This is the vast gray area of the field, in fact.

Those several kinds of shops are where the guns come from, in the main, leaving out those shooters expert and less so who do their own work.

What are they having built? Well, speaking now of bolt-actions and single shots, the most wanted general style is that of the "mountain rifle." By mountain rifle is meant a hunting arm for the long trails and the high country. That implies a usable weight tending toward the minimum, but not necessarily a skimpy barrel. It almost always means a medium caliber, and the classic mountain rifle caliber is the 270 Winchester. It may be that in the future the 7mm Express Remington will be the favored, but the 270 has been in the fight for a long time, and there is no reason it ought not continue to be.

It is a toss-up whether the next most-wanted category is the heavy rifle for heavy cartridges, or the extreme lightweight rifle or what one might call the standard sporter. The heavies are romantic and the featherweights are sometimes functional, but the people who make them know that it is the standard sporter that can be made most easily to shoot well and keep shooting well. The differences and the advantages are matters of weight and dimension, not usually cartridge.

There are other types, of course. Without getting into bench rest and competition rifles, which have been handled competently elsewhere, there are still varmint rifles and the various repeaters, principally lever-actions, which may be built to most of the functions.

Heavy guns, these days, start with the 338 Winchester Magnum and the 375 Holland & Holland Magnum and include, of course, the 458 Winchester Magnum. There is a considerable vogue for 416 Rigby's and wildcat 416s, as well as wildcats in 45 caliber. In fact, the heavy rifles in general are where the wildcats are these days, it seems. In single shots, the wildcat 9.74R case, and any number of larger capacity cases like the 460 Weatherby and the 416 Rigby and such are necked down and up to suit a buyer who is going to pay for

exactly what he wants. Sometimes the custom heavies are working guns; that means they are not overly decorated or highly refined or quite so expensive. Sometimes they share all the detail of the finest.

In general, heavy rifles made today show a British sort of heritage, with shorter forearms, somewhat more handfilling than usual, and more open pistol grips for fast handling. The actions, of course, must suit the cartridges. High on the list is a square bridge original Mauser; hardly to be thought of because of scarcity is a double-square bridge Mauser; the large Brevex Mauser action also works. Otherwise, standard Mausers and Model 70s are altered to suit. The guns made up on these actions are, considering the calibers, usually not heavyweights. They make up at 9 pounds and more, and are often completed without scope sights. In place of the scope there will be, generally, either a British- or Continental-style multi-leafed barrel sight, usually on a quarter-rib.

In the ultra-light rifles—rifles that, when scoped and loaded and ready for the field will weigh under 7 pounds, sometimes under 6 pounds—only the very, very expensive are made up on Mauser 98 actions, these considerably altered by metalsmithing. There are alternatives, most of them revolving around the use of the Remington Model 600 action, or another lightweight such as the Husqvarnas once imported to the United States. The lighter earlier Mauser actions, the 93s, 94s, 95s and 96s, are sometimes advocated, but most smiths realize that the lack of a safety lug in these actions renders them poor bets when a lot of money is going to be invested. The actions often have a very long striker fall, as well, to recommend against them.

For the most part, a lightweight rifle made with wood and steel—we leave aside, here, the fiberglass stock— demands at the most a straight-grained walnut, and often lighter woods are chosen. A few ounces can be gained with lighter woods, but lightweight rifle stocks are so dinky anyway that not as much saving can be realized as one might think. The rifle begins with the action, and the shortest, lightest possible action makes up, inevitably, into the lightest rifle. Good barrels, carefully worked down to minimum dimensions, still may not be too long if a true lightweight is to be achieved. It may not be necessary to go to the minimum 16⅛ inches, but it does seem to be difficult to hold a genuine lightweight concept and get a barrel much over 20 inches.

I myself use a very crude ultra-lightweight rifle with complete satisfaction. Mine is simply a butchered standard factory Model 600 Remington, with the ventilated rib torn off and the stock chopped. I have, through these devices and the use of Weaver top mounts and relatively light scopes, a rifle which weighs 6 pounds 6 ounces scoped, loaded and ready. It has been used to kill small deer and medium deer and medium elk and has a fine record of delivery. It helps that the rifle is quite

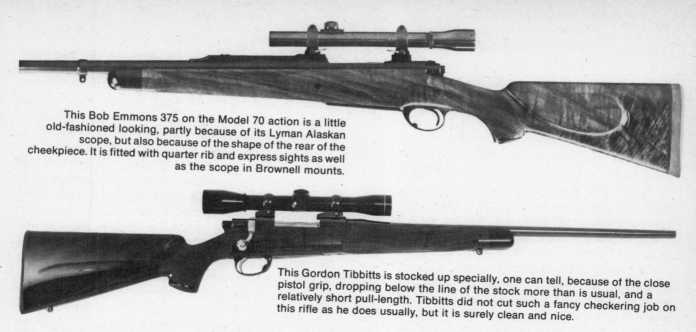

This Bob Emmons 375 on the Model 70 action is a little old-fashioned looking, partly because of its Lyman Alaskan scope, but also because of the shape of the rear of the cheekpiece. It is fitted with quarter rib and express sights as well as the scope in Brownell mounts.

This Gordon Tibbitts is stocked up specially, one can tell, because of the close pistol grip, dropping below the line of the stock more than is usual, and a relatively short pull-length. Tibbitts did not cut such a fancy checkering job on this rifle as he does usually, but it is surely clean and nice.

accurate, and that it was married sometime ago to a selected lot of handloads which deliver just about all the power the 308 cartridge can deliver.

Standard sporters tend to be 30-06s, 7mm Remington Magnums, 300 Winchester Magnums and the like. That is, they are rifles which will make up to about 8½ pounds, offer every convenience, including some considerable comfort while shooting, and carry enough weight in barrel and action and between the hands to assure steady holding and zero-holding as well. Such a rifle can be as handsome as any rifle and more so than most. It offers, really, the best compromise of weight, size and caliber to get the most done for the money. When you set out to build a standard sporter—and many do, the smiths tell me—you can permit yourself hard, dense and heavy wood of beautiful grain, a barrel contour which will deliver accuracy steadily, and you can get all the touches added in here and there, not regardless of weight, but without straining weight limits.

Varmint rifles are done in custom fashion less often than once. This is one place where there are wildcats, and it is also a place where a man with several custom rifles can spend some money and get a handsome piece to add to his battery without repeating himself. The cartridge above all other cartridges for a varmint gun remains the 22-250. This is the least often ordered style of sporting rifle, custom smiths say, but it is not unknown and, every once in a while, an artisan likes to do something a little different from his usual normal things.

There is distinctly a trend to single shot rifles, particularly and substantially the Ruger No. 1, although as a basis for a true custom job the Ruger No. 3 is often chosen. If an action is to be completely reserviced, resurfaced, completely timed and refurbished inside, have a new lever of particular and different shape, there is little reason, the gunsmiths think, for starting with the Ruger No. 1. They believe the No. 3 to be made internally to the same specifications and the difference in cost is noticeable.

All the variations of rifles discussed are here done up as single shots, from lightweights to extreme heavyweights or extreme cartridges. The resulting rifles are almost always distinctive, almost always distinctively custom, and entirely functional in use. It is necessary to keep saying that these guns are entirely functional in use despite the fact that very few of them see very much use.

That is not always so. The most recent full-custom single shot I saw, I took out of the case as its owner helped himself to a beer. He was hot and thirsty because he had just been at the range shooting this marvelous little creature. It is a 222 on the Winchester High Wall action and quite the fanciest old-time brand new varmint rifle I have seen in years. Its owner wouldn't go shooting groundhogs with it on a rainy day, but he certainly would do so on any sunny day. You can see it on our cover.

Custom work in lever-actions, slide-actions and the like, is for the most part reduced to either recreating no longer available models, such as takedown Winchester 94s and "baby" carbines, or to providing some shooter with a particular caliber he cannot find in the action he likes. That is how one gets Marlin Model 1894s in 45 ACP, 45 caliber wildcats in Model 1886 Winchester frames, and 35 Whelen slide-action rifles.

Somewhere in this book is pictured a considerably revamped Model 92 Winchester in 357 Magnum. It is a most handsome little gun, restocked in American walnut, checkered in a handsome point pattern, and blued over glass beading to reach an altogether pleasing proportion and appearance. That is rather the best kind of thing that is done with repeating rifles whose owners like custom work.

It would be nice here to print a chart that showed the

range of prices for the various possible custom jobs, so that one might select two from column A and three from column B and one from column C and arrive at a good idea of what the custom rifle of his particular dream might cost. In contrast, however, to such custom jobs as standard handgun work, rifle work is so variable in the demands of the buyers, and the work is charged at such different rates from one end of the country to the other and artisan by artisan that it is hardly possible. There are some broad general rules, and we will give it a little bit of a try right here.

For a top-grade gun, done first-class in every respect by only a top maker and workers, using exceptional wood from the very beginning, and stocking from the block, a suitable bolt-action can be made into a more than suitable rifle, any caliber, for between $4,000 and $5,000. That will break down to about—remember we are starting from scratch at current prices—$1,000 to $1,500 for materials and parts, including action, barrel, stock blank, stock furniture, sights, and the like; $1,200 to $2,000 to the stockmaker; $600 to $1,200 to the metal-smith. The seriously exceptional stock blank would add $500 or more to this total. Extreme efforts, such as handmade scope mounts, particular sorts of magazine releases and other furniture, and other metalsmith's art services could easily add another $500 to $900. And, of course, if one already owned a good action or good wood, he could reduce these costs by their value.

OK, that is the top. Where does one go from there?

At lower levels, the wood chosen assumes an out of proportion piece of the cost. There is no cheap wood. If one wants an exceptionally handsome rifle, one begins with exceptionally handsome $400 to $500 stock blanks, then buys a minimum, but complete metalsmithing, and finds a part-time or less busy gunsmith or stockmaker to do his work, and might get away for $600 apiece for

these gentlemen, which leaves only the barrel, action and furniture to buy. One can have, therefore, a high-quality rifle for under $3,000.

And so it goes. A little less wood, more or less standardized metalsmithing services, and an above-average rifle can be had for about $2,000. Below that price, if the end result is truly good, you have found a bargain.

We have spoken thus far only of guns made to order. There are many fine guns made for sale where the buyer gets no say in the detail of the rifle, and therefore buys the whole works cheaper. Still, a good one-of-a-kind rifle can often cost $1,000 to $2,000.

It is still possible, of course, to get a better than factory—in the sense that it is individually constructed, and may, depending on the artisan, shoot right up to a high standard—for not a great deal more than one might pay for a factory rifle new in the box. Of course, for that sort of money, one gets a nicely finished action with a standard contour barrel, but without any of the fine touches whatsoever and likely without—depending now on the individual artisan—a great deal of interior custom work to blueprint it, sitting in a good semi-inletted blank, the whole thing a very nice package indeed. This, however, is an entirely individual deal between the customer and the gunsmith. A lot of very nice rifles are turned out in whatever extra time is left in the gunsmith's departments of large sporting goods stores, or in home shops by professional gunsmiths who work for someone else and who build rifles for extra money on their own time.

We have not discussed some highly special finishes, extra high cost checkering patterns, or the ultimate embellishment, engraving, here. Those things are discussed elsewhere, but have to be added to the costs that are discussed in this section.

It is expensive business, but it is ordinarily good business. I do not know anybody who ever bought a first-class rifle and wound up having to sell it, lose money in so doing.

Ken Warner

**PRICE
AND
DEMAND
TRENDS** **Custom Shotguns**

WITHOUT question, the type and style of fine custom shotguns most sought in the United States is what the British call a game gun—a light and lively double, done up as close to the standards of a British best game gun as taste and pocketbook will allow. What comes out of that mix is a (preferably) sidelock double shotgun, in 12 or 20 gauge, with barrels 27 inches long or less, a modest fore-end, a straight-hand grip, all of this, of course,

gotten up in the best of wood and finish. There ought to be ejectors, but the U.S. shotgun world is divided on the subject of triggers. The classicists like double triggers; but many Americans vote for single triggers.

Such a gun will, as often as not, have a somewhat swamped rib if it does not have a somewhat high narrow solid rib in what is thought of as the Churchill style; where it is blue, it will be a somewhat soft rust blue; the ideal,

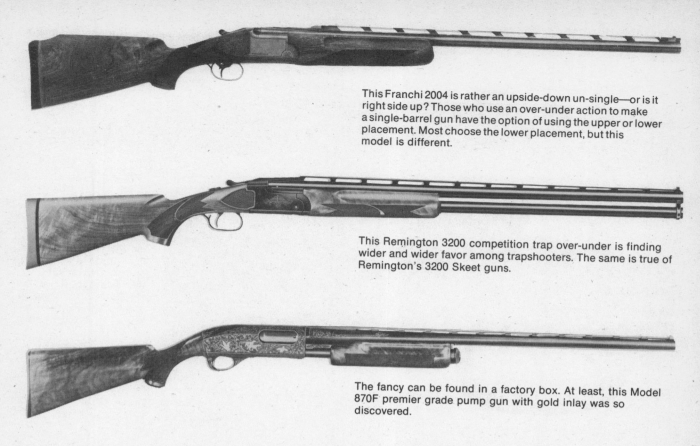

This Franchi 2004 is rather an upside-down un-single—or is it right side up? Those who use an over-under action to make a single-barrel gun have the option of using the upper or lower placement. Most choose the lower placement, but this model is different.

This Remington 3200 competition trap over-under is finding wider and wider favor among trapshooters. The same is true of Remington's 3200 Skeet guns.

The fancy can be found in a factory box. At least, this Model 870F premier grade pump gun with gold inlay was so discovered.

when it comes to embellishment, is probably small rosette English scroll, case-hardened in colors on the action, the sideplates and the trigger guard. As often as not, a pet showpiece will have a plain wood butt, checkered. Someone who intends to shoot and use such a gun, however, will more often choose to have a buttplate, or a solid, even leather-covered, recoil pad. A modest initial shield, perhaps oval, perhaps round, or even shield-shaped, is permitted along the belly of the buttstock.

Putting aside those Americans who, for sensible reasons of their own, prefer a form of pistol grip, the biggest difference one is likely to run into in the American version of a game gun is in the fore-end. The British hardly use a fore-end and prefer what is called in the United States a "splinter" there. Untold hours have been spent by stockmakers trying to install on game guns fore-ends that come near suiting the American preference for more bulk without totally destroying the look of the gun. Sometimes they succeed.

Such a gun, built and set up for American 2¾-inch cartridges, will weigh under 7 pounds and will put all its weight between the hands. Well, that is not exactly so, but that is how a good one feels. It points with rapidity and swings with style. Done up to fit, perhaps even to the extent of having cast-off, such a gun may be fired many times in a day without discomfort. It will not, of course, be happy with heavy American loads, but with loads up to 1⅛ ounces of shot it will be entirely comfortable. In fact, a limited amount of shooting with

3¼-1¼ loads will not, in a good one, unduly stress the gun or the shoulder.

All right—that is the big one. That is what a very high percentage of people want. What do they get? In a new gun, one can get somewhere near such handling qualities for about $1,000. That does not buy a sidelock, nor does it buy engraving, nor does it buy fine wood, but it will get you a nicely balanced, entirely functional, lightweight 12-gauge field double. Such a gun—friends of mine have some—is entirely sturdy enough and quick enough to stand the gaff in American shooting, yet deliver the blessings of a sophisticated upland gun.

Elsewhere we have discussed this whole question of what is available. Without going over that ground again, we can simply say that the biggest demand trend is for the deluxe field gun as described above.

That leads, of course, to sub-trends, and chief among them is the demand for and, on the part of many, an avid search for the basic materials with which to accomplish a game gun or a close approach thereto. That means that any once-good double in restorable condition is a desirable gun. "Good" in this case generally means a gun that has ejectors, and once-fine barrels. To a degree, this demand is met by older guns with Damascus barrels. The trick here is to have steel barrels installed, normally accomplished by sleeving, giving the benefit of being able to use the lumps of the original barrels. In a well-done job, it is hard to tell that such extensive reworking has occurred.

Eventually, all such guns are going to disappear into

Price and Demand Trends: Custom Shotguns

Dealing with the grace of a double gun grip, trigger guard and action, as seen from below here and then providing a wide and hand-filling fore-end, as has been done here, remains the principal aesthetic problem of those who want custom doubles these days.

This is the charm in old metalwork that brings men to spend thousands of dollars to restore the whole gun. This is the metalwork of a Scherping drilling restored to beauty by Bob Emmons.

the hands of collectors or shooters. At that point, there is going to be a demand for good boxlock guns, at which point a number of plain firearms of American make are going to start looking very good. People are already making Parker Trojans, the very plainest of Parkers, into shooting guns of some distinction by spending quite a bit of money on them. The same will be true of plain vanilla Ithacas, Lefevers and Foxes, meaning the A.H. Fox guns and not the later gun known as the Model B. All will be sought out for rebuilding.

All of this ought to be equally true of over-under guns, but it is not, perhaps because there are so many ways to acquire a good over-under these days. Old Remington Model 32s are an exception, but the people who pay the most money for them are Skeet shooters and that is where they go. For some reason, the fine gun market does not follow the general trend in the shooters market, and this is particularly so in the case of double-barrel shotguns.

There are other shotguns, of course. Older repeaters, the Remington 31s and Remington Model 10s, as well as the much-sought Model 12 Winchester, are likewise finding a market among those who wish to restore them. One more recent gun that is in a vogue all its own is the glass-barreled Model 59 Winchester. The writings of Frank Woolner, who made rather a specialty of chopping the Model 59 into what he—and many others—believes is the ideal close covert gun, are largely responsible for this mini-trend.

More than ever before, sophisticated shotgunners

are seeking artisans to accomplish boring to pattern and other interior barrel work. There are, it should be pointed out, a very great many high-grade shotguns around. Far earlier than they did with fine rifles and handguns, investors and collectors discovered the double gun. Certainly, at the high-roller gun shows it is the great double gun that is in evidence. In fact, a show like the one Wally Beinfeld puts on in Las Vegas is *the* place to view a lot of fine shotguns.

Fewer people are interested in the non-game gun. However, wildfowlers still search for the grand magnums of the past and occasionally have one built up once they find a suitable action and barrels. Virtually the same gun is made for the occasional turkey hunter who wants something a little special with him in the thickets.

All of that apart, the main thrust in shotguns is toward getting artisans to rework standard guns to better suit their owners, with Poly-Choke ribs, restocking and the like. In many ways, stemming from the nature of the guns themselves, the shotgun field is more limited in terms of what can be done to the guns than are rifles and handguns.

Thus, it could be expected that an increasing number of people will be looking for fewer and fewer opportunities, so it isn't going to get any easier in the shotgun business for those who search for their very own fine shotguns. On the other hand, the game will always be worth the candle because the shotgun is the gun of use over most of our continent.

Ken Warner

A DECADE OF CUSTOM GUNS 1969-1978

Here's a taste of what's been, enough to show—to a degree—where the field is going as well. There is no question about it, gunstocks are getting simpler profiles and more complicated detailing.

Over the long years, John Amber assembled "Custom Guns" each year in the *Gun Digest* by asking the makers to send photos of their work. What appeared, then, we must believe to be a fair sampling of what was going on. To his credit, and our benefit now, Amber gave the California styles and other less conservative efforts full play in these pages.

As the person now in charge of that effort, I can say that most of the photos that arrive in *Gun Digest's* "Custom Guns" file do show the conservative and traditional outline these days. There will no doubt be a counter-trend some time soon, and it, too, will be revealed in "Custom Guns" in *Gun Digest*.

On the three pages following you will find samples of work from the 1969, 1973, and 1978 issues, thus spanning a decade. The shapes and details tell their own stories, although the names, you will note, change. In the main, the classicist's point of view is sustained.

And below you will find a short essay on the subject by John Amber, written in 1969. It accompanied an article written about the acquisition of a Perazzi shotgun.

I haven't asked him, but I rather doubt Amber would change having said it if he could, particularly since 11 years later, it was proven to be prophetic.

Ken Warner

Styles and Fashions

If what I've written here carries a touch of arrogant belief in my own taste, I can only add that it derives from some 40 years of exposure to firearms of all kinds. Over that long span I've learned that the simpler elements of good line, deftly-handled proportions, economy and tautness of line and curve, blended together form a functional whole, make for a shotgun—or rifle—that epitomizes the ultimate in handling, shooting and visually attractive qualities.

These truly handsome examples of the gunmakers' art—the best gunmakers, to be sure—elegant in their rich simplicity, their restrained and subdued finishes—are not, as you might suppose, at all new. Far from it. Flintlock-ignition shotguns—the fowling pieces of the late 18th century—show a grace of form and style, a degree of functionality the equal of today's very best guns. The stock dimensions of early Mantons, for example, differ in no important degree from the standards found acceptable and useful today. True, the drop at heel is often rather more than American shooters find correct, but that's because of a stance and shooting style situation prevalent here in recent years. British and continental shotgunners shoot with the head held higher—more erect—than is our practice, and more drop at heel is required by them.

I realize—all too well—that the U.S. is full of garish and gaudy guns, more particularly rifles—guns bejeweled and bedizened, guns showing carving and/or checkering, often intermingled in ill-designed, even more ill-executed patterns, replete with exaggerated combs and roll-over cheekpieces, flared pistol grips, oddly-slanted fore-end tips, blinding piano finishes and other alluring aspects.

Alluring they must be to many. Thousands upon thousands are sold, almost all of them paying homage to Roy Weatherby in their adoption of style points he pioneered years ago. Some of them, indeed, are far more ostentatiously styled than Weatherby ever intended.

These things, too, will pass away—or so I keep telling myself! Styles and fashions change, though it may take years, but I'm confident that these glittering, glaring guns will eventually disappear—at least in good part—leaving the classic, traditional style once again pre-eminent in the field. *JTA*

Custom Guns 1969

Royal Arms

This is their basic RR20 custom rifle, made in all popular calibers, and starting at $200. Numerous extra-cost options are offered, including engraving.

Shaw's

A 458 Magnum on an F.N. Mauser, handsomely stocked in finest quality screwbean mesquite, the checkering combining skip-line and fleur de lis.

The Bartletts

Gale B. stocked this 280-cal. M70 Winchester for world traveler T. Siatos, Skip B. did the handsome checkering.

Earl Milliron

Winchester 70, cal. 270, made for Prince Abdorezza of Iran. Unusual fleur de lis checkering pattern, with cheekpiece flowing gracefully into grip area. Leupold scope and mount.

The Ruger 77 and *Gunfacts* magazine were announced; *Gun Digest* tested the Diamondback and the 788; and these six makers showed these guns. The Milliron is cleanly classic; the Shaw is close, except for that grip; the Kess and Bartlett rifles have Monte Carlos and other fancy details; the Royal and the Campbell are California all the way.

Campbell's Gun Shop

A custom-stocked Mauser with a very high heel line and roll-over Monte Carlo comb.

Kess Arms

Full length French walnut stock on a Mauser G33-40 action, cal. 7x57mm, Douglas barrel. Custom tang-safe locks both bolt and trigger. Weight only 7¼ lbs.

1973

Shaw's-Finest in Guns
Feather crotch Claro walnut, carved to oak leaves and acorns, was used to stock this Sako rifle, caliber 300 Win. Mag.

Reed Gun Shop
FN action, Apex-barreled in 22-250, stocked in well-figured American walnut.

Winchester's 9422 came out and so did Ruger's Old Army; George Wallace was shot; Pete Kuhlhoff of Argosy died; and of these five guns on a typical page, two—the Milliron and the Winter—are classic, then and now; the Reed solves some problems, but loses the line; Shaw and Talmage retain the full flavor of the Coast school.

Earl Milliron
Mauser 98 action, classically fashioned. Metal work—guard, floorplate release, scope bases—by Tom Burgess.

Talmage Enterprises
Stocked in birdseye maple, with rosewood trim, the 24″ Douglas Premium barrel is on a 98 Mauser action.

Robert M. Winter
Classic stocking in fancy American walnut of a Shilen-barreled Mauser, cal. 22-250. Double set triggers.

209

1978

BILL DOWTIN
This well-done classic is based on a Ruger 77 in 7mm Rem. Mag., the fancy-figure French walnut checkered 24 lpi in a multi-point pattern.

PACHMAYR GUN WORKS
A Douglas-barreled Mauser 98 stocked in fancy fiddle-back buttstock walnut, yet with the grain commendably straight through the grip and fore-end.

JOHN H. EATON
257 Robts. on a G-33-40 action, the barrel a Doublas. Circassian walnut classic stock, 24 lpi checkering. Metalsmithing by Homer Culver.

The NRA changed the guard at Cincinnati; Warren Page died; Remington introduced the Accelerator; and this page showed only one back-slider—Dave's Gun Shop. The rest, except perhaps for that Pachmayr forearm tip, not only are cleanly classic, but begin to show the intricate and sophisticated detailing that today's makers have in full flower.

GARY GOUDY
Made for Jim Carmichel, this pre-64 M70 has a Douglas barrel in 6mm Rem. The French walnut stock has a skeleton grip cap and buttplate plus a Blackburn straddle-type floorplate.

STEPHEN L. BILLEB
Light, 7¼ lb., rifle on Mexican 98 Mauser, Douglas Premium barrel, cal. 260 AAR, is 19" long. Paulson walnut, 24 lpi checkering, all fittings hand worked.

DAVE'S GUN SHOP
Sako-actioned 375 H&H, the barrel carrying a full length ventilated rib, topped by express sights. 26-lpi checkering plus carving.

BOOKS WORTH HAVING

THERE ARE not so many books on fine guns, but there are some, and to a degree they have served to put together a sort of continuity on the subject over the past 50 years. In his discussion of his custom guns, John Amber elsewhere in this volume discusses the importance to him of Captain Crossman's *Book of the Springfield.* It was and is an important book for someone who wants to understand the field.

There were others, roughly contemporary, such as Alvin Linden's book on stocking a rifle, those books of Townsend Whelen's which touched on the built-to-order gun, and some of the little books by Major Charles Askins, Sr. discussing the aims of the fine gun, if they did not discuss the details.

In the middle years of the past five decades, there was an outpouring of literature on sporting firearms, but very few books written specifically about fine guns. Jack O'Connor, Elmer Keith, Warren Page—all gave the subject some consideration in their published writings and in the complete books that they did.

Of late, with almost everything general having been said, there is what seems to be room for more specific, more detailed books and they are beginning to appear. In the past year, Dove Press has produced a book exclusively on the fine custom rifle; Mario Abbiatico has produced a milestone work on engraving; there is even this present work as evidence that a trend is among us.

Over the past two decades, *Gun Digest* has been a considerable influence on fine guns. There's scarcely an issue of those two decades which does not have a feature article on the construction or the detailing or the general design of fine guns as a group, and where that did not occur, there were almost always descriptions and tests of individual fine guns. Those pages in every edition since the 1950s titled "Custom Guns" constitute the only contemporary and continuous record of what was happening in the field during those years. Individual writers in individual issues of periodical publications, including the *American Rifleman,* the *Rifle,* and all the rest, did approach the subject. However, even the best of magazine articles, and many of these were very fine magazine articles indeed, concerning themselves at length with very fine guns, lack the permanence of an annual or a hardbound book. Only the very serious student can keep track through such media.

Since John Amber was in charge of *Gun Digest* during that whole period, obviously John Amber was a very important figure in the field. He helped shape it, he helped to make it work, he as much or more than any other single person made it possible for artisans to become known on a national level. Unfortunately, John Amber has not himself written a book.

We can look forward, I believe, to a continuing and enlarging trend of books on fine and custom guns. They will be better understood, and have more value to their readers, if those readers will know the books listed and described below. I do not pretend that this is a complete list, but knowing these books will provide a sound background for those who would know the custom gun in the future.
Ken Warner

African Rifles and Cartridges, by John Taylor.

It was first published by Samworth in Georgetown, SC, in 1948 and has 431 pages.

There is not so much on fine guns in this book, but its thinking pervades the custom rifle field when it comes to building the bigbore guns. Taylor's theories on ballistics in practical field use on big animals have rarely been seriously disputed; it is, beyond that, an immensely readable book which shows how a man of experience who makes his living with the rifle thinks.

American Engravers, by C. Roger Bleile. Beinfeld Publishing, Inc. 1980, 204 pp.

This new book is a compendium of available firearms engraving talent in the United States. It was created by mailing questionnaires to 160 artisans, and is made up of their replies and the photos they furnished, supplemented by much effort by the publisher and the author.

All 160 did not reply, of course, but there are profiles and specific illustrations of 73 people now working. All 160 addresses are furnished. There are 36 pages of four-color illustrations.

The Art of Engraving, by James B. Meek. F. Brownell & Son, Montezuma, IA, 1973.

This was the first book of its kind, and its publishers call it a complete, authoritative, imaginative and detailed study in *training* for gun engraving. In fact, engravers have told me that the book was of

considerable value; some young engravers told me it got them started. Certainly, there is much for the buyer of engraving to learn in discovering what beginners in such an art form must know.

The Bolt Action: A Design Analysis, by Stuart Otteson, Winchester Press, 1976.

There is no better book on the bolt-action than this by Stuart Otteson. Perhaps this reporter ought not say that, since he edited the book and was involved with it from its very inception. Otteson being a personal friend and sometime colleague. Nevertheless, the entirely original investigative approach, the marvelous drawings, and the expertise applied to the consideration of the function and the form of the bolt-action make this the best book on the subject.

The Book of the Springfield, by E.C. Crossman. Original 1932; rev. ed. 1951 by Samworth. (out of print)

Either edition of Crossman's Springfield book is worth the owning and the knowing. It is the book of the Springfield, but both the original and the revised edition covered almost all American-made firearms—and some others—that shot the 30-06 cartridge. The original is unalloyed Crossman, giving the contemporary knowledgeable man's view of the importance of the Springfield rifle, both as-issued, as constructed for match shooting in our own armories, and as refurbished, rebuilt and restocked, both commercially and by private gunsmiths. The revision by Dunlap brings the facts of the book up to the date of 1951 and adds what an important gunsmith thought to the available information.

Checkering and Carving of Gunstocks, by Monte Kennedy. Stackpole in 1962.

This was the revised and enlarged clothbound edition of what was called a sought-after dependable work, which was an accurate description. Kennedy's text says much of the middle years of this century thus far on custom rifles and shotguns themselves, as well as their finishing and embellishment. Certainly, the enthusiast ought to own or have read it.

Churchill's Shotgun Book, by Robert Churchill. Alfred A. Knopf, 1955.

This comprehensive volume follows *Game Shooting* by the same author and gunmaker. Churchill made his mark on shotguns, and still today one style of shooting in England is described as Churchill style. The earlier book has a great deal of the master's personal and hard-held opinions; *Churchill's Shotgun Book* handles all phases of gunning for birds and small game and the selection and care and handling of a shotgun from the point of view of a master in the business.

Contemporary American Stockmakers, by Ron Toews.

The author intended *Contemporary American Stockmakers* to be representative, not encyclopedic, on its subject. Toews is a photographer; he believes stocks and rifles to be best appreciated visually; the book is a picture book covering the work of thirteen craftsmen in considerable detail. There are 200 pages of photographs of 40 different rifles and shotguns and a foreword by Jim Carmichel. The book's 9- by 12-inch horizontal format is particularly good for the subject. Published in 1979. Dove Press, Enid, OK.

Custom Built Rifles, by R.F. Simmons, Stackpole, 1955. 2nd ed. rev.

This big book—346 pages—tells how it was in the custom business from the standpoint of 1955. The book did not make a big impact in its time; perhaps it came too early for large sales. It remains an interesting and useful historical document.

Custom Rifles, published by Trend Books (Petersen Publications) in 1957 by Jeff Cooper. (out of print)

This small paperback is hard to find, but it is one of the few books written about custom guns, as such, early on. Cooper took no strong position on style; he took a very strong position on function. It may be in this book that the terms "baroque" and "rococo" were invented for the ornate decoration of firearms which was so prevalent then, and so seldom seen these days. Printed in brown ink on reasonably good paper, *Custom Rifles* by Cooper is profusely illustrated, but shows many guns that enthusiasts today would not truly appreciate. It is an early work in an early field.

Firearm Design and Assembly, by Alvin Linden. 1938 by Samworth.

First printed in paper folders and three sections—Inletting, Shaping the Blank, and Finishing Gunstocks—this essential book for the custom gun enthusiast furnished full-scale drawings to follow and from the vantage point of 1980 is a charming addition to any library, whether the shapes then sought work today or not. The book was later published in hard cover by Stackpole under the title *Restocking a Rifle.* Either edition, or both, are good ideas.

Gough Thomas' Gun Book, by G.T. Garwood. A.&C. Black, London, England, 1969.

This wide-ranging survey is actually a sampling of the writings of G.T. Garwood, whose column appears in the *Shooting Times* of England every week and has appeared there for longer than even the author cares to think. He wrote, I believe, his one-thousandth column recently. He also wrote *Shotguns and Cartridges* and others. Any of them will give the American shotgunner pause for thought; they all could help one's shooting if he let them.

Gunsmithing, by Roy F. Dunlap. Samworth, 1950.

Dunlap's book gets into action shortening, opening up actions, and good stuff on barreling and chambering practices after WW II. Dunlap was a pioneering gunsmith in match rifle construction and is an original thinker always.

The Hunting Rifle, by Jack O'Connor. Winchester Press, 1970.

The world's principal 270 Winchester shooter here analyzes then-contemporary rifles, cartridges and accessories. In this book, O'Connor makes considerable statement about the ideal hunting rifle, its components, and its style and functioning expectations. It does not replace other books by O'Connor, but it does aim rather precisely at problems that concern the man who wants a custom rifle.

The Hunting Rifle, by Col. Townsend Whelen. Stackpole, Harrisburg, PA, 1948. (out of print)

A lifetime with rifles and hunting generated this book, done toward the end of Colonel Whelen's long and impressive career as a gun writer. *The Hunting Rifle* is not a treatise on custom guns, but throughout its pages one can find the good sense and observation that shaped the custom guns of the '30s and '40s, together with some pictures of Colonel Whelen's own guns. This book distills a great deal of the lore and fact generated by Townsend Whelen.

Modern Firearm Engravings, by Mario Abbiatico.

Described by John Amber as the "finest work of its type to be offered to the English-speaking world," *Modern Firearm Engravings* has hundreds of illustrations, many in full color, all handsomely printed.

Abbiatico's text is clear and simple on the history, the tools, and the techniques of engraving. The work is largely Italian, of course, but it is all fine work. The large format works well for the subject; so does the excellent reproduction. Edizioni Artistiche Italiane, Gardone Valtrompia, Italy, 1980.

The Modern Gunsmith, by James B. Howe. Funk & Wagnalls, 1954. Revised edition in two volumes.

This classic is chosen for this listing over the many other worthy gunsmithing books (there were a great many gunsmithing books, as opposed to books about guns in the middle years), because it is packed with the old formulae, as well as a good deal of work on early machining and the details of fine guns. Howe reveals, aside from details, the *attitude* of fine craftsmen.

The Modern Rifle, by Jim Carmichel. Winchester Press, 1975.

This book has a deal to say about custom rifles and fine rifles and even more to say about the proper expectations of Americans who shoot rifles well. Carmichel, of course, knows whereof he speaks. Recently, in a conversation, I found him somewhat fidgety. He said the reason was that it had been a couple of days since he had fired a gun. Carmichel likes to shoot every day God sends.

The Modern Shotgun, by Gerald Burrard. Herbert Jenkins, London, England, various printings.

This 3-volume study is seminal on the subject of shotguns and their cartridges. It is written from the British point of view, but it is so thoroughly written as to be a genuinely basic book for those involved in the shotgun from any point of view at all. It is comprehensive and authoritative and basic.

The Parker Gun, by Larry L. Baer. Beinfeld Publ., 1978.

This is a one-volume edition of what were originally two separate volumes. Insofar as the Parker and the interest in the Parker probably stimulated a great deal in the current interest in the fine double shotguns, it probably behooves a serious American shotgunner to know the Parker. One cannot, with a late start, overtake the genuine Parker aficionados in their detailed knowledge of the gun, but this book does get across the mystique and much of the construction and detail that did make the Parker a fine using gun.

The Shotgun Stock, by Robert Arthur. A.S. Barnes & Co., 1971.

With this work not everyone agrees, but it is the only work of its kind, devoted solely and strictly to the woodwork involved in a shotgun, its care and feeding, its fit and finish. It's part of the lore.

Shotgunning: The Art and the Science, by Bob Brister. Winchester Press, 1976.

Brister, who is an outstanding wingshot and an enthusiastic student of the gun, poured a lot of himself into this volume. Very little of it is a treatise on custom guns, though much of it concerns fine shotguns. What the shotgunning enthusiast can find here is good dope on smallbore shotguns and their use, and the clear and opinionated advice of a fine wingshot on his favorite subject. On feathered targets, Bob Brister is a stone killer, so he knows.

COMPONENTS AND ACCESSORIES CATALOG

Rifle Actions, Barrels & Metalsmithing
Sights & Mounts
Rifle Furniture & Accessories
Rifle & Shotgun Stocks
Shotgun Furniture & Accessories

Handgun Metalsmithing
Handgun Stocks & Accessories
Match Gun Specialties
Embellishment & Metal Finishes
Miscellaneous

NOTE: In this Components and Accessories Catalog, some of the addresses of individual, company or corporate custom makers are included in the listing of their product. To find the addresses of custom makers whose addresses are not listed in this section, consult the Directory of Artisans on pages 245-256.

Section 1:
RIFLE ACTIONS, BARRELS & METALSMITHING

P.O. Ackley Rebarreling Service

Many shooters are hesitant to give up a good gun just because the barrel has gone bad or been damaged through an unavoidable accident. The P.O. Ackley shop offers a complete rebarreling service; and, will even duplicate the contours of your original barrel

Prices: Approximate

.22 - .45	$100.00 approx
.17 - .20	$ 5.00 extra
Duplication of old barrel	$10.00 extra
Blueing of barrel	$10.00 extra
Building of recoil lugs	$20.00 extra
Rebarreling of single shots	$20.00 extra
Returning old barrel	$ 5.00 extra

From P.O. Ackley Barrels (Dennis Bellm).

Barreled Action

A commercial Mauser-type action with adjustable trigger and side safety. All-steel contoured trigger guard, hinged floorplate. In-the-white.

Price: $89.55 (Santa Barbara action)

From Federal Firearms.

Barreled Actions

These are barreled Mauser-type actions that are available in most popular standard calibers—magnum calibers are $10 and $20 more depending upon caliber requested. Premier Grade barrels cost an additional $3. All are in-the-white.

Prices:

1. Santa Barbara Federal Barreled Action $130
2. Mark X Federal Barreled Action $130
3. Mark X Federal Barreled Action with adjustable trigger. $170
4. Sako Federal Barreled Action $230

From Federal Firearms.

Barreled Action

Atkinson stainless steel barrels are available fitted to new Remington 700 actions or Wichita BR actions. All calibers available.

Prices:

A. Rem 700 ADL/SST-100 Stainless Steel Barrel $363.50
B. Rem 700 ADL/Mag/SST-100 Stainless Steel Barrel $363.50
C. Rem 700 BDL/SST-100 Stainless Steel Barrel $378.50
D. Rem 700 BDL/Mag/SST-100 Stainless Steel Barrel $398.50

From H.S. Precision

Custom Actions

Series of custom bolt actions are available in five sizes. From top to bottom: DGA Magnum-Length repeater, $439; DGA Medium-Length Repeater, $419; DGA Medium-Length Single Shot, $419; BP Medium-Length Single Shot, $419; and the BP Short-

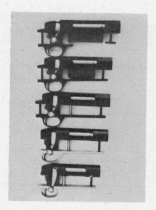

Length Single Shot, $419. Top three actions feature non-glare, blue-black trigger guards while the bottom two come in the white.

From Shilen Rifles, Inc.

Custom Barrels

Made exclusively from Douglas blanks. A wide variety of calibers are available. Barrels are in-the-white or blued. Classic tapered octagon barrels are also available. The maker advises he strives for total quality and will not be rushed; hence, a 12- to 14-week waiting period on regular barrels; and, a 6-month wait for tapered octagon barrels.

Write direct for prices.

From W.C. Strutz.

P.O. Ackley Barrel Blanks

These blanks are currently offered in calibers ranging from .17 to .45 in full round, rough tapered and contoured and semi-polished configurations. They are made of 4140 chrome moly steel, drilled and reamed slowly, then button rifled.

Prices: Approximate, only.

.22 - .45 Full round	$50.00
Rough tapered	$55.00
Contoured and semi polished	$60.00
Chambered	$10.00 extra
Threaded	$ 5.00 extra
.17 - .20 Caliber	$ 5.00 extra

From P.O. Ackley Barrels, (Dennis Bellm)

Douglas Barrels

Douglas barrels have an excellent, well-deserved reputation for accuracy. These barrels are available in most popular calibers in either rough blank, finished (turned and polished) or completely finished (turned, threaded, crowned, polished, chambered and cut to length) styles. As you will notice in the nearby chart, barrels carry numbers running from "1" through "9"—this indicates the weight of the barrel. "Featherweight" is the lightest with barrel weight increasing as the numbers ascend. The prices shown are for standard grade barrels—add $9 for premium grade; $32.25 for air gauging and $49.50 for stainless.
Prices:

Barrel No. or Type (See Reverse Side for Further Detail Information)	Rough Turned to Approx. Size (PRET)		Finished Turned & Polished (FT)		Turned, Threaded Chambered, Cut to Length, Crowned & Polished (FTC)	
	*M-S	*ENF.	*M-S	*ENF.	*M-S	*ENF.
FEATHERWEIGHT	77.25	N.A.	81.75	N.A.	103.00	N.A.
NO. #1	61.25	70.25	63.25	72.00	82.00	91.00
NO. #2 THRU #3	46.50	59.75	57.00	66.00	76.50	85.50
NO. #4 THRU #7	55.25	64.50	63.50	75.60	82.75	91.75
NO. #8	60.50	67.75	68.00	77.00	87.00	96.25
BENCHRESTER & #9	86.25	86.25	92.00	92.00	117.25	117.25
BASIC — SHORT	42.00	51.00	N.A.	N.A.	N.A.	N.A.
BASIC — MEDIUM	46.25	55.25	N.A.	N.A.	N.A.	N.A.
BASIC — LONG	51.50	60.50	N.A.	N.A.	N.A.	N.A.

*M-S & Enf. refers to breech diameter. The basic barrel is rough turned to straight cylinder shape 1⅛" to 1³/₁₆" diameter and comes in three lengths: 26" — 27½" — 30" to finish at 24", 26", and 28".

Custom Barrel Blanks

William H. Hobaugh makes barrel blanks in calibers ranging from .224 to .45—special twists to order, no extra charge. The steel used is 4140 chrome moly. Sporter, featherweight, target/varmint and benchrest blanks are available. Write for full list of services. May be installed by your gunsmith.
Prices: Approximate, only.
Basic Sporter Blank: 25" overall $50.00
Featherweight Blank: 25" overall 52.50
Featherweight Blank: 27" overall 52.00
Target/varmint Blank: 29" overall 55.00
Benchrest Blank: 31" overall 57.50
Barrels of 1⅜" Stock: to your specs up
 to 27" long 57.50
Sporter Barrels w/integral magnum lug 60.00
Chrome Moly Barrel: installed, chambered,
 blued, on your action—up to 26"
 barrel length 110.00
From The Rifle Shop (William Hobaugh)

Pre-64 Model 70 Quick Release Trigger Bow

These bows come in the white as shown and are designed primarily as a replacement unit for Pre-64 Model 70 rifles. May be installed by your gunsmith.
Price: Under $75
From Don Allen

Bolt Handle

Ready for your gunsmith to install, polish and blue. Nearby you'll see the bolt as shipped.
Price: $3.00
From Lenard M. Brownell.

Custom Trigger Guard for Mdl. 52 Winchester

Made of solid steel and milled, not stamped. All hand work. Features miniature floorplate (hinged) and hand checkered release.
Price: Write direct.
From N.B. Fashingbauer.

Pre-64 Model 70 Quick Release Trigger Bow & Floorplate Assembly

This entire assembly comes in the white as shown. It replaces trigger guard assemblies on Pre-64 Model 70 bolt action rifles; or, it can be used as a basic component for a custom rifle.
Price: Under $150
From Don Allen.

Steel Floorplate/Trigger Guard for 600 Series Remingtons

Made of steel and comes blued. Contoured to fit the stock cutout at the rear end and to be flatter than the original. Will fit any Remington 600, 660 or Mohawk 600.
Price: $31.50 ppd.
From Neil A. Jones, 686 Baldwin St., Meadville, PA 16335.

Magnum Drop Magazine for Mauser 98's

These all steel magazines hold five .375 H&H cartridges. Comes in the white with follower. (Also available as unfinished castings, adaptable to M70's, Enfields, Springfields, and others—less follower.)
Prices: Complete with Follower $150; Unfinished Casting $60.
From London Guns.

Mauser Rifle Floorplate Release

Add a push button floor plate release to your Mauser bolt rifle action with this easily-installed, blued tool steel release button.
Price: $4.95
From The Sight Shop. (John G. Lawson)

Custom Rifles, Rifle Accessories

Restocking, rebarreling and complete custom rifle building are all done by Lenard Brownell. He also manufactures a custom bolt handle and bolt stop for Mauser actions and a grip cap for sporter stocks. Custom rifle work is quoted on an individual basis.
From Lenard Brownell.

DeHaas Miller Rifles

Single shot sporting rifles using the De Haas Miller single shot action, built only to order on a custom basis only. Delivery 2-3 years.
Price: Write for quote.
From C-D Miller Guns

Antique Winchester Parts

Many parts for earlier Winchester lever and pump actions, High Wall single shots are available from Tommy Munsch. His detailed price list includes Henry; 1866, 1873, 1876, 1886, 1890, 1892, 1894, 1895, 1897, High Wall and Model 71.
From Tommy Munsch

Model 70 Type Safety for Mauser 98's

These safeties are much easier to use than the standard version. May be installed by your gunsmith.
Price: About $60
From Don Allen.

Custom Rifles

Custom sporting rifles built on surplus military or commercial actions to customer's specifications. The example pictured uses an Argentine Mauser action and a .270 Shilen barrel.
From Don Allen

Adjustable Triggers

Available for most brands of modern sporting rifles. Three styles: Improved, Set and Deluxe. Upper section of all three styles are mechanically the same—the difference is in the trigger shoe area and their width and functions.

Prices: Range depending upon the model of trigger and the gun they're going to be put on. As an example, for the Remington 700 the prices run: Set, $83.47; Deluxe, $64.71; Improved, $58.97.

From M.H. Canjar Co.

Adjustable Triggers

Fully adjustable. The "Super Liteweight" model features machined steel parts in an alloy housing. Integral safety. Available for most bolt action rifles. (See chart nearby for further information.)

Price: Model FD $32.

From Timney Manufacturing Co.

Adjustable Trigger

For the Husqvarna and Interarms Mark X rifles. Features machined parts, alloy housing and 3/16-inch trigger. Model H is shown. (See Master Chart nearby for further information.)

Price: About $35

From Timney Manufacturing Co.

Adjustable Trigger

Fits most military bolt actions and is fully adjustable. Alloy housing, machined steel working surfaces, 3/16-inch trigger. Model SP. (See chart nearby for further information).

Price: About $25

From Timney Manufacturing Co.

Rifle Making Services

A wide variety of rifle services, from bolt handle alteration to complete custom match and long range rifle building, is offered. Cloward also does hot bath bluing, rebarrels using Douglas or Hart barrels, and custom stocking. Write for his detailed price list.

From Jim Cloward, 4023 Aurora Ave., N., Seattle, WA 98103.

Herman Waldron, Custom Gunsmithing

Shown nearby are some excellent examples of this gunsmith's work. He makes custom bolt handles, safeties, trigger guards, sights and other items including complete rifles. He will modify your rifle to order. However, this work must be done on a scheduled (not mail order) basis. The prices are, of course, dependent upon the work to be done; we suggest you contact this gunsmith for more information.

Price: Write gunsmith direct.

From Herman Waldron, Gunsmith.

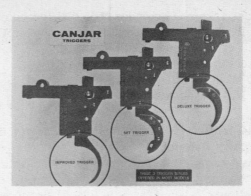

RIFLE MODEL NUMBER	RIFLE OR MFG. NAME	ADDITIONAL DATA	ORDER TIMNEY TRIGGER		
			MODEL SP	MODEL 15	MODEL FD
S03-A3	SPRINGFIELD	ALL MODELS EXCEPT .22 CALIBER	x	x	x
SM2-22	SPRINGFIELD	.22 CALIBER ONLY	x	x	x
M98-FN	MAUSER	THOSE WITH 2" TRIGGER GUARDS	x	x	x
M98-K	MAUSER	THOSE WITH 1¾" TRIGGER GUARDS	x	x	x
M98-8	MAUSER	BROWNING 400's J. C. HIGGINS M50's	x	x	x
M95-6	MAUSER	SWEDISH 94's SPANISH 95's	x	x	x
MS-98	MAUSER	MEXICAN M98 SHORT ACTIONS	x	x	x
M91-4	MAUSER	SPANISH M93's	x	x	x
M91-4K	MAUSER	SWEDISH M94's MODEL G33/50	x	x	x
M91-5	MAUSER	ARGENTINE M 91's	x	N/A	N/A
E1-4	ENFIELD	5 SHOT MAGAZINES N/A FOR BRITISH 303	x	x	N/A
E1-5	ENFIELD	6 SHOT MAGAZINES N/A FOR BRITISH 303	x	x	N/A
600 700	REMINGTON	PRESENT SAFETY USED IN INSTALLATION		MODEL R	
721 722	REMINGTON	PRESENT SAFETY USED IN INSTALLATION		MODEL R40X	
L461* L579-L61	SAKO	VIXEN-FORRESTER FINNEBEAR		MODEL SA	
70	WINCHESTER	MODEL 70 ONLY!		MODEL W7	
6.5 MM 7.7 MM	JAP	J5-WITH SAFETY J-WITH SAFETY	MODEL J		MODEL JS
ALL	HUSQVARNA	INTEGRAL SAFETY			MODEL H
MARK X	PRIOR TO 1977 INTERARMS	INTEGRAL SAFETY			MODEL HX

Custom Rifles

Custom rifles in classic style, custom modifications to standard guns are available as offered by Jay Frazier. Pictured is a custom pre-war Model 70 in .375, with low quarter rib mounted express sights. Quarter ribs with rear sights and matching front sights are also available separately.

Price: (Quarter Rib Sight, Multiple Leaves): From $300; Matching Machined Front Sight: From $75.

From Jay Frazier.

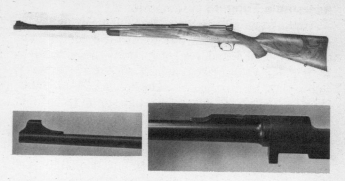

Custom Rifles

Mauser and Springfield bolt actions are rebuilt into sporters with Model 70 style safety, push button bolt stop, custom polish and blue, restocking. Price depends on individual requirements.

From H.L. "Pete" Grisel.

Custom Tapered Octagon Barrels

Top quality barrel blanks are cut to tapered octagon form with or without quarter- or full-length rib, draw filed and polished ready for bluing. Combinations other than those listed are also available; prices do not include barrel blank. Prices approximate.

Price: $96.50 (no rib); $146.50 (quarter rib); $176.50 (full rib).

Integral front sight ramp with dovetail, add $25; integral sling swivel lug or fore-end lug, $15 each.

From Ralph L. Carter.

Tapered Octagon Barrels

Existing barrel can be removed from action, cut to octagon shape and then reinstalled. New tapered octagon barrels are made from Douglas blanks. Prices approximate.

Price: $45 (pull, cut to octagon and reinstall customer's barrel); $85 (machined from Douglas blank); $115 (same, but half-octagon, half-round). Add $15 for polishing, $40 for blue.

From Kogot.

Rifle Barrel Reboring

Shot-out rifles can be restored to service by reboring to a larger caliber, for example .22 Hi-Power to .25-35 or .30-30 to .32 Special. Twists from 8 through 20 available.

Price: $80 up.

1892 Winchester can be converted to .357 Magnum by reboring and rechambering.

Price: $150 (.32-20); $160 (.25-20).

J.W. Van Patten offers a range of custom services for both bolt action and single shot rifles. Write for detailed price list.

From J.W. Van Patten.

Barrel Octagoning Service

Round barrels are made octagon without removing them from the action by Larry Forster. If desired the contour can also be changed at the same time.

Price: About $35 (sporter weight); $50 (target weight).

From Larry Forster.

Rebarreling

Douglas blanks, chambered for most standard and Magnum cartridges as well as the more popular wildcats, are offered in .17 through .460 caliber, Barrels and barreled actions, carefully finished and blued or in the white, are available in feather-weight through heavy bench rest styles. A classic tapered octagon contour can also be supplied. Delivery is at least 12-14 weeks on round barrels, six months on tapered octagons.

Price: From $105 (round); $215 (octagon).

From W.C. Strutz.

Rifle Barrel Reboring, Relining

Restore shot-out rifle barrels to service by reboring to a larger caliber, .22 through .50 caliber bores in 8, 9, 10-24 (even numbers) inch twists, six grooves, are available.

Price: $75

Low pressure barrels can be relined to the original caliber when preferred.

Price: $75 (.22 LR); $125 (.22-.32); $125 (.32 up).

From Robert G. West.

Rebarreling, Reboring

P.O. Ackley barrels are made from specially heat treated 4140 chrome Moly steel and are button rifled for proper bore dimensions. Prices approximate.

Price: $90 (.22-.45 caliber); $95 (.17-.20 caliber).

For: Duplication of old barrel ....add $10.00
Bluing 10.00
Recoil Lugs 20.00
Single Shot 20.00
Reboring: $50 (add $10 if rechambering is required).

From P.O. Ackley Barrels. (Dennis Bellm)

Rebarreling, Action Modifications

Actions are rebarreled with Shilen custom grade chrome-moly barrels, cut to desired length, and crowned, blued and installed. Bolts are altered by forging, high-polished or engine turned. Lawson Safety Shroud can be installed on most bolts, Lawson button safety installed in trigger, and Lawson muzzle brake installed.

Price: Prices approximate
   Rebarreling: $170
   Bolt Handle Alteration: $37.50 (add $15.00 for high polish bolt and extractor; $20 for engine turning).
   Lawson Safety Shroud: $20 (installed on Remington, Enfield, Sako; $23 on Model 70; $25 on Mauser, Springfield).
   Lawson Button Safety: $37.50 (installed in customer's guard).
   Lawson Muzzle Brake: $52.50 (installed).
From Harry Lawson.

Rebarreling, Action and Custom Stock Work

A Douglas premium barrel blank is turned to any standard weight and length, fitted to user-supplied action, chambered, lapped, throated, marked and test fired. Completed action and barrel assembly is then hand polished and deluxe blued, with mirror or matte finish as desired.

Price: $205 (add $33 for benchrest length and weight). Barrels can be rechambered to any practical caliber ($60) or turned to a new contour ($55 up). Shotgun barrels can be altered to a more open choke ($28), chambers lengthened ($28), and bores lapped ($28). Competition choking, which includes test firing, is $66 for single barrel guns; $120 for doubles. All prices listed are approximate.
Write for Heritage's detailed price list.
From Heritage Gunsmiths, 6441 Bishop Rd., Centerburg, OH 43011.

Barrel Restoration

Reboring and rerifling or relining a worn bore are a must if a shot-out but otherwise useful arm is to provide good accuracy. All rifling by Bruce Jones is six-groove, right-hand twist. Prices approximate.
Price:
Rebore and rifle: $45
Chambering: $5 to $10
Reline and rifle: $90 (larger calibers); $50 (.22, including chambering for any .22 rimfire)
Add $5 for shipping and handling.
From Bruce Jones.

Custom Rifle Actions

Bolt handle alteration, bolt knob checkering, Mauser action rework, and custom trigger guards for Model 70 Winchester, Remington 700, and Weatherby are offered.

Price: Prices approximate
   Bolt Handle Restyle and Polish $40
   Hand Checker Bolt Knob . . . .$20-$45
   Remove Mauser Charger Bridge and
      Polish Entire Action $35
   Polish and Checker Bolt Stop $15
From Dick Willis.

Section 2:

SIGHTS & MOUNTS

British Style Express Sight and Bases

Each sight comes in the white with one standing and three folding leaves. These sights will require the services of a competent gunsmith for regulating and installation. Small or large dovetail bases are also available.
Prices: Sight $49.95; Base $19.95
From London Guns.

Custom Claw-Style Scope Mount

This mount is specifically made for Mauser 98's with 1″ rings. Scope pivots to rear to detach; comes blued.
Price: $150 per set.
From London Guns.

Custom Scope Rings and Bases

Lenard Brownell hand makes these custom scope rings and bases for any gun/scope combination you have; they are beautifully made. Rings come with screws or levers (shown). Bases are available for most popular sporting rifles; left-hand Remington, Weatherby and Wichita actions as well.
Price: Rings $85; Bases $25 ($35 for unaltered 98 Mausers).
From Lenard M. Brownell Custom Rifles.

Conetrol 1-Piece and 2-Piece Scope Bases:

These bases are made of beautifully blued steel. They come in 1-piece (bridge) or 2-piece styles and are made to fit just about all popular actions—specify rifle when purchasing. Well made.
Price:

1- or 2-Piece Scope Bases

Huntur	$19.98
Gunnur	24.99
Custum	29.97

From Conetrol Scope Mounts.

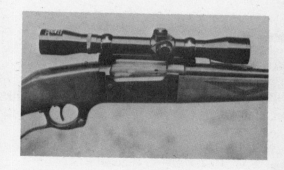

Conetrol Projectionless Scope Rings

These rings are beautifully made of high-polish blued steel. They come in high low and medium sizes and are offered in three grades—*Huntur, Gunnur* and *Custum.*
Price:

Solid Rings

Huntur	$ 8.49
Gunnur	10.47
Custum	12.48

Split Rings

Huntur	$ 9.99
Gunnur	12.48
Custum	14.97

From Conetrol Scope Mounts.

Scope Mount

Davidson's "Bridgemount" is made for the Remington 700, 721, 722, 40-X, 788, 600, 660, and XP-100; also Winchester Models 70 and 670; Wichita Mini and Shilen DGA rifles. Made to take Unertl "Posa" and Redfield 3200 external adjustment rings with 7.2 inches between spacing notches. Made of 7075-T6 alloy; hard anodized black.
Price: Under $20.
From Davidson, 2020 Huntington Dr., Las Cruces, NM 88001.

Griffin & Howe Top Mount

Each ring has an independent locking lever system allowing for fast attachment or removal. These mounts are completely hand crafted—one set at a time. They are offered on an installed basis only.
Price: $275 up.
From Griffin & Howe, Inc.

Griffin & Howe Scope Mounts

These mounts feature locking levers that allow for fast attachment or removal. The mount holds the scope immovable in its split ring brackets. It can be mounted high enough to enable the use of iron sights. Offered for most popular rifles. Also available are mounts (of this style) for the Winchester Model 94, Garand M-1 and the M-14.
Price: Mount only $110; installed $200.
From Griffin & Howe, Inc.

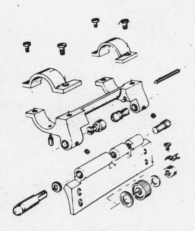

Bridge Mount

This bridge mount is intended for the longer scopes such as the Lyman LWBR and Leupold 24X when mounted on Remington 40X, 700, 722 actions using Weaver rings. Mount has ample cross section to insure a sturdy installation. It's 8 inches long. Weight 3½ ounces, black anodized aluminum.
Price: Under $30.
From K.W. Kleinendorst, Gunsmith.

Custom Rifle Ribs, Express Sights, Quarter Ribs and Ribs Machined for Scope Rings

All of these (and other) items and services are done by Ralph Carter. In the nearby photo you can see (top) a full-length rib with three-leaf express-type sight. The barrel on the bottom sports a quarter rib complete with three-leaf express-type sight—this rib has also been cut to accept Lenard Brownell custom rings or standard Ruger rings.
Prices: Write gunsmith direct.
From Ralph L. Carter.

Aperture Sight

Williams' Foolproof series of peep sights are made for just about every popular sporting rifle. They are available in either high- or low-sight line models. The FP sight shown, features micrometer adjustment knobs.
Price: $26.85; with Twilight aperture, $27.65; with target knobs (as shown), $31.95.
From Williams Gun Sight.

Aperture Sights

The Lyman Models 57 and 66 are identical except for the fact that the 57 is for round receivers while the 66 is for flat receivers. Features audible ¼-minute click adjustment for elevation and windage, quick-release slide and a set of aperture discs (2)—one for hunting, one for target.
Price: $34.95.
From Lyman Products Corp.

Lo-Swing Side Mount

Shown nearby is an exploded view of Pachmayr's Lo-Swing side mount. It's beautifully made and is designed for the hunter who knows what it's all about. There are moments in the field when you need iron sights; and, the Lo-Swing is perfect for that purpose. You simply swing the mount and scope off to one side and use your iron sights. This mount has received praise from some of the best known hunters.
Price: $30.
From Pachmayr's.

Section 3:

RIFLE FURNITURE & ACCESSORIES

Trap Butt Plate

Blued as shown, and made of chrome-moly steel, this trap buttplate is checkered 20-lines to the inch and is for professional fitting. Opening is large enough to accommodate ammo shown or sectioned cleaning rod.
Price: $24.95 ppd.
From Albright Products.

Custom Grip Cap

Bill Dyer, Engraver, makes this custom grip cap out of nickel silver along with a gold initial of your choice. The cap is most attractive—a nice touch for your favorite sporting rifle.
Price: Write maker direct.
From Bill Dyer, Engraver.

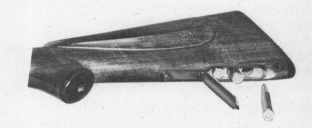

Cartridge Trap

The Fajen Cartridge Trap is big enough to take magnum rifle cartridges; holds 3 rounds of ammo and comes complete with sling swivel stud. This hinged trap comes in blued steel. May be professionally installed by a competent gunsmith.
Price: $38.50; $71.50 if installed by Fajen on one of their Semi-Finished stocks.
From Reinhart Fajen.

Trap-Type Grip Cap

These steel caps come in the white, ready for installation by a competent gunsmith. Handy for holding extra front sight blade or other items.
Price: $49.95.
From London Guns.

Custom Grip Caps

Two styles are available—plain and trap type. Both are in the white.
Price: Write direct.
From Hoenig & Rodman.

Custom Grip Cap

This cap comes with screws and is in the white as shown. It's made of steel and is ready for final fitting and bluing by your gunsmith.
Price: $20.65.
From Dave Talley.

Custom Grip Cap

Available in polished ($9.50), which is shown, or unpolished ($3.50) form.
From Lenard M. Brownell.

Q.D. Swivel Bases

These custom bases are in the white as shown. They are machined from cold drawn, bar stock. Screws have machine-cut threads with milled narrow slots. Ready to be polished, blued and installed by your gunsmith.
Price: $24 per set.
From Dave Talley.

Barrel Band Swivel Mount

Each band comes in the white and is ready to be sweated in place by your own gunsmith. Style "SD" fits standard Q.D. swivels; Style "W" fits old-style Winchester Q.D. swivels; Style "H" fits English hook swivels. Barrel bands are tapered .010 per inch. I.D. dimensions are nominal and are taken at the band's midpoint. Sizes available: .630, .655, .680, .705, .730, .755, .780, .805, .830, .855, .880 and .905.
Prices: $15.95 for "SD" & "W" Styles; $22.45 for "H" Style.
From London Guns.

White-Line Presentation Recoil Pad

This Pachmayr pad is designed expressly for heavy magnum rifles. It features a basket-weave face and smooth sides. Available in three thicknesses; .600", .800" and 1-inch. Comes in red, brown or black; small medium or large. Available with plain black base on special order.
Price: $9.75.
From Pachmayr Gun Works.

Skeleton Butt Plates

Each plate is made-to-order and custom-fitted to the owner's favorite rifle. The work is all hand done and expertly executed. We sincerely suggest you write the gunsmith direct for more information on this and other available services.
Price: Write gunsmith direct.
From Bill McGuire, Gunsmith.

Latigo Quick-Set Sling

Brownell's Latigo sling is made of top-quality leather and has an excellent reputation with hunters and sportsmen. It's quickly adjustable for almost any desired length. Well made, reasonably priced. Sling is 1-inch wide.
Price: $11.95.
From Brownell's Inc.

Carrying Straps

In the nearby photo from top to bottom are Lawrence's Models 2, 2F, and 2B carrying straps which represent plain, flower carved and basketweave styles. Straps taper to 1 inch at either end. Suede lined.
Price: Plain $11.55; Flower Carved $17.55; Basketweave $14.25. Prices approximate.
From Lawrence Leather, 306 S.W. 1st Ave., Portland, OR 97204.

Custom Trap-Type Butt Plate

The pad is of the stylish thin-rubber variety backed by black anodized aluminum, or ⅛" steel—customer's choice. The outside will be shaped to small, medium or large recoil pad sizes and white finished with brass screws furnished. Installed by maker.
Price: Write maker direct.
From Hubert J. Hecht.

Winchester Butt Plates

Accurate reproductions of both crescent and carbine type steel butt plates for older Winchester rifles. Available with or without trapdoor in blue or color case hardened finish (specify).
Price: Prices approximate

	Plain	With Trap Door
Crescent (2½" Tang)	$20.00	$22.50
Carbine	20.00	22.50

From Den-Rus Parts, P.O. Box 267, Cut & Shoot, TX 77302.

Rifle Slings

Hunter's Military Sling comes in both 1-inch and 1¼-inch sizes. These slings are made of beautiful leather that seems to resist cracking over long periods of time. They are well recognized by the experienced shooter. Come with brass hardware and leather keepers. Fully adjustable. *Well made.*
Price: 1-inch $12.50; 1¼-inch $14.65. (Model 200 slings).
From The Hunter Co., 3300 W. 71st Ave., Westminster, CO 80030.

Section 4:
RIFLE & SHOTGUN STOCKS

Fiberthane Rifle Stocks

No voids inside stock. Aluminum tube used internally to add rigidity. Come primer painted ready for bedding and final painting. Shown is the Silhouette Stock. Available for most modern rifles.

Prices:

F-100 "Fiberthane" FRP Benchrest Stock - Weight 2.0 pounds $85.00

F-200 "Fiberthane" FRP Sporter Stock - Weight 1.75 pounds $85.00

F-300 "Fiberthane" FRP Silhouette Stock - Weight 2.0 pounds $85.00

From H-S Precision, Inc.

Fiberglass Stocks

Available in a number of styles, from top to bottom:
BERGER BENCH REST

This pattern is made for a Rem. 40X, Witchita, Shilen DGA, Hart, etc. It has a full 3-inch wide flat forearm as well as 3-inch wide rear section.

Weight: 2 lbs. 4 oz.   *Price:* $80.00

HUNTER BENCH

Made to conform to Hunter Bench rules. 2¼-inch wide slightly oval forearm. This is also a good off-hand or Varmint stock. Made to fit the Rem. 40X, Rem. Varmint Special, or 700 short. The barrel channel will accept a full heavy barrel.

Weight: 1 lb. 7 oz.   *Price:* $80.50

WINCHESTER MODEL 70 CLASSIC

This is a Model 70 Winchester pre- and post-64 Classic stock.

Weight: 1 lb. 5 oz.   *Price:* $80.50

B.P.G.

This is a pistol-grip-less bench rest stock that has won so many championships. Will fit Rem 40X, XP100, Shilen DGA, Hart and other custom actions.

Weight: 1 lb. 10 oz.   *Price:* $70.50

From Brown Precision

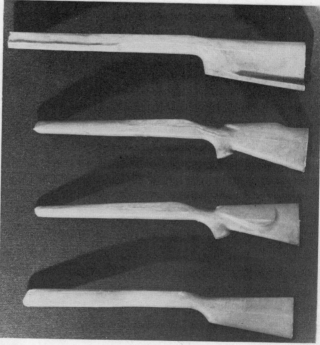

Silhouette Rifle Stock

If your taste runs to thumbhole stocks for a Silhouette rifle, you might want to consider Fajen's offerings. The stock is available in either walnut/walnut or walnut/maple lamination and can be bought in semi-finished, hand-fitted, or completely-finished form. They are made for the pre- or post-'64 Winchester, 98 Mauser, Ruger 77, 40X Remington, 700 Remington (Long or Short), Wichita Classic, Anschutz 54/64, Remington 580/581 or the Winchester Model 52.

Price: Depending on the laminate selected, and the degree of finish/fitting, the cost can run from approximate low of $75 up to about $375.

From Reinhart Fajen.

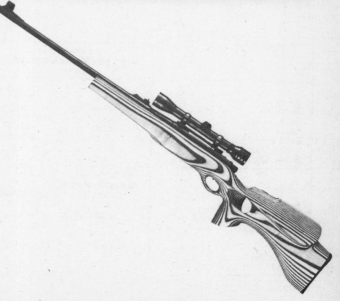

Fiberglass Stocks

Stocks made of this material are impervious to water and won't warp. Stocks are available inletted (about $150) or completely finished and painted (about $250). Models of stocks available are the Benchrest, Hunting/Silhouette and the Prone Position Stock (for small or large bore) with adjustable cheek piece. Also available is a Marine-style M-14 stock that sells for $275 complete with adjustable cheekpiece.
From Gale McMillan.

Custom Stocks

Most woods available; the following prices are approximate, write for exact quote.
Prices:
Stockmaking—1. Bolt action, 1-piece rifle stock: From about $350. 2. 2-piece rifle or shotgun stocks: from $375.
Checkering (20, 22 & 24 LPI)—1. Basic Pattern (similar to Ruger 77): about $50. 2. Wrap-around forend/grip panels: about $75. 3. Full coverage, Fleur-de-lis: about $100.
All From Fred D. Speiser.

Two-Piece Rifle Stocks

Available for Winchester 94, Savage 99, Remington pump and auto rifles and several popular single shot rifles as well. Shown nearby is a Winchester 94 that's wearing the best wood money can buy, complete with best checkering and carving. These two-piece stocks are available in a wide variety of grades of walnut.
Prices: See Below.

	100% Shaped 90% Machine Inletted Semi-finished		Custom Fitted to Customer's Gun Hand Fitted		Finished & Checkered	
	FIELD	**ISSUE**	**FIELD**	**ISSUE**	**FIELD**	**ISSUE**
Utility	$ 25.30	$ 27.50				
Supreme	27.50	29.70	$ 93.50	$120.45	$141.90	$168.85
Semi-Fancy	42.90	45.10	108.90	135.85	157.30	184.25
Fancy	66.55	68.75	140.80	167.75	197.45	224.40
Extra Fancy	100.10	102.30	182.60	209.55	247.50	274.45
Walnut/Maple Lam.	89.10	91.30	171.60	198.55	236.50	263.45
Cherry/Maple Lam.	85.80	88.00	168.30	195.25	233.20	260.15
	SPORTSMAN ARISTOCRAT CLASSIC	**FOREARM**	**SPORTSMAN ARISTOCRAT CLASSIC**	**FOREARM**	**SPORTSMAN ARISTOCRAT CLASSIC**	**FOREARM**
Utility	$ 31.35	$ 17.60				
Supreme	33.55	18.70	$132.55	$ 84.70	$197.45	$124.85
Semi-Fancy	48.95	27.50	147.95	93.50	212.85	133.65
Fancy	72.60	36.85	179.85	111.10	253.00	159.50
Extra Fancy	106.15	50.05	221.65	132.55	303.05	180.95
Walnut/Maple Lam.	95.15	50.05	210.65	132.55	292.05	180.95
Cherry/Maple Lam.	91.85	48.95	207.35	131.45	288.75	179.85

From Reinhart Fajen.

Stock Blanks

Johnson Wood products ofers a number of different types of suitable stock-blank woods. They also offer semi-inletted blanks for many action styles. Grades of American walnut are as follows and the nearby photo shows pieces of *Special Selection Grade* walnut (right) *"Rare Exhibition" Grade*).

Prices: Sporter length rifle stock blank:

Select	$ 15.00 (and up)
Semi-Fancy	$ 35.00 (and up)
Exhibition	$ 75.00 (and up)
Rare Exhibition	$100.00 (and up)

(Selected Mannlicher rifle blanks 40 to 44 inches are $10 above respective grade sporter blank).
From Johnson Wood Products.

Custom Walnut Blanks

These blanks are of some of the best walnut available to the trade. Shown nearby are "Standard," "XX" and "XXX" blanks. These blanks are properly dried and ready for use by your gunsmith.

Prices: In California English Walnut the "Standard" $35; "XX" $150; "XXX" $250. (Prices approximate.)
From Don Allen.

Custom English & Bastogne Walnut Blanks

Bill Dowtin has a reputation for providing some of the finest walnut blanks available. Each blank is air-dried and special care is taken to dry them out slowly and evenly. Each blank is also weighed every 3 months and turned for more even air circulation. Shown nearby are two full rifle blanks and one butt stock blank.
Prices: We suggest you write the firm.
From Custom Rifles by Bill Dowtin.

Custom Stock Woods

Paulsen Gunstocks offers a wide selection of quality stock making wood. Available woods: American Black Walnut, Claro Walnut, Bastogne Walnut, Circassian Walnut, Wild Black Cherry, Butternut, Myrtle, Maple and others. Availability is, of course, subject to the strains of demand—we urge you to contact this outfit directly to see what's available. A good selection of grades is also available.
Price: From as low as $50 on up to several hundred dollars, depending upon your choice of wood and grade.
From Paulsen Gun Stock & Shooters Supply.

Stock Making Service

Unique new pantograph can reproduce any stock to one-ten-thousandth of an inch accuracy. Service is available for all types of gun stocks; and, a broken stock may also be duplicated once repaired by Hoenig & Rodman.
Prices: Start at about $150—suggest you write for exact quote. (This is not a semi-inletting service—when stock is finished all metal will fit stock.)
From Hoenig & Rodman.

Custom Rifle Stocks

Complete stockmaking service using highest quality woods, individually fitted to the customer. Prices vary with individual requirements.
From Bill Dowtin.

Classic Sporter Stocks

Sporter stocks of simple, classic lines are David Dunlop's specialty. He prefers to work with European, French or Circassian walnut. Current delivery time is 12-18 months.
Price: About $600 (basic stock, including checkering).
From David R. Dunlop.

Custom Stocks

Custom rifle and shotgun stocks, and refinishing and recheckering of original stocks, are offered by Edward Hefti. Each job is quoted on an individual basis, so write him with your specific request.
From Edward O. Hefti.

Custom Stocks, Rifles

Hand-made sporter stocks of French, California, English or Claro walnut, complete with fleur de lis or point pattern checkering. Various grip caps, butt plates, and fore-end types are also available at additional cost; action work and rust or hot bluing are also offered.
Price: $1500 (stock work only; add $50 to $750 for blank. Other options quoted on request.)
From Dale W. Goens.

Custom Gunstocks, Inletting Service

Customer supplied blanks are precision machine inletted and shaped to customer's requirements, fully finished with recoil pad, grip cap and sling swivels. Checkering, Biesen butt plates and grip caps can also be supplied at additional cost.
Price:

One Piece Bolt Action Rifle	$ 725
Two Piece Rifle or Shotgun	$ 785
Sidelock Shotguns or Rifles	$1000

From Al Lind.

Custom Stocking

In addition to making stock blanks and stocks to fit practically every domestic and foreign rifle and shotgun, Reinhart Fajen will also fit a specified grade of wood to a customer's action and semi-finish or finish, with or without checkering, to his specifications. Prices vary considerably with grade of wood and the type of finishing required. Price for a shaped but unfinished stock of standard pattern, hand fitted to customer's action, is from $100 to $300 (depending on grade of wood); including hand checkering and finishing increases the price to $160 and $280. The "Aristocrat" style stock illustrated runs $15 to $20 more. Special finishes, other custom features are also available.
From Reinhart Fajen.

Quality Stock Wood

Some nice walnut is available from this source with prices ranging from $20 to $300.
From Jack Burres.

Custom Double and Over/Under Stocks

Shown nearby is an L.C. Smith double barrel shotgun completely re-stocked by Fajen. Made to original style with beavertail forearm and original checkering pattern. Stocks are available for just about every popular foreign or domestic double or over/under—past or present. Available to your dimensions in a wide variety of grades of walnut.

Prices: See below:

From Reinhart Fajen.

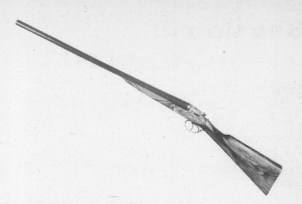

FIELD — MONTE CARLO TRAP STRAIGHT TRAP STYLES	Shaped and Machine Inletted Semi-finished		Custom Fitted to Customer's Gun Hand Fitted		Finished & Checkered	
Supreme	$ 44.55		$209.55		$274.45	
Semi-fancy	61.60		226.60		291.50	
Fancy	83.60		256.85		300.30	
Extra Fancy	116.60		298.10		379.50	
Walnut/Maple Lam.	114.40		295.90		377.30	
Cherry/Maple Lam.	111.10		292.60		374.00	
	ARISTOCRAT REGENT	**FOREARM**	**ARISTOCRAT REGENT**	**FOREARM**	**ARISTOCRAT REGENT**	**FOREARM**
Supreme	$ 51.15	$ 26.95	$240.90	$142.45	$274.45	$190.85
Semi-fancy	68.20	33.00	257.95	148.50	331.10	196.90
Fancy	90.20	44.00	288.20	167.75	369.60	224.40
Extra Fancy	123.20	58.30	329.45	190.30	419.10	255.20
Walnut/Maple Lam.	121.00	64.90	326.70	196.90	416.90	261.80
Cherry/Maple Lam.	117.70	64.90	326.15	196.90	413.60	261.80

Bishop Custom Rifle Stocks

Bishop has been making custom rifle stocks for years—it's that simple. The stocks listed below are available in any dimensions (various lengths of pull, drop at comb, etc.). They are also available in any specie of gunstock wood, in any stock style with a wide choice of options (various cheekpieces, checkering patterns, etc.).

Prices: See Chart

From E. C. Bishop & Son

CUSTOM RIFLE STOCKS

	PLAIN GRADE WALNUT			FANCY GRADE WALNUT					Walnut/ Maple Laminated
	Utility	Superior	Imperial	#5 Fancy	#4 Fancy	#3 Fancy	#2 Fancy	#1 Fancy	
SEMI-FINISHED, COMPLETELY SHAPED AND SEMI-INLETTED.									
Specialty True Classic	32.00	36.00	45.00	60.00	70.00	80.00	100.00	155.00	115.00
Specialty Sporter	32.00	36.00	46.00	61.00	75.00	85.00	105.00	160.00	115.00
Specialty Rollover	34.00	40.00	50.00	65.00	80.00	90.00	110.00	165.00	117.50
SF-2 Stockmakers Special	40.00	45.00	55.00	70.00	85.00	95.00	115.00	170.00	130.00
HAND-FITTED AND SHAPED, READY FOR SANDING.									
Specialty True Classic		135.00	155.00	170.00	190.00	210.00	235.00	290.00	240.00
Specialty Sporter		135.00	155.00	170.00	190.00	210.00	235.00	290.00	240.00
Specialty Rollover		140.00	160.00	175.00	195.00	220.00	240.00	295.00	242.50
Fancy Grades of Maple, Myrtlewood, French Walnut, Mesquite etc: prices available upon request.									

FINISHED CUSTOM RIFLE STOCKS

AMERICAN WALNUT
Superior Grade 225.00
Imperial Grade........ 250.00
No. 5 Fancy 275.00
No. 4 Fancy 300.00
No. 3 Fancy 325.00
No. 2 Fancy 375.00
No. 1 Fancy 425.00

CLARO WALNUT OR MYRTLEWOOD
No. 5 Fancy 300.00
No. 4 Fancy 325.00
No. 3 Fancy 350.00
No. 2 Fancy 400.00
No. 1 Fancy 475.00

FRENCH WALNUT
Imperial (Plain) 300.00
No. 5 Fancy 350.00
No. 4 Fancy 400.00
No. 3 Fancy 450.00
No. 2 Fancy 500.00
No. 1 Fancy 600.00

SCREWBEAN MESQUITE
.... 600.00

FANCY HARD MAPLE (Specify)
Fiddleback, Quilt or Birdseye)
No. 5 Fancy 275.00
No. 4 Fancy 300.00
No. 3 Fancy 325.00
No. 2 Fancy 375.00
No. 1 Fancy 425.00

LAMINATED WALNUT/MAPLE
.... 350.00
BLACK CHERRY 250.00

Section 5:
SHOTGUN FURNITURE & ACCESSORIES

Screw-In Choke

Wide range of chokes are available and installation costs vary from gun to gun when a ribbed barrel is converted.

Price: For installation on barrel without rib, $85.

From Stan Baker, 5303 Roosevelt Way NE, Seattle, WA 98105.

Adjustable Choke

Called the Economy Choke, it comes available for 12 or 20 gauge and allows you to change your shotguns patterning to suit a variety of needs. Your gunsmith can install it.

Price: $20 with tube of your choice; Adjustable tube $25; extra tubes $11.

From Lyman.

LYMAN Economy Choke for 12 or 20 Gauge

Adjustable Choke

The Cutts Compensator has been around for years—it's a favorite with shotgunners. The Cutts is available in 12 or 20 gauge only and comes complete with adapter, wrench and choke tube of your choice.

Price: $29.95 with fully adjustable tube; Spare tubes $6.95 each. Your gunsmith can install it.

From Lyman.

Cutts Magnum Full Tube   Cutts Superfull Tube   Cutts Full Choke Tube

Cutts Modified Tube   Cutts Improved Cylinder Tube   Cutts Spreader Tube

Adjustable Choke

Made for 12 or 20 gauge, the Lyman Adjustable Choke comes with three specific choke settings which can be selected with a turn of the hand.

Price: $35 with adjustable tube and wrench. Your gunsmith can install it.

From Lyman.

LYMAN Adjustable Choke with Recoil Chamber

Adjustable Shotgun Choke

Available in either vented or non-vented configuration. Each choke offers nine individual settings including extra-full and slug. Ventilated model reduces recoil by as much as 20%. Your gunsmith can install it.

Price: $39.95 for the vented model; $37.90 for the standard model. Available for most popular chokes.

From Poly Choke Company.

Snap Caps

These are functional as well as beautiful. Constructed of nickel plated brass, these snap caps are available in all popular gauges.

Price: $15 per pair.

From Wm. Larkin Moore, 31360 Via Colinas, Suite 109, Westlake Village, CA 91361.

Snap Caps

These fully nickeled snap caps are available in 12, 16, 20, 28 and .410 gauges. Construction is nickel plated solid brass. After cleaning, these caps may be inserted into the chambers of your favorite shotguns. You may dry fire without fear of damaging firing pins.
Price: Under $20 per pair.
From Bill McGuire & Associates.

Cased Cleaning Kit

Best quality English style cleaning kit comes with solvent/lube, oiler, snap caps, rod, stuck-shell remover, screwdriver, brush, jag and mop, all cased in mahogany presentation box. For shotguns, of course.
Price: $180, complete.
From Wm. Larkin Moore (See pg. 230 for address).

Shotgun Cleaning Set

Consists of 2-piece rod, split brass jag, brush, mop, patches, "Nevarust" oil and polishing cloth, all in a partitioned box. In 12, 16, 20, 28 and .410.
Price: $20.
From Wm. Larkin Moore (See pg. 230 for address).

Shotgun Sling

No swivels are necessary for this model. It simply slips over the barrel and butt of your favorite shotgun. Made of the best latigo leather, this strap is suede lined and comes with buckle adjustment.
Price: $22.95 (Model 560).
From Pioneer Products, 1033 W. Amity Rd., Boise, ID 83705.

Stuck Case Extractor

Nickel plated. For the removal of shotshell cases or portions of blown cases, from shotgun chambers.
Price: $12.
From Wm. Larkin Moore (See pg. 230 for address).

Spanish Shotgun Parts

An almost complete stock of Zabala Hermanos double barrel shotgun parts, along with many parts for a number of other European over-under and side-by-side shotguns, is maintained by R. J. Davis & Son. An illustrated price list is available for the Zabala Hermanos; many of its parts may be used on other current Spanish doubles but fitting is often required. For active shooters Davis offers a parts kit for Spanish doubles.
Price: $64.95
From R. J. Davis & Son, 758 College Ave., Adrian, MI 49221.

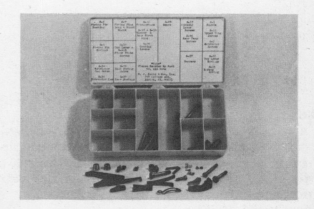

Section 6:
HANDGUN METALSMITHING

Custom Auto Pistols

Armand Swenson does accurizing and customizing work on .45 autos. In addition to action and trigger work and restyling, Swenson also offers ventilated ribs and his own patented ambidextrous safety for both Colt and Browning Hi Power pistols. Write for prices. **From Swenson's .45 Shop.**

Devel Model 39 Combat Conversion

Smith & Wesson Model 39 is shortened, lightened and extensively reworked to make a compact, reliable combat weapon. Conversion price includes holster, spare magazine, magazine holder and belt. Specify if for right- or left-handed shooter (ambidextrous safety available for $30.00 additional).
Price: $455 (buyer supplies Model 39 for conversion).
From Devel, 3441 W. Brainard Rd., Cleveland, OH 44122.

Clark Colt Combat Conversions

Includes accuracy job, reworked trigger, low mounted Bo-Mar or S&W sights, stippled front strap, altered feed ramp, lower ejection port, and beveled magazine well.
Price: $250.
From Jim Clark.

DiStefano Custom Colt .45 Auto

Compact conversions of Colt 1911 made to customer's specifications. Example shown is shortened to 4″ barrel, frame cut to 6-round magazine capacity, "K" sights, Gold Cup trigger, checkering and long safety.
Price: Open, based on individual requirements.
From Dominic DiStefano.

Seecamp 1911 Colt D/A Conversion, Modifications

Converts Colt 1911 or Combat Commander to double action lock without alteration to sear or safety linkage. Replacement wide trigger and short double-action pull make it unnecessary to shift trigger finger from double action to single action hold. Larger combat style trigger guard facilitates two-handed hold. For all calibers of Model 1911, Mark IV and Commanders except aluminum framed Commander.
Price: $166 (blue); $172 (nickel).

Combat Sights

Top of slide is milled flat and serrated like Gold Cup, Seecamp low-profile combat sight installed. Fully adjustable for windage, elevation.
Price: $92; with plastic, orange insert front sight add $23; with loaded cartridge indicator, add $29.

Shortened Slide

Slide is shortened 1-1/16″ in 1911, 11/16″ in Combat Commander. Uses Seecamp's unique "Spring Extender System."
Price: $126.50

Shortened Butt

Removes 7/16″ (approximately) from butt of Model 1911, decreasing magazine capacity by one round. One customer-supplied magazine is also altered, though full size Colt magazine will work as back up.
Price: $126.50; additional customer supplied magazine can be altered at $14 each.

From Seecamp.

Pistol and Revolver Work

A variety of services for 1911 pattern Colts and revolvers is available. These include:

1911 accurizing: $125-150

Adjust trigger pull to given weight: $15.

Mill for adjustable sights: $15 (1911); ;$20 (revolvers).

Drill and tap for Bo-Mar sights or scope mounts: $4 per hole.

Send $1.00 for detailed price list.

From J. Korzinek.

Adjustable Handgun Sights

MMC's adjustable pistol sights are designed to easily replace original, non-adjustable factory versions. Available for Ruger Standard Auto, High Standard automatics, Walthers, Browning Hi-Power, Colt 1911 and 1911 A1 autos, the S&W models 39 and 59 and other popular handguns. (S&W Model 39/59 sight shown.) Available with white outline rear leaf.
Price: Range from about $14.65, depending on the model desired. The S&W Model 39/59 shown, sells for $34.50 plain; $36.45 with white outline leaf.

From Miniature Machine Company.

Relining Pistol and Revolver Barrels

Handgun barrels can be relined to like-new firing condition without disturbing original outside finish or otherwise disturbing appearance. Relining also permits changing a gun chambered for an obsolete, unavailable cartridge to fire another that is readily available. Prices below are approximate.
Price: $19.50 for P.38, Nambu, Radom, Steyr, etc. to 9mm or 7.65mm Parabellum.

Mauser 1896 to 7.63mm or 9mm Mauser, 7.65mm or 9mm Parabellum, .38 Super: $24.50.

.25 ACP auto pistols: $8.50 (small); $11.50 (large)

.32 ACP auto pistol converted to .380: $19.50 (barrel only; be sure magazine will hold and feed .380 before sending barrel in for relining)

.22 Rimfire rifle barrels: $22.50

All prices plus postage.

From David Woodruff.

Walters Colt Conversions

Government Model combat conversions include trigger job, ejection port relief, barrel throat and feed ramp polish, speed safety, blocking grip safety (IPSC Combat Job); complete conversion also includes magazine well funneling, checkering mainspring housing, speed slide stop, fitted barrel bushing, fitting barrel lugs, and refinish (blue).
Price: $100 (IPSC); $250 (Complete).

Target Conversions

.45 Hard Ball	$260
.45 Standard with rib	$280
.45 Standard with extension rib	$295

From Walters Industries.

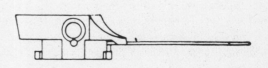

Section 7:
HANDGUN STOCKS & ACCESSORIES

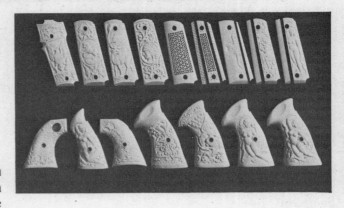

Custom Ivory Grips

Art Jewell offers a variety of grips for both revolvers and autos in carved ivory. (This same firm also offers rosewood grips.)

Price: Rosewood—under $40; Ivory (automatic)—$175
From Art Jewell Enterprises.

Custom Ivory S/A Grips

Jim Kelso, of Iron Age Craftsworks, can provide you with carved, inlaid or smooth grips. Depending upon the requested design or amount of coverage, the price will vary. Rare wood also available.

Price: For smooth, plain ivory, the cost will be under $150. Due to inflation and availability of materials, we do, however, suggest you write for the latest prices.

From Jim Kelso, P.O. Box 518, Preston, WA 98050.

Henri's Custom Grips

Jean St. Henri makes some of the most functional handgun grips you will ever see. The quiet, simplistic nature of those grips make them popular with handgunners everywhere. They are available in: walnut, zebrawood, rosewood, goncalo alves, cocobolo and macassar ebony. They are available for most popular autoloaders.

Price: $25 per pair
From Jean St. Henri

Genuine Stag Grips

These stag grips are available for most American made handguns. The grips shown are for a Colt 45 auto.

Price: $35
From Lock, Stock & Barrel, Box 1173, Kingsport, TN 37662.

Herrett's Handgun Stocks

Steve Herrett has been offering handgunners good grips for years. Their standard line of smooth or checkered grips is available in walnut; however, Steve's firm is capable of providing just what the customer wants. We would suggest you contact this outfit if something special is desired. They can, of course, handle your needs for all types of handguns.

Price: Under $35; Custom stocks over $35.
From Herrett's Stocks, Inc.

Newell's Custom Grips

These grips ae strictly custom made. The nearby photos speak for themselves. Walnut is standard, however, a large selection of exotic wood is available upon request. Keeping in mind these grips are strictly custom, you should know that delivery time runs from three to four months. The checkering job is superb. Revolvers and autos, of course.

Price: Under $80

From Robert H. Newell.

Custom Sight/Rib Combo

Available for the Walther PP series autos. The rib uses the S&W Kit sight milled into the rear of the rib which has a ramp-type blade pinned into the front. No ribbing of the slide is required and the added sight height is only ¼".

Price: Plain, $100 installed; triple dot $125.

From Austin Behlert Custom Gun Shop.

Adjustable Clark (Ruger) Rear Sight

Easy to install, the Clark rear sight is designed to replace all Ruger adjustable rear sights. Comes with large, flat rear blade with deeper sight notch. Improved sight picture, better click adjustments. (Also available to fit on current production model Mark I Ruger auto).

Price: $17.50; with white-outline blade $21 extra.

From James E. Clark.

Single-Unit Backstrap For Colt Autos

For combat competition. Solid blued steel one-piece backstrap eliminates grip safety feature. Available for all models of the Colt .45 auto.

Price: $40

From L. W. Seecamp Co.

Mag-Na-Port

Mag-na-port is a barrel muzzle venting process that reduces recoil and muzzle jump by altering the barrel itself rather than attaching an accessory device to it. The actual machining is by electrical discharge, which permits precise control of the cutting process and produces a clean, burr-less cut of the desired shape. It can be used with similar benefits on handguns, rifles and shotguns.

Price:

    Handguns .... $45 (two ports)
    Rifles .... $60 (four ports)

For bull barrels add $6.50 to above prices; return shipping, handling and insurance are not included.

From Mag-na-port.

Extended Slide Stop

Available for the Browning High Power, Star PD and the S&W Models 39/59. This unit will not interfere with the holster, nor will it protrude beyond conventional grip thickness; however, some grip modification may be necessary.

Price: In blue or chrome, the price is about $25
From Austin Behlert Custom Gun Shop.

Stainless Steel Auto Pistol Barrels

Available for all Colt .45 autos and the Browning High Power. Where applicable, bushing comes with barrel. The Bar-Sto barrels are precision made and have gained an excellent reputation for accuracy. They are available in .45 ACP, .38 Super, .38/.45 and 9mm. The list below contains *approximate* prices; those items with an asterisk take 6-12 weeks for delivery and any required fitting may be done by a competent gunsmith. (Shown nearby is the Browning 9mm Hi Power Barrel.)

Price: Approximate only

.45 ACP (Government Model & Commander	$85.00
.45 ACP (Gold Cup)	95.00
.45 ACP Match Target (Must be fitted)	95.00
.45 ACP Match Target Gold Cup (Must be fitted)	95.00
.45 ACP 6″ Match Target (Must be fitted)	150.00
.38 Super (Headspaced on case mouth)	85.50
9mm (Government Model & Commander)	85.50
.38/.45* (For all Models)	135.00
.45 ACP 6″* Match Target (Compensator Cuts at muzzle)	175.00
¾″ extra length barrel for Commander	115.00
Browning HI-Power barrel, 9mm	130.00

From Bar-Sto Precision Machine

Obsolete Rifle and Pistol Parts

Owners of discontinued, military surplus or foreign guns are often hard put to find replacement parts. Jack First Distributors attempts to meet this need by buying such guns for parts and offering the parts on an "as available" basis. At present, they have quantities of parts for 66 different guns, from 1900 Browning through more than two-dozen different Winchesters and including BSA, Colt, Dreyse, Martini, Mauser, Nambu and Webley. Prices vary widely, depending on availability, popularity and condition. Write for a quotation for a specific need. New manufacture parts for many more popular pistols are also offered.
From Jack First Distributors.

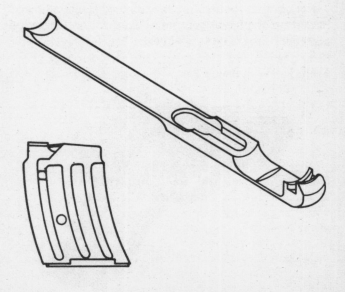

Section 8:

MATCH GUN SPECIALTIES

Light Pull Trigger

Designed as a reasonably-priced competition-type trigger, these units have an adjustment range between 2 and 12 ounces. Suitable for silhouette, bench rest, free rifle competition and some types of varmint shooting where the rifle is carefully handled. Available for most Remingtons and Winchester's Model 52 target rifles.
Price: About $70.
From M.H. Canjar Co.

Adjustable Trigger

For Remington rifles. Features a ¼-inch trigger, all steel construction and may be used with your existing safety. Available with ⅜-inch trigger ($2.50) and outside adjustment ($3). Model R.
Price: About $40.
From Timney Manufacturing Co.

Front Target Sight

The Lyman 17A target front sight is designed for use with dovetail mounting. Good range companion to the Lyman 57/66 receiver sight. Comes with 7 inserts that lock into place with a threaded cap. Available in 5 different sight heights ranging from .360″ to .532″.
Price: $13.95
From Lyman Products Company.

LYMAN Series 17A
Target Front Sight

Globe Front Sight

The Redfield International Small Bore front sight comes with six clear, distortion-free inserts and 6 skeleton inserts in vinyl insert holder. For the custom target rifle.
Price: $37.90.
From Redfield.

International
Small-Bore Front

Olympic Front Sight

Redfield's Olympic front sight comes with 10 inserts and is a top companion for any target-type aperture sight.
Price: $31.90.
From Redfield.

Olympic Front

Big-Bore Front Sight

The Redfield International Match Big-Bore front sight is specifically made for .30-caliber shooting events. Same as the Small Bore sight except for shortened tube to meet I.S.U. requirements. Comes with the same inserts—12 in all—as the Small Bore sight.
Price: $37.90.
From Redfield.

Clark Target Conversions

Ruger .22

Replaces factory barrel with 6¼″ Douglas premium barrel with muzzle brake. Includes deluxe Bo-Mar rear sight and ramp front, complete trigger job with steel trigger.

Price: $327

Same as above except 5½″ Douglas barrel with full length Bo-Mar rib and sights.

Price: $337

Long Heavy Slide 38 Special Colt

Colt Super .38 slide is lengthened 1″, 6″ Douglas barrel is fitted and gun completely accurized. Includes full length Bo-Mar rib with accuracy tuner.

Price: $735

Same as above except uses a shorter, lighter Bo-Mar Mini-Rib with accuracy tuner.

Price: $735

Standard Length .38 Special

Same as above except standard length slide with 5″ Colt .38 Special barrel.

Price: $640

Same as above except extension front sight that provides 8½″ sight radius.

Price: $650

Long Heavy Slide Custom .45

Same as long heavy slide .38 Special, except in .45 ACP.

Price: $735

Heavy Slide Custom .45

Same as above except standard length, standard front sight.

Price: $615

Same as above except extension front sight that provides 8½″ sight radius.

Price: $620

Custom .45 Long Slide

Similar to long heavy model, except uses a shorter, lighter Bo-Mar rib.

Price: $735

Custom .45

Same as above, except standard length slide and 5″ Colt barrel.

Price: $615

Extended Sight Custom .45

Same as above except extended front sight provides 8½″ sight radius.

Price: $620

.45 Hard Ball

Same as .45 Custom except uses a Bo-Mar Deluxe sight without Mini-Rib.

Price: $575

From Clark.

Clark Custom Combat Revolvers

Heavy Douglas barrel has full length Bo-Mar rib and sight protectors, complete action and trigger job. For Ruger Security-Six (regular or stainless), S&W Model 10, some Colts.

Price: Under $300.

From Clark.

XP-100 Conversions

A number of XP-100 conversions are offered, including a lightweight version of IHMSA and hunting models.

Price: From $260 to $850.

Threaded, chambered XP-100 barrels:	$ 85.00
Fiberglass XP-100 stock blanks:	$ 67.50
Fully inletted, ready for outside finish:	$187.50
Completely finished and inletted:	$217.50

From Jack B. Dever.

Replacement Trigger

The Hart 2-ounce trigger is for target shooters *only;* it has no *safety.* Pull is clean, sharp and consistent. Fits most modern Remington rifles including the 40X and 40XB. (Also fits all Hart actions.)

Price: $69.95

From Hart Products, 401 Montgomery St., Nescopeck, PA 18635.

Precision Target Aperture Sight

Redfield's Palma Metallic Target Sight is one of the last American made precision peep sights available to the man who wants to build a custom target rifle. Windage and elevation adjustment are crisp and have ¼-M.O.A. capability. The "clicks" are also adjustable for a hard or soft feel—shooters' choice. Repeatability error is limited to .001-inch per click. Precision made.

Price: $160.70; adjustable filter adapter, $4.90; SI disc ⅞″ x .046″, $3.30; SI disc ⅞″ x .093″, $3.30; Sure-X disc, $16.90.

From Redfield.

Section 9:
EMBELLISHMENT & METAL FINISHES

Rifle and Shotgun Finishing; Services

Blue and cold rust brown (for black powder arms), color case hardening, anodizing (for aluminum) and gold plating for triggers are all offered.

Price:

Standard blue: $55 (polish or matte)

Deluxe Blue: $65

Cold rust blue (doubles): $60

Stock refinishing: $55 (oil); $60 (high gloss or satin). Stock making in both wood and fiberglass is also available, along with a wide range of trigger, action and barrel work for both rifle and shotgun. A custom Remington Model 600, fitted with a Model 700 bolt handle and one of Korzinek's bolt sleeves (inset) and glued into a McMillen stock blank, is shown.

Write for detailed price list ($1.00).

From J. Korzinek

Teflon Firearms Finish

Teflon-S offers an alternative finish that is especially appropriate for guns that will see hard service. Its non-reflective surface offers excellent resistance to corrosion and has self lubricating properties. Available in black or olive drab.

Price: $55 (long guns); $45 (handguns). (A $4 discount is allowed for disassembled guns.)

From West Coast SECOA.

Color Case Hardening

Disassembled and polished actions and associated parts can be color case hardened in two to four weeks from receipt. Action heat treating, with emphasis on toughness rather than color, is also offered (specify).

Price: $20 (plus $2.50 return shipping).

From Twin City Steel Treating, 1114 S. Third St., Minneapolis, MN 55415.

Color Case Hardening

Terry Turnbull at Creekside Gunshop offers, on a strictly custom basis, color case hardening. Creekside's ability in this "specialty" area is such that they can come, " . . . very close," to duplicating original Winchester case colors. They specialize in case hardening quality rifles, shotguns and handguns. Write direct for prices.

From Creekside Gunshop, Main St., Holcomb, NY 14469.

Gun Engraving

A very wide range of stock patterns as well as custom design based on owner's suggestion are available from J.R. French. Prices depend on grade of engraving, area to be covered, and the percentage of coverage. Some examples are:

Handgun, Grade I engraving, 50% coverage: $200

Handgun; Grade II engraving, full coverage: $450.

Long Arms, Grade III, two-thirds coverage: $550.

Add 20% for stainless; gold or silver inlays are also available. A well-illustrated brochure and detailed price list are offered for $3 (refundable).

From J.R. French.

Gun Engraving

Traditional styles of engraving with a distinctly southwestern Indian motif is offered by Bryan Bridges. Though each job is quoted on an individual basis, some representative prices are:

Medium sized revolvers, fully engraved: $5000.

Grip Cap (illustrated): $400.

From Bryan Bridges.

Gun Engraving

Ben Shostle engraves both pistols and long guns in classic style, pricing his work by the amount of gun surface the engraving covers.
Representative prices are:
Class "A" (25%): $125 - $265
Class "B" (50%): $200 - $325
Class "C" (75%): $300 - $400
Class "D" (full): $325 - $625
From The Gun Room (Ben Shostle)

Gun and Knife Engraving

Engraving and precious metal inlaying in a variety of styles is offered by Master Engraver Ralph W. Ingle, who offers a photo-illustrated catalog of his work on both guns and knives for $2.
From Ralph W. Ingle.

Gun Engraving

Scroll engraving, with or without figures or gold or silver inlay, is offered by Ken Eyster on both long guns or pistols. Although each job must be quoted on an individual basis, some representative prices are:
Rifle or Shotgun: $1,450 - $1,600 (full coverage); from $500 up (partial coverage).
Pistols and Revolvers: $450 - $1,200 (full coverage, depending on size of gun); from $400 up (partial coverage).
From Heritage Gunsmiths, 6441 Bishop Rd, Centerburg, OH 43011.

Gun Engraving Inlays

Classic style gun engraving with a specialty in pearl grip inlays and custom ivory grips are offered by Jim Kelso of Iron Age Craftworks. Work is quoted on an individual basis.
From Iron Age Craftworks, P.O. Box 518, Preston, WA 98050.

Gun Engraving

Antique, modern and custom styles of engraving, with or without gold or silver inlays, are offered. Bill Johns also does relief carving of ivory grips. Work is quoted on an individual basis.
From Bill Johns.

Gun Engraving

Engraving in all traditional patterns, inlays of game scenes or monograms, special patterns to customer's request, are all available from E.C. Prudhomme's Shop. Prices vary widely so must be quoted on a job-by-job basis.
From E.C. Prudhomme.

Gun Engraving

George Sherwood specializes in floor plate and trigger guard, lever action rifle, shotgun and knife engraving, both line and relief. A profusely illustrated brochure showing examples and detailing prices is available for $1. Prices for the work illustrated are:
Ballard Rifle Receiver (both sides): $200.
Savage 99 (high relief, three different scenes): $875.
Floor Plate (line cut, including trigger guard): $85.
From George Sherwood.

Engraving, Stock Making

Traditional engraving and precious metal inlaying as well as custom classic-style stock making are services provided by John Vest. All work is quoted on a job-by-job basis.
From John Vest.

Gun Engraving

Scroll engraving of rifles, shotguns and pistols, with or without gold or silver inlays, is offered by Vernon Wagoner. Representative prices for scroll engraving over the action and part of the barrel (rifles and shotguns), the entire gun (pistols and revolvers) are:
Bolt Action Rifle: $575.
Pump or Auto Shotgun: $680.
Double or O/U Shotgun: $680-$750.
Pistol or Revolvers: $210-$475 (depending on size).
For Inlays, add $150 (silver); $175 (gold).
From Vernon G. Wagoner.

Gun Engraving

Traditional style engraving to customer's instruction is Mel Wood's forte. Price of the work on the example pictured is:
Stainless Rugers: $300 each.
From Mel Wood.

Section 10:

MISCELLANEOUS

Custom Oil Bottles

These oil bottles are made of nickel plated brass. They come in square or round configuration—your choice. This is a nice addition to your cleaning gear. Beautifully made.
Price: Under $30 each.
From Bill McGuire & Associates.

Repair and Restoration

Restoration of a valuable firearm requries repair of broken or badly worn parts and careful duplication of original polishing and blueing methods. J.J. Jenkins has long been a specialist in this kind of work, with emphasis on fine shotguns and rifles as well as the rarer variations of Luger, Mauser and other collectable automatic pistols. Restoration or duplication of original wood and custom stocks for sporting arms are also offered; a stock of replacement parts for all Merkel shotguns, other sporting arms is also maintained. Prices depend on individual job—call or write for quote.
From J.J. Jenkins.

Restoration Service

As the supply of fine rare and older firearms dwindles, collectors are turning to examples that have been badly used or are no longer complete. Rather than including such a less-than-adequate item in their collections, many collectors are turning to knowledgeable restorers like John Kaufield of Small Arms Engineering to put them back in factory-new condition. Old-time techniques provide a finish close to the original, while cut-off barrels can be restored to proper length, deep pits filled by welding, and original markings restamped or engraved.
Price on an individual job basis.
From Small Arms Engineering.

Repair, Restoration, Custom Rifle Making

Lester Womac also does repair and restoration work, specializing in commercial Mauser sporting rifles, including hand polish and reblue by original factory techniques. Classic style custom stocks are also offered. Write for detailed price list.
From Lester Womac.

Custom Stockmaking, Restoration

David Trevallion is an Englishman who learned his trade as an apprentice with England's top gunmakers. His specialty is custom stocks for fine shotguns and double rifles; he also does complete metal and wood restoration of antique as well as modern arms. All work is priced on an individual job basis.
From Trevallion Gunstocks, 6524 N. Carrollton Ave., Indianapolis, IN 46220.

Restoration, Refinishing And Custom Work

Complete refinishing services, with original type polishing and hot or rust blue as appropriate. Color case hardening. Prices vary depending on amount of preparation and type of blue, starting at $40 for a handgun. A wide range of gunsmithing services is also included. Write for detailed price list.
From Vic's Gun Refinishing.

Custom Gun Case

Each case is hand made of the best materials by Norbert Ertel. Shown is the Ertel oak and leather gun case. All sides of the lid and body are fully dovetailed for maximum strength. Only the finest oak and top grain hides are used in the construction of this case. Comes with the finest brass hinges, locks, buckles and corners. Mr. Ertel makes these cases one-at-a-time; and, he also

offers a number of accessories you might wish to order with your fully fitted case. (He also offers a complete restoration service for quality gun cases.) We urge you to write the craftsman direct for more information.
Price: As shown $640; two set of barrels case $690; "Pair-of-guns" case $790.
From Norbert Ertel.

Shotgun Case

Comes in several styles. Made from genuine bark tanned shearling and reinforced with top-grain cowhide. Fits most shotguns with barrel lengths up to 32 inches. *Well made.* Specify gun and barrel length when ordering. Model 27 series.
Price: About $70; with extra barrel pouch, about $85.
From Brauer Bros, 817 N. 17th, St. Louis, MO 63106.

Custom Gun Case

Bill McGuire's hand-made custom gun cases represent the epitome of the case-maker's art. Feature leather, brass and hardwood construction. Simply put, this maker will produce whatever you want for your favorite rifles, shotguns or handguns. We suggest you write to the maker direct for more information on prices and delivery schedule.
Price: From $400.
From Bill McGuire & Associates.

Best Quality Leather Trunk Gun Cases

These cases are beautifully made. In fact they are totally hand made. Built by Marion Huey, they are constructed of selected ash, best grade cowhide, choice wool and suede cloth linings. All bolsters, covers and pads are hand stitched. Comes with lidded compartments for loose parts and built-in brass lid stops and supports. *Many* options are available on request. Five different rifle, pistol, shotgun or ammo cases are available. Shown nearby is a classic "Hunting Case" for take-down shotguns.

Prices for Marion Huey's work are listed below; however, we must again mention the wide array of available options and suggest you write the maker direct for more information.

Prices are approximate only.

Pistol case	$425.00
Cartridge box	$425.00
Trunk case (single gun)	$485.00
Trunk case (pair of guns)	$575.00
Motorcase	$510.00
Full-length flat carbine case	$535.00
Bolt action rifle chest (open sights)	$550.00
Bolt action rifle chest (telescopic sights)	$575.00

From Huey Gun Cases.

Leg-O-Mutton Case for All Shotguns

Brauer's Model 41 and 141 cases are beautifully made of the best top-grain leather molded over a fiber base. Available with spare barrel compartment on special order. Model 41 fits all pumps, over unders and double barrel shotguns. Model 141 is specifically made for automatic shotguns.
Price: $175.00 for either model.
From Brauer Bros, 817 N. 17th, St. Louis, MO 63106.

Aluminum Gun Cases

Weatherby's series of top quality gun cases are made of sturdy aluminum, come fully foam lined and are lockable for maximum security. They come available in single and double rifle (shown) configurations along with one case specifically made for shotguns.
Price: Double rifle case $299.95, single rifle case $249.95; shotgun case $199.95.
From Weatherby, Inc.

Two-Gun Case

Featuring hard-shell, aluminum construction, Outers Model 525AX gun case is indeed a sturdy item. It comes with full foam padding, locks, aluminized finish and 6 bumper feet. It measures 53x13x4½ inches. Weighs 16½ pounds. Sturdy.
Price: $79.64.
From Outers Laboratories.

Gun Vault

The Pro-Steel 2436 vault features 12-gauge construction with a $3/16$-inch steel door. The door and frame are fully reinforced and 6 chrome finished locking pins secure the door—the lock is a combination type. Depending upon the type of rack you purchase, the vault will hold up to 23 guns. Weighs 425 pounds empty, stands upright.
Price: About $800 with shelving; 23-gun rack $145; 11-gun rack and 4 shelves around $200.
From Provo Steel & Supply Co.

Gun Storage Safe

Holds 12 guns; stands upright. Treadlok's Model 601 features 12-gauge welded steel construction, is 24-inches wide, 17-inches deep and is 63-inches high. The 601 also comes with three heavy-duty concealed hinges and a 2-point sliding bar lock secured by one "Medeco" high security lock. Weighs 225 pounds empty.
Price: $578 (with one shelf) holds 12 guns; with 4 shelves (holds 6 guns) $621.
From Tread Corporation.

Gun Vault

Se-Cur-All gun cabinets have double wall construction of heavy 14 and 18 gauge welded steel. It has a high-security door lock, double swinging doors, plug welded full length piano hinges and comes with shelving as shown. These vaults come in 6- and 12-gun models—12-gun models do not have the extensive shelving the 6-gun model has.
Price: $459 for either the 6- or 12-gun vault.
From A&A Sheet Metal Products, Inc. (Se-Cur-All)

Gun Storage Safe

The Treadlok Model 101R gun safe (as shown) comes complete with gun storage racks. This is the model that rests on the floor in a horizontal position. It's made of 12-gauge welded steel, comes with a set of locks and keys and features a full, piano-type hinge. May be bolted to the floor for additional security. Holds 16 guns. Weighs 180 pounds empty.
Price: $488; $559 with racks.
From Tread Corporation.

Custom Oil Bottles

Each bottle is made by James Dixon & Sons, Sheffield, England, of Britannia metal (highest quality pewter), polished to a silver-like shine, and marked with the maker's cartouche and style number on the bottom. The bottles feature a leak proof screw on cap with oil dropper, and are available in two styles and three sizes: The two square bottles measure 2 inches high x 2 inches wide x 1¾ inches deep on the larger; and 2 inches high x 1½ inches wide x 1½ inches deep on the smaller bottle. Round bottle is 2 inches high and 1¾ inches around.
Prices: Large Square Bottle $26.95; Small Square Bottle $22.95; Round Bottle $18.95. Prices *approximate*.
From Dixie Gun Works, Inc.

Scabbard With Hood

Triple K's Model 128 Scabbard is available with matching Model 129 hood. Scabbard and hood are made of heavy strap leather and will accommodate all scoped rifles. It's made for rifles with barrel lengths of up to 26 inches.
Price: $59.95 for the scabbard; $27.95 for the hood (specify barrel length when ordering).
From Triple K Manufacturing Company.

Rifle Scabbard For Scoped Rifles

Triple K's Model 121 scabbard is specifically made for scoped rifles and is available in sizes that will handle 20-, 22-, 24- or 26-inch barrel lengths. Made of the best oak-tanned saddle skirting. Walnut-oil finish only; comes with basketweave trim as standard.
Price: $84.95.
From Triple K Manufacturing Company.

Rifle Scabbard

The Bucheimer Model 104 scabbard is expressly made for scoped bolt action rifles. Comes with straps; hood available. Made of heavy, full-grain cowhide. Natural color.
Price: $83.50.
From J.M. Bucheimer, P.O. Box 280, Frederick, MD 21701.

Scabbard & Hood

Available for 20-, 22-, 24- and 26-inch barrel lengths. Solid, durable item that's made of the finest materials. Accommodates scoped rifle. Features a carrying handle. Two 23-inch saddle straps come with this scabbard. *Well made.*
Price: $149.70 (Model No. 27-179).
From The Hunter Co., 3300 W. 71st Ave., Westminster, CO 80030.

Leather Scabbard

This Lawrence product was designed by one of the top gun writers in the U.S.—Jack O'Connor. It's made from 9-10 ounce saddle leather and is hand molded to accommodate any scoped rifle. Comes with two extra long carrying straps; buckle-down hood or snap flap. Polished nickel hardware. Comes oiled, plain, or,

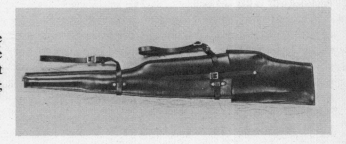

basketweave or flower carved styles. Send tracing of your rifle when ordering. Available with carrying handles, soft leather lining and hand carved initials. *Well made.*
Price: Plain with flap about $110; with hood around $200—prices go up to about $300 depending on style and options ordered. (Model 55.)
From Lawrence Leather, 306 S.W. 1st Ave., Portland, OR 97204.

DIRECTORY OF ARTISANS

AMMUNITION (Custom)

American Pistol Bullet, 133 Blue Bell Rd., Greensboro, NC 27406/919-272-6151
Bill Ballard, 830 Miles Ave., Billings, MT 59101 (ctlg. 50¢)
Ballistek, Weapons Systems Div., Box 11537, Tucson, AZ 85734/602-294-1991
Beal's Bullets, 170 W. Marshall Rd., Lansdowne, PA 19050 (Auto Mag Specialists)
Bell's Gun & Sport Shop, 3309-19 Mannheim Rd., Franklin Park, IL 60131
Brass Extrusion Labs. Ltd., 800 W. Maple Lane, Bensenville, IL 60106
C. W. Cartridge Co., 71 Hackensack St., Wood-Ridge, NJ 07075
Russell Campbell, 219 Leisure Dr., San Antonio, Tex. 78201
Collectors Shotshell Arsenal, E. Tichy, 365 So. Moore, Lakewood, CO 80226
Crown City Arms, P.O. Box 1126, Cortland, NY 13045
Cumberland Arms, Rt. 1, Shafer Rd., Blantons Chapel, Manchester, TN 37355
E. W. Ellis Sport Shop, RFD 1, Box 315, Corinth, NY 12822
Ellwood Epps Northern Ltd., 210 Worthington St. W., North Bay, Ont. PIB 3B4, Canada
Ramon B. Gonzalez, P.O. Box 370, Monticello, NY 12701
Gussert Bullet & Cartridge Co., Inc., P.O. Box 3945, Green Bay, WI 54303
J-4, Inc., 1700 Via Burton, Anaheim, CA 92806 (custom bullets)
Jensen's Custom Ammunition, 5146 E. Pima, Tucson, AZ 85716
R. H. Keeler, 817 "N" St., Port Angeles, WA 98362/206-457-4702
KTW Inc., 710 Foster Park Rd., Lorain, OH 44053 (bullets)
Dean Lincoln, P.O. Box 1886, Farmington, NM 87401
Lomont Precision Bullets, 4421 S. Wayne Ave., Ft. Wayne, IN 46807/219-694-6792 (custom cast bullets only)
Mansfield Gunshop, Box 83, New Boston, N.H. 03070
Numrich Arms Corp., 203 Broadway, W. Hurley, N.Y. 12491
Robert Pomeroy, Morison Ave., Corinth, ME 04427 (custom shells)
Precision Ammunition & Reloading, 122 Hildenboro Square, Agincourt, Ont. M1W 1Y3, Canada
Precision Prods. of Wash., Inc., N. 311 Walnut Rd., Spokane, WA 99206 (Exammo)
Anthony F. Sailer-Ammunition, 707 W. Third St., P.O. Box L, Owen, WI 54460
Sanders Cust. Gun Serv., 2358 Tyler Lane, Louisville, Ky. 40205
Geo. Spence, 202 Main St., Steele, MO 63877/314-695-4926 (box-primed cartridges)
The 3-D Company, Box 142, Doniphan, NB 68832 (reloaded police ammo)

AMMUNITION (Foreign)

K. J. David & Company, P.O. Box 12595, Lake Park, FL 33043
Dynamit Nobel of America, Inc., 105 Stonehurst Court, Northvale, NJ 07647/201-767-1660 (RWS, Geco, Rottweil)
Guilio Fiocchi S.p.A., 22053 Lecco-Belledo, Italy
Hirtenberger Patronen-, Zündhütchen- & Metallwarenfabrik, A.G., Leobersdorfer Str. 33, A2552 Hirtenberg, Austria
Hy-Score Arms Co., 200 Tillary, Brooklyn, N.Y. 11201
Paul Jaeger Inc., 211 Leedom St., Jenkintown, Pa. 19046
S. E. Laszlo, 200 Tillary, Brooklyn, N.Y. 11201
NORMA-Precision, 798 Cascadilla St., Ithaca, NY 14850
RWS (Rheinische-Westfälische Sprengstoff) see: Dynamit Nobel of America

BOOKS (ARMS), Publishers and Dealers

Arms & Armour Press, 2-6 Hampstead High Street, London NW3 1PR, England
Beinfeld Publishing, Inc., 12767 Saticoy St., No. Hollywood, CA 91605/213-982-3700
Blacktail Mountain Books, 42 First Ave. West, Kalispell, MT 59901/406-257-5573
DBI Books, Inc., one Northfield Plaza, Northfield, IL 60093/312-441-7010
EPCO Publ. Co., 75-24 64 St., Glendale, NY 11227
Empire Press, P.O. Box 2902, Santa Fe, NM 87501
Fairfield Book Co., Inc., P.O. Box 289, Brookfield Center, CT 06805/800-243-1318
Follett Publishing Co., 1010 W. Washington Blvd., Chicago, IL 60607
Fortress Publications Inc., P.O. Box 241, Stoney Creek, Ont. L8G 3X9, Canada
Guncraft Books, Div. of Ridge Guncraft, Inc., 125 E. Tyrone Rd., Oak Ridge, TN 37830/615-483-4024
Handgun Press, 5832 S. Green, Chicago, IL 60621
Jackson Arms, 6209 Hillcrest Ave., Dallas, TX 75205
Lyman, Route 147, Middlefield, CT 06455
John Olson Co., 294 W. Oakland Ave., Oakland, NJ 07436
Ridge Guncraft Inc., M. C. Wiest, 234 N. Tulane Ave., Oak Ridge, TN 37830
Ray Riling Arms Books Co., 6844 Gorsten St., Philadelphia, PA 19119
Rutgers Book Center, Mark Aziz, 127 Raritan Ave., Highland Park, NJ 08904
Stackpole Books, Cameron & Kelker Sts., Telegraph Press Bldg., Harrisburg, PA 17105
Stoeger Publishing Co., 55 Ruta Court, South Hackensack, NJ 07606
James C. Tillinghast, Box 568, Marlow, NH 03456
Ken Trotman, 2-6 Hampstead High St., London, NW3 1PR, England

CASES, CABINETS AND RACKS—GUN

Action Co., P.O. Box 528, McKinney, TX 75069
Alco Carrying Cases, 601 W. 26th St., New York, N.Y. 10001
Allen Co., Inc., 640 Compton St., Broomfield, CO 80020/303-469-1857
Art Jewel Enterprises, Box 819, Berkeley, IL 60163
Morton Booth Co., Box 123, Joplin, Mo. 64801
Boyt Co., Div. of Welsh Sportg. Gds., Box 1108, Iowa Falls, Ia. 50126
Brenik, Inc., 925 W. Chicago Ave., Chicago, IL 60622
Browning, Rt. 4, Box 624-B, Arnold, MO 63010
Cap-Lex Gun Cases, Capitol Plastics of Ohio, Inc., 333 Van Camp Rd., Bowling Green, OH 43402
Dara-Nes Inc., P.O. Box 119, East Hampton, CT 06424/203-267-4175 (firearms security chests)
East-Tenn Mills, Inc., 2300 Buffalo Rd., Johnson City, TN 37601 (gun socks)
Ellwood Epps (Orillia) Ltd., R.R. 3, Hwy. 11 North, Orillia, Ont. L3V 6H3, Canada/705-689-5333 (custom gun cases)
Norbert Ertel, Box 1150, Des Plaines, IL 60018 (cust. gun cases)
Flambeau Plastics Corp., 801 Lynn, Baraboo, Wis. 53913
Gun-Ho Case Mfg. Co., 110 East 10th St., St. Paul, Minn. 55101
Harbor House Gun Cabinets, 12508 Center St., South Gate, CA 90280
B. E. Hodgdon, Inc., 7710 W. 50 Hiway, Shawnee-Mission, Kans. 66202
Marvin Huey Gun Cases, Box 98, Reed's Spring, MO 65737/417-538-4233 (handbuilt leath. cases)
Ithaca Gun Co., Terrace Hill, Ithaca, N.Y. 14850
Jumbo Sports Prods., P.O. Box 280-Airport Rd., Frederick, MD 21701
Kalispel Metal Prods. (KMP), Box 267, Cusick, WA 99119 (aluminum boxes)
Kolpin Mfg., Inc., Box 231, Berlin, WI 54923/414-361-0400
Marble Arms Corp., 420 Industrial Park, Gladstone, Mich. 49837
Bill McGuire, 1600 No. Eastmont Ave., East Wenatchee, WA 98801 (custom cases)
W. A. Miller Co., Inc. (Wamco), Mingo Loop, Oguossoc, ME 04964 (wooden handgun cases)
National Sports Div., Medalist Ind., 19 E. McWilliams St., Fond du Lac, WI 54935
Nortex Co., 2821 Main St., Dallas, Tex. 75226 (automobile gun rack)
North American Case, Inc., Industrial Park Rd., Johnstown, PA 15904/814-266-8941
North Star Devices, Inc., P.O. Box 2095, North St., Paul, MN 55109 (Gun-Slinger portable rack)
Paul-Reed, Inc., P.O. Box 227, Charlevoix, Mich. 49720
Penguin Industries, Inc., Airport Industrial Mall, Coatesville, PA 19320/215-384-6000
Precise, 3 Chestnut, Suffern, NY 10901
Protecto Plastics, Inc., 201 Alpha Rd., Wind Gap, Pa. 18091 (carrying cases)
Provo Steel & Supply Co., P.O. Box 977, Provo, UT 84601 (steel gun cases)
Richland Arms Co., 321 W. Adrian, Blissfield, Mich. 49228
Saf-T-Case Mfg. Co., Inc., P.O. Box 5472, Irving, TX 75062
San Angelo Co. Inc., Box 984, San Angelo, TX 76901
Buddy Schoellkopf, 4949 Joseph Hardin Dr., Dallas, TX 75236
Se-Cur-All Cabinet Co., K-Prods., P.O. Box 2052, Michigan City, IN 46360/219-872-7957
Security Gun Chest, see: Tread Corp.
Sile Distr., 7 Centre Market Pl., New York, N.Y. 10013 (leg o'mutton case)
Stearns Mfg. Co., P.O. Box 1498, St. Cloud, MN 56301
Straight Shooter Gun Cases, P.O. Box 10, Teaneck, NJ 07666
Stowline Inc., 811 So. 1st, Kent, WA 98031
Tread Corp., P.O. Box 13207, 1734 Granby St. N.E., Roanoke, VA 24012 (security gun chest)
Trik Truk, P.O. Box 3760, Kent, WA 98301 (P.U. truck cases)
Vanguard Prods. Corp., 545 Cedar Lane, Box #10, Teaneck, NJ 07666 (Straight Shooter gun cases)
Weather Shield Sports Equipm. Inc., Rte. #3, Petoskey Rd., Charlevoix, MI 49720
Woodstream Corp., Box 327, Lititz, Pa. 17543
Yield House, Inc., RFD, No. Conway, N.H. 03860

CHOKE DEVICES & RECOIL ABSORBERS

Arms Ingenuity Co., Box 1; 51 Canal St., Weatogue, CT 06089/203-658-5624 (Jet-Away)
C&H Research, 115 Sunnyside Dr., Lewis, KS 67552/316-324-5445 (Mercury recoil suppressor)
Dahl's Gun Shop, 6947 King Ave., Route 4, Billings, MT 59102
Diverter Arms, Inc., P.O. Box 22084, Houston, TX 77027 (shotgun diverter)
Edwards Recoil Reducer, 269 Herbert St., Alton, Ill. 62002
Emsco Variable Shotgun Chokes, 101 Second Ave., S.E., Waseca, MN 56093/507-835-1481
Herter's Inc., Waseca, Minn. 56093. (Vari-Choke)
J & K Enterprises, Rte. 1, B.O.B. 202-A, Scappoose, OR 97056 (Mercury recoil absorbers)
Lyman Products Corp., Rte. 147, Middlefield, CT 06455 (Cutts Comp.)
Mag-Na-Port Arms, Inc., 30016 S. River Rd., Mt. Clemens, MI 48043 (muzzle-brake system)
Mag-Na-Port of Canada, 1861 Burrows Ave., Winnipeg, Manitoba R2X 2V6, Canada
Poly-Choke Co., Inc., Box 296, Hartford, Conn. 06101
Pro-Port Canada, 1861 Burrows Ave., Winnipeg, Manitoba R2X 2V6, Canada
Pro-Port U.S.A., 30016 South River Rd., Mt. Clemens, MI 48045/313-469-7323

CLEANING & REFINISHING SUPPLIES

A 'n A Co., Box 571, King of Prussia, PA 19406 (Valet shotgun cleaner)
Armite Labs., 1845 Randolph St., Los Angeles, CA 90001 (pen oiler)
Armoloy Co. of Ft. Worth, 204 E. Daggett St., Ft. Worth, TX 76104
Birchwood-Casey, 7900 Fuller Rd., Eden Prairie, MN 55344/612-927-1733
Bisonite Co., Inc., P.O. Box 84, Kenmore Station, Buffalo, NY 14217
Blue and Gray Prods., Inc., 817 E. Main St., Bradford, PA 16701
Jim Brobst, 299 Poplar St., Hamburg, Pa. 19526 (J-B Compound)
GB Prods. Dept. H & R, Inc., Industrial Rowe, Gardner, MA 01440
Browning Arms, Rt. 4, Box 624-B, Arnold, Mo. 63010
J. M. Bucheimer Co., P.O. Box 280, Airport Rd., Frederick, MD 21701/301-662-5101
Burnishine Prod. Co., 8140 N. Ridgeway, Skokie, Ill. 60076 (Stock Glaze)
Caddie Products Corp., Div. of Jet-Aer, Paterson, NJ 07524 (the Cloth)
Chem-Pak Inc., Winchester, VA 22601 (Gun-Savr. protect. & lubricant)
Chopie Mfg. Inc., 531 Copeland, La Crosse, Wis. 54601 (Black-Solve)
Clenzoil Co., Box 1226, Sta. C, Canton, O. 44708
Clover Mfg. Co., 139 Woodward Ave., Norwalk, CT 06856 (Clover compound)
Dri-Slide, Inc., Industrial Park, 1210 Locust St., Fremont, MI 49412
Durango U.S.A., P.O. Box 1029, Durango, CO 81301 (cleaning rods)
Forty-Five Ranch Enterpr., 119 S. Main St., Miami, Okla. 74354
Gun-All Products, Box 244, Dowagiac, Mich. 49047
Frank C. Hoppe Div., Penguin Ind., Inc., Airport Industrial Mall, Coatesville, PA 19320/215-384-6000
J & G Rifle Ranch, Box S 80, Turner, MT 59542
Jet-Aer Corp., 100 Sixth Ave., Paterson, N.J. 07524 (blues & oils)
Kellog's Professional Prods., Inc., P.O. Box 1201, Sandusky, OH 44870
K.W. Kleinendorst, 48 Taylortown Rd., Montville, N.J. 07045 (rifle clg. cables)
LPS Res. Labs. Inc., 2050 Cotner Ave., Los Angeles, Calif. 90025
LEM Gun Spec., Box 31, College Park, Ga 30337 (Lewis Lead Remover)
Liquid Wrench, Box 10628, Charlotte, N.C. 28201 (pen. oil)
Lynx Line Gun Prods. Div., Protective Coatings, Inc., 20626 Fenkell Ave., Detroit, MI 48223
Marble Arms Co., 420 Industrial Pk., Gladstone, Mich. 49837
Micro Sight Co., 242 Harbor Blvd., Belmont, Ca. 94002 (bedding)
Mirror-Lube, P.O. Box 693, San Juan Capistrano, CA 92675
New Method Mfg. Co., Box 175, Bradford, Pa. 16701 (gun blue)
Northern Instruments, Inc., 6680 North Highway 49, Lino Lake, MN 55014 (Stor-Safe rust preventer)
Numrich Arms Co., West Hurley, N.Y. 12491 (44-40 gun blue)
Old World Oil Products, 3827 Queen Ave. No., Minneapolis, MN 55412
Original Mink Oil, Inc., P.O. Box 20191, 10652 N.E. Holman, Portland, OR 97220/503-255-2814
Outers Laboratories, Route 2, Onalaska, WI 54650/608-783-1515 (Gun-slick kits)
Radiator Spec. Co., 1400 Independence Blvd., Charlotte, N.C. 28201 (liquid wrench)
Reardon Prod., 103 W. Market St., Morrison, IL 61270 (Dry-Lube)
Rice Gun Coatings, 1521-43rd St., West Palm Beach, FL 33407
Rig Products Co., Div. of Mitann, Inc., 21320 Deering Ct., Canoga Park, CA 91304/213-883-4700
Rusteprufe Labs., Sparta, WI 54656
San/Bar Corp., Chemicals Div., P.O. Box 11787, 17422 Pullman St., Santa Ana, CA 92711 (Break-Free)
Saunders Sptg. Gds., 338 Somerset, No. Plainfield, NJ 07060 (Sav-Bore)
Schultea's Gun String, 67 Burress, Houston, TX 77022 (pocket-size rifle cleaning kit)
Service Armament, 689 Bergen Blvd., Ridgefield, N. J. 07657 (Parker-Hale)
Silicote Corp., Box 359, Oshkosh, Wis. 54901 (Silicone cloths)
Silver Dollar Guns, P.O. Box 475, 10 Frances St., Franklin, NH 03235 (Silicone oil)
Sportsmen's Labs., Inc., Box 732, Anoka, Minn. 55303 (Gun Life lube)
Taylor & Robbins, Box 164, Rixford, Pa. 16745 (Throat Saver)
Testing Systems, Inc., 220 Pegasus Ave., Northvale, NJ 07647/201-767-7300 (gun lube)
Texas Platers Supply Co., 2453 W. Five Mile Parkway, Dallas, TX 75233 (plating kit)
Totally Dependable Prods., Inc., P.O. Box 277, Zieglerville, PA 19492
C. S. Van Gorden, 120 Tenth Ave., Eau Claire, Wis. 54701 (Instant Blue)
WD-40 Co., 1061 Cudahy Pl., San Diego, CA 92110
West Coast Secoa, 3915 U S Hwy. 98S, Lakeland, FL 33801 (Teflon coatings)
Williams Gun Sight, 7389 Lapeer Rd., Davison, Mich. 48423 (finish kit)
Winslow Arms Inc., P.O. Box 783, Camden, SC 29020 (refinishing kit)
Wisconsin Platers Supply Co., see: Texas Platers Supply Co.
Woodstream Corp., P.O. Box 327, Lititz, Pa. 17543 (Mask)
Zip Aerosol Prods., 21320 Deering Court, Canoga Park, CA 91304

CUSTOM GUNSMITHS

Ahlman Cust. Gun Shop, R.R. 1, Box 20, Morristown, Minn. 55052
Don Allen, Rte. 1, Timberland, Northfield, MN 55057
Amrine's Gun Shop, 937 Luna Ave., Ojai, CA 93023
Anderson's Guns, Jim Jares, 706 S. 23rd St., Laramie, WY 82070
Antique Arms, D. F. R. J. Anton, 874 Olympic Dr., Waterloo, IA 50701
Armas Erbi, S.C.I., Box 45, Elgoibar, Spain
John A. Armbrust, 313 E. 11th St., Mishawaka, IN 46544
Atkinson Gun Co., P.O. Box 512, Prescott, AZ 86301
E. von Atzigen, The Custom Shop, 890 Cochrane Crescent, Peterborough, Ont., K9H 5N3 Canada/705-742-6693
Austrian Gun Works Reg'd., P.O. Box 136, Eastman, Que. JOE 1PO, Canada/514-297-2492

Richard W. Baber, 28 Dudley Ave., Colorado Springs, CO 80909
Bacon Creek Gun Shop, Cumberland Falls Rd., Corbin, Ky. 40701
Bain and Davis Sptg. Gds., 599 W. Las Tunas Dr., San Gabriel, Calif. 41776
Stan Baker, 5303 Roosevelt Way NE, Seattle, WA 98105 (shotgun specialist)
Joe J. Balickie, Rte. 2, Box 56-G, Apex, NC 27502
Wm. G. Bankard, 4211 Thorncliff Rd., Baltimore, MD 21236 (Kentuckys)
Barta's, Rte. 1, Box 129-A, Cato, Wis. 54206
Roy L. Bauer, c/o C-D Miller Guns, St. Onge, SD 57779
Bell's Gun & Sport Shop, David Norin, 3319 Mannheim Rd., Franklin Park, IL 60131 (handguns)
Bennett Gun Works, 561 Delaware Ave., Delmar, N.Y. 12054
Irvin L. Benson, Saganaga Lake, Pine Island Camp, Ontario, Canada (via Grand Marais, MN 55604)
Gordon Bess, 708 River St., Canon City, Colo. 81212
Bruce Betts Gunsmith Co., 100 W. Highway 72, Rolla, MO 65401
Al Biesen, W. 2039 Sinto Ave., Spokane, WA 99201
Roger Biesen, W. 2039 Sinto Ave., Spokane, WA 99201
John Bivins, Jr., 200 Wicklow Rd., Winston-Salem, NC 27106
Boone Mountain Trading Post, 118 Sunrise Rd., Saint Marys, PA 15857/814-834-4879
Victor Bortugno, Atlantic & Pacific Arms Co., 4859 Virginia Beach Blvd., Virginia Beach, VA 23462
Art Bourne, see: Guncraft
Breckheimers, Rte. 69-A, Parish, NY 13131
John P. Brown, Jr., Brown's Gun Shop, 3107 Elinore Ave., Rockford, IL 61103/815-962-1236
L. H. Brown, Brown's Rifle Ranch, 1820 Airport Rd., Kalispell, MT 59901
Lenard M. Brownell, Box 25, Wyarno, WY 82845 (Custom rifles)
E. J. Bryant, 3154 Glen St., Eureka, CA 95501
David Budin, Main St., Margaretville, NY 12455
George Bunch, 7735 Garrison Rd., Hyattsville, Md. 20784
Samuel W. Burgess, 25 Squam Rd., Rockport, MA 01966 (bluing repairs)
Leo Bustani, P.O. Box 8125, W. Palm Beach, Fla. 33407
Cache La Poudre Rifleworks, 168 No. College Ave., Ft. Collins, CO 80524/303-482-6913/303-482-6913 (cust. ML)
Cameron's Guns, 16690 W. 11th Ave., Golden, CO 80401
Lou Camilli, 4700 Oahu Dr. N.E., 4700 Oahu Dr. N.E., Albuquerque, NM 87111/505-293-5259 (ML)
Carter Gun Works, 2211 Jefferson Pk. Ave., Charlottesville, VA 22903
Ralph L. Carter, Carter's Gun Shop, 225 G St., Penrose, CO 81240/303-372-6240
R. MacDonald Champlin, P.O. Box 74, Wentworth, NH 03282 (ML rifles and pistols)
Mark Chanlynn, Bighorn Trading Co., 1704-14th St., Boulder, CO 80302
N. C. Christakos, 2842 N. Austin, Chicago, IL 60634
Jim Clark, Custom Gun Shop, 5367 S. 1950 West, Roy, UT 84067
Classic Arms Corp., P.O. Box 8, Palo Alto, CA 94302/415-321-7243
Kenneth E. Clark, 18738 Highway 99, Madera, Calif. 93637
Richard G. Cole, Box 159, Saegertown, PA 16433
John Corry, P.O. Box 109, Deerfield, IL 60015/312-541-6250 (U.S. agent for Frank E. Malin & Son)
The Country Gun Shoppe Ltd., 251 N. Front St., Monument, CO 80132
Crest Carving Co., 14849 Dillow St., Westminster, Ca. 92683
Crocker, 1510 - 42nd St., Los Alamos, NM 87544 (rifles)
Philip R. Crouthamel, 513 E. Baltimore, E. Lansdowne, PA 19050
Jim Cuthbert, 715 S. 5th St., Coos Bay, Ore. 97420
Dahl's Custom Stocks, Rt. 4, Box 187, Schofield Rd., Lake Geneva, WI 53147
Dahl's Gunshop, 6947 King Ave., Billings, MT 59102
Homer L. Dangler, Box 254, Addison, MI 49220 (Kentucky rifles)
Davis Gun Shop, 7213 Lee Highway, Falls Church, VA 22046
Dee Davis, 5658 So. Mayfield, Chicago, Ill. 60638
Jack Dever, 8520 N.W. 90, Okla. City, OK 73132
R. H. Devereaux, 475 Trucky St., St. Igance, MI 49781
Dominic DiStefano, 4303 Friar Lane, Colorado Springs, CO 80907
Bill Dowtin, P.O. Box 72, Celina, TX 75009
Drumbore Gun Shop, 119 Center St., Lehighton, PA 18235
Charles Duffy, Williams Lane, W. Hurley, N.Y. 12491
David R. Dunlop, Rte. 1, Box 199, Rolla, ND 58367
D. W. Firearms, D. Wayne Schlumbaum, 1821 - 200th S.W., Alderwood Manor, WA 98036
John H. Eaton, 8516 James St., Upper Marlboro, MD 20870
Bob Emmons, 238 Robson Rd., Grafton, OH 44044
Bill English, 4411 S. W. 100th, Seattle, Wash. 98146
Ken Eyster, Heritage Gunsmiths Inc., 6441 Bishop Rd., Centerburg, OH 43011/614-625-6131
N. B. Fashingbauer, P.O. Box 366, Lac Du Flambeau, WI 54538/715-588-7116
Ted Fellowes, Beaver Lodge, 9245-16th Ave., S.W., Seattle, WA 98106/206-763-1698 (muzzleloaders)
H. J. and L. A. Finn, 12565 Gratiot Ave., Detroit, MI 48205
Jack First Distributors Inc., 44633 Sierra Highway, Lancaster, CA 93534/805-942-2016
Marshall F. Fish, Rt. 22 North, Westport, NY 12993
Jerry Fisher, 1244—4th Ave. West, Kalispell, Mont. 59901
Flynn's Cust. Guns, P.O. Box 7461, Alexandria, LA 71306/318-445-7130
Larry L. Forster, Box 212, Gwinner, ND 58040
Clark K. Frazier/Matchmate, RFD 1, Rawson, OH 45881
Jay Frazier, Box 8644, Bird Creek, AK 99540
Freeland's Scope Stands, 3737—14th Ave., Rock Island, Ill. 61201
Fredrick Gun Shop, 10 Elson Drive, Riverside, R.I. 02915
R. L. Freshour, P.O. Box 2837, Texas City, TX 77590
Frontier Arms, Inc., 420 E. Riding Club Rd., Cheyenne, Wyo. 82001
Frontier Shop & Gallery, The Depot, Main St., Riverton, WY 82501/307-856-4498

Fuller Gunshop, Cooper Landing, Alas. 99572
Garcia Natl. Gun Traders, Inc., 225 S.W. 22nd Ave., Miami, Fla. 33135
Gentry's Bluing and Gun Shop, 314 N. Hoffman St., Belgrade, MT 59714/406-388-4806
Ed Gillman, R.R. 6, Box 195, Hanover, PA 17331
Dale Goens, Box 224, Cedar Crest, NM 87008
A. R. Goode, 12845 Catoctin Furnace Rd. Thurmont, MD 21788/301-271-2228
Gordie's Gun Shop, Gordon Mulholland, 1401 Fulton St., Streator, IL 61364/815-672-7202
Charles E. Grace, 10144 Elk Lake Rd., Williamsburg, MI 49690
Roger M. Green, Box 984, Glenrock, WY 82637/307-436-9804
Griffin & Howe, 589 Broadway, New York, N.Y. 10012
H. L. "Pete" Grisel, 61912 Skyline View Dr., Bend, OR 97701/503-389-2649 (rifles)
Gun City, 504 Main Ave., Bismarck, ND 58501
Guncraft (Kamloops) Ltd., 127 Victoria St., Kamloops, B.C. V2C 1Z4, Canada/604-374-2151
Guncraft (Kelowna) Ltd., 1771 Harvey Ave., Kelowna, B.C. V1Y 6G4, Canada
The Gunshop, R. D. Wallace, 320 Overland Rd., Prescott, AZ 86301
H & R Custom Gun Serv., 68 Passaic Dr., Hewitt, N.J. 07421
Paul Haberly, 2364 N. Neva, Chicago, IL 60635
Martin Hagn, Herzogstandweg 41, 8113 Kochel a. See, W. Germany (s.s. actions & rifles)
Chas. E. Hammans, Box 788, Stuttgart, AR 72160
Harkrader's Cust. Gun Shop, 825 Radford St., Christiansburg, VA 24073
Harp's Gun Repair Shop, 3349 Pio-Nono Circle, Macon, GA 31206 (cust. rifles)
Rob't W. Hart & Son Inc., 401 Montgomery St., Nescopeck, PA 18635 (actions, stocks)
Hal Hartley, 147 Blairs Fork Rd., Lenoir, NC 28645
Hartmann & Weiss KG, Rahlstedter Str. 139, 2000 Hamburg 73, W. Germany
Hubert J. Hecht, 55 Rose Mead Circle, Sacramento, CA 95831
Edw. O. Hefti, 300 Fairview, College Sta., Tex. 77840
Iver Henriksen, 1211 So. 2nd St. W., Missoula, MT 59801
Wm. Hobaugh, Box M, Philipsburg, MT 59858
Hodgson, Joseph & Assoc., 1800 Commerce St. 7S, Boulder, CO 80301
Richard Hodgson, 5589 Arapahoe, Unit 104, Boulder, CO 80301
Hoenig Rodman, 6521 Morton Dr., Boise, ID 83705/208-375-1116
Dick Holland, 422 N.E. 6th St., Newport, OR 97365/503-265-7556
Hollingsworth's Guns, Route 1, Box 55B, Alvaton, KY 42122/502-842-3580
Hollis Gun Shop, 917 Rex St., Carlsbad, N.M. 88220
Bill Holmes, Rt. 2, Box 242, Fayetteville, AR 72701/501-521-8958
Douglas Hough, 3626 W. 4th Ave., Vancouver, B.C. V6R 1P1, Canada
Huntington's, P.O. Box 991, Oroville, CA 95965
Hyper-Single Precision SS Rifles, 520 E. Beaver, Jenks, OK 74037
Independent Machine & Gun Shop, 1416 N. Hayes, Pocatello, Ida. 83201
Jackson's, Box 416, Selman City, TX 75689
Paul Jaeger, 211 Leedom St., P.O. Box 67, Jenkintown, PA 19046
J. J. Jenkins Ent. Inc., 375 Pine Ave. No. 25, Goleta, CA 93017/805-967-1366
Jerry's Gun Shop, 9220 Ogden Ave., Brookfield, Ill. 60513
Bruce Jones, 389 Calla Ave., Imperial Beach, CA 92032
Joseph & Associates, 4810 Riverbend Rd., Boulder, CO 80301/303-332-6720
Jos. Jurjevic, Gunshop, 605 Main St., Marble Falls, TX 78654
John Kaufield Small Arms Eng. Co., 7698 Garden Prairie Rd., Garden Prairie, IL 61038 (restorations)
Ken's Gun Specialties, K. Hunnell, Lakeview, AR 72642/501-431-5606
Kennedy Gun Shop, Rte. 12, Box 21, Clarksville, TN 37040/615-647-6043
Monte Kennedy, P.O. Box 214, Kalispell, MT 59901
Kennon's Custom Rifles, 5408 Biffle, Stone Mtn., GA 30083/404-469-9339
Stanley Kenvin, 5 Lakeville Lane, Plainview, NY 11803/516-931-0321
Kerr Sport Shop, Inc., 9584 Wilshire Blvd., Beverly Hills, Calif. 90212
Kesselring Gun Shop, 400 Pacific Hiway No., Burlington, WA 98233/206-724-3113
Don Klein Custom Guns, Box 277, Camp Douglas, WI 54618
K. W. Kleinendorst, 48 Taylortown Rd., Montville, NJ 07045
J. Korzinek, RD #2, Box 73, Canton, PA 17724/717-673-8512 (riflesmith)
L&W Casting Co., 5014 Freeman Rd. E., Puyallup, WA 98371
Sam Lair, 520 E. Beaver, Jenks, OK 74037
Maynard Lambert, Kamas, UT 84036
LanDav Custom Guns, 7213 Lee Highway, Falls Church, VA 22046
Harry Lawson Co., 3328 N. Richey Blvd., Tucson, Ariz. 85716
John G. Lawson, 1802 E. Columbia, Tacoma, Wa. 98404
Gene Lechner, 636 Jane N.E., Albuquerque, NM 87123
LeDel, Inc., Main and Commerce Sts., Cheswold, Del. 19936
Mark Lee, c/o Don Allen, Inc., RR 1, Timberlane, Northfield, MN 55057/507-645-9216
Bill Leeper, see: Guncraft
Art LeFeuvre, 1003 Hazel Ave., Deerfield, Ill. 60015
LeFever Arms Co., R.D. 1, Lee Center-Stokes Rd., Lee Center, NY 13363/315-337-6722
Lenz Firearms Co., 1480 Elkay Dr., Eugene, OR 97404
Al Lind, 7821—76th Ave. S.W., Tacoma, WA 98498
Max J. Lindauer, R.R. 2, Box 27, Washington, MO 63090
Robt. L. Lindsay, J & B Enterprises, 9416 Emory Grove Rd., Gaithersburg, MD 20760/301-948-2941 (services only)
Ljutic Ind., Box 2117, Yakima, WA 98902 (Mono-Wads)

Llanerch Gun Shop, 2800 Township Line, Upper Darby, PA 19082/215-789-5462
Jim Lofland, 2275 Larkin Rd., Boothwyn, PA 19061 (SS rifles)
London Guns, 1528—20th St., Santa Monica, CA 90404
R. J. Maberry, 511 So. K, Midland, Tex. 79701
Harold E. MacFarland, Route #4, Box 1249 Cottonwood, AZ 86326/602-634-5320
Frank E. Malin & Son (see: John Corry)
Monte Mandarino, 4946 Pinewood Drive, Winston Salem, NC 27106 (Penn. rifles)
McCann's Muzzle-Gun Works, 200 Federal City Rd., Pennington, NJ 08354/609-737-1070 (ML)
McCormick's Gun Bluing Service, 609 N.E. 104th Ave., Vancouver, WA 98664
Bill McGuire, 1600 N. Eastmont Ave., East Wenatchee, WA 98801
Marcos Gunsmithing, 438 Main St., Paterson, NJ 07501
Dale Marfell, 107 N. State St., Litchfield, IL 62056
Marquart Precision Co., Box 1740, Prescott, AZ 86301
Marsh Al's, Rt. #3, Box 729, Preston, ID 83263
E. H. Martin's Gun Shop, 937 S. Sheridan Blvd., Lakewood, CO 80226
Mashburn Arms Co., 1218 N. Pennsylvania, Oklahoma City, OK 73107
Seely Masker, Custom Rifles, 261 Washington Ave., Pleasantville, NY 10570
Geo. E. Mathews & Son Inc., 10224 S. Paramount Blvd., Downey, CA 90241
Maurer Arms, 2366 Frederick Dr., Cuyahoga Falls, Ohio 44221 (muzzleloaders)
John E. Maxson, Box 332, Dumas, TX 79029/806-935-5990 (high grade rifles)
Eric Meitzner, c/o Don Allen, Inc., Rt. 1, Timberlane, Northfield, MN 55057/507-645-9216
Miller Custom Rifles, 655 Dutton Ave., San Leandro, CA 94577
Miller Gun Works, P.O. Box 7326, Tamuning, Guam 96911
C.D. Miller Guns, Purl St., St. Onge, SD 57779
David Miller Co., 3131 E. Greenlee Rd., Tucson, AZ 85716/602-326-3117 (classic rifles)
Earl Milliron, 1249 N.E. 166th Ave., Portland, Ore. 97230
Wm. Larkin Moore Co., 31360 Via Colinas, Suite 109, Westlake Village, CA 91360/213-889-4160
Larry Mrock, R.F.D. 3, Woodhill-Hooksett Rd., Bow, NH 03301/603-224-4096 (broch. $3)
Clayton N. Nelson, R.R. #3, Box 119, Enid, OK 73701
Newman Gunshop, 119 Miller Rd., Agency, Ia. 52530
William J. Nittler, 290 More Drive, Boulder Creek, CA 95006 (shotgun repairs)
Jim Norman, Jim's Gunstocks, 11230 Calenda Rd., San Diego, CA 92127/714-487-4173
Nu-Line Guns, Inc., 1053 Caulkshill Rd., Harvester, MO 63303/314-441-4500
O'Brien Rifle Co., 324 Tropicana No. 128, Las Vegas, Nev. 89109
Warren E. Offenberger, Star Route, Reno, Oh 45773 (ML)
Vic Olson, 5002 Countryside Dr., Imperial, MO 63052/314-296-8086
Pachmayr Gun Works, 1220 S. Grand Ave., Los Angeles, Calif. 90015
Charles J. Parkinson, 116 Wharncliffe Rd. So., London, Ont., Canada N6J2K3
Byrd Pearson, 191 No. 2050 W., Provo, UT 84601
John Pell, 410 College Ave., Trinidad, CO 81082
C. R. Pedersen & Son, Ludington, Mich. 49431
Al Petersen, Box 8, Riverhurst, Sask., Canada S0H3P0
A. W. Peterson Gun Shop, 1693 Old Hwy. 441, Mt. Dora, FL 32757 (ML rifles, also)
Phillip Pilkington, P.O. Box 2284, University Station, Enid, OK 73701
Ready Eddie's Gun Shop, 501 Van Spanje Ave., Michigan City, IN 46360
R. Neal Rice, 5152 Newton, Denver, CO 80221
Ridge Guncraft, Inc., 125 E. Tyrone Rd., Oak Ridge, Tenn. 37830/615-483-4024
Rifle Ranch, Jim Wilkinson, Rte. 5, Prescott, AZ 86301
Rifle Shop, Box M, Philipsburg, MT 59858
Wm. A. Roberts II, Rte. 4, Box 34, Athens, AL 35611 (ML)
W. Rodman, 6521 Morton Dr., Boise, ID 83705
Carl Roth, 4728 Pineridge Ave., Cheyenne, WY 82001 (rust bluing)
Royal Arms, Inc., 10064 Bert Acosta, Santee, Calif. 92071
Murray F. Ruffino, Rt. 2, Milford, ME 04461
Rush's Old Colonial Forge, 106 Wiltshire Rd., Baltimore, MD 21221 (Ky.-Pa. rifles)
Russell's Rifle Shop, Route 5, Box 92, Georgetown, TX 78626/512-778-5338 (gunsmith services)
Lewis B. Sanchez, Cumberland Knife & Gun Works, 5661 Bragg Blvd., Fayetteville, NC 28303
Sanders Custom Gun Serv., 2358 Tyler Lane, Louisville, Ky. 40205
Sandy's Custom Gunshop, Rte. #1, Rockport, Ill. 62370
Saratoga Arms Co., R.D. 3, Box 387, Pottstown, Pa. 19464
Roy V. Schaefer, 965 W. Hilliard Lane, Eugene, OR 97404
N.H. Schiffman Cust. Gun Serv., 963 Malibu, Pocatello, ID 83201
SGW, Inc. (formerly Schuetzen Gun Works), 624 Old Pacific Hwy. S.E., Olympia, WA 98503/206-456-3471
Schumaker's Gun Shop, Rte. 4, Box 500, Colville, WA 99114/509-684-4848
Schwartz Custom Guns, 9621 Coleman Rd., Haslett, Mich. 48840
Schwarz's Gun Shop, 41-15th St., Wellsburg, W. Va. 26070
Shaw's, Rt. 2, Box 407-L, Escondido, CA 92025/714-728-7070
Shell Shack, 113 E. Main, Laurel, MT 59044
George H. Sheldon, P.O. Box 489, Franklin, NH 03235 (45 autos & M-1 carbines only)
Lynn Shelton Custom rifles, P.O. Box 681, Elk City,, OK 73644
Shilen Rifles, Inc., 205 Metropark Blvd., Ennis, TX 75119

Harold H. Shockley, 204 E. Farmington Rd., Hanna City, IL 61536 (hot bluing & plating)
Shootin' Shop, Inc., 1169 Harlow Rd., Springfield, OR 97477/503-747-0175
Walter Shultz, 1752 N. Pleasantview Rd., Pottstown, PA 19464
Silver Dollar Guns, P.O. Box 475, 10 Frances St., Franklin, NH 03235 (45 autos & M-1 carbines only)
Simmons Gun Spec., 700 Rogers Rd., Olathe, Kans. 66061
Simms Hardware Co., 2801 J St., Sacramento, Calif. 95816
Skinner's Gun Shop, Box 30, Juneau, Alaska 98801
Markus Skosples, c/o Ziffren Sptg. Gds., 124 E. Third St., Davenport, IA 52801
Jerome F. Slezak, 1290 Marlowe, Lakewood (Cleveland), OH 44107
Small Arms Eng., 7698 Garden Prairie Rd., Garden Prairie, IL 61038 (restorations)
John Smith, 912 Lincoln, Carpentersville, Ill. 60110
Snapp's Gunshop, 6911 E. Washington Rd., Clare, Mich. 48617
Southern Blueing, 6027-B N.W. 31st Ave., Ft. Lauderdale, FL 33309 (blueing)
Southern Penna. Sporting Goods Center, R.D. No. 1, Spring Grove, PA 17362/717-225-5908
Fred D. Speiser, 2229 Dearborn, Missoula, MT 59801
Sport Service Center, 2364 N. Neva, Chicago, IL 60635
Sportsman's Bailiwick, 5306 Broadway, San Antonio, TX 78209
Sportsmens Equip. Co., 915 W. Washington, San Diego, Calif. 92103
Sportsmen's Exchange & Western Gun Traders, Inc., P.O. Box 111, 560 S. "C" St., Oxnard, CA 93030/805-483-1917
George B. Spring, RFD #4, Rt. 82, Salem, CT 06415/203-859-0561
Jess L. Stark, 12051 Stroud, Houston, TX 77072
Ken Starnes, Rt. 1, Box 89-C, Scorggins, TX 75480/214-365-2566
Keith Stegall, Box 696, Gunnison, Colo. 81230
Victor W. Strawbridge, 6 Pineview Dr., Dover Point, Dover, NH 03820 (antique arms restoring)
W. C.Box 606, Fallbrook, CA 92028
T-P Shop, 212 E. Houghton, West Branch, Mich. 48661
Talmage Ent., 43197 E. Whittier, Hemet, CA 92343
Taylor & Robbins, Box 164, Rixford, Pa. 16745
Gordon Tibbitts, 1378 Lakewood Circle, Salt Lake City, UT 84117
Daniel Titus, 119 Morlyn Ave., Bryn Mawr, PA 19010
Tom's Gunshop, 4435 Central, Hot Springs, AR 71901
Trinko's Gun Serv., 1406 E. Main, Watertown, Wis. 53094
Herb. G. Troester's Accurizing Serv., 2292 W. 1000 North, Vernal, UT 84078/801-789-2158
Dennis A. "Doc" Ulrich, 2511 S. 57th Ave., Cicero, IL 60650
Brent Umberger, Sportsman's Haven, R.R. 4, Cambridge, OH 43725
Upper Missouri Trading Co., Inc., Box 181, Crofton, MO 68730
Chas. VanDyke, 201 Gatewood Cir. W., Burleson, TX 76028/817-295-7373 (shotgun & recoil pad specialist)
Milton Van Epps, Rt. 69-A, Parish, NY 13131
VanHorn, 5124 Huntington Dr., Los Angeles, CA 90032
J. W. Van Patten, Box 145, Foster Hill, Milford, Pa. 18337
Vic's Gun Refinishing, 6 Pineview Dr., Dover, NH 03820 (antique arms restorations)
Walker Arms Co., R. 2, Box 73, Selma, AL 36701
Walker Arms Co., 127 N. Main St., Joplin, MO 64801
R. D.57, Mineral Wells, TX 76067
Wells Sport Store, 110 N. Summit St., Prescott, Ariz. 86301
R. A. Wells, 3452 N. 1st, Racine, Wis. 53402
Robert G. West, 27211 Huey Lane, Eugene, OR 97402/503-689-6610
Western Gunstocks Mfg. Co., 550 Valencia School Rd., Aptos, CA 95003
Duane Wiebe, P.O. Box 497 Lotus, CA 95651/916-626-6240
M. Wiest & Son, 125 E. Tyrone Rd., Oak Ridge, TN 37830/615-483-4024
W. C. Wilber, 400 Lucerne Dr., Spartanburg, SC 29302
Williams Gun Sight Co., 7389 Lapeer Rd., Davison, Mich. 48423
Bob Williams, P.O. Box 143, Boonsboro, MD 21713
Williamson-Pate Gunsmith Service, 117 W. Pipeline, Hurst, TX 76053/817-268-2887
Wilson Gun Store Inc., R.D. 1, Rte. 225, Dauphin, Pa. 17018
Thomas E. Wilson, 644 Spruce St., Boulder, CO 80302 (restorations)
Robert M. Winter, Box 484, Menno, SD 57045
Lester Womack, Box 17210, Tucson, AZ 85731/602-298-2036
Stan Wright, Billings Gunsmiths Inc., 421 St. Johns Ave., Billings, MT 59101/406-245-3337
J. David Yale, Ltd., 2618 Conowingo Rd., Bel Air, MD 21014/301-838-9479 (ML work)
Mike Yee, 4700-46th Ave. S.W., Seattle, WA 98116
York County Gun Works, RR 4, Tottenham, Ont., L0G 1W0 Canada (muzzleloaders)
Russ Zeeryp, 1601 Foard Dr., Lynn Ross Manor, Morristown, TN 37814
John G. Zimmerman, 60273 N.W. 31st Ave., Ft. Lauderdale, FL 33309

CUSTOM METALSMITHS

Ted Blackburn, 85 E. 700 South, Springfield, UT 84663 (precision metalwork)
Tom Burgess, 180 McMannamy Draw, Kalispell, MT 59901
Dave Cook, Dave's Gun Shop, 720 Hancock Ave., Hancock, MI 49930
Homer Culver, 1219 N. Stuart, Arlington, VA 22201
John H. Eaton, 8516 James St., Upper Marlboro, MD 20870
Geo. M. Fullmer, 2499 Mavis St., Oakland, CA 94601/415-533-4193 (precise chambering—300 cals.)
Harkrader's Custom Gun Shop, 825 Radford St., Christiansburg, VA 24073
Huntington's, P.O. Box 991, Oroville, CA 95965
Ken Jantz, Rt. 1, Sulphur, OK 73086/405-622-3790
Terry K. Kopp, Highway 13, Lexington, MO 64067/816-259-2083
R. H. Lampert, Rt. 1, Box 61, Guthrie, MN 56451

Mark Lee, c/o Don Allen, Inc., R.R. 1, Timberlane, Northfield, MN 55057
Paul's Precision Gunworks, 420 Eldon, Corpus Christi, TX 78412
Dave Talley, 124 Whitehaven Dr., Greenville, SC 29611/803-246-4648
John Vest, 6715 Shasta Way, Klamath Falls, OR 97601/503-884-5585
Herman Waldron, Box 475, Pomeroy, WA 99347
Edward S. Welty, R.D. 2, Box 25, Cheswick, PA 15024
Dick Willis, 141 Shady Creek Rd., Rochester, NY 14623

ENGRAVERS, ENGRAVING TOOLS

John J. Adams, 47 Brown Ave., Mansfield, MA 02048/617-339-4613
Aurum Etchings, P.O. Box 401059, Garland, TX 75040 (acid engraving)
Joseph C. Bayer, 439 Sunset Ave., Sunset Hill Griggstown, RD 1, Princeton, NJ 08540/201-359-7283
Sid Bell Originals, R.D. 2, Tully, NY 13159
Weldon Bledsoe, 6812 Park Place Dr., Fort Worth, Tex. 76118
Carl Bleile, Box 11285, Cincinnati, OH 45211/513-662-0802
Roger C. Bleile, Box 5112, Cincinnati, OH 45205/513-251-0249
Erich Boessler, Am Vogeltal 3, 8732 Münnerstadt, W. Germany
Henry "Hank" Bonham, 218 Franklin Ave., Seaside Heights, NJ 08751
Bryan Bridges, 6350 E. Paseo San Andres, Tucson, AZ 85710
Burgess Vibrocrafters (BVI), Rt. 83, Grayslake, Ill. 60030
Winston Churchill, Twenty Mile Stream Rd., RFD Box 29B, Proctorsville, VT 05153/802-226-7772
Crocker Engraving, 1510 - 42nd St., Los Alamos, NM 87544
Art A. Darakis, RD #2, Box 165D, Fredericksburg, OH 44627/216-695-4271
Tim Davis, 230 S. Main St., Eldorado, OH 45321
James R. DeMunck, 3012 English Rd., Rochester, NY 14616
Gerald R. Desquesnes, 4890 Pompana Ave., Venice, FL 33595/813-484-5391
Howard M. Dove, 402 Roanoke St., Blacksburg, VA 24060
Ernest Dumoulin-Deleye, 8 rue Florent Boclinville, 4410 Herstal (Vottem), Belgium
Bill Dyer, P.O. Box 75255, Oklahoma City, Okla. 73107
Wilton L. English, 12009-B Barksdale Dr., Omaha, NB 68123
Ken Eyster, Heritage Gunsmiths Inc., 6441 Bishop Rd., Centerburg, OH 43011/614-625-6131
John Fanzoi, P.O. Box 25, Ferlach, Austria 9170
Jacqueline Favre, 3111 So-Valley View Blvd., Suite B-214, Las Vegas, NV 89102
Armi FERLIB, 46 Via Costa, 25063 Gardone V.T. (Brescia), Italy
Lynn Fliger, 5036 Hughes Ave. NE, Fridley, MN 55421
Heinrich H. Frank, 210 Meadow Rd., Whitefish, MT 59937/406-862-2681
Leonard Francolini, P.O. Box 32, West Granby, CT 06090/203-653-2336
J. R. French, 2633 Quail Valley, Irving TX 75060
GRS Corp., P.O. Box 1153, Emporia, KS 66801/316-343-1084 (Gravermeister tool)
Ed F. Giles, 204 Tremont St., Rehoboth, MA 02769
Donald Glaser, 1520 West St., Emporia, Kans. 66801
Eric Gold, Box 1904, Flagstaff, AZ 86002
Daniel Goodwin, P.O. Box 66, Kalispell, MT 59901
Howard V. Grant, P.O. Box 396, Lac Du Flambeau, WI 54538
John Gray, 3923 Richard Dr. NE, Cedar Rapids, IA 52402
Griffin & Howe, 589 Broadway, N.Y., N.Y. 10012
F. R. Gurney Engraving Method Ltd., #2301, 9925 Jasper Ave., Edmonton, Alberta, Can. T5J 2X4/403-426-7474
Neil Hartleip, Box 733, Fairmont, Minn. 56031
Frank E. Hendricks, Inc., Rt. 2, Box 189J, San Antonio, TX 78229
Heidemarie Hiptmayer, P.O. Box 136, Eastman, Que. J0E 1P0, Canada/514-297-2492
Steve Huff, P.O. Box 8663, Missoula, MT 59807/406-721-1740
Ralph W.211 Leedom, Jenkintown, Pa. 19046
Bill Johns, 2217 No. 10th, McAllen, TX 78501
T. J.79
Ben Lane, Jr., 2118 Lipscomb St., Amarillo, TX 79109
Beth Lane, 201 S. Main St., Pontiac, IL 61764
Herb Larsen, 2021 Guilford Dr., Abbotsford, B.C. V2S 5K5, Canada
W. Neal Lewis, Rt. 8, Box 5-B, Bowers Rd., Newnan, GA 30263/404-251-3045
Frank Lindsay, 1326 Tenth Ave., Holdrege, NB 68949
London Guns, 1528-20th St., Santa Monica, CA 90404
Ed. J. Machu, Jr., Sportsman's Bailiwick, 5306 Broadway, San Antonio, TX 78209
Lynton S.M. McKenzie, 5589 Arapahoe, Unit 104, Boulder, CO 80301
Wm. H. Mains, 3111 So. Valley View Blvd., Suite B-214, Las Vegas, NV 89102
Robert E. Maki, 814 Revere Rd., Glenview, IL 60025/312-724-8238
Rudy Márek, Rt. 1, Box 1, Banks, Ore. 97106
Franz Marktl, P.O. Box 716, Kalispell, MT 59901
S. A. Miller, Miller Gun Works, P.O. Box 7326, Tamuning, Guam 96911
Frank Mittermeier, 3577 E. Tremont Ave., New York, N.Y. 10465
NgraveR Co., 879 Raymond Hill Rd., Oakdale, CT 06370 (engr. tool)
New Orleans Jewelers Supply, 206 Chartres St., New Orleans, LA 70130
Hans Obiltschnig, 12. November St. 7, 9170 Ferlach, Austria
Warren E. Offenberger, Star Route, Reno, OH 45773
Oker's Engraving, 280 Illinois St., Crystal Lake, IL 60014
Gale Overbey, 612 Azalea Ave., Richmond, VA 23227
Pachmayr Gun Works, Inc., 1220 S. Grand Ave., Los Angeles, CA 90015/213-748-7271
Marcello Pedini, 470 Deer Park Ave., Dix Hills, NY 11746
Barbara Pierce, 248 E. Ridgeway, Hermiston, OR 97838/503-567-1661
Arthur Pitetti, Hawk Hollow Rd., Denver, NY 12421
Jeremy W. Potts, 912 Poplar St., Denver, CO 80220/303-355-5462
Wayne E. Potts, 912 Poplar St., Denver, CO 80220/303-355-5462
E. C. Prudhomme, 513 Ricou-Brewster Bldg., Shreveport, LA 71101

Martin Rabeno, Spook Hollow Trading Co., Box 37F, RD #1, Ellenville, NY 12428/914-647-4567

Wayne Reno, c/o Blackhawk Mtn., 1337 Delmar Parkway, Aurora, CO 80010

John and Hans Rohner, Sunshine Canyon, Boulder, Colo. 80302

Joe Rundell, 6198 Frances Rd., Clio, MI 48420/313-687-0559

Robert P. Runge, 94 Grove St., Ilion, N.Y. 13357

A. E. Scott, 609 E. Jackson, Pasadena, TX 77506

Shaw-Leibowitz, Rt. 1, Box 421, New Cumberland, W.Va. 26047 (etchers)

George Sherwood, Box 735, Winchester, OR 97495/503-672-3159

Ben Shostle, The Gun Room, 1201 Burlington Dr., Muncie, IN 47302

Ron Skaggs, 508 W. Central, Princeton, IL 61536

Russell J. Smith, 231 Springdale Rd., Westfield, Mass. 01085

George B. Spring, RFD #4, Rte. 82, Salem, CT 06415/203-859-0561

Robt. Swartley, 2800 Pine St., Napa, Calif. 94559

George W. Thiewes, 1846 Allen Lane, St. Charles, IL 60174/312-584-1383

Anthony Tuscano, 1473 Felton Rd., South Euclid, OH 44121

Robert Valade, Rte. 1, Box 30-A, Cove, OR 97824

John Vest, 6715 Shasta Way, Klamath Falls, OR 97601

Ray Viramontez, 4348 Newberry Ct., Dayton, OH 45432

Louis Vrancken, 30-rue sur le bois, 4531 Argenteau (Liege), Belgium

Vernon G. Wagoner, 12271 N. Chama Dr., Fountain Hills, AZ 85268/602-837-1789

Terry Wallace, 385 San Marino, Vallejo, CA 94590

Floyd E. Warren, 1273 St. Rt. 305 N.E. Rt. #3, Cortland, OH 44410

John E. Warren, P.O. Box 72, Eastham, Mass. 02642

Rachel Wells, 110 N. Summit St., Prescott, AZ 86301

Sam Welch, Box 2152, Kodiak, AK 99615

Mel Wood, 3901 Crestmont Dr., Santa Maria, CA 93454

Dwain Wright, 67168 Central, Bend, OR 97701/503-389-5558 (ctlg. $3)

GUNMAKERS, FERLACH, AUSTRIA

Ludwig Borovnik, Dollichgasse 14, A-9170

Johann Fanzoj, Griesgasse 1, A-9170

Wilfried Glanznig, Werkstr. 9, A-9170

Josef Hambrusch, Gartengasse 2, A-9170

Karl Hauptmann, Bahnhofstr. 5, A-9170

Gottfried Juch, Pfarrhofgasse 2, A-9170

Josef Just, Hauptplatz 18, A-9170

Jakob Koschat, 12.-November-Str. 2, A-9170

Johann Michelitsch, 12.-November-Str. 2, A-9170

Josef Orasche, Lastenstr. 5, A-9170

Komm.-Rat A. Sch. Outschar, Josef-Orgis-Gasse 23, A-9170

Valentin Rosenzopf's Erbe, Griesgasse 2, A-9170

Helmut Scheiring-Düsel, 10.-Oktober-Str. 8, A-9170

R. Franz Schmid, Freibacherstr. 10, A-9170

Anton Sodia, Uterferlach 39, A-9170

Vinzenz Urbas, Neubaugasse 6, A-9170

Benedikt Winkler, Postgasse 1, A-9170

Josef Winkler, Neubaugasse 1, A-9170

GUN PARTS, U. S. AND FOREIGN

Badger Shooter's Supply, Box 397, Owen, WI 54460

Behlert Custom Guns, Inc., 725 Lehigh Ave., Union, NJ 07083 (handgun parts)

Philip R. Crouthamel, 513 E. Baltimore, E. Lansdowne, Pa. 19050

Charles E. Duffy, Williams Lane, West Hurley, N.Y. 12491

Federal Ordnance Inc., 9649 Alpaca St., So. El Monte, CA 91733/213-283-3880

Jack First Distributors Inc., 44633 Sierra Highway, Lancaster, CA 93534/805-942-2016

Gun-Tec, P.O. Box 8125, W. Palm Beach, FL 33407 (Win. mag. tubing; Win. 92 conversion parts)

Hunter's Haven, Zero Prince St., Alexandria, Va. 22314

Walter H. Lodewick, 2816 N.E. Halsey, Portland, OR 97232

Marsh Al's, Rte. #3, Box 729, Preston, ID 83263 (Contender rifle)

Numrich Arms Co., West Hurley, N.Y. 12491

Pacific Intl. Merch. Corp., 2215 "J" St., Sacramento, CA 95816 (Vega 45 Colt mag.)

Potomac Arms Corp. (see Hunter's Haven)

Martin B. Retting, Inc., 11029 Washington, Culver City, Cal. 90230

Sarco, Inc., 323 Union St., Stirling, NJ 07980

Sherwood Intl. Export Corp., 18714 Parthenia St., Northridge, CA 91324

Simms, 2801 J St., Sacramento, CA 95816

Clifford L. Smires, R.D., Box 39, Columbus, NJ 08022 (Mauser rifles)

Springfield Sporters Inc., R.D. 1, Penn Run, PA 15751/412-254-2626

N. F. Strebe Gunworks, 4926 Marlboro Pike, S.E., Washington, D.C. 20027

Triple-K Mfg. Co., 568-6th Ave., San Diego, CA 92101 (magazines, gun parts)

GUNS (Foreign)

Abercrombie & Fitch, 2302 Maxwell Lane, Houston, TX 77023 (Ferlib)

Alpha Arms, Inc., 1602 Stemmons, Suite "D," Carrollton, TX 75006/214-245-3115

American Arms International P.O. Box 11717, Salt Lake City, UT 84147/531-0180

Action Arms, 4567 Bermuda, Philadelphia, PA 19124/215-744-3400

AYA (Aguirre y Aranzabal) see: IGI Domino or Wm. L. Moore (Spanish shotguns)

Pedro Arrizabalaga, Eibar, Spain

Armoury Inc., Rte. 202, New Preston, CT 06777

Armsport, Inc., 3590 N.W. 49th St., Miami, FL 33142/305-592-7850

Beeman's Precision Airguns, Inc., 47 Paul Dr., San Rafael, CA 94903/415-472-7121 (FWB, Weihrauch firearms)

Benelli Armi, S.p.A., via della Stazione 50, 61029 Urbino, Italy

Beretta Arms Co., Inc., P.O. Box 697, Ridgefield, CT 06877

Blaser/Vinzenz Huber GmbH, P.O. Box 2245, D-7900 Ulm, W. Germany

Britarms, Ltd., Unit 1, Raban's Close, Raban's Lane Industrial Estate, Aylesbury, Bucks., England

Bretton, 21 Rue Clement Forissier, 42-St. Etienne, France

Browning (Gen. Offices), Rt. 1, Morgan, UT 84050/801-876-2711

Browning, (parts & service), Rt. 4, Box 624-B, Arnold, MO. 63010/314-287-6800

Carlo Casartelli, 25062 Concesio (Brescia), Italy

Century Arms Co., 3-5 Federal St., St. Albans, Vt. 05478

Champlin Firearms, Inc., Box 3191, Enid, OK 73701

Ets. Chapuis, 42380 St. Bonnet-le-Chateau, France (see R. Painter)

Commercial Trading Imports, Inc., 2125 Center Ave., Suite 201, Fort Lee, NJ 07024/201-461-8833 (Russian shotguns)

Connecticut Valley Arms Co., Saybrook Rd., Haddam, CT 06438 (CVA)

Walter Craig, Inc., Box 927-A Selma, AL 36701

Creighton & Warren, P.O. Box 15723, Nashville, TN 37215 (Krieghoff combination guns)

Morton Cundy & Son, Ltd., P.O. Box 315, Lakeside, MT 59922

Charles Daly (see: Outdoor Sports HQ.)

Davis Gun Shop, 7213 Lee Highway, Falls Church, VA 22046 (Fanzoj, Ferlach; Spanish guns)

Dikar s. Coop. (see: Connecticut Valley Arms Co.)

Dixie Gun Works, Inc., Hwy 51, South, Union City, TN 38261/901-885-0561 ("Kentucky" rifles)

Dynamit Nobel of America, Inc., 105 Stonehurst Court, Northvale, NJ 07647/201-767-1660 (Rottweil)

Ernest Dumoulin-Deleye, 8 rue Florent Boclinville, 4410 Herstal (Vottem), Belgium

Peter Dyson Ltd., 29-31 Church St., Honley, Huddersfield, Yorkshire HD7 2AH, England (accessories f. antique gun collectors)

Elko Arms, 28 rue Ecole Moderne, 7400 Soignes, Belgium

Excam Inc., 4480 E. 11 Ave., P.O. Box 3483, Hialeah, FL 33013

Armi Fabbri, Casella 206, Brescia, Italy 25100

Famars, Abbiatico & Salvinelli, Via Cinelli 29, Gardone V.T. (Brescia), Italy 25063

J. Fanzoj, P.O. Box 25, Ferlach, Austria 9170

F.E.T.E. Corp., 2867 W. 7th St., Los Angeles, CA 90005 (A. Zoli guns)

Armi FERLIB, 46 Via Costa, 25063 Gardone V.T. (Brescia), Italy

Ferlach (Austria) of North America, P.O. Box 430435, S. Miami, FL 33143

Firearms Center Inc. (FCI), 308 Leisure Lane, Victoria, TX 77901

Firearms Imp. & Exp. Corp., 4530 NW 135th St., Opa-Locka, FL 33054/305-685-5966

Flaig's Lodge, Millvale, Pa. 15209

Auguste Francotte & Cie, S.A., 61 Mont St. Martin, 4000 Liege, Belgium

Freeland's Scope Stands, Inc., 3737 14th Ave., Rock Island, Ill. 61201

J. L. Galef & Son, Inc., 85 Chambers, New York, N.Y. 10007

Renato Gamba, Fabbrica d'Armi, via Petrarca, 25060 Ponte Zanano di Sarezzo (Brescia), Italy

Armas Garbi, Urki #12, Eibar (Guipuzcoa) Spain (shotguns, see W. L. Moore)

Gastinne Renette, 39 Ave. F.D. Roosevelt, 75008 Paris, France

Golden Eagle Firearms, 5803 Sovereign, Suite 206, Houston, TX 77036

Georges Granger, 66 Cours Fauriel, 42 St. Etienne, France

Hawes National Corp., 15424 Cabrito Rd., Van Nuys, CA 91406

Healthways, Box 45055, Los Angeles, Calif. 90061

Gil Hebard Guns, Box 1, Knoxville, IL 61448 (Hammerli)

Heckler & Koch Inc., 933 N. Kenmore St., Suite 218, Arlington, VA 22201

A. D. Heller, Inc., Box 56, 2322 Grand Ave., Baldwin, NY 11510

Herter's, Waseca, Minn. 56093

Heym, Friedr. Wilh., Box 861, Bolton, Ont. L0P 1A0, Canada

Hunting World, 16 E. 53d St., New York, NY 10022

IGI Domino Corp., 200 Madison Ave., New York, NY 10016/212-889-4889 (AYA, Breda)

Incor, Inc., P.O. Box 132, Addison, TX 75001/214-386-7000

Interarmco, see: Interarms (Walther)

Interarms Ltd., 10 Prince St., Alexandria, Va. 22313 (Mauser, Valmet M-62/S)

International Distr., Inc., 7290 S.W. 42nd St., Miami, FL 33155 (Taurus rev.)

Italguns, Via Voltabo, 20090 Cusago (Milano), Italy

Ithaca Gun Co., Terrace Hill, Ithaca, NY 14850

Paul Jaeger Inc., 211 Leedom St., Jenkintown, Pa. 19046

Jana Intl. Co., Box 1107, Denver, Colo. 80201 (Parker-Hale)

J. J. Jenkins Enterprises, Inc., 375 Pine Ave. No. 25, Goleta, CA 93017/805-967-1366 (Gebrüder Merkel)

Kassnar Imports, 5480 Linglestown Rd., Harrisburg, PA 17110

Kimel Industries, P.O. Box 335, Matthews, NC 28105

Kleinguenther's, P.O. Box 1261, Seguin, TX 78155

Knight & Knight, 5930 S.W. 48 St., Miami, FL 33155 (made-to-order only)

L. A. Distributors, 4 Centre Market Pl., New York, N.Y. 10013

La Paloma Marketing, 4500 E. Speedway Blvd., Suite 93, Tucson, AZ 85712/602-881-4750 (K.F.C. shotguns)

S. E. Laszlo, 200 Tillary St., Brooklyn, N.Y. 11201

Lever Arms Serv. Ltd., 771 Dunsmuir, Vancouver, B.C., Canada V6C 1M9

Liberty Arms Organization, Box 306, Montrose, Calif. 91020

McQueen Sales Co. Ltd., 1760 W. 3rd Ave., Vancouver, B.C., Canada V6J 1K5

Mandall Shtg. Suppl. Corp., 3616 N. Scottsdale Rd., Scottsdale, AZ 85251/602-945-2553

Mannlicher Div., Steyr Daimler Puch of Amer., 85 Metro Way, Secaucus, NJ 07094

Manu-Arm, St. Etienne, France

Manufrance, 100-Cours Fauriel, 42 St. Etienne, France

Mendi s. coop. (see: Connecticut Valley Arms Co.)

Merkuria, P.O. Box 18, 17005 Prague, Czechoslovakia (BRNO)

Mitchell Arms Corp., 116 East 16th St., Costa Mesa, CA 92627/714-548-7701 (Uberti pistols)

Wm. Larkin Moore, 31360 Via Colinas, Suite 109, Westlake Village, CA 91360/213-889-4160 (AYA, Garbi, Ferlib, Piotti, Lightwood)

Navy Arms Co., 689 Bergen Blvd., Ridgefield, N.J. 07657

Outdoor Sports Headquarters, Inc., 2290 Arbor Blvd., Dayton, OH 45439/513-294-2811 (Charles Daly shotguns)

P.M. Air Services, Ltd., P.O. Box 1573, Costa Mesa, CA 92626

Pachmayr Gun Works, 1220 S. Grand Ave., Los Angeles, CA 90015

Pacific Intl. Merch. Corp., 2215 "J" St., Sacramento, CA 95816

Rob. Painter, 2901 Oakhurst Ave., Austin, TX 78703 (Chapuis)

Parker-Hale, Bisleyworks, Golden Hillock Rd., Sparbrook, Birmingham B11 2PZ, England

Ed Paul Sptg. Goods, 172 Flatbush Ave., Brooklyn, N.Y. 11217 (Premier)

Picard-Fayolle, 42-rue du Vernay, 42100 Saint Etienne, France

Pragotrade, a Div. of Molokov Canada, Inc., 307 Humberline Dr., Rexdale, Ont. M9W 5V1, Canada/416-675-1322

Precise, 3 Chestnut, Suffern, NY 10901

Precision Sports, 798 Cascadilla St., Ithaca, NY 14850/607-273-2993

Premier Shotguns, 172 Flatbush Ave., Brooklyn N.Y. 11217

Leonard Puccinelli Co., 11 Belle Ave., San Anselmo, CA 94960/415-456-1666 (I.A.B., Rizzini shotguns of Italy)

RG Industries, Inc., 2485 N.W. 20th St., Miami, FL 33142 (Erma)

L. Joseph Rahn, Inc., First Natl. Bldg., Room 502, 201 S. Main St., Ann Arbor, MI 48104 (Garbi, Astra shotguns)

Ravizza Caccia Pesca Sport, s.p.a., Via Volta 60, 20090 Cusago, Italy

Richland Arms Co., 321 W. Adrian St., Blissfield, Mich. 49228

F.lli Rizzini, 25060 Magno di Gardone V.T., (Bs.) Italy

Rottweil, see: Dynamit Nobel of America

Ruko Sporting Goods Inc., 195 Sugg Rd., Buffalo, NY 14225 (Tikka)

SKB Sports Inc., 190 Shepard, Wheeling, IL 60090

Sanderson's, 724 W. Edgewater, Portage, Wis. 53901

Victor Sarasqueta, S.A., P.O. Box 25, 3 Victor Sarasqueta St., Eibar, Spain

Sarco, Inc., 323 Union St., Stirling, NJ 07980/201-647-3800

Savage Arms Corp., Westfield, Mass. 01085 (Anschutz)

W. C. Scott & Co. (British shotguns), see: Griffin & Howe

Security Arms Co., See: Heckler & Koch

Service Armament, 689 Bergen Blvd., Ridgefield, N.J. 07657 (Greener Harpoon Gun)

Sherwood Intl. Export Corp., 18714 Parthenia St., Northridge, CA 91324

Shore Galleries, Inc., 3318 W. Devon Ave., Chicago, IL 60645

Shotguns of Ulm, 7 Forest Glen, Highland Park, NJ 08904/201-297-0573

Sile Distributors, 7 Centre Market Pl., New York, 10013

Simmons Spec., Inc., 700 Rogers Rd., Olathe, Kans. 66061

Sloan's Sprtg. Goods, Inc., 10 South St., Ridgefield, CT 06877

Franz Sodia Jagdgewehrfabrik, Schulhausgasse 14, 9170 Ferlach, (Kärnten) Austria

Solersport, 23629 7th Ave. West, Bothell, WA 98011 (Unique)

Steyr-Daimler-Puch of America, Inc., see: Mannlicher

Stoeger Industries, 55 Ruta Ct., S. Hackensack, NJ 07606/201-440-2700

Tradewinds, Inc., P.O. Box 1191, Tacoma, Wash. 98401

Uberti, Aldo & Co., Via G. Carducci 41 or 39, Ponte Zanano (Brescia) Italy

Ignacio Ugartechea, Apartado 21, Eibar, Spain

Valmet Sporting Arms Div., 7 Westchester Plaza, Elmsford, NY 10523/914-347-4440

Valor Imp. Corp., 5555 N.W. 36th Ave., Miami, FL 33142

Valtra Inc., One Rockefeller Plaza, Suite 1715, New York, NY 10020/212-765-4660 (Valmet)

Ventura Imports, P.O. Box 2782, Seal Beach, CA 90740 (European shotguns)

Verney-Carron, B.P. 88, 17 Cours Fauriel, 42010 St. Etienne Cedex, France

Waffen-Frankonia, Box 6780, 87 Wurzburg 1, W. Germany

Weatherby's, 2781 Firestone Blvd., So. Gate, Calif. 90280 (Sauer)

Fabio Zanotti di Stefano, Via XXV Aprile 1, 25063 Gardone V.T. (Brescia) Italy

Zavodi Crvena Zastava, 29 Novembra St., No. 12, Belgrade, Yugosl.

Antonio Zoli & Co., 39 Via Zanardelli, 25063 Gardone V.T., Brescia, Italy

GUNS, SURPLUS—PARTS AND AMMUNITION

Century Arms, Inc., 3-5 Federal St., St. Albans, Vt. 05478

Walter Craig, Inc., Box 927-A, Selma, AL 36701

Eastern Firearms Co., 790 S. Arroyo Pkwy., Pasadena, Calif. 91105

Garcia National Gun Traders, 225 S.W. 22nd, Miami, Fla. 33135

Lever Arms Serv. Ltd., 771 Dunsmuir St., Vancouver, B.C., Canada V6C IM9

Mars Equipment Corp., 3318 W. Devon, Chicago, Ill. 60645

Pacific Intl. Merch. Corp., 2215 "J" St., Sacramento, CA 95816

Plainfield Ordnance Co., Box 447, Dunellen, N.J. 08812

Sarco, Inc., 323 Union St., Stirling, NJ 07980/201-647-3800

Service Armament Co., 689 Bergen Blvd., Ridgefield, N.J. 07657

Sherwood Intl. Export Corp., 18714 Parthenia St., Northridge, CA 91324

Springfield Sporters Inc., R.D. 1, Penn Run, PA 15765/412-254-2626

GUNS, U.S.-made

A.I.G. Corp., 7 Grasso Ave., North Haven, CT 06473

AMT (Arcadia Machine & Tool), 11666 McBean Dr., El Monte, CA 91732

A. R. Sales Co., 9624 Alpaca St., South El Monte, CA 91733 (Mark IV sporter)

Accuracy Systems, Inc., 2105 S. Hardy Dr., Tempe, AZ 85282

American Arms & Ammunition Co., 1015 N.W. 72nd St., Miami, FL 33150 (Budischowski)

ArmaLite, 118 E. 16th St., Costa Mesa, Calif. 92627

Artistic Arms, Inc., Box 23, Hoagland, IN 46745 (Sharps-Borchardt)

Auto-Ordnance Corp., Box ZG, West Hurley, NY 12491

Bauer Firearms, 34750 Klein Ave., Fraser, MI 48026

Bortmess Gun Co., Inc., RD #2, Box 3, Scenery Hill, PA 15360/412-945-5175

Brown Precision Co., P.O. Box 270W; 7786 Molinos Ave. Los Molinos, CA 96055/916-384-2506 (High Country rifle)

Browning (Gen. Offices), Rt. 1, Morgan, UT 84050/801-876-2711

Browning (Parts & Service), Rt. 4, Box 624-B, Arnold, MO 63010/314-287-6800

Challanger Mfg. Corp., 118 Pearl St., Mt. Vernon, NY 10550 (Hopkins & Allen)

Champlin Firearms, Inc., Box 3191, Enid, Okla. 73701

Charter Arms Corp., 430 Sniffens Ln., Stratford, CT 06497

Classic Arms Ltd., 20 Wilbraham St., Palmer, MA 01069/413-596-9691 (BP guns)

Colt, 150 Huyshope Ave., Hartford, CT 06102

Commando Arms, Inc., Box 10214, Knoxville, Tenn. 37919

Coonan Arms, Inc., 570 S. Fairview, St. Paul, MN 55116/612-699-5639 (357 Mag. Autom.)

Crown City Arms, P.O. Box 1126, Cortland, NY 13045 (45 auto handgun)

Cumberland Arms, Rt. 1, Shafer Rd., Blanton Chapel, Manchester, TN 37355

Day Arms Corp., 2412 S.W. Loop 410, San Antonio, TX 78227

Leonard Day & Co., 316 Burts Pits Rd., Northampton, MA 01060 (ML)

Detonics 45 Associates, 2500 Seattle Tower, Seattle, WA 98101 (auto pistol)

DuBiel Arms Co., 1724 Baker Rd., Sherman, TX 75090/214-893-7313

EE-DA-How Long Rifles, Inc., 3318 Camrose Lane, Boise, ID 83705

EMF Co. Inc., Box 1248, Studio City, CA 91604 (T.D.A. rev.)

FTL Marketing Corp., 12521-3 Oxnard St., No. Hollywood, CA 91601/213-985-2939

Falling Block Works, P.O. Box 22, Troy, MI 48084

Firearms Imp. & Exp. Corp., 4530 NW 135th St., Opa-Locka, FL 33054/305-685-5966 (FIE)

Freedom Arms Co., Freedom, WY 83120 (mini revolver, Casull rev.)

Freshour Mfg. Co., 1914 - 15th Ave. N., Texas City, TX 77590 (Ranger rifle)

Golden Age Arms Co., 14 W. Winter St., Delaware, OH 43015

Gwinn Firearms, #19 Freedom Industrial Park, Bangor, ME 04401/207-848-3333

Harrington & Richardson, Industrial Rowe, Gardner, MA 01440

Hatfield's, 2028 Frederick Ave., St. Joseph, MO 64501 (squirrel rifle)

A. D. Heller, Inc., Box 268, Grand Ave., Baldwin, NY 11510

High Standard Sporting Firearms, 31 Prestige Park Circle, East Hartford, CT 06108

Holmes Firearms Corp., Rte. 6, Box 242, Fayetteville, AR 72701

Hopkins & Allen Arms, #1 Melnick Rd., Monsey, NY 10952

Hyper-Single Precision SS Rifles, 520 E. Beaver, Jenks, OK 74037

Ithaca Gun Co., Ithaca, N.Y. 14850

Iver Johnson Arms Inc., P.O. Box 251, Middlesex, NJ 08846

J & R carbine, (see: PJK Inc.)

Paul Jaeger, Inc., 211 Leedom St., Jenkintown, PA 19046

Kimber of Oregon, Inc., 9039 S.E. Jannsen Rd., Clackamas, OR 97015/503-656-1704

H. Koon, Inc., 1602 Stemmons, Suite D, Carrollton, TX 75006

L.E.S., 2301 Davis St., North Chicago, IL 60064/312-473-9484

Ljutic Ind., Inc., P.O. Box 2117, Yakima, WA 98902 (Mono-Gun)

Ljutic Intl., Inc., 101 Carmel Dr., Suite 120, Carmel, IN 46032/317-848-5051

M & N Distributors, 3040 Lomita Blvd., Torrance, CA 90505/213-530-9000 (Budischowsky)

Marlin Firearms Co., 100 Kenna Dr., New Haven, Conn. 06473

Merrill Co. Inc., 704 E. Commonwealth, Fullerton, CA 92631/714-879-8922

O. F. Mossberg & Sons, Inc., 7 Grasso Ave., No. Haven, Conn. 06473

Mowrey Gun Works, Box 28, Iowa Park TX 76367

Navy Arms Corp., 689 Bergen Blvd., Ridgefield, N.J. 07657

North Star Arms, R.2, Box 74A, Ortonville, MN 56278 (The Plainsman)

Numrich Arms Corp., W. Hurley, N.Y. 12491

PJK, Inc., 1527 Royal Oak Dr., Bradbury, Ca 91010 (J&R Carbine)

Plainfield Machine Co., Inc., Box 447, Dunellen, N.J. 08812

Plainfield Inc., 292 Vail Ave., Piscataway, NJ 08854

R G Industries, 2485 N.W. 20th SE., Miami, FL 33142

Raven Arms, 1300 Bixby Dr., Industry, CA 91745

Remington Arms Co., Bridgeport, Conn. 06602

Ruger (see Sturm, Ruger & Co.)

Savage Arms Corp., Westfield, Mass. 01085

Sears, Roebuck & Co., 825 S. St. Louis, Chicago, Ill. 60607

Semmerling Corp., P.O. Box 400, Newton, MA 02160

Sharon Rifle Barrel Co., P.O., Springfield, MA 01101

Sporting Arms, Inc., 9643 Alpaca St., So. El Monte, CA 91733 (M-1 carbine)

Springfield Armory, 111 E. Exchange St., Geneseo, IL 61254

Sterling Arms Corp., 211 Grand St., Lockport, NY 14094/716-434-6631

Sturm, Ruger & Co., Southport, Conn. 06490

Thompson-Center Arms, Box 2405, Rochester, N.H. 03867

Trail Guns Armory, 1634 E. Main St., League City, TX 77573 (muzzleloaders)

United Sporting Arms, Inc., 35 Gilpin Ave., Hauppauge, L.I., NY 11787

United States Arms Corp., Doctors Path and Middle Road, Riverhead, NY 11901 (Abilene SA rev.)
Universal Firearms, 3740 E. 10th Ct., Hialeah, FL 33013
Ward's, 619 W. Chicago, Chicago, Ill. 60607 (Western Field brand)
Weatherby's, 2781 E. Firestone Blvd., South Gate, Calif. 90280
Dan Wesson Arms, 293 So. Main St., Monson, Mass. 01057
Wichita Arms, 333 Lulu, Wichita, KS 67211
Wildey Firearms Co., Inc., P.O. Box 4264, New Windsor, NY 12250/203-272-7215
Wilkinson Arms, 803 N. Glendora Ave, Covina, CA 91724 (Diane 25 ACP auto pistol)
Winchester Repeating Arms Co., New Haven, Conn. 06504
Winslow Arms Co., Inc., P.O. Box 783, Camden, SC 29020

GUNSMITHS, CUSTOM (see Custom Gunsmiths)

GUNSMITHS, HANDGUN (see Pistolsmiths)

GUNSMITH SCHOOLS

Colorado School of Trades, 1545 Hoyt, Lakewood, CO 80215
Lassen Community College, P.O. Box 3000, Susanville, CA 96130
Modern Gun Repair School Inc., 4225 N. Brown Ave., Scottsdale, AZ 85252
Montgomery Technical Institute, P.O. Drawer 487, Troy, NC 27371
Murray State College, Tishomingo, OK 73460
North American School of Firearms, 4401 Birch St., Newport Beach, CA 92663 (correspondence)
Oregon Institute of Technology, Small Arms Dept., Klamath Falls, OR 97601
Penn. Gunsmith School, 812 Ohio River Blvd., Avalon, Pittsburgh, Pa. 15202
Police Sciences Institute, 4401 Birch St., Newport Beach, CA 92660/714-546-7360 (General Law Enforcement Course)
Trinidad State Junior College, Trinidad, Colo. 81082
Yavapai College, 1100 East Sheldon St., Prescott, AZ 86301/602-445-7300

GUNSMITH SUPPLIES, TOOLS, SERVICES

Albright Prod. Co., P.O. Box 1144, Portola, CA 96122 (trap buttplates)
Alley Supply Co., Carson Valley Industrial Park, Gardnerville, NV 89410
Ametek, Hunter Spring Div., One Spring Ave., Hatfield, PA 19440/215-822-2971 (trigger gauge)
Anderson Mfg. Co., P.O. Box 3120, Yakima WA 98903 (tang safe)
Armite Labs., 1845 Randolph St., Los Angeles, Cal. 90001 (pen oiler)
B-Square Co., Box 11281, Ft. Worth, Tex. 76110
Jim Baiar, 490 Halfmoon Rd., Columbia Falls, MT 59912 (hex screws)
Behlert Custom Guns, Inc., 725 Lehigh Ave., Union, NJ 07083
Al Biesen, W. 2039 Sinto Ave., Spokane, WA 99201 (grip caps, buttplates)
Bonanza Sports Mfg. Co., 412 Western Ave., Faribault, Minn. 55021
Brookstone Co., 125 Vose Farm Rd., Peterborough, NH 03458
Brownell's, Main & Third, Montezuma, Ia. 50171
Lenard M. Brownell, Box 25, Wyarno, WY 82845/307-737-2468 (cust. grip caps, bolt handle, etc.)
W. E. Brownell, 1852 Alessandro Trail, Vista, Calif. 92083 (checkering tools)
Maynard P. Buehler, Inc., 17 Orinda Hwy.,St., Pittsburgh, PA 15201 (Chubb Multigauge)
Chubb (see Chase Chem. Co.)
Chicago Wheel & Mfg. Co., 1101 W. Monroe St., Chicago, Ill. 60607 (Handee grinders)
Christy Gun Works, 875-57th St., Sacramento, Calif. 95819
Clover Mfg. Co., 139 Woodward Ave., Norwalk, CT 06856 (Clover compound)
Clymer Mfg. Co., 14241 W. 11 Mile Rd., Oak Park, Mich. 48237 (reamers)
Colbert Industries, 10107 Adella, South Gate, Calif. 90280 (Panavise)
A. Constantine & Son, Inc., 2050 Eastchester Rd., Bronx, N.Y. 10461 (wood)
Dave Cook, 720 Hancock Ave., Hancock, MI 49930 (metalsmithing only)
Cougar & Hunter, G 6398 W. Pierson Rd., Flushing, Mich. 48433 (scope jigs)
Alvin L. Davidson Prods. f. Shooters, 1215 Branson, Las Cruces, NM 88001 (action sleeves)
Dayton-Traister Co., 9322 - 900th West, P.O. Box 593, Oak Harbor, WA 98277 (triggers)
Delta Arm Sporting Goods, Highway 82 West, Indianola, MS 38751/601-887-5566 (Lightwood/England)
Dem-Bart Checkering Tools, Inc., 6807 Hiway #2, Snohomish, WA 98290/206-568-7536
Dremel Mfg. Co., 4915-21st St., Racine, WI 53406 (grinders)
Chas. E. Duffy, Williams Lane, West Hurley, N.Y. 12491
Peter Dyson Ltd., 29-31 Church St., Honley, Huddersfield, Yorksh. HD7 2AH, England (accessories f. antique gun coll.)
E-Z Tool Co., P.O. Box 3186, 25 N.W. 44th Ave., Des Moines, Ia. 50313 (lathe taper attachment)
Edmund Scientific Co., 101 E. Glouster Pike, Barrington, N.J. 08007
F. K. Elliott, Box 785, Ramona, Calif. 92065 (reamers)

Emco-Lux, 2050 Fairwood Ave.; P.O. Box 07861 Columbus, OH 43207/614-445-8328
Forster Products, Inc., 82 E. Lanark Ave., Lanark, IL 61046/815-493-6360
Keith Francis Inc., 1020 W. Catching Slough Rd., Coos Bay, OR 97420/503-269-2021 (reamers)
G. R. S. Corp., P.O. Box 1153, Emporia, KS 66801/316-343-1084 (Graver-meiste)
Gager Gage and Tool Co., 27509 Industrial Blvd., Hayward, CA 94545 (speedlock triggers f. Rem. 1100 & 870 pumps)
Gilmore Pattern Works, P.O. Box 50234, Tulsa, OK 74150/918-245-7614 (wagner safe-T-Planer)
Glendo Corp., P.O. Box 1153, Emporia, KS 66801/316-343-1084 (Accu-Finish tool)
Gold Lode, Inc., 181 Gary Ave., Wheaton, IL 60187 (gold inlay kit)
Gopher Shooter's Supply, Box 278, Faribault, MN 55021 (screwdrivers, etc.)
Grace Metal Prod., 115 Ames St., Elk Rapids, MI 49629 (screw drivers, drifts)
Gunline Tools Inc., 719 No. East St., Anaheim, CA 92805
Gun-Tec, P.O. Box 8125, W. Palm Beach, FL 33407
Half Moon Rifle Shop, 490 Halfmoon Rd., Columbia Falls, MT 59912 (hex screws)
Hartford Reamer Co., Box 134, Lathrup Village, Mich. 48075
Paul Jaeger Inc., 211 Leedom St., Jenkintown, PA. 19046
Jeffredo Gunsight Co., 1629 Via Monserate, Fallbrook, CA 92028 (trap buttplate)
Jerrow's Inletting Service, 452 5th Ave., E.N., Kalispell, MT 59901
K&D Grinding Co., P.O. Box 1766, Alexandria, LA 71301/318-487-0823 (cust. tools f. pistolsmiths)
Kasenite Co., Inc., 3 King St., Mahwah, N.J. 07430 (surface hrdng. comp.)
J. Korzinek, RD #2, Box 73, Canton, PA 17724 (stainl. steel bluing)
LanDav Custom Guns, 7213 Lee Highway, Falls Church, VA 22046
John G. Lawson, 1802 E. Columbia Ave., Tacoma, WA 98404
Lea Mfg. Co., 237 E. Aurora St., Waterbury, Conn. 06720
Lightwood (Fieldsport) Ltd., Britannia Rd., Banbury, Oxfordsh. OX16 8TD, England
Lock's Phila. Gun Exch., 6700 Rowland Ave., Philadelphia, Pa. 19149
John McClure, 4549 Alamo Dr., San Diego, CA 92115 (electric checkering tool)
Marker Machine Co., Box 426, Charleston, Ill. 61920
Michaels of Oregon Co., P.O. Box 13010, Portland, Ore. 97213
Viggo Miller, P.O. Box 4181, Omaha, Neb. 68104 (trigger attachment)
Miller Single Trigger Mfg. Co., R.D. on Rt. 209, Millersburg, PA 17061
Frank Mittermeier, 3577 E. Tremont, N.Y., N.Y. 10465
Moderntools Corp, Box 407, Dept. GD, Woodside, N.Y. 11377
N&J Sales, Lime Kiln Rd., Northford, Conn. 06472 (screwdrivers)
Karl A. Neise, Inc., 5602 Roosevelt Ave., Woodside, N.Y. 11377
Palmgren Prods., Chicago Tool & Eng. Co., 8383 South Chicago Ave., Chicago, IL 60167 (vises, etc.)
Panavise Prods., Inc., 2850-29th St., Long Beach, CA 90806/213-595-7621
C. R. Pedersen & Son, Ludington, Mich. 49431
Richland Arms Co., 321 W. Adrian St., Blissfield, Mich. 49228
Riley's Supply Co., 121 No. Main St., Avilla, Ind. 46710 (Niedner butt-plates, caps)
Ruhr-American Corp., So. Hwy #5, Glenwood, Minn. 56334
A. G. Russell, 1705 Hiway 71N, Springdale, AR 72764 (Arkansas oil-stones)
Schaffner Mfg. Co., Emsworth, Pittsburgh, Pa. 15202 (polishing kits)
SGW, Inc. (formerly Schuetzen Gun Works), 624 Old Pacific Hwy. S.E., Olympia, WA 98503/206-456-3471
Shaw's, Rt. 2, Box 407-L, Escondido, CA 92025/714-728-7070
Shooters Specialty Shop, 5146 E. Pima, Tucson, AZ 85712/602-325-3346
Southern Blueing, 6027-B N.W. 31st Ave., Ft. Lauderdale, FL 33309 (gun blueing & repairs)
L. S. Starrett Co., 121 Crescent St. Athol, MA 01331
Texas Platers Supply Co., 2453 W. Five Mile Parkway, Dallas, TX 75233 (plating kit)
Timney Mfg. Co., 2847 E. Siesta Lane, Phoenix, AZ 85024
Stan de Treville, Box 33021, San Diego, Calif. 92103 (checkering patterns)
Twin City Steel Treating Co., Inc., 1114 S. 3rd, Minneapolis, Minn. 55415 (heat treating)
Will-Burt Co., 169 So. Main, Orrville, OH 44667 (vises)
Williams Gun Sight Co., 7389 Lapeer Rd., Davison, Mich. 48423
Wilson Arms Co., 63 Leetes Island Rd., Branford, CT 06405
Wisconsin Platers Supply Co., see: Texas Platers
W. C. Wolff Co., Box 232, Ardmore, PA 19003 (springs)
Woodcraft Supply Corp., 313 Montvale, Woburn, MA 01801

HANDGUN ACCESSORIES

A. R. Sales Co., P.O. Box 3192, South El Monte, CA 91733
Baramie Corp., 6250 E. 7 Mile Rd., Detroit, MI 48234 (Hip-Grip)
Bar-Sto Precision Machine, 633 S. Victory Blvd., Burbank, CA 91502
Behlert Custom Guns, Inc., 725 Lehigh Ave., Union, NJ 07083
Belt Slide, Inc., 1301 Brushy Bend Dr., Round Lake, TX 78664
Bingham Ltd., 1775-C Wilwat Dr., Norcross, GA 30093 (magazines)
C'Arco, P.O. Box 308, Highland, CA 92346 (Ransom Rest)
Central Specialties Co., 6030 Northwest Hwy., Chicago, Ill. 60631
D&E Magazines Mgf., P.O. Box 4579, Downey, CA 90242 (clips)
Essex Arms, Box 345, Phaerring St., Island Pond, VT 05846 (45 Auto frames)
R. S. Frielich, 211 East 21st St., New York, NY 10010/212-777-4477 (cases)
Jafin Prods., Jacob & Tiffin Inc., P.O. Box 547, Clanton,, AL 35045 (Light Load)

Laka Tool Co., 62 Kinkel St., Westbury, L.I., NY 11590 (stainless steel 45 Auto parts)

Lee Custom Engineering, Inc., 46 E. Jackson St., Hartford, WI 53027

Lee's Red Ramps, 7252 E. Ave. U-3, Littlerock, CA 93543 (illuminated sights)

Lee Precision Inc., 4275 Hwy. U, Hartford, WI 53027 (pistol rest holders)

Kent Lomont, 4421 So. Wayne Ave., Ft. Wayne, IN 46807/219-694-6792 (Auto Mag only)

Los Gatos Grip & Specialty Co., P.O. Box 1850, Los Gatos, CA 95030 (custom-made)

Mascot rib sights (see: Travis R. Strahan)

Mellmark Mfg. Co., P.O. Box 139, Turlock, CA 95380 (pistol safe)

W. A. Miller Co., Inc., Mingo Loop, Oguossoc, ME 04964 (cases)

No-Sho Mfg. Co., 10727 Glenfield Ct., Houston, TX 77096

Pachmayr, 1220 S. Grand, Los Angeles, Calif. 90015 (cases)

Pacific Intl. Mchdsg. Corp., 2215 "J" St., Sacramento, CA 95818 (Vega 45 Colt comb. mag.)

Platt Luggage, Inc., 2301 S. Prairie, Chicago, Ill. 60616 (cases)

Sile Distributors, 7 Centre Market Pl., New York, NY 10013

Sportsmen's Equipment Co., 415 W. Washington, San Diego, Calif. 92103

Travis R. Strahan, Rt. 7, Townsend Circle, Ringgold, GA 30736/404-937-4495 (Mascot rib sights)

M. Tyler, 1326 W. Britton, Oklahoma City, Okla. 73114 (grip adaptor)

Whitney Sales, Inc., P.O. Box 875, Reseda, CA 91335

Dave Woodruff, Box 5, Bear, DE 19701 (relining and conversions)

HANDGUN GRIPS

Art Jewel Enterprises, Box 819, Berkeley, IL 60163

Beeman's Precision Airguns, Inc., 47 Paul Dr., San Rafael, CA 94903/415-472-7121 (airguns only)

Bingham Ltd., 1775-C Wilwat Dr., Norcross, GA 30093

Fitz, 653 N. Hagar St., San Fernando, CA 91340

Gateway Shooters' Supply, Inc., 10145-103rd St., Jacksonville, FL 32210 (Rogers grips)

The Gunshop, R. D. Wallace, 320 Overland Rd., Prescott, AZ 86301

Herrett's, Box 741, Twin Falls, Ida. 83301

Mershon Co., Inc., 1230 S. Grand Ave., Los Angeles, Calif. 90015

Mustang Custom Pistol Grips, 1334 E. Katella Ave., Anaheim, CA 92805/ 714-978-7474

Robert H. Newell, 55 Coyote, Los Alamos, NM 87544 (custom)

Rogers Grips (see: Gateway Shooters' Supply)

Jean St. Henri, 6525 Dume Dr., Malibu, CA 90265 (custom)

Schiermeier, Box 704, Twin Falls, ID 83301 (Thompson/Contender)

Sile Dist., 7 Centre Market Pl., New York, N.Y. 10013

Southern Gun Exchange, Inc., 4311 Northeast Expressway, Atlanta (Doraville), GA 30340 (Outrider brand)

Sports Inc., P.O. Box 683, Park Ridge, IL 60068 (Franzite)

MISCELLANEOUS

Accurizing Service, Herbert G. Troester, 2292 W. 1000 North, Vernal, UT 84078/801-789-2158

Action Sleeves, Alvin L. Davidson, 1215 Branson, Las Cruces, NM 88001

Arms Restoration, J. J. Jenkins Ent. Inc., 375 Pine Ave. No. 25, Goleta, CA 93017/805-967-1366

Barrel Band Swivels, Phil Judd, 83 E. Park St., Butte, Mont. 59701

Bedding Kit, Bisonite Co., P.O. Box 84, Kenmore Station, Buffalo, NY 14217

Bedding Kit, Fenwal, Inc., Resins Systems Div., 400 Main St., Ashland, MA 01721

Benchrest & Accuracy Shooters Equipment, Bob Pease Accuracy, P.O. Box 787, Zipp Road, New Braunfels, TX 78130/512-625-13

Chrome Brl. Lining, Marker Mach. Co., Box 426, Charleston, Ill. 61920

Bill Dyer, 503 Midwest Bldg., Oklahoma City, Okla. 73102 (grip caps)

Grip caps, Knickerbocker Enterprises, 16199 S. Maple Ln. Rd., Oregon City, OR 97045

Gun Bedding Kit, Fenwal, Inc., Resins System Div., 400 Main St., Ashland, MA 01721/617-881-2000

Gun Jewelry, Sid Bell Originals, R.D. 2, Tully, NY 13159

Gun Jewelry, Pilgrim Pewter Inc., R.D. 2, Tully, NY 13159

Gun Jewelry, Al Popper, 614 Turnpike St., Stoughton, Mass. 02072

Gun Jewelry, Sports Style Assoc., 41 Jackson, Elmont, L.I., NY 11003

Gun Sling, Kwikfire, Wayne Prods. Co., P.O. Box 247, Camp Hill, PA 17011

Gun Slings, Torel, Inc., 1053 N. South St., Yoakum, TX 77995

Insert Barrels, Sport Specialties, H. Owen, Box 5337, Hacienda Hts., CA 91745/213-330-0782

Monte Carlo Pad, Frank A. Hoppe Div., Penguin Ind., Airport Industrial Mall, Coatesville, PA 19320/215-384-6000

Powderhorns, Kirk Olson, Ft. Woolsey Guns, P.O. Box 2122, Prescott, AZ 86302/602-778-3035

Pressure Testg. Machine, M. York, 5508 Griffith Rd., Gaithersburg, MD 20760

Ransom Handgun Rests, C'Arco, P.O. Box 308, Highland, CA 92346

Rifle Slings, Bianchi Leather Prods., 100 Calle Cortez, Temecula, CA 92390

Rifle Slings, Chace Leather Prods., 507 Alden St., Fall River, MA 02722

Scrimshaw Engraving, C. Milton Barringer, 217-2nd Isle N., Port Richey, FL 33568

Shotgun Sight, bi-ocular, Trius Prod., Box 25, Cleves, O. 45002

Shotshell Adapter, PC Co., 5942 Secor Rd., Toledo, OH 43623 (Plummer 410 converter)

Silver Grip Caps, Bill Dyer, P.O. Box 75255, Oklahoma City, Okla. 73107

Single Shot Action, John Foote, Foote-Shephard Inc., P.O. Box 6473, Marietta, GA 30065

Snap Caps, Edwards Recoil Reducer, 269 Herbert St., Alton, IL 62002

Springfield Safety Pin, B-Square Co., P.O. Box 11281, Ft. Worth, Tex. 76110

Springs, W. Wolff Co., Box 232, Ardmore, Pa. 19003

Stock pad, variable, Meadow Industries, Dept. 92, Meadow Lands, PA 15347

Swivels, Michaels, P.O. Box 13010, Portland, Ore. 97213

Swivels, Sile Dist., 7 Centre Market Pl., New York, N.Y. 10013

Swivels, Williams Gun Sight Co., 7389 Lapeer Rd., Davison, Mich. 48423

MUZZLE-LOADING GUNS, BARRELS OR EQUIPMENT

A&K Mfg. C., Inc., 1651 N. Nancy Rose Ave., Tucson, AZ 85712 (ctlg. $1)

Luther Adkins, Box 281, Shelbyville, IN 47176/317-392-3795 (breech plugs)

Anderson Mfg. Co., P.O. Box 3120, Yakima WA 98903

Armoury, Inc., Rte. 202, New Preston, CT 06777

Beaver Lodge, 9245 16th Ave. S.W., Seattle, WA 98106

John Bivins, Jr., 200 Wicklow St., Winston-Salem, NC 27106

Blue and Gray Prods., Inc., 817 E. Main St., Bradford, PA 16701

G. S. Bunch, 7735 Garrison, Hyattsville, Md. 20784 (flask repair)

Butler Creek Corp., Box GG, Jackson, WY 83001 (poly patch)

CAI, Conversion Arms, Inc., P.O. Box 449, Yuba City, CA 95991 (stainl. steel BP shotshell adaptors)

Cache La Poudre Rifleworks, 168 N. College, Ft. Collins, CO 80521/303-482-6913 (custom muzzleloaders)

Challanger Mfg. Co., 118 Pearl St., Mt. Vernon, NY 10550

R. MacDonald Champlin, P.O. Box 74, Wentworth, NH 03282 (custom muzzleloaders)

Chopie Mfg. Inc., 531 Copeland Ave., LaCrosse, WI 54601 (nipple wrenches)

Classic Arms Ltd., 20 Wilbraham St., Palmer, MA 01069/413-596-9691 (BP guns and kits)

Connecticut Valley Arms Co. (CVA), Saybrook Rd., Haddam, CT 06438 (kits also)

Earl T. Cureton, Rte. 2, Box 388, Willoughby Rd., Bulls Gap, TN 37711 (powder horns)

DJ Inc., 1310 S. Park Rd., Fairdale, KY 40118

Leonard Day & Co., 316 Burt Pits Rd., Northampton, MA 10160

Dixie Gun Works, Inc., P.O. Box 130, Union City, TN 38261

EMF Co., Inc., Box 1248, Studio City, CA 91604

Eagle Arms Co., 136 Westward Ho Dr., Northlake, IL 60164/312-562-2708

Euroarms of America, Inc., 14 W. Monmouth St., Winchester, VA 22601

The Eutaw Co., Box 608, U.S. Highway 176W, Holly Hill, SC 29059 (accessories)

Excam, Inc., 4480 E. 11th Ave., Hialeah, FL 33012

Ted Fellowes, Beaver Lodge, 9245 16th Ave. S.W., Seattle, Wash. 98106

Firearms Imp. & Exp. Corp., 4530 N.W. 135th St., Opa-Locka, FL 33054/ 305-685-5966

Marshall F. Fish, Rt. 22 N., Westport, NY 12993 (antique ML repairs)

Clark K. Frazier/Matchmate, RFD. 1, Rawson, OH 45881

C. R. & D. E. Getz, Box 88, Beavertown, PA 17813 (barrels)

Golden Age Arms Co., 14 W. Winter St., Delaware, OH 43015 (ctlg. $2)

A. R. Goode, 12845 Catoctin Furnace Rd., Thurmont, MD 21788/301-271-2228 (ML rifle bbls.)

Green River Forge, Ltd., P.O. Box 885, Springfield, OR 97477 (Forge-Fire flints)

The Flintlock Muzzleloading Gun Shop, 1238 S. Beach, Anaheim, CA 92804/714-821-6655

Harper's Ferry Arms Co., 256 E. Broadway, Hopewell, VA 23860 (guns)

Hopkins & Allen, #1 Melnick Rd., Monsey, NY 10952

International Arms, 23239 Doremus Ave., St. Clair Shores, MI 48080

JJJJ Ranch, Wm. Large, Rte. 1, State Route 243, Ironton, Ohio 45638/614-532-5298

Kern's Gun Shop, 319 E. Main St., Ligonier, PA 15658/412-238-7651 (ctlg. $1.50)

Art LeFeuvre, 1003 Hazel Ave., Deerfield, Ill. 60015 (antique gun restoring)

Les' Gun Shop (Les Bauska), Box 511, Kalispell, Mont. 59901

Lever Arms Serv. Ltd., 771 Dunsmuir, Vancouver, BC V6C 1M0, Canada

Log Cabin Sport Shop, 8010 Lafayette Rd., Lodi, OH 44254/216-948-1082 (ctlg. $3)

Loven Firearms Corp., Del Mar Dr., Brookfield, CT 06804

Lyman Products Corp., Rte. 147, Middlefield, CT 06455

McCann's Muzzle-Gun Works, 200 Federal City Rd., Pennington, NJ 08354/609-737-1707

McKeown's Guns, R.R. 4, Pekin, IL 61554/309-347-3559 (E-Z load rev. stand)

Judson E. Mariotti, Beauty Hill Rd., Barrington, NH 03825 (brass bullet mould)

Maurer Arms, 2366 Frederick Dr., Cuyahoga Falls, OH 44221 (cust. muzzleloaders)

Mountain State Muzzleloading Supplies, Box 154-1, Williamstown, WV 26187

Mowrey Gun Works, Box 28, Iowa Park, TX 76367

Muzzleloaders Etc., Inc., Jim Westberg, 9901 Lyndale Ave. S., Bloomington, MN 55420

Numrich Corp., W. Hurley, N.Y. 12491 (powder flasks)

Kirk Olson, Ft. Woolsey Guns, P.O. Box 2122, Prescott, AZ 86302/602-778-3035 (powderhorns)

Ox-Yoke Originals, 130 Griffin Rd., West Suffield, CT 06093 (dry lubr. patches)

Orrin L. Parsons, Jr., Central Maine Muzzle-Loading & Gunsmithing, RFD #1, Box 787, Madison, ME 04950

A. W. Peterson Gun Shop, 1693 Old Hwy. 441 N., Mt. Dora, FL 32757 (ML guns)

Richland Arms, 321 W. Adrian St., Blissfield, MI 49228

Rush's Old Colonial Forge, 106 Wiltshire Rd., Baltimore, MD 21221

Directory of Artisans

Salish House, Inc., P.O. Box 27, Rollins, MT 59931
H. M. Schoeller, 569 So. Braddock Ave., Pittsburgh, Pa. 15221
Sharon Rifle Barrel Co., P.O. Box 106, Kalispell, MT 59901
Shiloh Products, 37 Potter St., Farmingdale, NY 11735 (4-cavity mould)
Shore Galleries, Inc., 3318 W. Devon Ave., Chicago, IL 60645/312-676-2900
Sile Distributors, 7 Centre Market Pl., New York, NY 10013
C. E. Siler Locks, Rt. 6, Box 5, Candler, NC 28715 (flint locks)
Ken Steggles, 17 Bell Lane, Byfield, Near Daventry, Northants NN11 6US, England (accessories)
T.E.S. Firearms, Inc., 2807 N. Prospect St., Colorado Springs, CO 80907 (underhammer target rifle)
Ten-Ring Precision, Inc., 1449 Blue Crest Lane, San Antonio, TX 78232/512-494-3063
Upper Missouri Trading Co., 3rd and Harold Sts., Crofton, NB 68730
R. Watts, 826 Springdale Rd., Atlanta, GA 30306 (ML rifles)
W. H. Wescomb, P.O. Box 488, Glencoe, CA 95232 (parts)
Thos. F. White, 5801 Westchester Ct., Worthington, O. 43085 (powder horn)
Williamson-Pate Gunsmith Serv., 117 W. Pipeline, Hurst, TX 76053/817-268-2887
York County Gun Works, R.R. #4, Tottenham, Ont. L0G 1W0, Canada (locks)

PISTOLSMITHS

Allen Assoc., 7502 Limekiln Pike, Philadelphia, PA 19150 (speed-cock lever for 45 ACP)
Bain and Davis Sptg. Gds., 559 W. Las Tunas Dr., San Gabriel, Cal. 91776
Lee Baker, 7252 East Ave. U-3, Littlerock, CA 93543/805-944-4487
Bar-Sto Precision Machine, 633 So. Victory Blvd., Burbank, CA 91502 (S.S. bbls. f. 45 Acp)
Behlert Custom Guns, Inc., 725 Lehigh Ave., Union, NJ 07083 (short actions)
F. Bob Chow, Gun Shop, 3185 Mission, San Francisco, Calif. 94110
Steven N. Brown, 8810 Rocky Ridge Rd., Indianapolis, IN 46217/317-881-2771 aft. 5 PM
J.E. Clark, Rte. 2, Box 22A, Keithville, LA 71047
Custom Gun Shop, 725 Lehigh Ave., Union, NJ 07083
Davis Co., 2793 Del Monte St., West Sacramento, CA 95691/916-372-6789
Day Arms Corp., 2412 S.W. Loop 410, San Antonio, TX 78227
Dominic DiStefano, 4303 Friar Lane, Colorado Springs, CO 80907 (accurizing)
Dan Dwyer, 915 W. Washington, San Diego, Calif. 92103
Ehresman Tool Co., Inc., 5425 Planeview Dr., Ft. Wayne, IN 46805 (custom)
Ken Eversull Gunsmith, Inc., P.O. Box 1766, Alexandria, LA 71301/318-442-0569
Giles' 45 Shop, Rt. 2, Box 847, Odessa, FL 33556
The Gunshop, R. D. Wallace, 320 Overland Rd., Prescott, AZ 86301
Gil Hebard Guns, Box 1, Knoxville, Ill. 61448
Lee E. Jurras & Assoc., Inc., P.O. Drawer F, Hagerman, NM 88232
Kart Sptg. Arms Corp., RD 2, Box 929-Broad Ave., Riverhead, NY 11901 (handgun conversions)
Lenz Firearms Co., 1480 Elkay Dr., Eugene, OR 97404
Kent Lomont, 4421 So. Wayne Ave., Ft. Wayne, IN 46807/219-694-6792 (Auto Mag only)
Mag-Na-Port Arms, Inc., 30016 S. River Rd., Mt. Clemens, MI 48043/313-469-6727
Rudolf Marent, 9711 Tiltree, Houston, TX 77075 (Hammerli)
Nu-Line Guns, 3727 Jennings Rd., St. Louis, MO 63121
Pachmayr Gun Works, 1220 S. Grand Ave., Los Angeles, Calif. 90015
L. W. Seecamp Co., Inc., Box 255, New Haven, CT 06502 (DA Colt auto conversions)
Silver Dollar Guns, P.O. Box 475, 10 Frances St., Franklin, NH 03235 (45 ACP)
Spokhandguns Inc., E. J. Christensen, East 1911 Sprague Ave., Spokane, WA 99202/509-534-4112
Sportsmens Equipmt. Co., 915 W. Washington, San Diego, Calif. 92103
Irving O. Stone, Jr., 633 S. Victory Blvd., Burbank, CA 91502
Victor W. Strawbridge, 6 Pineview Dr., Dover Pt., Dover, NH 03820
A. D. Swenson's 45 Shop, P.O. Box 606, Fallbrook, CA 92028
Dennis A. "Doc" Ulrich, 2511 S. 57th Ave., Cicero, IL 60650
Vic's Gun Refinishing, 6 Pineview Dr., Dover, NH 03820
Walters Industries, 6226 Park Lane, Dallas, TX 75225
Dave Woodruff, Box 5, Bear, DE 19701

REBORING AND RERIFLING

P.O. Ackley (see: Successor Dennis M. Bellm Gunsmithing, Inc.
Atkinson Gun Co., P.O. Box 512, Prescott, AZ 86301
Bain & Davis Sptg. Gds., 559 W. Las Tunas Dr., San Gabriel, Calif. 91776
Dennis M. Bellm Gunsmithing Inc., 2376 So. Redwood Rd., Salt Lake City, UT 84119
Charles P. Donnelly, Siskiyou Gun Works, 405 Kubli Rd., Grants Pass, OR 97526
Fuller Gun Shop, Cooper Landing, Alaska 99572
Bruce Jones, 389 Calla Ave., Imperial Beach, CA 92032
Les' Gun Shop, (Les Bauska), Box 511, Kalispell, MT 59901

Morgan's Cust. Reboring, 707 Union Ave., Grants Pass, OR 97526
Nu-Line Guns, 1053 Caulkshill Rd., Harvester, MO 63303/314-441-4500 (handguns)
Al Petersen, Box 8, Riverhurst, Saskatchewan, Canada S0H3P0
SGW, Inc. (formerly Schuetzen Gun Works), 624 Old Pacific Hwy. S.E., Olympia, WA 98503/206-456-3471
Sharon Gun Specialties, 14587 Peaceful Valley Rd., Sonora, CA 95370
Siegrist Gun Shop, 2689 McLean Rd., Whittemore, MI 48770
Snapp's Gunshop, 6911 E. Washington Rd., Clare, Mich. 48617
J. W. Van Patten, Box 145, Foster Hill, Milford, Pa. 18337
Robt. G. West, 27211 Huey Lane, Eugene, OR 97402

RIFLE BARREL MAKERS

P.O. Ackley Rifle Barrels (see: David M. Bellm Gunsmithing Inc.)
Atkinson Gun Co., P.O. Box 512, Prescott, AZ 86301
Jim Baiar, 490 Halfmoon Rd., Columbia Falls, MT 59912/406-892-4409
Dennis M. Bellm Gunsmithing Inc., 2376 So. Redwood Rd., Salt Lake City, UT 84119
Ralph L. Carter, Carter's Gun Shop, 225 G St., Penrose, CO 81240/303-372-6240
Christy Gun Works, 875 57th St., Sacramento, Calif. 95819
Clerke Prods., 2219 Main St., Santa Monica, Calif. 90405
Cuthbert Gun Shop, 715 So. 5th, Coos Bay, Ore. 97420
B. W. Darr, Saeco-Darr Rifle Co., Ltd., P.O. Box 778, Carpinteria, CA 93013
Douglas Barrels, Inc., 5504 Big Tyler Rd., Charleston, W. Va. 25312
Douglas Jackalope Gun & Sport Shop, Inc., 1048 S. 5th St., Douglas, WY 82633
Federal Firearms Co., Inc., Box 145, 145 Thomas Run Rd., Oakdale, PA 15071
C. R. & D. E. Getz, Box 88, Beavertown, PA 17813
A. R. Goode, 12845 Catoctin Furnace Rd., Thurmont, MD 21788/301-271-2228
Half Moon Rifle Shop, 490 Halfmoon Rd., Columbia Falls, MT 59912/406-892-4409
Hart Rifle Barrels, Inc., RD 2, Lafayette, N.Y. 13084
Wm. H. Hobaugh, Box M, Philipsburg, MT 59858
David R. Huntington, RFD #1, Box 23, Heber City, UT 83032
Kogot, John Pell, 410 College Ave., Trinidad, CO 81082/303-846-9006 (custom octagon)
Gene Lechner, 636 Jane N.E., Albuquerque, NM 87123
Les' Gun Shop, (Les Bauska), Box 511, Kalispell, MT 59901
Marquart Precision Co., Box 1740, Prescott, AZ 86301
Nu-Line Guns, Inc., 1053 Caulkshill Rd., Harvester, MO 63303/314-441-4500
Numrich Arms, W. Hurley, N.Y. 12491
Al Petersen, The Rifle Ranch, Box 8, Riverhurst, Sask., Canada SOH3PO
Sanders Cust. Gun Serv., 2358 Tyler Lane, Louisville, Ky. 40205
SGW, Inc., D. A. Schuetz, 624 Old Pacific Hwy. S.E., Olympia, WA 98503/206-456-3471
Sharon Gun Specialties, 14587 Peaceful Valley Rd., Sonora, CA 95370/209-532-4139
Ed Shilen Rifles, Inc., 205 Metropark Blvd., Ennis, TX 75119
W. C. Strutz, Rte. 1, "Woodland", Eagle River, WI 54521
Titus Barrel & Gun Co., R.F.D. #1, Box 23, Heber City, UT 84032
Bob Williams, P.O. Box 143, Boonsboro, MD 21713
Wilson Arms Co., 63 Leetes Island Rd., Branford, CT 06405

SCOPES, MOUNTS, ACCESSORIES, OPTICAL EQUIPMENT

Aimpoint U.S.A., 29351 Stonecrest Rd., Rancho Palos Verdes, CA 90274 (electronic sight)
Alley Supply Co., Carson Valley Industrial Park, Gardnerville, NV 89410 (Scope collimator)
American Import Co., 1167 Mission, San Francisco, Calif. 94103
Anderson Mfg. Co., P.O. Box 3120, Yakima, WA 98903 (lens cap)
Armsport, Inc., 3590 N.W. 49th St., Miami, FL 33122/305-592-7850
B-Square Co., Box 11281, Ft. Worth, TX 76109 (Mini-14 mount)
Bausch & Lomb Inc., 1400 Goodman St., Rochester, NY 14602/716-338-6000
Beeman's Precision Airguns, Inc., 47 Paul Dr., San Rafael, CA 94903/415-472-7121
Bennett, 561 Delaware, Delmar, N.Y. 12054 (mounting wrench)
Lenard M. Brownell, Box 25, Wyarno, WY 82845/307-737-2468 (cust. mounts)
Browning Arms, Rt. 4, Box 624-B, Arnold, Mo. 63010
Maynard P. Buehler, Inc., 17 Orinda Highway, Orinda, Calif. 94563
Burris Co., 331 E. 8th St., Box 1747, Greeley, CO 80631
Bushnell Optical Co., 2828 E. Foothill Blvd., Pasadena, Calif. 91107
Butler Creek Corp., Box GG, Jackson Hole, WY 83001 (lens caps)
Kenneth Clark, 18738 Highway 99, Madera, Calif. 93637
Clearview Mfg. Co., Inc., 20821 Grand River Ave., Detroit, MI 48219 (mounts)
Clear View Sports Shields, P.O. Box 255, Wethersfield, CT 06107 (shooting/testing glasses)
Colt's, Hartford, Conn. 06102
Compass Instr. & Optical Co., Inc., 104 E 25th St., New York, N.Y. 10010
Conetrol Scope Mounts, Hwy 123 South, Seguin, TX 78155
D&H Prods. Co., Inc., P.O. Box 22, Glenshaw, PA 15116/412-443-2190 (lens covers)
Davis Optical Co., P.O. Box 6, Winchester, Ind. 47934
Del-Sports Inc., Main St., Margaretville, NY 12455/914-586-4103 (Kahles)
M. B. Dinsmore, Box 21, Wyomissing, PA 19610 (shooting glasses)

Eder Instrument Co., 5115 N. Ravenswood, Chicago, IL 60640 (borescope)
Flaig's, Babcock Blvd., Millvale, Pa. 15209
Fontaine Ind., Inc., 11552 Knott St., Suite 2, Garden Grove, CA 92641/714-892-4473 (traj. compensator dials)
Freeland's Scope Stands, Inc. 3734 14th, Rock Island, Ill. 61201
Griffin & Howe, Inc., 589 Broadway, New York, N.Y. 10012
H&H Assoc., P.O. Box 447, Strathmore, CA 93267 (target adj. knobs)
H. J. Hermann Leather Co., Rt. 1, Skiatook, OK 74070 (lens caps)
Herter's Inc., Waseca, Minn. 56093
J. B. Holden Co., 295 W. Pearl, Plymouth, MI 48170
The Hutson Corp., P.O. 1127, Arlington, Tex.76010
Hy-Score Arms Corp., 200 Tillary St., Brooklyn, N.Y. 11201
Interarms, 10 Prince St., Alexandria, VA 22313
Paul Jaeger, 211 Leedom St., Jenkintown, Pa. 19046 (Nickel)
Jana Intl. Co., Box 1107, Denver, Colo. 80201
Jason Empire Inc., 9200 Cody, P.O. Box 12370, Overland Park, KS 66212/913-888-0220
Jennison TCS (see Fontaine Ind., Inc.)
Kahles of America, Div. of Del-Sports, Inc. Main St., Margaretville, NY 12455/914-586-4103
Kesselring Gun Shop, 400 Pacific Hiway No., Burlington, WA 98283/206-724-3113
Kris Mounts, 108 Lehigh St., Johnstown, PA 15905
Kuharsky Bros. (see Modern Industries)
Kwik-Site, 5555 Treadwell, Wayne, MI 48185 (rings, mounts only)
LanDav, 7213 Lee Highway, Falls Church, VA 22046 (steel leverlock side mt.)
S. E. Laszlo House of Imports, 200 Tillary St., Brooklyn, NY 11201
Leatherwood Bros., Rte. 1, Box 111, Stephenville, TX 76401
T. K. Lee, 2830 S. 19th St., Off. #4, Birmingham, AL 35209 (reticles)
E. Leitz, Inc., Rockleigh, N.J. 07647
Leupold & Stevens Inc., P.O. Box 688, Beaverton, Ore. 97005
Jake Levin and Son, Inc., 9200 Cody, Overland Park, KS 66214
W. H. Lodewick, 2816 N.E. Halsey, Portland, OR 97232 (scope safeties)
Lyman Products Corp., Route 147, Middlefield, CT 06455
Mandall Shooting Supplies, 7150 E. 4th St., Scottsdale, AZ 85252
Marble Arms Co., 420 Industrial Park, Gladstone, MI 49837
Marlin Firearms Co., 100 Kenna Dr., New Haven, Conn. 06473
Robert Medaris, P.O. Box 309, Mira Loma, CA 91752/714-685-5666 (side mount f. H&K 91 & 93)
Modern Industries, Inc., 613 W-11, Erie, PA 16501
O. F. Mossberg & Sons, Inc., 7 Grasso Ave., North Haven, Conn. 06473
Normark Corp., 1710 E. 78th St., Minneapolis, Minn. 55423 (Singlepoint)
Numrich Arms, West Hurley, N.Y. 12491
Nydar, see: Swain Nelson Co.
PEM's Mounts, 6063 Waterloo, Atwater, PA 44201
Pachmayr Gun Works, 1220 S. Grand Ave., Los Angeles, Calif. 90015
Precise, 3 Chestnut, Suffern, NY 10901
Ranging Inc., 90 Lincoln Rd. North, East Rochester, NY 14445/716-385-1250
Ray-O-Vac, Willson Prod. Div., P.O. Box 622, Reading, PA 19603 (shooting glasses)
Redfield Gun Sight Co., 5800 E. Jewell Ave., Denver, Colo. 80222
S & K Mfg. Co., Box 247, Pittsfield, Pa. 16340 (Insta-mount)
Sanders Cust. Gun Serv., 2358 Tyler Lane, Louisville, Ky. 40205 (MSW)
Savage Arms, Westfield, Mass. 01085
Sears, Roebuck & Co., 825 S. St. Louis, Chicago, Ill. 60607
Sherwood Intl. Export Corp., 18714 Parthenia St., Northridge, CA 91324 (mounts)
W. H. Siebert, 22720 S.E. 56th Pl., Issaquah, WA 98027
Singlepoint (see Normark)
Southern Precision·Inst. Co., 3419 E. Commerce St., San Antonio, TX 78219
Spacetron Inc., Box 84, Broadview, IL 60155 (bore lamp)
Stoeger Industries, 55 Ruta Ct., S. Hackensack, NJ 07606/201-440-2700
Strieter Corp., 2100 - 18th Ave., Rock Island, IL 61201/309-794-9800 (Swarovski, Habicht)
Supreme Lens Covers, Box GG, Jackson Hole, WY 83001 (lens caps)
Swain Nelson Co., Box 45, 92 Park Dr., Glenview, IL 60025 (shotgun sight)
Swift Instruments, Inc., 952 Dorchester Ave., Boston, Mass. 02125
Tasco, 1075 N.W. 71st, Miami, Fla. 33138
Ted's Sight Aligner, Box 1073, Scottsdale AZ 85252
Thompson-Center Arms, P.O. Box 2405, Rochester, N.H. 03867 (handgun scope)
Tradewinds, Inc., Box 1191, Tacoma, Wash. 98401
John Unertl Optical Co., 3551-5 East St., Pittsburgh, Pa. 15214
United Binocular Co., 9043 S. Western Ave., Chicago, Ill. 60620
Verano Corp., Box 270, Glendora, CA 91740
Vissing (see: Supreme Lens Covers)
Weatherby's, 2781 Firestone, South Gate, Calif. 90280
W. R. Weaver Co., 7125 Industrial Ave., El Paso, Tex. 79915
Wide View Scope Mount Corp., 26110 Michigan Ave., Inkster, MI 48141
Williams Gun Sight Co., 7389 Lapeer Rd., Davison, Mich. 48423
Boyd Williams Inc., 8701-14 Mile Rd. (M-57), Cedar Springs, MI 49319 (BR)
Willrich Precision Instrument Co., 95 Cedar Lane, Englewood, NJ 07631/201-567-1411 (borescope)
Carl Zeiss Inc., 444 Fifth Ave., New York, N.Y. 10018 (Hensoldt)

SIGHTS, METALLIC

Accura-Site Co., Inc., Box 193, Neenah, WI 54956
B-Square Eng. Co., Box 11281, Ft. Worth, Tex. 76110
Beeman's Precision Airguns, Inc., 47 Paul Dr., San Rafael, CA 94903/415-472-7121 (airguns only)
Behlert Custom Sights, Inc., 725 Lehigh Ave., Union, NJ 07083

Bo-Mar Tool & Mfg. Co., Box 168, Carthage, Tex. 75633
Maynard P. Buehler, Inc., 17 Orinda Highway, Orinda, Calif. 94563
Christy Gun Works, 875 57th St., Sacramento, Calif. 95819
Jim Day, 902 N. Bownen Lane, Florence, SD 29501 (Chaba)
E-Z Mount, Ruelle Bros., P.O. Box 114, Ferndale, MT 48220
Freeland's Scope Stands, Inc., 3734-14th Ave., Rock Island, Ill. 61201
Paul T. Haberly, 2364 N. Neva, Chicago, IL 60635
Paul Jaeger, Inc., 211 Leedom St., Jenkintown, PA 19046
Lee's Red Ramps, 7252 E. Ave. U-3, Littlerock, CA 93543/805-944-4487 (illuminated sights)
Jim Lofland, 2275 Larkin Rd., Boothwyn, PA 19061
Lyman Products Corp., Rte. 147, Middlefield, Conn. 06455
Marble Arms Corp., 420 Industrial Park, Gladstone, Mich. 49837
Merit Gunsight Co., P.O. Box 995, Sequim, Wash. 98382
Micro Sight Co., 242 Harbor Blvd., Belmont, Calif. 94002
Miniature Machine Co., 210 E. Poplar, Deming, NM 88030/505-546-2151
Modern Industries, Inc., 613 W-11, Erie, PA 16501
C. R. Pedersen & Son, Ludington, Mich. 49431
Poly Choke Co., Inc., P.O. Box 296, Hartford, CT 06101
Redfield Gun Sight Co., 5800 E. Jewell St., Denver, Colo. 80222
S&M Tang Sights, P.O. Box 1338, West Babylon, NY 11704
Schwarz's Gun Shop, 41 - 15th St., Wellsburg, W. Va. 26070
Simmons Gun Specialties, Inc., 700 Rodgers Rd., Olathe, Kans. 66061
Slug Site Co., Whitetail Wilds, Lake Hubert, MN. 56469
Sport Service Center, 2364 N. Neva, Chicago, IL 60635
Tradewinds, Inc., Box 1191, Tacoma, WA 98401
Williams Gun Sight Co., 7389 Lapeer Rd., Davison, Mich. 48423

STOCKS (Commercial and Custom)

Abe and VanHorn, 5120¾ Huntington Dr., Los Angeles, CA 90032/213-227-4870
Adams Custom Gun Stocks, 13461 Quito Rd., Saratoga, CA 95070
Ahlman's Inc., R.R. 1, Box 20, Morristown, MN 55052
Don Allen, Rte. 1, Northfield, MN 55057 (blanks)
Anderson's Guns, Jim Jares, 706 S. 23rd St., Laramie, WY 82070
R. J. Anton, 874 Olympic Dr., Waterloo, IA 50701
Jim Baiar, 490 Halfmoon Rd., Columbia Falls, MT 59912
Joe J. Balickie, Custom Stocks, Rte. 2, Box 56-G, Apex, NC 27502
Bartas, Rte. 1, Box 129-A, Cato, Wis. 54206
Beeman's Precision Airguns, Inc., 47 Paul Dr., San Rafael, CA 94903/415-472-7121 (airguns only)
John Bianchi, 100 Calle Cortez, Temecula, CA 92390 (U. S. carbines)
Al Biesen, West 2039 Sinto Ave., Spokane, Wash. 99201
Stephen L. Billeb, Box 219, Philipsburg, MT 59858/406-859-3919
E. C. Bishop & Son Inc., Box 7, Warsaw, Mo. 65355
John M. Boltin, P.O. Box 1122, No. Myrtle Beach, SC 29582
Border Gun Shop, Garry Simmons, 2760 Tucson Hiway, Nogales, AZ 85621/602-281-0045 (spl. silueta stocks, complete rifles)
Brown Precision Co., P.O. Box 270W; 7786 Molinos Ave., Los Molinos, CA 96055/916-384-2506
Lenard M. Brownell, Box 25, Wyarno, WY 82845
E. J. Bryant, 3154 Glen St., Eureka, CA 95501
Jack Burres, 10333 San Fernando Road, Pacoima, CA 91331 (English, Claro, Bastogne Paradox walnut blanks only)
Calico Hardwoods, Inc., 1648 Airport Blvd., Windsor, Calif. 95492 (blanks)
Dick Campbell, 365 W. Oxford Ave., Englewood, CO 80110
Winston Churchill, Twenty Mile Stream Rd., Rt.1, Box 29B, Proctorsville, VT 05153
Crane Creek Gun Stock Co., 25 Shephard Terr., Madison, WI 53705
Reggie Cubriel, 15502 Purple Sage, San Antonio, TX 78255/512-695-8401 (cust. stockm.)
Dahl's Custom Stocks, Rt. 4, Box 187, Schofield Rd., Lake Geneva, WI 53147 (Martin Dahl)
Jack Dever, 8520 N.W. 90, Oklahoma City, OK 73132
Charles De Veto, 1087 Irene Rd., Lyndhurst, O. 44124
Bill Dowtin, P.O. Box 72, Celina, TX 75009
Gary Duncan, 1118 Canterbury, Enid, OK 73701 (blanks only)
David R. Dunlop, Rte. 1, Box 199, Rolla, ND 58367
Bob Emmons, 238 Robson Road, Grafton, OH 44044 (custom)
Reinhart Fajen, Box 338, Warsaw, MO 65355/814-438-5111
N. B. Fashingbauer, P.O. Box 366, Lac Du Flambeau, WI 54538/715-588-7116
Ted Fellowes, Beaver Lodge, 9245 16th Ave. S. W., Seattle, Wash. 98106
Clyde E. Fischer, Rt. 1, Box 170-M, Victoria, Tex. 77901
Jerry Fisher, 1244-4th Ave. W., Kalispell, MT 59901
Flaig's Lodge, Millvale, Pa. 15209
Donald E. Folks, 205 W. Lincoln St., Pontiac, IL 61764
Larry L. Forster, Box 212, Gwinner, ND 58040
Horace M. Frantz, Box 128, Farmingdale, N.J. 07727
Freeland's Scope Stands, Inc., 3734 14th Ave., Rock Island, Ill. 61201
Dale Goens, Box 224, Cedar Crest, N.M. 87008
Gary Goudy, 263 Hedge Rd., Menlo Park, CA 44025
Gould's Myrtlewood, 1692 N. Dogwood, Coquille, Ore. 97423 (gun blanks)
Charles E. Grace, 10144 Elk Lake Rd., Williamsburg, MI 49690
Rolf R. Gruning, 315 Busby Dr., San Antonio, Tex. 78209
The Gunshop, R. D. Wallace, 320 Overland Rd., Prescott, AZ 86301 (custom)
Half Moon Rifle Shop, 490 Halfmoon Rd., Columbia Falls, MT 59912
Harper's Custom Stocks, 928 Lombrano St., San Antonio, Tex. 78207
Harris Gun Stocks, Inc., 12 Lake St., Richfield Springs, N.Y. 13439
Hal Hartley, 147 Blairsfork Rd., Lenoir, NC 28645
Hayes Gunstock Service Co., 914 E. Turner St., Clearwater, Fla. 33516
Hubert J. Hecht, 55 Rose Mead Circle, Sacramento, CA 95831
Edward O. Hefti, 300 Fairview, College Sta., Tex. 77840

Herter's Inc., Waseca, Minn. 56093
Klaus Hiptmayer, P.O. Box 136, Eastman, Que., JOE 1PO Canada/514-297-2492
Richard Hodgson, 5589 Arapahoe, Unit 104, Boulder, CO 80301
Hollis Gun Shop, 917 Rex St., Carlsbad, N.M. 88220
Henry Houser, Ozark Custom Carving, 117 Main St., Warsaw, MO 65355
Jackson's, Box 416, Selman City, Tex. 75689 (blanks)
Paul Jaeger, 211 Leedom St., Jenkintown, Pa. 19046
JL Woods, Jim Jackson, 144 Colorado, Spearfish, SD 57783/605-642-2251 (blanks)
Johnson Wood Products, R.R. #1, Strawberry Point, IA 52076/319-933-4930 (blanks)
Monte Kennedy, P.O. Box 214, Kalispell, MT 59901
Don Klein, Box 277, Camp Douglas, WI 54618
LeFever Arms Co., Inc., R.D. 1, Lee Center-Stokes Rd., Lee Center, NY 13363/315-337-6422
Lenz Firearms Co., 1480 Elkay Dr., Eugene, OR 97404
Stanley Kenvin, 5 Lakeville Lane, Plainview, NY 11803/516-931-0321 (custom)
Philip D. Letiecq, AQ 18 Wagon Box Rd., P.O. Box 251, Story, WY 82842/307-683-2817
Al Lind, 7821 76th Ave. S.W., Tacoma, WA 98498 (cust. stockm.)
Bill McGuire, 1600 N. Eastmont Ave., East Wenatchee, WA 98801
Gale McMillan, 28638 N. 42 St., Box 7870 - Cave Creek Stage, Phoenix, AZ 85020/602-585-4684
Maurer Arms, 2366 Frederick Dr., Cuyahoga Falls, OH 44221
John E. Maxson, Box 332, Dumas, TX 79029/806-935-5990 (custom)
Leonard Mews, Spring Rd., Box 242, Hortonville, WI 54944
Robt. U. Milhoan & Son, Rt. 3, Elizabeth, W. Va. 26143
C. D. Miller Guns, Purl St., St. Onge, SD 57779
Nelsen's Gun Shop, 501 S. Wilson, Olympia, Wash. 98501
Oakley and Merkley, Box 2446, Sacramento, CA 95811 (blanks)
Jim Norman, Jim's Gunstocks, 11230 Calenda Road, San Diego, CA 92127/714-487-4173
Maurice Ottmar, Box 657, 113 E. Fir, Coulee City, WA 99115
Pachmayr Gun Works, 1220 S. Grand Ave., Los Angeles, CA 90015 (blanks and custom jobs)
Paulsen Gunstocks, Rte. 71, Box 11, Chinook, MT 59523 (blanks)
Peterson Mach. Carving, Box 1065, Sun Valley, Calif. 91352
Phillip Pilkington, P.O. Box 2284, University Station, Enid, OK 73701
R. Neal Rice, 5152 Newton, Denver, CO 80221
Richards Micro-Fit Stocks, P.O. Box 1066, Sun Valley, CA. 91352 (thumb-hole)
Carl Roth, Jr., 4728 Pineridge Ave., Cheyenne, Wy. 82001
Matt Row, Lock, Stock 'N Barrel, 8972 East Huntington Dr., San Gabriel, CA 91775/213-287-0051
Royal Arms, Inc., 10064 Bert Acosta Ct., Santee, Calif. 92071
Sanders Cust. Gun Serv., 2358 Tyler Lane, Louisville, Ky. 40205 (blanks)
Saratoga Arms Co., R.D. 3, Box 387, Pottstown, Pa. 19464
Roy Schaefer, 965 W. Hilliard Lane, Eugene, OR 97404 (blanks)
Shaw's, Rt. 2, Box 407-L, Escondido, CA 92025/714-728-7070
Hank Shows, The Best, 1202 N. State, Ukaih, CA 95482
Walter Shultz, 1752 N. Pleasantview Rd., Pottstown, PA 19464
Sile Dist., 7 Centre Market Pl., New York, N.Y. 10013
Six Enterprises, 6564 Hidden Creek Dr., San Jose, CA 95120 (fiberglass)
Ed Sowers, 8331 DeCelis Pl., Sepulveda, CA 91343 (hydro-coil gunstocks)
Fred D. Speiser, 2229 Dearborn, Missoula, MT 59801
Sport Service Center, 2364 N. Neva, Chicago, IL 60635/312-889-1114 (custom)
Sportsmen's Equip. Co., 915 W. Washington, San Diego, Calif. 92103 (carbine conversions)
Keith Stegall, Box 696, Gunnison, Colo. 81230
Stinehour Rifles, Box 84, Cragsmoor, N.Y. 12420
Surf N' Sea, Inc., 62-595 Kam Hwy., Box 268, Haleiwa, HI 96712 (custom gunstocks blanks)

Swanson Cust. Firearms, 1051 Broadway, Denver, Colo. 80203
Talmage Enterpr., 43197 E. Whittier, Hemet, CA 92343
Brent L. Umberger, Sportsman's Haven, R.R. 4, Cambridge, OH 43725
John Vest, 6715 Shasta Way, Klamath Falls, OR 97601/503-884-5585 (classic rifles)
Weatherby's, 2781 Firestone, South Gate, Calif. 90280
Cecil Weems, Box 657, Mineral Wells, TX 76067
Frank R. Wells, 3019 W. Bartlett Pl., Tucson, AZ 85704 (custom stocks)
Western Gunstocks Mfg. Co., 550 Valencia School Rd., Aptos, CA 95003
Duane Wiebe, P.O. Box 497, Lotus, CA 95651
Bob Williams, P.O. Box 143, Boonsboro, MD 21713
Williamson-Pate Gunsmith Service, 117 W. Pipeline, Hurst, TX 76053/817-268-2887
Robert M. Winter, Box 484, Menno, S.D. 57045
Mike Yee, 4700-46th Ave. S.W., Seattle, WA 98116
Russell R. Zeeryp, 1601 Foard Dr., Lynn Ross Manor, Morristown, TN 37814

TRAP & SKEET SHOOTERS EQUIP.

Wm. J. Mittler, 290 Moore Dr., Boulder Creek, CA 95006 (shotgun choke specialist)
Multi-Gauge Enterprises, 433 W. Foothill Blvd., Monrovia, CA 91061 (shotgun specialists)
William J. Nittler, 290 More Dr., Boulder Creek, CA 95006 (shotgun repairs)
Herb Orre, Box 56, Phillipsburg, OH 45354 (shotgun specialist)
Purbaugh Sporting Goods, 433 W. Foothill Blvd., Monrovia, CA 91016 (shotgun barrel inserts)

TRIGGERS, RELATED EQUIP.

Ametek, Hunter Spring Div., One Spring Ave., Hatfield, PA 19440/215-822-2971 (trigger gauge)
M. H. Canjar Co., 500 E. 45th Ave., Denver, CO 80216 (triggers)
Central Specialties Co., 6030 Northwest Hwy., Chicago, IL 60631/312-774-5000 (trigger lock)
Custom Products, 686 Baldwin St., Meadville, PA 16335/814-724-7045 (trigger guard)
Dayton-Traister Co., 9322-900th West, P.O. Box 593, Oak Harbor, WA 98277 (triggers)
Electronic Trigger Systems, (Franklin C. Green), 530 W. Oak Grove Rd., Montrose, CO 81401
Flaig's, Babcock Blvd. & Thompson Run Rd., Millvale, PA 15209 (trigger shoe)
Gager Gage & Tool Co., 27509 Industrial Blvd., Hayward, CA 94545 (speedlock triggers f. Rem. 1100 and 870 shotguns)
Franklin C. Green, See Electronic Trigg. System
Bill Holmes, Rt. 2, Box 242, Fayetteville, AR 72701/501-521-8958 (trigger release)
Paul Jaeger, Inc., 211 Leedom St., Jenkintown, PA 19046
Michaels of Oregon Co., P.O. Box 13010, Portland, OR 97213 (trigger guards)
Miller Single Trigger Mfg. Co., R.D. 1 on Rte. 209, Millersburg, PA 17061
Viggo Miller, P.O. Box 4181, Omaha, NB 68104 (trigger attachment)
Ohaus Corp., 29 Hanover Rd., Florham Park, NJ 07932 (trigger pull gauge)
Pachmayr Gun Works, 1220 S. Grand Ave., Los Angeles, CA 90015 (trigger shoe)
Pacific Tool Co., P.O. Box 2048, Ordnance Plant Rd., Grand Island, NE 68801 (trigger shoe)
Richland Arms Co., 321 W. Adrian St., Blissfield, MI 49228 (trigger pull gauge)
Sport Service Center, 2364 N. Neva, Chicago, IL 60635 (release triggers)
Timney Mfg. Co., 2847 E. Siesta Lane, Phoenix, AZ 85024 (triggers)
Melvin Tyler, 1326 W. Britton Ave., Oklahoma City, OK 73114 (trigger shoe)
Williams Gun Sight Co., 7389 Lapeer Rd., Davison, MI 48423 (trigger shoe)